Harvard Studies in Urban History

Series Editors: Stephan Thernstrom and Charles Tilly

The Lyon Uprising of 1834

Social and Political Conflict in the Early July Monarchy

ROBERT J. BEZUCHA

Harvard University Press   Cambridge, Massachusetts   1974

For My Mother and Father

Preface

This book is about a community of artisans who organized in order to resist proletarianization and consequently found themselves at the barricades. Its intellectual structure is meant to be like a nest of three childrens' blocks which fit one within the next larger.

The smallest represents a subject familiar to historians of nineteenth century France. The standard works on the political and worker societies of the early years of the July Monarchy—books such as those by Dolléans (1945), Festy (1908), Perreux (1931), Tchernoff (1902), and Weill (1928)—agree that the city of Lyon was a storm center in this period. Access to a complete collection of the Lyonnais press as well as to a rare source in the municipal archives, the papers and official correspondence of Adrien Étienne de Gasparin, prefect of the Rhône department from December 1831 until 1835, has allowed me to expand and on several occasions to correct previous knowledge of the local worker movement and the Republican party between the Revolution of 1830 and the so-called *procès monstre* in 1835. Much of this material is a refinement of a doctoral dissertation which I completed at the University of Michigan in 1968.

The second block is a contribution to the history of popular violence. Twice within three years—in November 1831 and April 1834—the second city of France was the scene of bloody resistance. The first rebellion of the Lyonnais silk workers, or *canuts* as they were called, has had a constant fascination for historians. Beginning with the young Karl Marx,[1] many have referred to it as the earliest example of open warfare between the working class and bourgeois society. The second uprising, on the other hand, has generally been neglected. The probable explanation is that scholars have mistakenly tended to accept the contemporary conclusion that while the first

revolt had been "essentially industrial" in character, the second was
not only "political" but also the result of a Republican conspiracy.[2]
The implication was that a presumed political conflict was intrinsi-
cally less important than an apparently spontaneous worker uprising.
A generation ago Fernand Rude's *Le Mouvement ouvrier à Lyon de
1827 à 1832* (1944; revised edition 1969) overturned much of the
accepted interpretation of November 1831. A critical examination
of the Lyon uprising of 1834, therefore, is doubly overdue.

Thirty years' development in historical methodology separates my
work from Rude's, however. Recent studies by scholars such as
Maurice Agulhon, Rémi Gossez, Eric Hobsbawm, Jacques Rougerie,
George Rudé, David Pinkney, Edward Thompson, and Charles Tilly
have suggested new ways for me to study the mobilization of the
Lyonnais worker community and to analyze the composition and
behavior of the crowd. Much of my data has been extracted from
two sets of sources: first, the dossiers of more than 500 persons
arrested in April 1834, which are found in the records of the Chamber of Peers in the Archives Nationales in Paris; second, the unpublished fiscal census of Lyon, the *Recensement de la population,*
preserved in the attic of the Hôtel-de-Ville. In using them my intention has been not only to describe what happened in April 1834, but
also to explain why, after November 1831, trouble came again so
soon to the city. The first block fits inside the second one in this
manner.

The largest block is an attempt to set the Lyon uprising of 1834
within the emerging framework of social history. I hope that this
book will not be consigned to that unjustly denigrated corner of the
profession called "local history" merely because the occupational
structure of Lyon makes the city appear to be unique at first glance.
I am convinced that some of the answers (or at least a more precise
statement of the problems) can be found there for some significant
questions concerning European institutions and mentalities during
the transition period between traditional and modern society.

These questions fall into three broad categories: (1) Urban development: How did the character of urban life change in the half century
after the French Revolution? Did cities develop new occupational
and residential patterns before the arrival of modern industry? How
were they administered and defended? (2) Economic and social
change: How did handwork industries respond to the abolition of
traditional corporations and the introduction of open competition?
To the threat of factories and mechanization? How was official
economic policy actually administered in the era of laissez-faire?

What was the nature of economic and social relationships within the artisan community? To what extent was there a sense of solidarity or class feeling? (3) Social and political movements: Why were voluntary associations such a popular and characteristic form of organization at this time? What did the worker community believe they would accomplish? What formulas did bourgeois radicals such as the members of the Republican party propose for the solution of economic and social problems? How successful was their appeal for support from the workshops? Why were local and national officials so concerned to prevent the politicization of the masses? To what extent were their fears well-founded or based on misapprehension and self-deception?

Lyon is not so unique after all. Instead, I believe we can perceive in the context of a specific city and industry an example of a set of tensions which widely accompany the process of modernization. As Wolfram Fischer has suggested, what contemporaries called "the social question" was "the crisis of a society in transition . . . At the beginning of industrialization the labor problem of all western European countries was essentially the same."[3] It applied, moreover, to threatened handwork industries such as the manufacture of silk cloth as well as to the burgeoning factory system. The articulate, coherent expression of the *canuts'* goals and the remarkable vigor of their associations suggest that historians should not assume that the victims of change were simply a tabula rasa for the political agitators and social theorists of the day. It is worth emphasizing that the Lyonnais workers' powerful sense of association as the means of collective freedom in a nascent industrial society antedated Proudhon's theory of "mutualist" society and Marx's ideas on proletarian self-emancipation by a decade.

Finally, the Lyon uprising of 1834 can be seen as a benchmark in the development of collective violence. The largest urban disturbance in France between the Revolutions of 1830 and 1848, this six-day politicized confrontation between a preindustrial crowd and a government intent on repression stands at the interstices between what has been described as "reactionary" and "modern" violence.[4] The *canuts* were neither contesting the introduction of jurisdictional claims by the state nor protesting the revocation of archaic rights (both standard examples of reactionary violence); rather they were struggling to establish a claim to control over their work in the future. As we shall learn, the protoindustrial concentration and conscious organization of the Lyonnais worker community give claim that this was the first modern insurrection in European history.

Acknowledgements

More than six years have passed since I began to work in the reading room of the Archives Nationales. I have accumulated debts of gratitude to a number of persons and institutions during this period and I want to acknowledge some of them here.

The French government, the United States government (Hays-Fulbright Act), and the Horace H. Rackham School of Graduate Studies of the University of Michigan supported fourteen months of predoctoral research in France in 1966 and 1967. The Faculty Research Council of Northwestern University gave me a grant for three months of postdoctoral research during the summer of 1969. The History Departments of the University of Michigan and Northwestern University provided funds for microfilming and typing; the latter was done by Anne Potter.

The fledgling historian working abroad for the first time is often influenced by the example of more experienced colleagues whom he meets. I was most fortunate that Natalie Davis, Edward Gargan, and Alan Spitzer offered their advise and encouragement during my *rite du passage.* In Lyon, M. and Mme. Robert Joanny, Bernard Chardère, Paul Bouchet, and M. le Docteur Croizat opened their homes to us; so much for the false reputation that Lyon is a cold city. The municipal archivist, Henri Hours, and his capable assistant, Maurice Vanario, uncovered a number of sources and offered suggestions concerning my project on their own initiative.

The members of my dissertation committee were helpful and considerate. I realize better now than I did then that David Bien, Raymond Grew, and Roy Pierce did more work than their duties as readers required. John Bowditch was more than a supervisor; he was a teacher and a good friend.

Roderick Aya, Georges Haupt, David Katzman, Leo Loubère, Joan

Scott, James Sheehan, Richard Sinkin, and Charles Tilly each read all or parts of the manuscript at various stages. They share the credit for whatever forest is visible through the trees. Richard Press and Russell Maylone of the Northwestern University Library have demonstrated their interest in social history on many occasions.

My parents, to whom this book is dedicated, have done more to make it possible than I can say. The parents of my wife, Elbridge and Margaret Vance, also offered inspiration and support. My wife, Susan, waited with patience and understanding to begin her own career. Finally, our children, Tom and Meg, are a constant reminder that there is more to life than writing books.

R.J.B.
Evanston, Illinois

Contents

Illustration

Map

Figures

Tables

The Lyon Uprising of 1834

1   The *Canuts,* the Silk Industry, and the City of Lyon

In *Les Français peint par eux-mêmes*, a popular series portraying social types, Joanny Augier wrote:

> Ten years ago the *canut* was almost unknown in France and Europe. One day he took up arms, wrote on his banner the terrible words *Vivre en travaillant ou mourir en combattant,* and the bloody disorders in the second city of the kingdom called general attention to the worker of the Lyonnais silk industry. Until then he went unnoticed; no one took account of his labor, his perseverance, or his long resignation . . . Then the *canut* fought; the gun replaced the shuttle in his hands; he fanned the flames of civil war and revolt obtained for him a reknown his work had not acquired. Henceforth he became the object of studies by economists; the grave questions raised by the insurrections of November 1831 and April 1834 divided businessmen, journalists, and legislators into two camps.[1]

Thus were the *canuts,* the silk industry, and the city of Lyon inseparably linked in the mind of an audience fascinated by the spectacle of working class rebellion. This introductory chapter explains some of the reasons why, around the year 1830, they fit together in such an explosive manner. Much of the discussion concerns urban development and economic and social trends after 1789. Nevertheless, the current historical canon that asserts that the Revolution was less revolutionary than commonly assumed compels us to speak of change with less facile resort to 1789 as the Great Turning Point. We must set our historical stage by examining the city and the silk industry under the Old Regime before we can identify and measure those changes which were truly revolutionary.

1

I

Situated at the confluence of the Saône and Rhône rivers three
hundred miles southeast of Paris, Lyon stands at one of the natural
crossroads of the continent. The placid Saône is shaped like a tree
with its branches nearly touching the Rhine, the Seine, the Marne,
and the Moselle, its trunk a valley traversing eastern France, and its
base where it meets the turbulent Rhône. The Rhône flows west
from the Lake of Geneva and then south to the Mediterranean.
Throughout European history travelers and goods on route from
London to Rome, from Paris to Marseille, from Frankfurt to Madrid
were all likely to pass through Lyon.

An alluvial peninsula has formed over the centuries at the rivers'
confluence and today they flow parallel for nearly two miles
before meeting. The northern base of the peninsula is formed by a
hill (300 feet above river level) called the Croix Rousse after a cross
of reddish stone erected at its peak by a religious mission in 1560.
To the west, along the right bank of the Saône, there is a belt of level
ground between the river and a second, steeper hill (400 feet) called
Fourvière after the Roman forum which stood on its upper plateau.
Fourvière is a spur of the Monts du Lyonnais, the eastern extension
of the Massif Central. To the east of the peninsula, on the left bank
of the Rhône, lies the plain of Dauphiné which continues until the
Alps. If geography guaranteed Lyon's role as a commercial capital,
complex topography—two rivers, two hills, peninsula, and plain—
contributed to the fragmented pattern of her urban development.

The Roman city of Lugdunum, the capital of Gaul after 43 *B.C.*,
was built on the two hills. The principal government buildings, the
forum, and a theater for 10,000 persons stood on the plateau of
Fourvière. There was a larger theater on the slopes of the Croix
Rousse where representatives of the tribes of Gaul came each year to
renew their allegiance to the cult of Rome and Augustus. At that
time the peninsula ended near the base of the Croix Rousse hill and
it was there that Saint Pontin established the city's first Christian
church in *A.D.* 175. Merchants and traders lived along the river banks
and on an island at the confluence. Lugdunum was a frequent victim of the political struggles of the Roman Empire. Saint Pontin was
among those martyred during the persecutions of Marcus Aurelius
and 18,000 Christians were said to have been killed when the city
was sacked and burned by Septimus Severius. Rebuilt during the
reigns of Nero and Trajan, Lugdunum fell from the first rank of

European cities when Constantine transferred the capital of Gaul to Arles under the threat of barbarian invasions.

Lying at the interstices of a number of natural regions, Lyon was buffeted by the vicissitudes of medieval politics. The Treaty of Verdun placed her within Lotharingia, the weakest of the three successor kingdoms to the Carolingian Empire. From the tenth to the twelfth centuries the Counts of Forez waged an ultimately unsuccessful contest with the Archbishop for control over the city. The church celebrated its victory at two Lyonnais councils during the thirteenth century. At the one held in 1245, Pope Innocent IV consecrated the Cathedral of Saint John (Saint Jean) and chose the occasion to declare the excommunication of the Emperor Frederick II. The new cathedral stood on the narrow ground between Fourvière and the right bank of the Saône. Its consecration symbolized the emergence of a new urban axis, the Saône, which was to influence the city's development until the middle of the eighteenth century.

Ecclesiastical control weighed heavily on the Lyonnais merchants, however. In 1312 they sought the protection of the Capetian King, Phillip the Fair, and received the right to form a city government called the Consulate. Although she surrendered her municipal independence when Henry IV installed a provost, Lyon flourished with the support of the Crown. From the fourteenth to the seventeenth centuries goods flowed through her markets and gold into her banks from around the world. Rabelais, a physician at the Hôtel-Dieu, took advantage of the local printing industry to publish his tales of Gargantua and Pantagruel for sale at her great fairs. The public buildings and private residences erected during this period indicate that Renaissance Lyon was a city on the Saône. The Hôtel-Dieu, built on the peninsula along the right bank of the Rhône, was an exception. Only the bridge of La Guillotière linked the city with the rural plain of Dauphiné.

Although the archbishop had surrendered his temporal power, the church continued to exert an influence which was as much physical as it was spiritual. A large number of religious orders maintained chapters in Lyon. By the eighteenth century there were thirty-three houses and their chapels, cloisters, orchards, and gardens literally ringed the city;[2] Louis Trénard has estimated that the church owned and occupied three-quarters of the local land.[3] Thus, Lyon was an enclosed community, unable to expand naturally across her urban site in response to the pressure of a growing population and the introduction of a new industry, silk weaving.

The city held a monopoly on the sale of imported silk cloth from the middle of the fifteenth century. Weaving, however, was considered to be an Italian art. In 1536, one Étienne Turquet, a native of Piedmont who had made his fortune selling cloth, established twenty looms in Lyon. Exempt from taxes and militia duty by order of Francis I, the weaver community grew quickly. By 1559, the date of the Treaty of Cateau-Cambrèsis, there may have been as many as 7,000 looms in the city. For the next two and a half centuries the periods of prosperity and crisis in the Grande Fabrique (so-called to indicate its status as the city's most important corporation) were linked to the domestic and international fortunes of the Crown.[4]

The milestones in the history of the Grande Fabrique are its Regulations (*Règlements*) and ordinances, which mark both its institutional evolution and the development of social and economic conflict. The Regulation of 1554 described an open, infant industry. There were no rules to define the occupational prerequisites of a master or an apprentice, no limit to the number of looms a master could operate, and no restriction on their location. Furthermore, there was nothing to differentiate between a cloth merchant and a master weaver. The economic crisis which accompanied the civil wars of the late sixteenth century brought demands for more restrictive statutes. Henry IV responded in 1598 with an ordinance which set seven years' training (five as an apprentice and two as a journeyman) as a prerequisite for master status, limited each master to two apprentices, and excluded foreign weavers unless they had served apprenticeship elsewhere. An additional Regulation of 1619 imposed a limit of twelve looms for each workshop and restricted them to within the city's boundaries.

The seventeenth century was truly the *Grand Siècle* of the Lyon silk industry. From a postwar nadir of 1,800 looms in 1600, the Grande Fabrique had grown ten-fold by 1660. Although many workshops were occupied by the production of *unies* (plain cloth) or operated the small shuttle (*petite navette*) to manufacture ribbons, the most important impulse to economic growth came with the introduction of the Dangon loom (1605), which improved and made less expensive the production of *façonnes* (brocaded material). Rapid expansion made it difficult to control the quality of weaving, however. In 1667, Colbert imposed a new Regulation designed to correct the abuses and irregularities which he believed harmful to Lyonnais sales. In preparing the statutes Colbert refused to call a general assembly of the corporation; instead he relied on the advice of the provost, the Consulate, and a commission of silk merchants.

The main purpose of Colbert's edict was to create a strong governing body for the Grande Fabrique. At this time the corporation was composed of a pyramid of three economic groups, exclusive of apprentices and journeymen: at its peak were the merchants (*marchands*), who had no weaving training and bought and sold only finished cloth; next came the merchant-masters (*maîtres-fabricants* or *maîtres-ouvriers marchands*), who sold cloth commercially and also supervised its production on their looms; and at its base were the master weavers (*maîtres-ouvriers à façon*), who tended the looms in their workshops under short-term contracts with the merchants. The new board of six overseers (*maîtres-gardes*) was composed of four men chosen directly by the Consulate, which also selected thirty master weavers who were to elect the two remaining members.

The introduction of the board of overseers had three important results. First, the master weavers, numerically the vast majority of the corporation, were legally reduced to a minority on its governing body. Second, the nature of the selection process welded an alliance between the silk merchants and other elements of the commercial elite which dominated local political life. Using the overseers' power to regulate the quality of all cloth produced by the corporation and to inspect the records of each master weaver, this bourgeois coalition now controlled the industry. Third, the hybrid middle group, the merchant-masters, disappeared over time.[5] As the merchant-masters set their sights on becoming full-time merchants and, thereby, entering the group from which the overseers were directly chosen, their ranks were not renewed because the Regulation of 1667 made it nearly impossible for a master weaver to open a sales office without first abandoning his looms. By the mid-eighteenth century the number of basic groups in the Grande Fabrique had been reduced to two: merchants and master weavers.

Colbert had sacrificed the interests of the master weavers upon the altar of mercantilism. Little wonder that the publication of the Regulation of 1667 triggered a minor riot.[6] Agitation over restrictions and inherent inequalities never subsided before the Revolution. A virtual pattern emerged in the master weavers' struggle to win concessions from the Consulate and the overseers: first they appealed to the royal government, which persuaded the local authorities to yield to their demands; then, sometime later, the merchants would succeed in having these gains reduced or nullified. We will later see how this pattern reappeared with tragic results in October and November 1831.

The Regulations introduced, altered, or withdrawn during the eighteenth century are an accurate indication of the polarization of the Grande Fabrique. In 1698, the Consulate began to require a deposit of 5,000 *livres* from each overseer during his term in office. In 1700, the master weavers had this rule nullified and also won equal representation on the governing board. The Regulation of 1702, however, not only swept away these gains but also restricted the number of looms and apprentices per workshop. The merchants' intention was to limit the number of master weavers in the corporation.[7]

The cycle was renewed by the Regulation of 1737, which increased to eight the number of overseers and again gave equal representation to merchants and masters. But the Regulation of 1744 reduced to six the number of overseers (four merchants and two masters) and required a deposit to the corporation of 800 *livres* from all merchants and 200 *livres* from all merchant-masters; this money was nonrefundable if, in the latter case, a man closed his sales office and limited his work to that of a master weaver. The Regulation of 1744 was the final blow to the merchant-masters and climaxed the merchants' campaign to separate formally sales and weaving functions; with it disappeared the master weavers' opportunity for significant social ascension.[8] On the day the new statute was to go into effect there was a spontaneous strike in the workshops and a crowd of angry weavers gathered near the home of the provost. Their protest soon became a riot in which warehouses were pillaged and finished cloth was slashed. The Royal Council revoked the hated Regulation and restored the "democratic" one of 1737, but the next year troops were sent to place the city under martial law and to reimpose the Regulation of 1744.[9]

These controversies should be recalled when we later discuss the master weavers' campaign for equal representation on the *Conseil des Prud'hommes* in 1832 and 1833. The demand for an equal voice in the government of the silk industry persisted from the Old Regime into the modern era.

II

In the last half of the eighteenth century the Grande Fabrique was perhaps the most highly restricted and closely regulated corporation in France. Each type of job performed, cloth woven, thread spun, or dye blended, was subject to statutes governing preparation, production, and sale. And there was good reason for such controls. In 1789, Lyon and its suburbs had a population of 143,000, three-sevenths of whose lives depended in some way on the manufacture and sale of a luxury commodity, silk cloth.[10] For the same date Maurice Garden has collected precise information concerning the occupational structure of this remarkable large industry.[11] At the top of the pyramid of 34,762 persons directly employed by the Grande Fabrique were 308 silk merchants. Only 42 merchant-masters—those who combined sales and weaving—survived. Below them were the *canuts,* as the weavers as a group were by then described: 5,575 master weavers, 3,924 of their wives who worked the looms, 5,575 of their children who likewise wove, 507 apprentices, 1,796 journeymen, 1,015 female weavers without apprentice or journeyman status (a practice legal only after 1786, but present before nonetheless), 2,236 male and female corders, 4,993 female reelers, and 1,355 female throwers. In addition, there were thousands of persons engaged in spinning, carding, and dying thread. Thus, approximately 300 merchants controlled the industry by setting the weaving rates for 5,500 workshop masters, who in turn supervised the labor of more than 20,000 other workers in what Pierre Goubert has described as "the cascade of dependency" of preindustrial life.[12] According to information collected by the Consultate in 1788, there were 9,335 looms in operation in Lyon: 5,583 were for *unies,* 1,283 for *façonnes,* 2,007 for gauzes, and 257 for velours.[13]

From these sets of figures we can observe four important characteristics of the Lyon silk industry on the eve of the Revolution. First, cloth production was carried out in thousands of small shops of virtually equal size. The Regulations that until recently had restricted the number of looms in each workshop had produced their intended result of maintaining a homogeneous group of master weavers. Second, apprentices and journeyman constituted only one-fifth of the weaver population. The rules that required five years' training at each rank made them a small and relatively stable part of the community. At this time, according to Maurice Garden, there were few distinctions between the master weaver and his *compagnon;* "the latter was younger, but his condition was only transitory, he was always a master in preparation."[14] Third, weaving was generally a family operation. The urban home-workshop lay at the heart of the Grande Fabrique. Fourth, a majority of those who worked on or around the looms were women, many of whom were considered to be domestic servants with no status whatsoever in the corporation. When we speak of the *canuts* we should not forget that more than half of them were actually *canutes.* By 1830, significant change had occurred with regard to each of these pre-Revolutionary characteristics.

Attention to the details of Regulations and occupational structures should not lull us into the assumption that the Grande Fabrique had become static. During the generation before the Revolution the silk industry experienced a social upheaval, an internal revolution, which was related only indirectly to the political crisis of the French monarchy.

In 1784, an anonymous report noted that the Grande Fabrique was "in the most dreadful state of anarchy since the revolution of 1777" and that "a spirit of independence [was] rising rapidly among workers in every category."[15] The reference to the "revolution of 1777" meant the corporation restored after the fall of Turgot, who had abolished all guilds during the previous year in the hope of reviving the economy. Separate commissions of merchants and master weavers prepared new statutes. Compromise was impossible as each group appealed to its own self-interest in a period of economic crisis. Many merchants were willing to sacrifice their concern for strict regulation of the quality of dye and thread in order to compete for the reduced market by lowering production costs; the masters complained of receiving inferior materials and then being blamed and penalized for the resulting finished cloth. The masters, for their part, established the right to move their looms to the suburbs, operate an unlimited number of looms in each workshop, and hire women as weavers; the merchants lamented that the corporation had surrendered all control over weaving. A common line was drawn, however, at admitting Protestants to the industry. As a merchants' report commented: "They do not know anything yet about silk manufacture and will never know anything they do not learn from Catholics."[16]

Having lost the hope of becoming merchant-masters and having abandoned for the moment the demand for equal representation as overseers, the master weavers' principal goal was now to secure what they called a *tarif,* a fixed minimum rate for finished cloth. They first won permission for such a contractual agreement from the Consulate in 1779. In 1785, after their repeated requests for an adjustment and stronger enforcement had been ignored, the master overseers wrote directly to the Count of Vergennes (as Secretary of

State for Foreign Affairs he had the city under his jurisdiction), who requested that the mayor of Lyon, Tolozan, negotiate a settlement. To the latter's mind, however, a new *tarif* would establish a dangerous precedent. In words that might have come as easily from the pen of Dr. Prunelle, the mayor of Lyon fifty years later, Tolozan wrote that the weavers "would soon be raising new demands perhaps less justifiable than the present ones without considering that they must compete equally with the merchants in the business fortunes of the industry."[17] Promises were made, but the Consulate was clearly reluctant to accede for fear not only of raising the market price of Lyonnais cloth but also of triggering wage demands in other trades.

The *tarif* dispute became a crisis in August 1786, when the archbishop decided to invoke his feudal right to collect the wine tax (*le banvin*). Saddled with higher prices for their beverages, workers in a number of trades went on strike for a raise in wages or rates. On the evening of August 8 there were unruly demonstrations by silk weavers and hatters in the Place des Terreaux in front of the Hôtel-de-Ville and in the aristocratic Place Bellecour. Windows were smashed, the militia disarmed, and, after the mounted police fired into the crowd, a serious riot ensued.

Alarmed by the "two sous riot" (*l'émeute des deux sous*), for that was the additional rate demanded for a finished yard of taffeta cloth, the Consulate approved a temporary increase. But the strikes continued and the mayor was obliged to call for military protection. A certain Lieutenant Bonaparte was assigned to the unit which arrived. All workers were forbidden to assemble, to carry arms, or to make any mutual agreement "contrary to public order." On August 12, two leaders of the riot (a hatter and a journeyman taffeta weaver) were executed on the Place des Terreaux. According to Mayor Tolozan's account of the "two sous riot," "it was the journeymen who rioted to demand higher rates, [but] it was not against their masters with whom they have much in common, but against the merchants who determine the rates. One cannot overlook the fact that the masters themselves encouraged their journeymen in order to achieve their goal more easily."[18] If this analysis is correct—and there is no reason to question it—there was an important element of continuity in the composition of the Lyonnais "crowd": in 1786, as well as in the larger disturbances of 1831 and 1834, it was the journeymen silk weavers who actually took to the streets when an industrial dispute gave way to violence.[19]

The mayor changed his mind about the necessity for a new *tarif* as

a result of the "two sous riot." "It is unthinkable today," he wrote,
"after all that has happened, that a number of merchants in this
city persist in the injustice of refusing a slight increase to the unfortunate workers to whom they owe their brilliant and rapidly acquired
fortunes."[20] Before an agreement could be reached, however, an
edict of the Royal Council arrived nullifying all concessions by the
Consulate. Whether or not the king's intention was to remove all
restrictions on weaving rates—the fact that he later agreed to a *tarif*
in November 1789 strongly suggests it was not[21] —the merchants
interpreted the edict as giving them complete freedom to set rates
as low as the labor market would allow. And in a period of severe
unemployment this was very low indeed. Public works projects were
opened, private contributions for relief were solicited (Mayor Tolozan, for example, gave 4,000 *livres*), and a theater manager named
Collot d'Herbois organized a benefit performance for the unemployed *canuts*. Five years later he would return to Lyon as a member
of the Committee of Public Safety and launch the Terror. The overseers of the Grande Fabrique noted: "All writers, publicists, and
economists agree . . . that it would be better to make sacrifices . . . in
order to keep the worker occupied, than to turn him loose to live
a life in idleness and sloth which often leads to the worst consequences."[22] The appeal fell on deaf ears.

The conflict between merchants and master weavers was renewed
at the time of the selection of electors to the local Assembly of
the Third Estate. In February 1789, the members of the Grande
Fabrique gathered in the Cathedral of Saint Jean where the large
number of masters outvoted the merchants and chose a delegation
composed only of weavers. The merchants complained in vain to
Necker, the king's chief adviser, that they, who owned property
valued at sixty million *livres*, were unrepresented. The Consulate
refused to intervene for fear of more violence.[23] Thus, on the eve
of the Revolution, the threat of a worker uprising was an implicit
part of the city's life.

Encouraged by this victory, the master weavers again demanded
and this time received a *tarif* from the king. The new collective contract was supposed to take effect in January 1790, but the merchants
chose to ignore it. Finally, on 3 May, 3,500 master weavers gathered
in the Cathedral and voted to secede from the Grande Fabrique and
to form a separate corporation. Delegates were selected from each
quarter and charged with organizing the weavers into sections.[24]
When the National Assembly later passed the Le Chapelier law abol-
ishing all guilds the master weavers' schism was stillborn.

During the eighteenth century the *canuts* had united in opposition
to the silk merchants. Twice they saw their gains annulled and twice
their frustration boiled over into serious violence. But in 1744 they
reacted as members of a corporation refusing to admit the superi-
ority of the merchants, whereas in 1786 they were acting as workers
demanding a fixed wage. "Between the two dates," Maurice Garden
states, "there was a true *prise de conscience*, a radically different
social analysis of the condition of work in the Lyonnais *fabrique.*"[25]
Nevertheless, the *canuts*—masters, apprentices, and journeymen
alike—were opposed to what the merchants called "economic liberty"
and remained committed to the traditional world of regulation;
when they asserted their collective strength by seceding from the
Grande Fabrique it was for the purpose of starting a corporation of
their own. The search for an alternative form of organization would
dominate the future of their community. Thus, to cite Garden again,
"in the evolution of the [Grande] Fabrique there germinated all the
difficulties and combats of . . . the first half of the nineteenth
century."[26] The Revolution, in fact, broke the momentum created
prior to 1789 and may have retarded the development of a worker
movement in Lyon.

With the exception of Paris, Lyon suffered more than any other
city during the Revolution. Because she was already beset with a
social crisis it is remarkable that there was little serious violence for
nearly four years after the fall of the Bastille. But the old antagonisms did not disappear, they merely took new forms. At the review
of the National Guard in 1790, for example, the units from the
working class quarters carried the white flag of the Bourbons (associated with Louis XVI and the *tarif*), while those from the bourgeois
quarters displayed the new tricolored banner.[27] Profiting from the
municipal revolutions which occurred after 1789, the merchant elite
supported increased local and regional autonomy, a program associated with the ideas of the Girondist leader Roland de la Platière,
who came from the Lyonnais region.[28] But Louis XVI was executed
in January 1793, and the Mountain replaced the Girondists in control
of the Convention. In March, a band of local Jacobins seized the
Hôtel-de-Ville and placed their leader, J. Chalier, in power in Lyon.
On 29 May, in the same week as the Jacobins seized control of the
Commune of Paris, the Lyonnais Girondists staged a successful
countercoup. Chalier was executed in July and Lyon found herself
at the center of the federalist revolt.

Thousands of refugees, many of them weavers who had supported
Chalier, sought shelter in the surrounding countryside as the guns

of the arriving French army were trained on the city from the heights
of her two hills. From 8 August until 9 October, Lyon was first
besieged, then bombarded, and finally captured by military assault.
The Committee of Public Safety decided to make a grim example of
the nation's second city. On 12 October, the Convention passed a
decree which read, in part:

> The city of Lyon shall be destroyed. Every habitation of the
> rich shall be demolished; there shall remain only the homes of
> the poor, the houses of patriots . . . , the buildings employed in
> industry, and the monuments devoted to humanity and public
> instruction.
>
> The name of Lyon shall be effaced from the list of cities of the
> Republic. The collection of houses left standing shall hence-
> forth bear the name of Ville-Affranchie—the Liberated City.[29]

When the Committee's Representative on Mission, Georges
Couthon, requested to be transferred rather than enforce the decree,
two men with greater revolutionary zeal were sent to carry out the
task; one was the future Imperial Prefect of Police, Joseph Fouché,
the other was Collot d'Herbois. Not since the revenge of Septimus
Severius had Lyon witnessed such destruction. The popular Parisian
army (the *armée révolutionnaire*) poured into the city to support
the local worker sections as they stripped the marble façades from
the residences on the Place Bellecour and otherwise symbolically
"destroyed" the Ville-Affranchie.[30] Within six months of the end
of the siege nearly 2,000 men, women, and even children were
executed—more than 10 per cent of the total number killed in all
of France during the entire Terror. The most deplorable incidents—
comparable only to the mass drowning at Nantes—occurred in early
December when hundreds of prisoners were taken across the Rhône
to the suburb of Les Brotteaux where they were slaughtered by
cannon fire and buried in a common grave. The Lyonnais Terror,
moreover, had a greater class bias than elsewhere; whereas members
of the bourgeois and aristocratic classes constituted only 28 per cent
of the executions in the rest of France, they made up 64 per cent
of those killed in Lyon.[31] It was with some reason, therefore, that
the silk merchants later equated the Republic with the Terror.

For those who had sown the wind by their support of Chalier or
Collot d'Herbois Thermidor was a time to reap the whirlwind of
the White Terror.[32] The silk industry was almost destroyed in this

unhappy period. Not only was the domestic market disrupted by inflation and political uncertainty, but also the war cut off most international sales. The number of looms fell to 2,000, a figure which approached the nadir reached in 1600.[33] Recovery came only under the Empire when Lyon sent her silk and her sons across Europe; in the absence of a sufficient number of apprentices and native journeymen the bulk of the weaving was done by women and immigrant Savoyards.[34] To restore the grandeur of what had been the nation's richest industry, the Emperor introduced a number of programs, ranging from the European monopoly under the Continental System to the *tarifs* of 1808 and 1811. By the time of the first Treaty of Paris (1814) the annual value of Lyonnais production had reached 40 million francs and the industry was poised for a take-off period in which this figure would double by 1830.[35]

But this is to get ahead of our story. For the city and the silk industry had been transformed in a number of ways as a result of the Revolutionary and Napoleonic experience.

III

A visitor returning to Lyon in 1815 after a twenty-five year absence would have found her appearance strikingly different. There was little physical evidence of the siege and its aftermath—the Place Bellecour, for example, had been rebuilt during the Empire—but the axis of the community no longer lay along the Saône. New buildings, in fact entire quarters, were under construction near the confluence of the rivers, on the slopes of the Croix Rousse, and in the suburbs.

The community had already begun to break the ring of church-owned land during the eighteenth century. As early as 1714, fields belonging to the Benedictine abbey of Ainy were purchased for the construction of the Place Bellecour. In 1778, the six monks who remained in the Celestin abbey on the left bank of the Saône were secularized to allow the city to build a quai, a square, and a theater which later bore the name of their order.[36] The most ambitious pre-Revolutionary projects, however, were those of Antoine Perrache and Antoine Morand.[37] The former had plans for a new quarter at the confluence of the rivers, to be built on the islands as well as on the land made available when Louis XV closed the Benedictine abbey of Ainy. The Perrache family went bankrupt before 1789. After 1815, the city constructed a prison and slaughterhouses on this marshy land and residential neighborhoods and new industries followed. In 1852, Napoleon III inaugurated the city's main rail-

road station there, climaxing the delayed development of the
Perrache quarter. The latter urban planner, Morand, envisioned the
future growth of the city on the left bank of the Rhône. At this
time, however, the bridge of the Guillotière was the only span across
the river. In 1774, Morand supervised the construction of a wooden
bridge bearing his name, which linked the center of the peninsula
with the open area called Les Brotteaux, most of which belonged to
the Hôtel-Dieu. Land values rocketed as elaborate street plans were
drawn for this suburb. By 1789, however, Les Brotteaux was still an
area of open air cafes and pleasure gardens. The balloon flights of
Mongolfier, for example, rose from this site. A strong deterrent to
the development of Les Brotteaux lay in the fact that the area was
administered from Grenoble. The inclusion of La Guillotière and Les
Brotteaux in the new Rhône department after 1794 did much to
stimulate their post-Revolutionary growth.[38]
   If the full influence of the projects of Perrache and Morand lay in
the future, it was the sale of church property during the Revolution
which had an immediate effect on the city and the silk industry.
During the sixteenth and seventeenth centuries the weavers lived and
worked on the upper floors of buildings in the Renaissance city on
the peninsula between the Place des Terreaux and the site of future
Place Bellecour, as well as on the right bank of the Saône. Workers,
merchants, and aristocrats, in other words, shared social space.[39]
During the latter half of the eighteenth century the silk merchants
constructed magnificent warehouse—residences for themselves at
the base of the Croix Rousse hill; some of these buildings were along
the Saône, but the most impressive ones were along the Rhône on
the quai Saint Clair near the new Morand bridge. Some master
weavers had also moved their workshops into this northern section
of the city by 1789. Approximately 700 *ateliers* (around 15 per cent
of the total number in the Grande Fabrique) were situated on the
Grande Côte, the single street which ran from the base to the crest
of the Croix Rousse hill.[40] The Grande Côte ended at the *oc troi*
barrier (municipal tax station) formed by part of the sixteenth
century city wall which still separated Lyon from the suburb of
the Croix Rousse. The total population of Lyon's four principal
suburbs (La Croix Rousse, La Guillotière, and Les Brotteaux, and
Vaise) was 6,000 persons; the suburbs housed around 500 silk looms,
most of them having been installed within the decade as a result of
the liberalized regulation.[41] The vast majority of weavers, however,
continued to live in the old quarters of the city, particularly those

nestled between the Fourvière hill and the right bank of the Saône.
It was here in 1808 that a master weaver named Laurent Mourguet
first carved a *canut* puppet which he named Guignol.

In 1789, most of the Croix Rousse hillside was covered by religious
houses, orchards, and gardens. Its appearance was that of the countryside.[42] By 1820, however, this area had become the Jardin-des-
Plantes arrondissement with a population of 25,454 persons and
4,138 silk looms; by 1834, these figures had grown to 33,059 and
6,352 respectively.[43] Similar, if less spectacular, changes also had
occurred in the center of the peninsula where the demolition of the
Jacobin and Cordeliers abbeys permitted the construction of the
major squares which bore their names. On the right bank of the
Saône the confiscation of the church's vineyards on the side of
Fourvière opened a residential area built on the stairway-streets
called *montées*.

With the resurgence of the silk industry in the early years of the
Empire those who had purchases land on the slopes of the Croix
Rousse became speculators in real estate. New streets running lat-
erally across the hillside were opened and entire blocks of buildings
designed to accommodate looms and workshops were raised. A
network of passageways called *traboules*, a unique feature of Lyonnais architecture, were constructed to permit a person to walk from
the base to the crest of the hill without exposing the cloth he was
carrying to the elements.[44] In most cases materials garnered from the
destruction of religious houses were used for the construction of
these projects.[45]

One of these new streets was the rue Tolozan (the present day rue
Gabriel Marcel), a single block of twenty, nearly uniform buildings.
Because this street was a center of resistance during the uprising of
April 1834, it is appropriate that we examine the dimensions of life
there in detail. The rue Tolozan was atypical only in the fact that
it stood at the northern fringe of the urban development; above it lay
only the empty fields of a Carthusian monastery and the wall sep-
arating Lyon from the Croix Rousse suburb. (See Lyon in 1830,
pp. 16–17.) At its western end was another new street, the rue des
Flesselles, and at its eastern end ran the montée des Carmelites.
Across this ancient roadway were the new municipal gardens, the
Jardin-des-Plantes, formerly the property of a Carmelite house.
Further down the hillside was the Place Sathonay, whose outlines
followed those of the old cloister. Here the residents of the rue
Tolozan drew their water from a municipal fountain.[46] When com-

A drawing of Lyon in 1830. The buildings in the right foreground
are those of the rue Tolozan.

pared to the streets of the old city, this must have seemed a pleasant neighborhood indeed.

In 1834, the rue Tolozan was packed with 1,427 residents and 678 silk looms, a density which it had maintained for nearly a decade.[47] Two hundred and thirty-two master weavers (by this time called workshop masters, or *chefs d'atelier*) and 227 resident journeymen filled the air with the sound of the shuttle. Only twenty-six masters owned more than four looms: thirteen of them owned five, nine owned six, two owned seven, and one owned eight. Almost half of them were the new Jacquard model. Three hundred and ninety-six children—a remarkably small number for so many families— worked alongside their parents or played in the rocky field above their homes. Seven persons listed as "domestics" lived in this street; one or two might have worked for a master who retained the eighteenth century custom of keeping a servant girl to perform odd jobs in the workshop,[48] but it is likely that the rest worked elsewhere for a bourgeois family.

Table 1 reconstructs one of the buildings of the rue Tolozan. This six-story building with 69 residents and 35 silk looms was in no way unusual: the twenty buildings on the block ranged from five to seven stories and their average number of residents and looms was 71.35 and 33.9 respectively. What is remarkable about Number 3 of the rue Tolozan is not so much its size or its cramped quarters, but the fact that it was like a small factory. Residents with bourgeois occupations were nowhere to be seen; everywhere there were *canuts* weaving silk cloth in small workshops. An industrial setting had been created on the slopes of the Croix Rousse to produce what remained a preindustrial commodity. The *canuts* recognized these conditions as a part of their collective experience. As one of their newspapers apothesized:

> Who has never seen these houses of seven or eight stories, veritable hives of activity . . . Thousands of men, women, and children are crowded into these narrow, airless, dirty buildings and it is a pity to see in what holes live these ingenious workers, who produce velours, satins, gauzes . . . and all the other magnificent cloths. The nation does not know . . . how many men of genius are hidden in this glorious and unfortunate town of Lyon.[49]

The development of new quarters was only one aspect of the transformation of Lyon and the silk industry. By 1815, a series of national

laws and Lyonnais institutions had created a new structure for the
regulation of cloth production, replacing that of the Grande Fabrique
which had been abolished a quarter of a century earlier. Three institutions pertained principally to the concerns of the silk merchants:
the Chamber of Commerce (1802) was a restoration of a pre-Revolutionary body of the same name; the Commercial Court (1791) heard
cases of disputes involving more than 100 francs; and *La Condition
Public* (1804) tested samples of raw silk, thread, and cloth for quality
and weight. The latter was in a special building on the Croix Rousse
hillside and the merchants regarded its monthly reports as "a sure
thermometer of the health of the industry."[50]

The *Conseil des Prud'hommes* (1804) was a court of conciliation
with final judgment on disputes involving less than 100 francs.[51]
Under the original statute the board was composed of four silk merchants and three master weavers; in 1808, it was enlarged to include
representatives from the hosiery (one merchant and one master),
ribbon weaving (two merchants and one master), and hatters (two
merchants and one master) trades. Until its reorganization in 1832,
there were technically fifteen *Prud'hommes,* but the seven men
representing the *fabrique,* as the silk industry was now called, played
the most important role. The *Prud'hommes* were chosen by con-
stituent elections. In the case of the weavers, the franchise was
limited to masters who had paid the patent duty (less than 1 per
cent of their number)[52] and the journeymen were totally excluded.
In addition, the statutes noted that the merchants were always to
have at least one more representative than the masters. The *Conseil
des Prud'hommes* was a quasi-restoration of the overseers (*maîtres-
gardes*) of the Grande Fabrique and both the prestige and rancor
which surrounded the earlier institution soon were attributed to the
new one. The master weaver who wore the ceremonial emblem of a
Prud'homme became *de facto* a leader of the worker community.

All Frenchmen were theoretically equal in civic rights, but the
inherent inequality of the *Conseil des Prud'hommes* reflected the
general attitude of early nineteenth century law with regard to the
workingman.[53] In sweeping away the guilds the Le Chapelier law
(1791) had denied citizens the right to strike or associate in any
manner in order to advance "their pretended common interests."
That class bias influenced the interpretation of this statute may be
seen in the fact that workingmen's associations were forbidden as
obstacles to a free economy, while commercial organizations such as
the Chamber of Commerce were permitted. Imperial legislation also

TABLE 1. Number 3, rue Tolozan (corner of rue des Flesselles)

	Occupation of head of household	Number in household: family/resident journeymen	Number of rooms	Number of looms
Ground floor				
Cook-shop (*gargotier*)				
Charcuterie				
Apartment 1.	concierge-porter	1/0	1	1
2.	cooper	5/0	1	0
First floor				
Apartment 1.	master weaver	2/0	2	2
2.	designer	3/0	2	0
3.	empty			
4.	day laborers (bachelors)	2/0	1	0
5.	journeyman weaver	1/0	1	0
6.	master weaver	3/2	1	2
Second floor				
Apartment 1.	master weaver (widow)	1/2	1	2
2.	master weaver	2/2	2	2
3.	master weaver	3/1	2	2
4.	journeymen weavers (bachelors)	2/0	1	2
5.	empty			
6.	master weaver	1/1	1	2

Third floor				
Apartment 1.	master weaver	3/3	1	4
2.	master weaver	1/0	1	1
3.	master weaver	2/0	1	2
4.	master weaver	3/1	1	2
5.	master weaver	2/0	1	1
Fourth floor				
Apartment 1.	master weaver	1/1	1	1
2.	cobbler (master)	1/2	1	0
3.	master weaver	1/3	2	3
4.	master weaver	2/0	1	1
5.	master weaver	1/1	2	2
6.	clerk (bachelor)	1/0	1	0
7.	master weaver	1/0	1	1
8.	master weaver	1/1	1	2
9.	journeyman weaver	4/0	1	0
10.	empty			
Fifth floor				
Apartment 1.	washerwoman (widow)	1/0	1	0

Summary

Number of apartments	30
Number of occupied apartments	27
Number of rooms occupied	32
Number of residents	69
Number of silk looms	35

Source: AM K, "Recensement de la ville," 1834.

made specific distinctions between the rights of the worker and the
employer. The Penal Code (1810) forbade all "coalitions" to raise or
suppress wages; penalties for workers, however, were more severe
than for their employers. The Civil Code (1803) permitted courts to
accept an employer's word in a wage dispute, while a worker was
obliged to present physical evidence. Articles 291–294 of the Penal
Code prohibited all unauthorized associations of more than twenty
members whether for "religious, literary, political or any other
purpose." Although the authorities tolerated traditional worker
organizations such as the *compagnonnages,* this legislation prevented
the legal formation of more militant associations. Finally, each
worker was obliged to carry an identification booklet called a *livret,*
in which his employer noted the terms of his service, his conduct,
and his debts. In France as a whole these laws were commonly used
by master tailors, cobblers, and other artisans to regulate the activities of their journeymen. But in Lyon, the structure of the *fabrique*
meant that they also applied to the masters in their transactions
with the merchants. Each master weaver, for example, had a booklet
called a *livret d'acquit* for each of his looms in which the terms of
the weaving contracts were recorded.[54] If upon reading its contents
a merchant believed a master was rebellious or a poor risk he could
refuse to give him work. What the *canuts* themselves called "the
double character" of the workshop master—employer on the one
hand, employee on the other—was the most distinctive feature of the
Lyonnais weaver community.[55]

   The *canuts* were thus deprived of the recourse and protection—
frequently exaggerated in their minds—they had enjoyed under the
Regulations of the Grande Fabrique, and were sent into the world of
laissez-faire wearing the manacles of legal inequality. Little wonder
that their mentality was Janus-like: looking backward toward the
"moral order" of the world they believed they had lost, while at the
same time searching for new means of collective survival. As late as
1859, one observer came upon an eighty-year-old weaver who told
him: *"Monsieur, tout le mal vient de la liberté du commerce!"*[56]

   Commercial freedom also meant the end of the professional requirements of the Grande Fabrique. The master weavers were no
longer men who had been admitted to the corporation after years
of training. Now anyone who could afford to rent or purchase a
loom might call himself a "master" weaver. To the horror of some
chefs d'atelier, the institution of apprenticeship itself was fast dying
out. In the opinion of others, however, the education of these young

men was an economic burden which offered no reward.[57] This was
the era of the journeymen weavers, who, unlike the *compagnons* of
the Grande Fabrique, arrived in Lyon when the industry flourished
and abandoned the city when it languished. Often untrained and
with few roots in the community, they were called "the floating population" by the local authorities. Most of them came from the rural
regions of France, but a considerable number came from abroad.
According to statistics compiled by the prefect in 1833, among the
3,297 journeymen living in the Croix Rousse suburb only 547 had
been born there and 1,100 were foreigners.[58] The *canuts,* or at least
their leaders, recognized that the structure of the labor force was less
stable than it had been under the Old Regime. Throughout the
Restoration and the early years of the July Monarchy there was discussion about the "license" and "insubordination" which reigned
in the workshops; there were complaints, for example, about the
"capricious" journeyman who quit his job and demanded payment
for an unfinished piece still on the loom, or an apprentice who
wished to return to the farm and care for his sick parents.[59] Much
of the energy of the post-Revolutionary worker movement, therefore, was internally directed toward the self-regulation of masters and
journeymen.

A third aspect of the transformation of the *fabrique* resulted from
the introduction of the Jacquard loom. This important innovation,
a complex mechanism which transferred the pattern to the cloth by
means of punched cardboard forms, made possible the production
of brocaded cloth (*façonnes*) at a moderate price and permitted the
fabrique to compete for the new market among the middle classes.[60]
Jacquard was not an instant hero to his fellow Lyonnais, however.
When he first displayed his loom in 1804, the *Conseil des Prud'
hommes* ordered it publicly destroyed. This hostility was due to
three facts. First, the Jacquard loom was expensive; depending on
the model it cost between 400 and 4,000 francs. Second, it created
technological unemployment by making semiautomatic tasks previously done by the loomtenders. Third, even if he could afford one,
the master weaver might have no place to put it; its great height
and weight meant that most of the buildings in the old quarters were
physically incapable of housing a Jacquard loom.[61] Apartments in
the new buildings outside the central city, on the other hand, were
designed with tall ceilings and reinforced floors. The result was a
migration of the best-equipped *façonnes* workshops. By 1829 (a year
for which we have complete information concerning types of looms),

over 40 per cent of the 5,035 looms in the Jardin-des-Plantes arrondissement on the Croix Rousse hillside were Jacquard models as
compared with less than 10 per cent of the 5,847 looms in the
traditional worker quarters of the Métrople arrondissement on the
right bank of the Saône.[62] The Jacquard loom was in large part
responsible for the resurgence of the *fabrique,* but it also contributed
to the structural differentiation and physical displacement of the
weaver community.

This migration did not stop at the city boundaries and the growth
of the suburbs was the fourth aspect of the transformation of Lyon
and the silk industry. Although it began when the corporate statutes
were loosened after 1777, the movement of workshops to Vaise,
La Guillotière, Caluire, and the Croix Rousse suburb was largely a
post-Revolutionary response to the cost of living in the city. With the
exception of Paris, the central quarters of Lyon were likely the
most expensive place for a workingman to live in all of France.[63]
Particularly when compared to the situation of silk weavers elsewhere contemporary observers agreed that rents were high (double
those in Avignon, for example) and food and fuel far too expensive.[64] The principal cause of these high prices was the municipal tax
on goods which entered the city.[65] The *octroi* was so strictly collected that workers returning after a Sunday afternoon in the country had their market baskets inspected at the barriers.[66] While only
a successful master could install a Jacquard loom in a new building
on the slopes of the Croix Rousse, even the humblest weaver could
move to the suburbs; rents and taxes were cheaper there and he
could often cultivate a garden for his family. As the prefect reported
in 1833: "The suburbs are in the midst of prosperity; the town is
suffering. People are leaving the sober, humid, and stuffy town and
seeking breathing space."[67]

The disappearance of the rules restricting all looms to the city did
not uniformly work to the *canuts'* benefit, however. The silk merchants were no longer obliged to hire urban workers. Table 2 measures the growth of rural weaving between 1790 and 1870. Although
some of the specific figures compiled by Lévy-Leboyer differ from
those presented elsewhere in this book, the general pattern cannot be
disputed. Table 2 indicates that the uprisings of 1831 and 1834 seem
to have accelerated, but clearly did not initiate, the migration of
manufacture. The social and economic consequences of the development of rural weaving will be treated in the discussion of merchant
attitudes below.

TABLE 2. Growth of rural weaving, 1790–1870 (by number of looms)

Date	Lyon	Suburbs	Urban region	Rural	Total	Percent
1790	16,000	500	16,500	30	16,530	—
1800	5,000	100	5,100	42	5,142	—
1810	16,120	1,400	17,520	696	18,216	4
1820	19,200	3,500	22,700	2,568	25,268	10
1825	18,990	3,800	22,790	6,177	28,967	21
1830	18,000	11,278	29,278	8,265	37,543	22
1835	17,000	14,523	31,523	17,983	49,506	36
1840	—	—	27,450	30,050	57,500	52
1870	—	—	30,000	90,000	120,000	75

Source: Lévy-Leboyer, *Les Banques européenes,* 143.

The construction of new urban quarters, the post-Revolutionary framework of laws and institutions for the regulation of labor and production, the introduction of the Jacquard loom, the growth of the suburbs, and the development of rural weaving were five aspects of the transformation of Lyon and the *fabrique* which might have impressed our hypothetical visitor. This nexus of change had introduced powerful centrifugal forces in what had been previously a restricted community and industry. Now we must examine their impact on Lyonnais life.

IV

Around the year 1830, Lyon was among the world's largest and most important manufacturing centers. Approximately a quarter of her population was employed by the *fabrique* and silk and silk-related products accounted for half of the city's total commercial income and a third of the value of all French exports.[68] Three sets of questions suggest themselves. First, was Lyon growing steadily, in demographic equilibrium, or losing population? Second, had the creation of new quarters altered residential patterns, or were the silk weavers still distributed throughout the city? Third, was her occupational structure still that of a preindustrial city, or were men and women whose jobs are associated with modern industry already present in significant numbers?

A fluctuating population and a significant shift in its physical
distribution were the most important local demographic trends during the first half of the nineteenth century.[69] Lyon lost as much as
a quarter of her population as a result of the siege of 1793 and its
aftermath. Between 1800 and 1852, however, the city grew by 61.8
per cent, that is to say from 109,500 to 177,190 persons; in the same
period the population of the Rhône department increased by 115.3
per cent. By means of comparison, the population of Paris (inside
the *octroi* walls) rose from 546,856 to 1,053,064 between 1800 and
1851, and that of Toulon went from 20,500 to 69,404. Marseille,
which was likely the fastest growing city in France, went from
109,483 to 195,138 persons between 1821 and 1851, an increase
of 77 per cent in only thirty years.[70] Lyon's expansion, in other
words, was rapid but by no means exceptional.

Due to the fact that the excess of births over deaths was slight in
major cities in this period, we know that the principal cause of
French urban growth was rural immigration. The fluctuating rate
of increase in the population of Paris, for example, was tied directly
to the changing rate by which men and women left (or were forced
out of) the countryside for the capital. Table 3 shows that Lyon's
expansion was uneven and that there were times when her population actually decreased. These negative fluctuations (periods of either
slowed growth or loss of population) were caused by out-migration.
The 15.4 per cent loss of population between 1821 and 1831, in
fact, came at a time when there was an excess of births over deaths
in France as a whole.[71] When the Lyonnais authorities lamented
about the "floating population" of journeymen weavers they were
not only identifying the social group which characterized the post-
Revolutionary silk industry, but also the one principally responsible

TABLE 3. Pattern of population growth, Lyon, 1800–1851

1800–1821	+39.7%
1821–1831	−15.4%
1831–1836	+17.1%
1836–1841	+ 5.1%
1841–1846	+22.0%
1846–1851	− .8%

Source: Ch. Pouthas, *La Population française*, p. 101.

for the expansion and contraction of the community. It is significant that the uprisings of 1831 and 1834 occurred in a period when there was a marked increase in the local population; it is likely that this influx was tied directly to the economic recovery of the *fabrique* from the setbacks of the late 1820s.

The shift in the distribution of the population in the Lyonnais urban area is shown in table 4. The precision of the first set of figures is questionable, but the second set, compiled by the prefect and cited often in his correspondence, is the most accurate information available. Taken together they indicate the growth of the suburbs at the expense of the city. The subsequent annexation of La Guillotière (and Les Brotteaux), La Croix Rousse, and Vaise in 1852 climaxed nearly half a century of efforts toward administrative centralization in response to this phenomenon.[72]

Under the Old Regime the constraints on urban expansion (principally the extent of church-owned property) and the restriction of looms within the city boundaries had meant that the *canuts* shared social space with the other residents of Lyon; a significant number of weavers lived and worked in all quarters of the city. This description of residential patterns was no longer valid by 1830; instead there had developed distinctly working class neighborhoods—entire quarters devoted only to weaving. Having already examined a number of explanations for this transformation, we must measure the degree of social and economic polarization that had occurred.

The map of the quarters of Lyon has been drawn according to the boundaries indicated in the fiscal census of the city and may be used in interpreting figures 1 and 2, which are taken from the same

TABLE 4. Population of Lyon and its suburbs, 1789 and 1833

	1789	1833
Lyon	174,000	133,075
Suburbs	6,000	47,835[a]
Total	180,000	180,900

Source: AMDG, t.1, "Rapport sur le projet de réunion des communes suburbaines à la ville de Lyon," 27 November 1833.

[a] La Guillotière (including Les Brotteaux) 21,638; La Croix Rousse, 16,449; Caluire, 5,000; Vaise, 4,748.

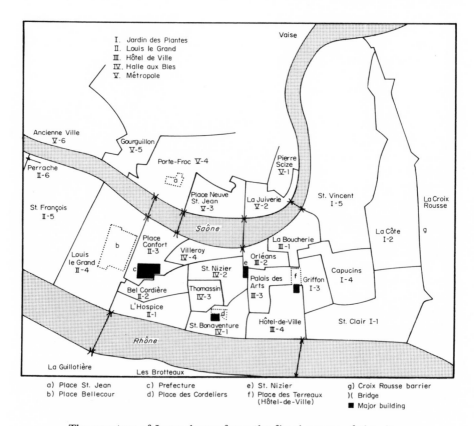

I. Jardin des Plantes
II. Louis le Grand
III. Hôtel de Ville
IV. Halle aux Bles
V. Métropole

a) Place St. Jean   c) Prefecture   e) St. Nizier   g) Croix Rousse barrier
b) Place Bellecour   d) Place des Cordeliers   f) Place des Terreaux   )(Bridge
                                                          (Hôtel-de-Ville)   ■ Major building

The quarters of Lyon drawn from the fiscal census of the city.

source.[73] Sequential data concerning the suburbs of La Guillotière (and Les Brotteaux) and Vaise are unavailable and these areas are therefore not represented here. Only the censuses of 1831 and 1834 exist for the suburb of the Croix Rousse.

The rapid expansion of the silk industry during the middle years of the Restoration, the severe crisis of the late 1820s, and the recovery after 1830, are the principal economic characteristics of the fifteen year period charted on the figures. These fluctuations can be seen in the flow of population and looms in the first and fifth arrondissements, as well as in the Croix Rousse suburb; these were the *canuts'* quarters and by 1830 they were growing rapidly again. But in the second, third, and fourth arrondissements—the entire peninsula from the Hôtel-de-Ville to the Perrache project—the changing fortunes of

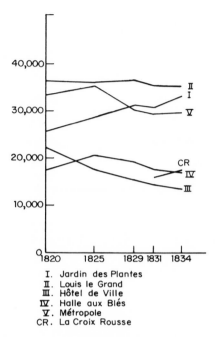

I.   Jardin des Plantes
II. Louis le Grand
III. Hôtel de Ville
IV. Halle aux Blés
V.   Métropole
CR. La Croix Rousse

FIGURE 1. Population of Lyon by arrondissement, 1820–1834
Source: AM K, "Recensement de la Population," 1820, 1825, 1829, 1831, 1834.

the *fabrique* are nowhere as apparent. There was, in fact, a net loss of population and looms with no suggestion there would be subsequent recovery. The polarization in residential patterns was clearly the result of the *canuts'* emmigration from the center of the city.

In order to grasp the social dimensions of the changing residential patterns on the peninsula we must recognize that in some quarters the emmigration was almost total, while in others the weaver population remained stable or actually increased. In the Hôtel-de-Ville quarter of the third arrondissement, for example, the population declined by 60 per cent and the number of looms by 85 per cent in less than a decade. All but 2 of the 18 looms which remained there by 1834 were clustered on a single street, the rue de l'Arbre Sec. In the Orléans quarter the number of residents fell about a quarter, while the number of looms plummeted from 128 in 1825 to only 2 in 1834—a loss approaching 99 per cent. In some cases the boundaries between quarters obscure the degree of polarization. The wealthy quarter of Louis le Grand in the second arrondissement,

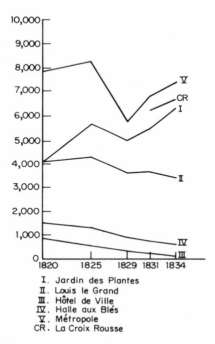

I. Jardin des Plantes
II. Louis le Grand
III. Hôtel de Ville
IV. Halle aux Blés
V. Métropole
CR. La Croix Rousse

FIGURE 2. Number of looms in Lyon by arrondissement, 1820–1834
Source: AM K, "Recensement de la Population," 1820, 1825, 1829, 1831, 1834.

where nearly 20 per cent of the population was composed of domestic servants, still retained 221 looms in 1834; but they were confined to two streets, the rue des Marronniers and the rue de la Sarre, which were contiguous with the Hospice quarter, one of the toughest neighborhoods in Lyon. Around the Hôtel-Dieu were a number of small, crowded streets such as the rue Noir (770 residents) and the rue Petit Soulier (845 residents) with the highest crime rates in the city.[74] In fact, if one were to trace a semi-circle on the map—beginning and ending at the Rhône and including all or parts of the Louis le Grand, L'Hospice, Bel-Cordière, Thomassin, Saint Nizier, and Saint Bonaventure quarters—he would mark an area characterized by a large number of recent arrivals to the city and a mixture of artisan trades. This area came closest to being a Lyonnais equivalent of those central quarters of Paris during the same period that have been described by Louis Chevalier.[75] On the other hand, a large number of workshops were introduced in the Perrache project at the same time as the *canuts* were rapidly abandoning other quarters of

the peninsula. Between 1820 and 1834, the number of looms in the
Saint François and Perrache quarters actually rose from 809 to 1,580.
Social space was shared with other classes in these new neighborhoods and, significantly, the weavers residing there played almost no
role in the worker movement.

The *canuts'* neighborhoods within the city lay in the first and fifth
arrondissements. There were important differences in the economic
character of the two areas, however. We have already noted that the
number of Jacquard looms in the new buildings of the first arrondissement suggest its relative affluence when compared to the
fifth arrondissement. The graphs substantiate this judgment. By
1834, the quarters on the right bank of the Saône housed the poorest
canuts. Nowhere on the Croix Rousse hillside can one find conditions such as those in the rue Saint Georges (2,955 residents and
1,109 looms) of the Gourgillon quarter; in 1831, only 39 of the
1,956 looms in the entire quarter were Jacquard models. Villermé
described the living conditions in this neighborhood as among the
worst in all of Europe.[76] The weavers of the fifth arrondissement had
to cross the city to deliver their finished cloth to the merchants,
while those in the first arrondissement had only to traverse the hillside to reach the major warehouses which lay in the Griffon, Capucins, and Saint Clair quarters.[77] In fact, one can draw an east-west
line bisecting the latter two quarters to mark where the looms
abruptly stopped and the warehouses began; north of the line were
the *canuts* and south of it were the bourgeois neighborhoods. To
conclude with an unanswerable question: did the residents of the
first arrondissement play such a prominent role in the worker movement, as well as in the uprisings of 1831 and 1834, because they
lived in closest proximity to the silk merchants?

The polarization in residential patterns, which anticipated by half
a century the post-Haussmann transformation of Paris, was complex and is difficult to recapture. Nevertheless, enough information
has been presented here to indicate that by 1830 it had a powerful
influence on the character of Lyon. As an economist later described
it: "This is a city unlike any other . . . The different areas (*parties*)
are separated from one another by natural barriers. One could say
that each social class is lodged separately like the Jews of the Middle
Ages."[78]

During the early years of the July Monarchy Lyon remained a preindustrial city with no significant group in her labor force whose
occupation is associated with modern industry. Table 5 is an abstract

TABLE 5. Abstract of the population of Lyon and its suburbs, 1833

	Rentiers, liberal professions, and employers	Professions under the patent	Workers outside the fabrique	Silk workers	Total
Lyon	20,771	36,943	39,041	36,320	133,075
La Croix Rousse	1,580	2,350	2,471	10,048	16,449
La Guillotière (including Les Brotteaux)	967	5,359	10,780	4,532	21,638
Vaise	615	1,719	1,486	918	4,738
Total	23,933	46,371	53,778	51,818	175,900[a]

Source: AMDG, t.1, "Rapport sur la situation industrielle."
[a]If the population of the commune of Caluire (5,000) is included the total is 180,900.

(Relevé de la population) prepared by the prefect in 1833. It divides the Lyonnais into two groups, bourgeois (70,304 persons) and workers (105,196 persons). Table 6 redivides the latter group into thirty occupational categories. The entire document is taken from the prefectoral papers with only the addition of eight subheadings. The apparent discrepancy in the figures—51,818 silk workers in table 5 and 40,650 in table 6—is attributable to the fact that the former includes all persons dependent on the fabrique (excluding the merchants), while the latter lists only those actually employed by it.

Five features of Lyonnais occupational structures after 1830 deserve comment. First, the tables confirm the persistence of a traditional artisanate. Only the masons, carpenters, joiners, and cloth printers worked in a mass labor or factory setting. In the case of the latter, we have found a police report that mentions six shops employing 200 printers in the Saint Clair commune behind the Croix Rousse suburb.[79] The tables do not include the men who repaired the Croix Rousse barrier and built the fortresses around the city at this time. Although they numbered as many as 5,000, they were seasonal laborers who returned to their villages for the winter.[80]

TABLE 6. Working classes of Lyon and its suburbs

	Masters	Journeymen	Women	Working children
Silk industry				
silk weavers	8,000	8,000	7,000	12,000
spinners (*tourneurs*)	80	100	80	150
dyers (*teinturiers*)	70	400	150	250
tulles weavers	100	300	500	400
cloth printers	70	1,000	1,600	400
Total	8,320	9,800	9,330	13,200
			Total	40,650
Clothing trades				
cobblers	400	2,000	4,000	2,000
tailors	400	1,000	3,000	1,600
hatters	300	800	2,000	1,500
wigmakers	300	400	150	200
Total	1,400	4,200	9,150	5,300
			Total	20,050
Food sellers				
bakers	200	300	200	400
butchers	300	400	300	500
Total	500	700	500	900
			Total	2,600
Building trades				
masons	150	1,200	200	800
carpenters	100	1,200	200	600
plasterers	80	300	100	300
stone cutters	20	150	30	50
marble cutters	40	100	400	100
Total	390	2,950	930	1,850
			Total	6,120

(continued)

TABLE 6, continued

	Masters	Journeymen	Women	Working children
Transportation and delivery				
curriers	50	300	70	150
wheelwrights	100	300	100	200
blacksmiths	100	250	100	250
saddlers	80	200	100	200
porters	–	800	500	700
Total	330	1,850	870	1,500
			Total	4,550
Heavy shop trades				
coopers	100	250	100	200
iron founders	50	600	400	600
tinsmiths	150	400	120	250
Total	300	1,250	620	1,050
			Total	3,220
Skilled shop trades				
printers	50	400	200	300
jewellers	150	200	250	500
joiners and woodworkers	300	3,000	600	1,500
scalemakers	50	100	60	120
locksmiths	150	400	200	400
Total	700	4,100	1,310	2,820
			Total	8,930
Miscellaneous (ouvriers divers)	3,000	4,700	4,500	8,000
TOTALS[a]	14,940	29,550	27,210	38,890

Source: AMDG, t. 7, "Tableau statistique des ouvriers de Lyon et des faubourgs en 1833," n.d.

[a]In table 5 the working classes of Lyon and its suburbs totals 105,596; in table 6 the total is 110,590. The discrepancy of 4,994 persons appears in the original documents, apparently an error made by Prefect Gasparin or a member of his staff.

Second, women and children constituted a majority of local workers, not only in the silk industry but in the city as a whole. While it is evident that the family work-unit remained in operation, additional research would be necessary to learn how much of it was devoted to "sweated" or "dishonorable" labor.[81] Third, Lyon's second largest occupational group was employed in the clothing trades. The hatters had been among the most volatile local trades during the eighteenth century (recall their role in the "two sous" riot of 1786) and the tailors and cobblers were to be part of the attempt to rejuvenate the *compagnonnages* with a wave of strikes in the fall of 1833. Fourth, a comparison of the work force in La Guillotière and La Croix Rousse (table 5) reveals that the *canuts* had moved less readily across the Rhône than up the hillside and beyond the *octroi* barrier. The growth of the suburbs, in other words, was uneven in terms of occupation.

Fifth and finally, the tables show the extraordinary presence of the *canuts.* Excluding the cloth printers (who were not considered to be *canuts*[82]), we can see that since 1789 the ratio of masters to journeymen and apprentice weavers had gone from 2/1 to 1/1, while the number of children employed had risen sharply. This confirms the important change in the structure of the weaver community. Furthermore, it is remarkable—perhaps unique—that at this time a large urban area should have a quarter of its population dependent on a single industry. That the *canuts* were dispersed in 8,000 or more separate shops, each of them devoted to hand manufacture, is a fact of considerable significance. While the residents of the rue Tolozan technically remained artisans, they daily experienced many features of industrial life without either factories or machines. This proto-industrial concentration of labor made life there unlike that in any other major city. Of the two French urban areas with which Lyon can properly be compared, Paris and Marseille had far greater economic diversity; neither approached her dependence on a single trade.[83]

Lyon in 1830, like Paris and Marseille, was still a preindustrial city. Her rate of growth, in fact, lagged behind the other two. But Lyon had special demographic trends, residential patterns, and an occupational structure that rendered her peculiarly explosive. Prefect Gasparin articulated this fact when he wrote: "The unfortunate position of Lyon is that it has really only one industry and thus discontent here is never partial, but soon becomes general."[84]

V

In order to plumb the depths of this discontent we must move
"inside" the silk industry and follow the merchants, the master
weavers, and the journeymen through the manufacturing process.
It will be important to see how each group perceived its work in
relation to that of the others, as well as how they articulated the
problems of the industry.

The silk merchants were commercial capitalists seeking to market
goods of high quality at the lowest possible cost. As tempting as it
might be to picture them in such a way, most were not French
counterparts of the infamous Mr. Bounderby in Dickens' novel *Hard
Times,* grinding out huge profits on the sweat of their weavers'
brows.[85] Silk, unlike cotton cloth, was a luxury product at the mercy
of the sensitive mechanisms of the international market. One report
issued by the Chamber of Commerce in 1832, noted the cholera
epidemic in Paris, revolutions in Latin America, the banking crisis
in the United States, tariff debate in England, and the growth of
Swiss and German competition as all directly affecting the *fabrique*
of Lyon.[86] Figure 3 charts the annual quantity of raw silk registered
at *La Condition Public* from 1806 until 1835. Figure 4 measures
the monthly quantity between January 1832 and June 1834. It is
true that only samples (perhaps a half or a third of a given lot[87])
were registered and that a portion of the registered silk was resold
directly on the market for weaving in other cities.[88] In fact, the
editor of the *canuts'* newspaper believed that the records of *La
Condition Public* were not an accurate means of judging the weavers'
situation in Lyon.[89] Nevertheless, the graphs do reveal the principal
economic characteristic of the *fabrique* in the first half of the nineteenth century: seasonal fluctuations and recurrent short-term crises
within a long-term trend of expansion. Between 1824 and 1826,
for example, the amount of registered silk fell nearly 25 per cent,
threatening bankruptcy for many merchants and unemployment or
lower rates for the weavers. "The *canuts,*" commented Villermé,
"pass rapidly from an excess of misery to prosperity and back again
to distress."[90]

The merchants were both puzzled and angered that a militant
worker movement reemerged in precisely those years (1831–1834)
when the *fabrique* was recovering from half a decade of stagnation,
but faced increased foreign competition. Between 1828 and 1830,
the value of English silk cloth (principally in the form of bandannas
and other cheap items) imported in France had risen from 119,570

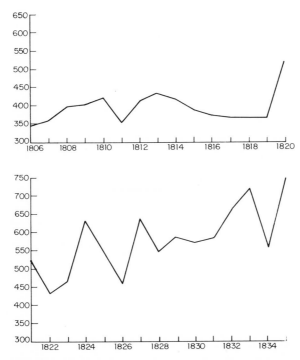

FIGURE 3. Raw silk registered by *La Condition Public,* 1806–1835 (in thousands of kilograms)

Source: *Archives statistiques du ministère des Travaux publics de l'Agriculture et du Commerce* (Paris, 1837), p. 267.

to 643,730 francs.[91] Table 7 reveals that French exports had successfully met the British challenge on the international market by mid-century. Seen from the perspective of the years immediately after 1830, however, the short-term trend appeared threatening indeed.

Between 1815 and 1830, the annual value of Lyonnais sales doubled at the same time as the number of silk merchants grew ten-fold.[92] In the latter year, French silk cloth exports to the United States were valued at 37,563,665 francs, 18,309,636 to the German states, and 15,204,388 to England, with a total export figure of 111,118,802 francs.[93] While the major Lyonnais firms were able to weather the brief periods of lower sales, around them were clustered hundreds of small houses with little capital margin. The result, in the words of a spokesman, was "a continual war of merchant against

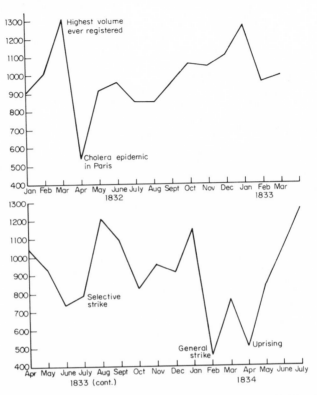

FIGURE 4. Volume of raw silk registered by *La Condition Public*, January 1832–June 1834 (in number of bales)
Source: Monthly reports in *Le Courrier de Lyon*.

merchant."[94] This multiplicity, one might even say excess, of firms made the average silk merchant hostile to any demand for higher weaving rates or a *tarif*. While publicly rejecting them out of a statesmanlike concern for liberal principles and the economic health of the nation, privately he was as likely as not seeking to prevent his business from going under.

In the merchants' minds the future of the industry depended on thwarting foreign competition by maintaining high quality and moderate prices in the brocaded cloth called *façonnes* and developing cheaper production methods for the plain cloth called *unies*. In addition to encouraging the use of the Jacquard loom, firms which specialized in the sale of *façonnes* had their own designers who

TABLE 7. Proportional value of exported silk cloth, Great Britain and France, 1825-1845

	Great Britain	France
1825	—	100[a]
1826-1829	6	91
1830-1833	11	84
1834-1835	16	93
1836-1838	20	117
1839-1841	20	128
1842-1843	17	117
1844-1845	19	137

Source: Adapted from Lévy-Leboyer, *Les Banques européenes,* p. 148.
[a] The year 1825 = 100. British values are converted to francs.

patented their intricate and beautiful creations. The municipal government supported an art school where local children were trained for employment by the merchants; a student with exceptional talent for design might even be offered a partnership in a firm.[95] Although mounting the pattern and weaving *façonnes* required the work of a skilled artisan operating a special loom, the merchants considered these functions to be of secondary importance. As their newspaper stated, "the merchants compose the intellectual portion of the industry. The difference between a master weaver and a merchant is that between a construction worker and an architect."[96] This condescending attitude severely poisoned relations between merchants and masters.

The vast majority of the *canuts* continued to operate the simpler *unies* looms. The exact number of looms in Lyon and its suburbs, as well as the proportion of *façonnes* to *unies* looms, is difficult to discover. In 1832, the *Courrier de Lyon* lamented that estimates varied widely and encouraged the *Conseil des Prud'hommes* to make an annual survey.[97] Late in 1833, the prefect undertook this task as part of his industrial report on the city. Tables 8 and 9 are drawn from this document.[98]

The *unies* weavers were the ones threatened by the growth of rural weaving (see table 2). Cheap foreign cloth for handkerchiefs, hats, and simple clothing was cutting into what once had been a secure

TABLE 8. Number of looms in Lyon and its suburbs, 1833

Lyon		16,087
Suburbs		
La Croix Rousse	6,259	
La Guillotière (including Les Brotteaux)	2,200	
Vaise	400	8,859

TABLE 9. Number of looms by category in Lyon, 1833

Unies	10,855
Façonnes	2,911
Velours	711
Crapes	359
Tulles	614
Bas	231
Passementerie	473
en repos	1,358
Total	17,512

Source: AMDG, t.1, "Rapport sur la situation industrielle."

Lyonnais market. The merchants believed that the local *unies* houses could only survive by radically reducing production costs. Despite the fact that the master weavers had begun to employ cheap female labor for these items,[99] some merchants were convinced that it was no longer a question of paying lower rates, but that *unies* production itself had no future within the urbanized industry. As a result they began to employ part-time rural labor. With cottage industry growing at their expense the *canuts* did not appreciate the irony that their fate at the hands of "economic progress" was the opposite of most nineteenth century handloom weavers.[100] Instead their newspaper lectured on the dangers which lay in the disperson of production.[101] As one report noted: "To carry the Lyonnais *fabrique* outside Lyon is to want to transport Lyon herself outside her walls."[102]

The factory system was only anticipated in the *fabrique*. Mechanization (for winding thread—a development that many masters applauded because it freed young children to attend school) and large sheds (for printing designs on plain cloth) had been introduced, but in 1830 there was little weaving done outside the small workshops. One exception was the installation of 200 looms for weaving plain crepe cloth at a waterfall twelve miles outside Lyon. A second was the proposal to establish a factory staffed by female weavers to make plush cloth for hats in a nearby village; one woman, who was asked to work as a foreman, refused *"pour ne faire pas tort à la classe ouvrière."*[103] A third exception suggested that factories were as yet unprofitable. In 1828, a philanthropic merchant named Charles Berna installed perhaps as many as 500 Jacquard looms in a chateau called La Sauvagère, which stood along the Saône about a mile upstream from Lyon. Calling his enterprise a *Grand Atelier,* Berna opened men's and women's dormitories and a cheap restaurant for the weavers, who worked in shifts under the supervision of foremen, or *contre-maîtres.* By the time Berna died in 1832, La Sauvagère was already a financial failure. Although the workers were known to be satisfied, his successor, Charles Depouilly, could not save the experiment. Decades later, when factories had arrived in Lyon, the legend had it that the *Grand Atelier* had failed because Berna and Depouilly had been too "liberal" with the *canuts.*[104] Nevertheless, many merchants regarded the concentration and mechanization of weaving to be the wave of the future.

The silk merchants believed themselves to be the central figures of the *fabrique.* Commercial considerations dictated their decisions, whether to pay minimum weaving rates, to disperse the looms in the countryside, or eventually to mechanize them. From their point of view the destruction of traditional workshop production was to be desired because the master weavers were now little more than "parasites" and "useless intermediaries" between themselves and the journeymen.[105] The *canuts,* on the other hand, saw things another way.

"The *canuserie,* or class of weavers, is divided and subdivided like society," wrote the *chef d'atelier,* Pierre Charnier. "It has its rich and its poor, its aristocrats and its humble subjects."[106] While the fundamental distinction was between journeymen and master weavers, there were important differences within the latter group. The "aristocrats" were the handful who owned a large number of looms. Acting as virtual subcontractors for the merchants, in theory nothing prevented them from amassing enough capital to become *fabricants* themselves. Although such mobility had, in fact, disappeared along with the merchant-masters of the Grande Fabrique,

TABLE 10. Number of master weavers owning four or more looms, 1832

Looms	13	12	11	10	9	8	7	6	5	4
Masters	1	4	0	2	8	12	8	53	82	614

Source: House of Commons, *Silk Trade,* p. 541.

the merchants continued to use it as a scourge with which to chastise the masters for their "idleness." [107]

The middle rank of master weavers was composed of those who owned four or more looms. Eligible for election to the *Conseil des Prud'hommes* after the reform of December 1831, these men were the "active citizens" of the weaving community.

From table 10 we can see that the average master weaver (seven-eights of the *chefs d'atelier*) owned fewer than four looms. Fiercely defensive of the fact that he was not an *ouvrier,* a simple worker, his absolute dependence on the merchants' rates brought this "humble subject" close to the economic position of a piece-work laborer.

The master weavers were constantly reminded of the power which the merchants held over their lives. Conflict between them was a by-product of the industry. Here is a dramatized conversation which appeared in the weavers' newspaper, *L'Écho de la Fabrique.* A *unies* weaver has just delivered a rush order to a merchant, who is sitting behind the iron grill (the *canuts* called it "the cage") of his warehouse:

> *Chef d'atelier:* "Here is the piece I've brought you."
>
> *Fabricant:* "Well, it's about time. It was due at eight o'clock this morning and it's already noon. Because of you I won't be able to send the order out today."
>
> *Chef:* "Please excuse me, Monsieur, but my wife and I have worked on nothing else for the last twelve days. We haven't even left the loom to eat. We had many problems because the thread was so poor and the weave so fine. And my wife, who is pregnant, intended to weave all night, but she fell asleep at the loom. That is why I am late."
>
> *Fabricant:* "That's all well and good. Nevertheless you've caused my order to be late." (Looks over the cloth.) "Here's a stain. What did you do, eat your stew over the loom?"

Chef: "Oh, Monsieur! If it's there it's because we were so pressed for time. My wife didn't even have time to make soup. We haven't eaten anything but bread while we worked on your order."

Fabricant: "Ah, here's a thread out of line." (To his clerk) "Monsieur Léon, mark this man down ten centimes per aune for waste."

Chef: "But Monsieur, have you no conscience? After we worked all night with such poor thread there are bound to be mistakes. It isn't fair to mark us down for that."

Fabricant: "Fair or not, that's the way it's going to be. When I pay good money I expect good work. And if you're as poorly paid as you claim, let me remind you that you didn't have to take the job. You could have refused it."

Chef: "But you know very well that I haven't worked for three months and that I took it because my savings are gone. I couldn't refuse it because my wife is pregnant."

Fabricant: "That is not my affair. I'm in business to make money, not to give you charity. What you are saying means little to me."

Chef: "Will you give me another order?"

Fabricant: "Give you another order? After the way you made me late on a commission! You dare ask for another order. No, my dear man. We only give orders to those who appreciate what we give them. Here is your payment.

Chef: "Dog of a merchant! If good times come you'll hear from me again."

Fabricant: (To his clerks) "Messieurs, you will be heads of commerce some day. I cannot recommend more highly such severity with the workers . . . It is the only way to force them to weave well. It is the only way that our industry can prosper."[108]

Such a confrontation was not pure fiction. We know, for example, that the harsh treatment given Pierre Charnier by a clerk of the Bouila firm in 1827 led directly to the foundation of the masters' Society of Mutual Duty.[109]

Secure inside his "cage" the merchant was on guard against all of the abuses of domestic manufacture: sloppy work, the theft of thread (in Lyon it was called *piquage d'once*), the artificial weighting or stretching of the cloth. From the *canuts'* point of view, however, those which the merchants built into the system were far more serious. Among the more vexing were the refusal either to permit the master to write the weight of the thread and the terms of each contract in the merchants' books or to weigh the finished cloth in his presence (although both were required by law), the failure to return bobbins which were the masters' property, and the refusal to pay higher rates for rush orders which required nighttime weaving— work which cost the *canuts* oil for their lamps and coal for their stoves, as well as their sleep.[110] Furthermore, the warehouses dispensed orders and received cloth only within fixed hours so that poor masters were known to pawn their tools in order to eat before being paid and anyone who disputed a merchant's decision risked angering his fellow weavers waiting in line behind him.[111]

Masters who owned Jacquard looms had special grievances. By custom the *chef d'atelier,* not the *fabricant,* bore the cost of mounting *façonnes* patterns on the looms. This was an operation which could idle a loom for a week or more and required a considerable investment; in the case of a major order, an outlay of 100 francs was not unknown. Most masters were obliged to seek a cash advance, thereby tying themselves to a specific firm. Should the merchant cancel the contract, the master simply lost his investment and found himself indebted for future work. Risks such as these reduced competition to weave the latest *façonnes* designs. Not only did the merchants fine them severely for damage to the cardboard forms (the *cartons*) which transferred the pattern to the cloth, but the masters also knew that working with a new pattern increased the chance of unexpected mounting costs and problems. Some masters with the equipment and training to weave *façonnes* actually confined themselves to *unies* cloth because the latter promised them more working days at less financial risk.[112] Complaints such as these accumulated at the heart of the conflict between silk merchants and masters in Lyon.

The master weavers were no longer the homogeneous group they had been in the era of the Grande Fabrique. There was now a hierarchy of status based on the number and type of looms owned. Masters who had a number of Jacquard looms frequented different cafés than did those who were less successful. The wives of more affluent masters sometimes refused to recognize in the street women

whose husbands had only one or two *unies* looms.[113] The "aristocrats" among them were united with the "humble subjects," however, in the conviction that they performed the critical function
in the manufacturing process. The key to the development of the
Lyonnais worker movement lay in their ability to convince the
journeymen that it was the merchants and not themselves who were
the real "parasites" of the industry.

The lives of the journeymen weavers cannot be described in simple
terms. The old image of the *compagnon*—a young bachelor who
called his master *mon bourgeois,* worked for half the rate paid for
the finished cloth, and lived in the same room as the looms—simply
does not work by 1830. In a large shop housing four or five looms
one might find the master and his wife operating two looms, an
apprentice (more often than not the master's son) being trained at
another loom, an experienced journeyman renting a loom from the
master by the month, and an unskilled weaver signed on for the
preparation of a single order. In this example (table 1 shows it is not
merely hypothetical) the apprentice could live with the master's
family, the experienced journeyman with his wife in a furnished
room, and the unskilled weaver alone in a garret or with others from
his rural region or country. The experienced weaver may have been
saving to purchase a loom, while the unskilled weaver was as likely to
move to another shop or take a job on a construction project for
the next week as he was to continue working for the same master.[114]
In another shop one could discover a well-trained female weaver, a
female apprentice, or an unskilled *canute* who might have had to
sleep with the master to gain work. There were even female masters
who specialized in a material called *shalls.* [115]

The critical question with regard to the journeymen is why, despite
the separation of social status and economic interest which potentially existed between them, they did not consider the masters as
"useless intermediaries" but instead were united with them against
the merchants? The answer revolves around the negative and positive
poles of a single fact: the journeymen weavers were indeed a "floating population." Seeking to explain the relative absence of class
consciousness among immigrant laborers in nineteenth century Bos-
ton, Stephan Thernstrom has observed that unskilled workers who
had the greatest grievances "are precisely those who never stay put
very long in any one place."[116] So it was with the *canuts.* While the
journeymen came and went, strangers to one another and often
literally not speaking the same language, the masters remained to

define and articulate the problems of the community. In 1789, there
had been 1,796 journeymen, each of them "a master in preparation";
in 1830, there were more than four times that number and few had
the possibility of advancement. In addition, there were no longer
legal restraints on their movement. This is not to say that they were
a *classe dangereuse* (in fact, Savey-Casard has estimated that in an
era of rapidly rising crime rates weavers committed only 15.5 per
cent of the reported crimes in Lyon[117]) but that the stable world of
the *compagnon* had given way to a fluid one of piece-work laborers.
In 1832, as we shall later learn, the journeymen formed their own
organization. Because it was abolished along with most other worker
associations in 1834, we cannot know whether they would have
continued to follow their masters' lead as they acquired a sense of
institutional continuity for themselves.

A more positive explanation is that the *canuts* not only experienced mutual hardships, but also shared social goals. If one were
to regard the structure of the workshop in the crudest economic
terms the master was a petit-bourgeois craftsman whose property
(his looms) placed him in constant conflict with the journeyman, a
sort of preproletarian with only his labor to sell. Yet, they worked
side by side and their income was determined by a third party, the
merchant. While the weaver could complain about the irregularity of
his work or even demand more than the traditional half of the
established rate, he could not accuse the master of reaping idle
profits. It is indicative of workshop relations that Joseph Benoit, a
canut elected to the Chamber of Deputies from Lyon in 1848, should
refer to the *chef d'atelier* as "a worker [an *ouvrier,* a term which
the masters themselves felt was demeaning] and one of the most mis-
treated in our economic society," and describe the plight of the
journeyman by saying that "his life, like that of the master weaver,
is a continual struggle, a constant fear for the future."[118]

In what became a litany on social conflict the merchants charged
that "the alliance which exists today between the masters and the
weavers is clearly contrary to the interests of the latter group"[119]
and the masters replied that the journeymen were satisfied with the
wage arrangement and that with hard work they could achieve the
goal of owning a loom and becoming masters themselves.[120] No
matter that this defense was nearly as unrealistic as the merchants'
vow that any *chef d'atelier* might become a *fabricant,* for, as Joseph
Benoit tells us, "the trials endured collectively" created "a solidarity
and a community of sentiments capable of uniting the world of the

canuts."[121] So far as generalization is possible about so diverse a group, the weavers mirrored the masters' perception of the problems of the silk industry. And that view, as stated by the *Écho de la Fabrique,* was that "without contradiction, the most direct and scandalous [abuse] is the IMMORAL AND ARBITRARY EXPLOITATION OF THE MASTER WEAVER BY THE MERCHANT, . . . who by virtue of the laws which govern us . . . exploits the industry as he chooses."[122]

In 1830, the *canuts,* the silk industry, and the city of Lyon were like a latent, but potentially explosive compound. The concerted demand for the restoration of a *tarif* by the worker community soon furnished the catalyst which triggered the rebellion of November 1831.

2   The Rebellion of November 1831

On 3 August 1830, the tricolor was raised over the Hôtel-de-Ville in Lyon. Without waiting for direction from the capital, local liberals had called out the National Guard against the government and encouraged the master weavers to close their workshops and send their journeymen to demonstrate against the July Ordinances. By the time representatives of the new monarch, Louis Philippe, arrived a provisional government was already functioning. In both Paris and Lyon the participation of the working class was crucial in toppling the Bourbons. In the euphoria of victory the silk merchants and *canuts* together hailed the new regime. But their unity was to be short-lived. The July Days helped rekindle the weavers' hopes and reminded them of their potential power.[1] In November 1831, after their successful demand for a *tarif* had been thwarted by the merchants, the *canuts* rose in rebellion, drove out the garrison, and unexpectedly found themselves in control of the city. Although they voluntarily yielded to the authorities, the rebels with their motto "Live Working or Die Fighting (*Vivre en travaillant ou mourir en combattant*)" had presented a frightening spectacle to the supporters of the *juste-milieu*. The *Journal des Débats* warned: "The barbarians who menace society are neither in the Caucasus nor on the Tartar steppes; they are in the suburbs of our manufacturing cities."[2]

But the *canuts* were not a wild horde suddenly descended from the hills. In the first chapter we sketched the histories of Lyon and of her silk industry from their origins until 1789, examined their post-Revolutionary transformation, and traced the economic and social structure of the city around the year 1830. We are now prepared to discuss the character of the worker community, the rebellion of November 1831, and the attempt to restore order by the new prefect, Gasparin. This chapter—in fact, the entire book—questions two familiar interpretations of nineteenth century French social history.

The first asserts that the early worker movement was more a product of the political activity generated by the Revolution of 1830 than the result of the internal development of the working class itself.[3] The second implies that the urban disorders of the July Monarchy were primarily caused by widespread social dislocation.[4] Neither seems accurate in the case of Lyon. The thesis presented here is that in the early 1830s the *canuts* constituted a protoindustrial class whose formation was related only indirectly to political developments.[5] Furthermore, their resort to violence grew directly from their life in Lyon and their labor in the *fabrique*. The uprisings of 1831 and 1834 are evidence, not of dislocation, but of attempts at community organization.

I

Economic and social antagonisms exist in every labor arrangement and it is obvious that the Lyonnais worker movement was not generated solely from the conflict between the silk merchants and the *canuts*. In seeking a broader explanation we can turn to the cumulative effect of four factors which molded the character of the worker community: continuity, occupational concentration, a distinct popular culture, and a relative affluence among the weavers. The first two factors have already been treated and we need only review them here in a different context. The latter two, however, require more discussion.

First, Lyon was an old city, not a new industrial town like Manchester and other places commonly associated with the origins of the working class. The laws and customs which regulated silk cloth production in 1830 could be and were compared to those of the Grande Fabrique. In a rapidly changing world, in other words, the *canuts* lived with a sense of the past. Second, the outstanding characteristics of the city's occupational structure were the concentration of nearly half of the labor force in a single trade and the solidarity between the master weavers and journeymen. Other historians have recently suggested that the strangeness of factory life (for the textile workers of Lille), antagonisms between masters and journeymen (for German workers in 1848 and 1849), and conflicts of interest between rival artisan groups (for the Chartists in London) severely retarded the development of class consciousness and an organized worker movement.[6] None of these problems apply to the Lyonnais *canuts* in the early 1830s.

A persistent theme weaves itself through contemporary descriptions of Lyon in this period: the "typical" *canut,* a docile, diligent, and colorful sort of local character had disappeared. In his place one found a belligerent fellow, spouting slogans (supplied him by the meddlesome Republicans or Saint Simonians, since the "typical" *canut* was presumed to have never had a thought in his head), and declaring himself at war with the merchants. Writers enjoyed slumming in the old quarters of the city in search of some toothless wreck whom they could unveil to their readers as "the last of the Mohicans."[7] Because we know that the Grande Fabrique was beset with social and economic conflict—that a worker movement was perhaps stillborn by the Revolution—in one sense these accounts were merely painting over the harsh present with a mythical golden past. In another sense, however, they are evidence for the presence of a popular culture among the *canuts.*

The life of the weavers revolved around the workshop and the café. At first glance their working conditions seem to have been unrelentingly grim. The working day might last fourteen or eighteen hours; even twenty hours were not unknown during peak periods.[8] Seated in an awkward position at the loom, the bar striking his chest repeatedly, and breathing air filled with silk dust (windows in the shops were often kept closed to protect the thread from humidity), the *canut* was said by contemporary physicians to have a pale, unhealthy appearance and to be the frequent victim of pulmonary ailments.[9] Such examples are only part of the story, however. It is equally important to note that the journeymen never struck over working conditions and that the masters never made female or child labor an issue because they were intent on preserving the family work-unit and also retaining the cheap services of the *canutes.* In addition, the rhythm of artisanal production was different from that of the factory. Daily labor did not have to keep pace with a tireless machine. The Sunday holiday might be extended through "Holy Monday." Given seasonal fluctuations, holidays, and the slack time between major contracts, an *unies* master likely worked around 300 days and a *façonnes* master 240 days annually.[10] To paraphrase E. P. Thompson's insightful comment, the *canuts* had not yet learned the lesson that one spends time and so they were still able to pass time.[11]

The social hubs of the worker community were the cafés. Some were dingy wineshops where immigrant weavers congregated; the local police kept close watch on these *estaminets,* particularly the ones frequented by Savoyards and Piedmontese.[12] Others were neighborhood establishments where the masters passed their evenings with their favorite drink, *piquette,* and even brought their wives on Sunday afternoon.[13] In the suburbs there were inns where the *canuts* could play a game of *boules,* watch a performance by Père Thomas, the so-called "Molière of the workers," or hold dances and banquets, which the *Écho de la Fabrique* said were "to civilized men what communion is to a devout Christian."[14] The illicit meetings of worker associations were also held there in order to escape surveillance by the city police.[15] Recreation center, meeting place, and reading room, the café was where Lyonnais popular culture was often articulated.[16]

The café was not in Gin Lane, moreover. The physician and economist Villermé spent an entire Sunday in 1835 listening and watching in the cafés of the Croix Rousse and failed to find a single drunken *canut.* "One must conclude," he wrote,

> that far from being morally degraded and of meager intelligence as has been said, they are on the contrary men most advanced in true civilization, not only superior to the majority of the workers of Paris, but also, I dare say, to many men whose fortune and social position have elevated them above the rank of worker.[17]

In the French puppet theater it is Gnafron the cobbler, not Guignol the *canut,* who has a red nose.

What Villermé called their "true civilization" was also evident in the *canuts'* traditional concern for education. From his analysis of marriage and apprenticeship contracts Maurice Garden has estimated that around 70 per cent of male silk workers were literate in the second half of the eighteenth century.[18] By 1830, at a time when three-quarters of all Frenchmen were still unable to read and write, illiteracy was a social stigma in the weaving community. One member of the Executive Committee of the masters' Society of Mutual Duty, for example, resigned because his opinion was ignored due to his inability to read.[19] Two-thirds of the workers arrested after the uprising of April 1834 could read and sign their names.[20] That Lyon supported two worker newspapers when there were none in Paris is testimony to the high level of popular culture.[21] And in the period before the Guizot laws regarding primary schools (1833) had taken effect the *canuts'* instruction was voluntary and often autodidactic.

Among the most popular social experiments in Lyon were the ten

schools using the Bell-Lancastrian method which were established
by Charles Berna, the founder of the *Grand Atelier* at La Sauvagère,
at a cost of 60,000 francs. Working with a single teacher and several
older pupils who served as monitors, groups of fifty to one hundred
children spent up to ten hours a day at their lessons. The fact that
eight-year-olds were able to recite *Télémaque* from memory was
cited as proof that mutual education was effective.[22] Religious training as well as instruction in reading and writing was provided by
the eight schools operated by the Society of Elementary Education
of the Rhône. Although figures from our period are unavailable,
in 1857, 3,543 worker children attended these institutions.[23] In
1825, the government encouraged the foundation of adult evening
schools in geometry and mechanics; in Lyon these were supple-
mented by Saint Simonian classes in mathematics and accounting.
And Eugène Baune, the future president of the local Society of the
Rights of Man, directed a Special Commercial School with a curric-
ulum devoted to the improvement of the *fabrique*.[24] Education,
in fact, was one issue on which the merchant and worker communities agreed. To the former it had a moral value which might
serve to prevent social unrest, while to the latter it helped to create
an equality of opportunity. The *Écho de la Fabrique* heaped scorn
on the "stupid" peasants and illiterate weavers who doomed themselves to be governed by others and the *Écho des Travailleurs* called
"instruction . . . the pivot of the emancipation of the laboring
classes."[25] To cite Garden again: "The very great extention of instruction" was "one of the most original characteristics" of the
canuts.[26]

The *canuts'* popular culture also extended over their personal
behavior and family lives. Villermé, who criticized their lack of
economy in other matters, noted that the average marriage age of
Lyonnais weavers was high when compared with other French textile workers (although, in fact, it was substantially lower than it had
been a century earlier) and applauded their "moral restraint" with
regard to procreation.[27] Indeed, the small number of children (396
out of a population of 1,497) living in the rue Tolozan supports the
impression that the *canuts* limited the size of their families by intention. "The Lyonnais workers," wrote Joseph Benoit, "are the most
moral in France because of the family life that surrounds their daily
work."[28] While this statement cannot be tested, we can accept
Benoit's point that the presence of the masters' wives and children
demanded relatively high standards of behavior. Numerous letters

and articles in the worker newspapers indicate that many masters
continued to take a paternalistic attitude toward the activities of
their journeymen.[29] There is even evidence of an emerging interest
in the rights and protection of female workers; one *canute,* for
example, was permitted to end her apprenticeship because she was
the only woman in the *atelier.*[30]

There is another, uglier side to the story, however. Women were
paid less than male journeymen and some were driven to prostitution
during slack periods in the *fabrique.* In addition, Lyon ranked second
to Paris in the number of illegitimate births and each year around
sixty mothers left their legitimate children in the delivery room of
the Hôtel-Dieu. Citing "unquestionable progress," the hospital
director reported an annual average of almost 2,000 foundlings in
Lyon; in December 1831, 9,434 *enfants trouvés* were supported by
local charity.[31] The necessity that wives return to work quickly and
the fact that children were an economic burden until they were old
enough to perform light tasks caused many weaver families to send
their new-born infants to wet nurses in the countryside where they
were often neglected and died. We do not know whether the mor-
tality rate was as high as the horrifying figure which Maurice Garden
has established for the eighteenth century; nevertheless, a kind of
institutionalized infanticide remained a part of Lyonnais popular
culture.[32] The children of the rue Tolozan, in other words, were
more likely survivors than the result of planned parenthood.

The *canuts* were not content with this cruel custom, however. In
1832, day-care centers (*salles d'asile*) were introduced for worker
children under the leadership of Madame Gasparin, the wife of the
prefect. The Municipal Council contributed 6,000 francs to the
project. The first centers were established in the poorest quarters of
the fifth arrondissement and two others were later opened on the
Croix Rousse hillside. Free to any child between the ages of two and
six who had been vaccinated and examined by a doctor, the centers
were endorsed by the worker press, which assured parents that their
children would not be proselytized by the church. Although no solution to the plight of new-born infants, the *salles d'asile* proved so
popular that private charity was sought to supplement public
funds.[33]

To suggest there existed a distinct popular culture is to imply that
the *canuts* had (or were developing) a conscious sense of community.
Nowhere was this more evident than in their speech and songs. According to Justin Godart, Guignol's speech pattern (slow pronunciation

with emphasis on the final syllable) originated in *canuts'* attempts to make themselves understood over the noise of the loom.[34] Lyonnais work songs were dominated by the rhythm of the loom; in the chorus of *La Chanson de ma cousin Mariette* the weavers sang *Je puis rimer sans rien craindre/Mes cartons et mon cylindre/Tout ça tourne/Tout ça tourne en même temps.*[35] Even the humor column of the *Écho de la Fabrique* was called "Shuttle Blows" (*Coups de navette*). In 1832, the paper, which called itself "the journal of the PROLETARIAN CASTE," offered a free subscription to the person who suggested the best word to describe all silk workers. Other "classes" had an "honorable" term for themselves, it explained, and because *canuts* was used by the merchants many weavers considered it insulting. Forty-two words were entered in the contest, most of them pretentious ones with Greek or Latin roots such as *textoricarien* and *bombixier.*[36] Language plays a critical role in social cohesion and the fact that many believed it important to have an "honorable" term for the weaver community tells us much about its level of consciousness. As Monfalcon noted: "In their customs and especially in their language the silk workers of Lyon present a character entirely foreign to persons in other parts of France."[37]

The fourth factor in the development of the Lyonnais worker movement was the relative affluence of the *canuts.* Villermé, who had observed textile workers throughout France, noted that the cotton weavers of Lille wore wooden clogs and slept in cellars while the silk weavers of Lyon wore boots and lived in apartments. "They believe themselves unfortunate," he wrote, "because they have created new habits for themselves, new needs."[38] While some callous defenders of the silk merchants claimed that the *canuts* were irresponsible and drank and gambled away their wages, more responsible critics were sympathetic to the fact that dances, banquets, newspaper subscriptions, and fraternal dues were a traditional part of their social obligations. According to Prefect Gasparin, it was this *aisance* rather than *impôt* which was responsible for the high cost of living.[39]

Wages, that is to say weaving rates, were the most important issue in the worker community. The exact income of a master weaver or journeyman is difficult to reconstruct, however, not only because weaving was done at a piece rate but also because of the variety of types of cloth, many of which are no longer woven today.[40] Villermé lamented: "There is no subject in all my research on which I had as much difficulty getting an opinion as the salaries paid by the Lyon-

nais *fabrique* and on the relationship of these to the price of the
necessities of life."[41] Had he consulted the best sources available at
the time he would have found a mass of contradictory evidence,
particularly with regard to the income of a *façonnes* master. In 1833,
for example, the Republican lawyer Jules Favre calculated that the
profit per day of a *façonnes* loom was one franc and ten centimes,
while Prefect Gasparin responded to these figures by citing six francs,
fifty centimes as a "more just" estimate. This discrepancy stems
from the fact that Favre's source of information was a group of *chefs
d'atelier* he was defending after a strike against the merchants, while
the prefect had consulted a wealthy master who owned eight looms
and assumed that each would be mounted for a single contract which
would take a year to weave. In addition, Favre's figures were based
on the production of one kind of cloth and pattern and the prefect's
on another type.[42] There exist other contemporary examples where
a master actually lost money on a *façonnes* loom after paying mounting costs, heat and light, rent, interest on a loan for the loom, and
one half of the contracted rate to the journeyman weaver.[43]

In the case of the income of a *unies* loom owner Villermé might
have consulted the estimate prepared for the Council of Ministers by
the master weaver Pierre Charnier.[44] The production of *shalls* was
paid at a rate of twenty-five centimes per 1,000 rows. An experienced
journeyman could weave 12,000 rows in a day, for a gross income
per loom of three francs. This amount was divided between the
master and the journeyman, and the former was also obliged to pay
the *lanceur* (the youth who threw the shuttle back across the loom)
and the woman who fed thread onto the loom. After other minor
expenses were deducted the master might make a profit of forty
centimes per loom daily. If he wove a cheaper *unies* cloth than *shalls*,
moreover, he might have to pay the journeyman two-thirds of the
contracted rate.[45] The master controlled the means of production,
but unless he owned a number of looms his fixed expenses could
bring his net income to the same level or below that of a skilled
journeyman. He would not have been amused to learn that the prefect considered him to be a member of a "parasite class" which "lives
at the expense of the weaver."[46]

The wage issue was also colored by the memory of better times.
When the press reported that the local deputy Fulchiron had told the
Chamber of Deputies that the *canuts* were more prosperous than in
1789, an elderly master refuted him by presenting figures which
suggested that food costs, rents, and the price of a loom had trebled

in fifty years. Others declared that the weaving rates paid by the merchants for some of the most popular *façonnes* materials had fallen 50 to 75 per cent in the past decade.[47] It scarcely matters to what degree these figures are accurate. What is significant is that at a time when the *canuts* were among the best-paid workers in France they perceived that things were getting worse. An objective affluence made possible their popular culture while a subjective sense that their standard of living was deteriorating and that their economic and social goals were threatened gave impulse to the worker movement. This is almost a classic example of what Walter Runciman calls "relative deprivation."[48]

It is little wonder that most *canuts* looked for salvation in the restoration of a *tarif,* the fixed minimum rate for finished cloth. Imperial *tarifs* were established for *unies* in 1807 and for *façonnes* in 1811 and the Bourbons had seemingly reaffirmed their principle when they adjusted these rates in 1818. After that date, however, the Restoration prefects enforced and ignored the *tarif* with so little apparent system that its legality became questionable and its impact on rates negligible.[49] Furthermore, the act which for fifty years had successfully regulated the wages of the Spitalfields silk weavers in London was abolished by Parliament in 1824 and the Lyonnais merchants were able to cite this decision to their advantage.[50] The appearance of the Citizen King, Louis Philippe, understandably raised the weavers' hopes that the *tarif* issue would be settled in their favor. Their demands, as we shall soon see, posed an early test of the economic and social policies of the new regime.

Voluntary worker associations were a part of Lyonnais life during the Empire and the Restoration, but their programs were far from militant. The *compagnonnages,* the centuries-old fraternities of journeymen existed in a number of local trades, but not in the silk industry.[51] The *canuts*, however, did belong to mutual aid societies which were established with the permission of the mayor and whose meetings were attended by the police. These groups were devoted to providing sickness and accident protection by means of regular contributions to a common fund. Their multiplicity, as well as their constant surveillance, left them weak and unable to transform themselves into societies of "resistance," that is to say, to use their treasuries as strike funds.[52] Indeed, after the unrest which had dominated the final decades of the Grande Fabrique it is remarkable that there were no strikes recorded in the silk industry between 1800 and 1830.

This post-Revolutionary inertia did not end abruptly with the July Days, rather gradually after the foundation of the masters' secret Society of Surveillance and Mutual Indication in 1827. By the time it was suppressed after the uprising of 1834 it had become one of the most powerful workingmens' associations in France. At its start, however, it was the dream-child of a royalist *chef d'atelier,* Pierre Charnier, who intended it to be "a worker masonry" to "neutralize the revolutionary intentions of the bourgeoisie" and "inspire in the workers defiance and hatred of commerce whose only goal is to gain power in order to abuse it."[53] All of the original mutualists (as they later called themselves) were master weavers who owned several Jacquard looms. The location of their workshops underlines what was said earlier about Lyon's residential patterns: fifty-three lived in the Croix Rousse suburb, thirty-two in the first arrondissement, fourteen in the fifth arrondissement, four on the peninsula, and two in La Guillotière.[54] Although the society was launched during an economic depression, its earliest members were less concerned with a *tarif* than the "moral regeneration of the *fabrique*" and the restoration of harmony between all social classes.[55] As the "aristocrats" of the worker community they could afford such untypical sentiments. Nevertheless, Mutualism, which emerged from Charnier's personal experience as a *canut,* was an autonomous Lyonnais creation and owed little or nothing to the social and political theories of the day.[56]

II

As an urban commercial center it is not surprising that a liberal current flowed through Lyon in the first half of the nineteenth century. Political life, however, was considered the preserve of an elite minority. During the Restoration many merchants, doctors, and lawyers read the *Précurseur,* the most successful provincial journal of the day, and voted for opposition candidates. In 1830, they duplicated the behavior of Parisian voters by sending a solidly liberal delegation from the Rhône department to the Chamber of Deputies which was dissolved by the July Ordinances.[57] The Revolution unleashed the divergent forces which had been united in opposition to the Bourbons. In fact, the political history of the first years of the July Monarchy is largely the story of the breakup of this coalition into the party of Order (the supporters of Louis Philippe), the party of Movement (the liberal monarchist opposition), and the Republican party.[58]

The Lyonnais supporters of the parties of Order and Movement agreed on two fundamental rules of local politics. First, they believed that the worker community was apolitical and should remain so. "The masses are neither legitimist, Republican, nor *juste-milieu;* they are profoundly indifferent and egotistical," said the *Courrier de Lyon*.[59] Second, the city's bitter experience had taught them to equate a Republic with the Terror. "Republican ideas are far from popular in Lyon because of the memories of '93," wrote the prefect.[60] In fact, there was no Republican party in Lyon until the middle of 1832. After the July Days the local authorities were more concerned with the Carlists (supporters of the deposed Bourbons) and Bonapartists. Incidents such as the singing of the *Marseillaise* under the mayor's window or the planting of a Liberty Tree in the Place Bellecour were the work of individuals or small groups at best.[61] We will postpone discussion of the activities of the local Republican party, therefore, until the next chapter.

In the legislative elections of July 1831 the Rhône's voters supported the stern policies associated with the Minister of the Interior, Casimir Perier, and his "System of 13 March."[62] Three "ministerials" and two "liberals" were sent to the Chamber of Deputies by 2,117 male electors (out of 2,988 eligible to vote).[63] At the time of the two Lyon uprisings, in other words, the party of Order controlled the departmental delegation in Paris.

In Lyon herself power flowed less along party lines than between the Hôtel-de-Ville and the Prefecture, for the local July Days had reawakened the tradition of decentralization. From 1830 until after the uprising of 1834, the mayor and the Municipal Council sought to retain authority over local affairs and keep it out of the hands of the prefect, who represented the centralized national bureaucracy.[64] The mayor during the entire period was Dr. Gabriel Prunelle, whose appointment by the local provisional government was later confirmed in Paris.[65] Prunelle had a reputation as a difficult, even unpleasant, man whose simultaneous service as a deputy from the Isère department gave him considerable influence. Daumier placed him in the front row in his drawing of the *Ventres legislatifs*. The Municipal Council was composed of twenty-nine locally elected men whose occupations suggest they represented the commercial interests of the city.[66] The deputy mayor for much of the period was Vachon-Imbert, a capable administrator whose responsibilities were increased by Prunelle's frequent absence.[67] Far less talented was Commissioner of Police Prat, who was appointed and stoutly defended by the mayor. With French law enforcement already plagued by overlapping jurisdictions and procedures, Prat's incompetence made matters worse in Lyon.[68] The first round in the local struggle for authority went to the Hôtel-de-Ville: the mayor was able to force the resignation of the first Orleanist prefect.[69] As Adolphe Thiers later commented: "It is not easy to be prefect in Lyon when M. Prunelle is the mayor."[70]

The Municipal Council lost little time in asserting that established barriers had not fallen on account of the July Days. The king's son was to visit the city in November 1830 and the National Guard drilled diligently for a military review to be followed by a gala ball. All guardsmen were invited, but at the last moment it was announced that only ten franc tickets would be honored; those purchased for lesser amounts were annulled. The implication was obvious. One *canut* wrote to the *Journal de Commerce*: "Aren't we worthy enough to assist in a celebration offered to our Prince? Weren't we the equals of the rich at the moment of danger?" As Fernand Rude has commented, the Idyll of July was already only a memory.[71]

The Idyll was indeed over for the silk industry. The *fabrique*, struck by severe depression from 1826 to 1828, showed signs of recovery in 1829 and the first months of 1830. But the number of weaving contracts plunged again in the aftermath of the Revolution.[72] By November local officials reported spreading unemployment and in December a commission was appointed to organize public work projects on the city's fortifications.[73] In January 1831 the National Guard had to maintain order when a crowd of two thousand workers marched on the Hôtel-de-Ville demanding work. The crisis subsided a bit in February with the arrival of domestic orders for National Guard uniforms and international contracts from America.[74] By this time, however, some workers had become mercenaries in an invasion to liberate Savoy and Piedmont.

The expedition of the Legion of the Volunteers of the Rhône was intended as one of a series of revolts planned throughout Europe in early 1831.[75] The conspiracy, which involved Mazzini, Buonarroti, Lafayette, and the *Carbonari*, was prepared with the complicity of the French government. In Lyonnais taverns such as the Café du Phénix and the Café della Fenice, French and Italian tricolors were interwoven as decorations and men were enrolled for twenty-five *sous* a day.[76] The expedition was scheduled to leave on 25 February, but at the last moment the king had second thoughts. When the 700 to 1,000 legionnaires, many of them foreign-born journeymen, marched out of Lyon they were stopped by the authorities. Some immediately volunteered for military service in Algeria, while the rest returned to the city. Their leaders were taken before the prefect, but were promptly released when they produced a favorable letter from General Lafayette. An order for the police to expel all Italian refugees was never enforced.

The first of many attempts to alter forcibly the Restoration territorial settlement thus ended in failure. Nevertheless, the episode not only demonstrated the strength of Lyonnais popular nationalism, but also introduced politics directly into the worker community and mobilized a portion of it for concerted action. The veterans of the expedition refused to disband, moreover, remaining a loosely-organized paramilitary force in the city. Nine months later they played an important role in the November rebellion.

III

Faced with the depression in the silk industry during the winter of 1830–1831, most *canuts* focused their attention on economic issues. In February, 3,000 to 4,000 master weavers signed a petition to the Chamber of Deputies in favor of lower electoral requirements and equal representation on the *Conseil des Prud'hommes.*[77] On 20 May, a worker audience heard a Saint Simonian speaker say that the reign of private property was over: "It is time to pull down the golden calf . . . Idols can no longer keep the people satisfied." By the time the so-called *Mission du Midi* completed its lecture series in late June an *Église Saint-Simonienne*, largely supported by bourgeois converts, had been established.[78] And in October, members of the masters' Society of Surveillance and Mutual Indication began to press for a restoration of the *tarif.*[79] Attendance at a series of public meetings rose from 300 to 1,500 masters and a Central Commission on the *Tarif* was elected. This group presented a petition to the prefect, Bouvier Dumolard (sometimes written du Molard), on 21 October. Unfamiliar with the history of labor relations in the city, the prefect convened a commission composed of himself, the deputy mayor, the mayors of the suburban communes, and representatives of the master weavers and silk merchants to discuss the *canuts'* request. When the merchants present said they had no authority to speak for their colleagues the meeting was adjourned to permit the election of official delegates to the *tarif* negotiations.

The election period was filled with rumors of possible violence, including an alleged plot to burn down the *Grand Atelier* at La Sauvagère. When the meeting reconvened on 25 October several thousand *canuts,* organized by the Central Commission on the *Tarif,* marched in formation to the Prefecture to await the outcome.[80] Laboring under the encouragement of the prefect, the commission reached a general agreement on minimum rates for the scores of types of cloth. When the news reached the waiting crowd the *canuts* shouted praise for the prefect and the king and began a night of celebration. Bouvier Dumolard was pleased that his intervention had apparently reinforced the weavers' allegiance to the new regime. As he wrote to Paris: "I played the role of mediator and conciliator. My voice was heard . . . [and] not a soldier, not a gendarme, not a National Guardsman was put into action."[81] For the moment it appeared that the *canuts* had won an unexpectedly easy victory.

The *tarif* was scheduled to take effect on 2 November. In the interval between the merchants' agreement and that date two events occurred which were to influence the direction of the Lyonnais worker movement for years to come. First, on 30 October the *Écho de la Fabrique* began publication. Controlled by thirty-seven stock-holders (*actionnaires*), thirty of whom were master weavers, the city's first worker newspaper was edited by a *chef d'atelier* named Falconnet, a resident of the rue Tolozan and vice-president of the Central Commission on the *Tarif.* Twelve of the stockholders had been original members of the Society of Surveillance and Mutual Indication in 1827. In its first issue the *Écho de la Fabrique* printed the text of the *tarif* and proposed that every master post a copy in his shop.[82] Second, on the same date a meeting was held of the General and Mutual Association of *Chefs d'Atelier* of the City of Lyon and its Suburbs. Chaired by another member of the Central Commission on the *Tarif,* a master weaver named Bouvery, this group was dedicated not only to provide mutual aid but also to refuse to accept weaving contracts from merchants who failed to honor the *tarif.* Although the new organization was a direct descendent of his own society, Pierre Charnier attended only to denounce the *tarif* as an "ephemeral" solution and a "false calculation."[83] He soon became the personal enemy of his former friends, Falconnet and Bouvery.[84]

With their concerted demand for a *tarif,* the appearance of the *Écho de la Fabrique,* and the rejuvenation of Mutualism the *canuts* had demonstrated a renewed intention to organize for their economic self-protection. Equally important, they still believed they might bring about change by appealing to the government.

The second of November came and passed while the silk merchants generally ignored the *tarif*. On the 5th they sent a petition to Paris and informed the prefect that they considered the *tarif* illegal and predicted it would ruin them. Minister of the Interior Perier was already furious with Bouvier Dumolard for his intervention in the dispute. When he received the merchants' petition he wrote to the prefect: "it is evident that the *tarif* cannot continue . . . It is thus necessary that you find a way of getting rid of it in good faith."[85] On the 17th, a letter from the prefect was read during a session of the *Conseil des Prud'hommes* stating that the agreement of 25 October was only "an engagement of honor" and was not legally binding. Some merchants temporarily closed their warehouses rather than pay rates approximating the *tarif*. They advised the master weavers to take their complaints to the Prefecture.[86] This duplicity amounted to an illegal lockout and only served to deepen the resentment felt by the workers.

Rumors were widespread of possible trouble on Sunday or Monday, 20 and 21 November. Placards calling for a journeymens' strike until the *tarif* was reinstated were seized in the Croix Rousse suburb, on the Grande Côte, and in the rue Tolozan.[87] A black flag was seen flying in Les Brotteaux. On Sunday, while the National Guard drilled on the Place Bellecour, a notice was posted in the worker neighborhoods:

> In the name of fifteen thousand workers the master weavers are hereby informed that all looms will stop until further notice on Monday the 21st. That same day the workers will gather in the principal square of their quarter at seven in the morning in order to climb to the Croix Rousse [suburb]. Good order is recommended.
>
> By the workers, 1831[88]

The authorities knew that a strike and a public demonstration had been called. Nevertheless, when the *canuts* began to make their way up the hillside toward the Grande Place of the Croix Rousse the prefect allowed them to assemble. Had he chosen to bar the demonstration he might have avoided the subsequent disaster. Instead, his strategy was to place soldiers and National Guardsmen at the *octroi* barrier to prevent the weavers from descending en masse into the city. His error in judgment was compounded by the fact that the First Legion of the National Guard, a unit largely composed of silk merchants and clerks from the Saint Clair quarter, was sent to guard the entrance to the Grande Côte. At approximately eleven o'clock a column of *canuts* began to march toward the *octroi* barrier, singing the *Parisienne* (a song as popular after 1830 as the *Marseillaise* was after 1789) on their way to the Prefecture.[89] As they reached the entrance to the Grande Côte the commander of the First Legion, a silk merchant named Gentlet, waved his sword and shouted to his fellow guardsmen: "My friends, help me sweep away this rabble (*canaille*)." Bayonets were fixed, but the crowd continued to advance, hurling stones as it came. The regular troops stood aside rather than become involved in a skirmish.[90] Shots rang out and the *canuts* retreated, carrying their dead and wounded. The November rebellion had begun.

What he lacked in judgment Prefect Bouvier Dumolard owned in personal courage and for a moment it appeared that he might quell the rebellion. Less than an hour after the fighting began the prefect and the commander of the National Guard marched in full uniform up the Grande Côte and past the barricades toward the town hall of the Croix Rousse. Relying on his popularity to calm the situation, Bouvier Dumolard ascended a balcony and began to address the crowd. Shots rang out nearby and in the ensuing panic both the prefect and the commander were taken prisoner. Although they were later released unharmed their capture had the effect of paralyzing the troops and guardsmen at the very time when the uprising began to spread to other quarters of the city.[91]

The worker neighborhoods had been tense for days and the news of the skirmish on the Grande Côte triggered the formation of insurgent bands throughout Lyon. The defection of the National Guard of the Croix Rousse, largely composed of master weavers, gave the workers control of that suburb at the start of the uprising. Residents of the first arrondissement threw up barricades and forced the troops to retreat down the hillside to the Place des Terreaux in front of the Hôtel-de-Ville. On either side of the city, workers from the fifth arrondissement and the suburbs of La Guillotière and Les Brotteaux seized the bridges and began to invade the peninsula. By evening the troops and the few remaining members of the National Guard were surrounded in the neighborhood of the Hôtel-de-Ville.[92]

The next day, the 22nd of November, the situation failed to

improve and at midnight the members of the Municipal Council who were able to reach the Hôtel-de-Ville recommended that the army evacuate the city. The march was carried out under the eyes of the workers, who trained weapons out their windows on the retreating soldiers. The *tocsin* sounded from many churches and at three o'clock on the morning of 23 November the crowd took control of the Hôtel-de-Ville. Bouvier Dumolard remained powerless in the Prefecture. Lyon was without a government.[93]

This vacuum was quickly filled, however, by a motley band of Republicans, Volunteers of the Rhône, Carlists, and other miscellaneous conspirators, who simply occupied the Hôtel-de-Ville and proclaimed themselves the Provisional General Staff.[94] The following day they distributed an *affiche* which read in part:

> Lyonnais! The perfidious magistrates have lost their right to public confidence; a barrier of bodies has been raised between us and them. Any arrangement should thus be impossible. Lyon, gloriously emancipated by her brave children, should have magistrates of her choice; magistrates whose habit is not to defile the blood of their brothers.
>
> Those who have defended us will nominate officials (*syndics*) to preside over all corporations for the representation of the city and the department of the Rhône.
>
> Lyon will have committees or primary general assemblies; the needs of provincial people will finally be heard and a new citizens' guard will be organized. No longer will ministerial charlatanism be imposed on us . . .
>
> Long live liverty![95]

The proclamation was signed by Lacombe, Lachapelle, and Charpentier, who were known to the worker community as leaders of the Volunteers of the Rhône.[96]

This seditious placard failed to have its intended effect, however. As Fernand Rude has convincingly concluded, the overwhelming majority of *canuts* were not interested in a revolution.[97] Sensing that the Provisional General Staff had no authority over those it claimed to lead, Prefect Bouvier Dumolard called a meeting of influential master weavers, many of whom were officers of the National Guard or members of the Central Commission on the *Tarif*. By the evening of the 23rd the Provisional General Staff had the support of the Volunteers of the Rhône and some journeymen from the Croix

Rousse suburb and the first arrondissement. The rest of the community looked toward the Prefecture for guidance.[98]

On 24 November the prefect established a Council of Sixteen, a body of moderate master weavers, to govern the city. Thwarted in their attempted coup the members of the Provisional General Staff abandoned the Hôtel-de-Ville and were soon arrested. On the 29th the Council of Sixteen returned power to the prefect. When Minister of War Soult and the Duc d'Orléans reached the city at the head of the returning army on 2 December they found its gates open and many *canuts* in holiday dress. The first Lyonnais rebellion had ended.

The rebellion of November 1831 was not a purely spontaneous event. The strike and demonstration on the morning of the 21st had been organized by groups of journeymen, the rejuvenated mutualist masters, and the Central Commission on the *Tarif*. Once the fighting started, however, their influence quickly faded. Napoleonic veterans, worker members of the National Guard, and the paramilitary Legion of the Volunteers of the Rhône provided all the leadership that was necessary.[99] The lack of military preparation by the authorities permitted the *canuts* and other workers to leave their own neighborhoods and threaten other parts of the city. This influenced the outcome more than any other factor. But the garrison and bourgeois units of the National Guard did not surrender without a struggle. Government casualties were 75 men killed and 263 wounded. Civilian victims were established at around 200 persons.[100]

In the absence of the *dossiers* of persons killed, wounded, and arrested we cannot test Fernand Rude's contention that the journeymen *canuts* were at the heart of the crowd and that workers from many other professions—particularly day laborers on the city's fortifications—participated in the fighting. Only his statement that the master weavers directed the crowd because they were "the most instructed, the most capable" seems worth qualifying, however.[101] During the fighting there was considerable looting of *octroi* stations, casernes, and food and weapon shops; such selective destruction is to have been expected. More remarkable was the discipline of the worker community after the troops evacuated the city. Two buildings belonging to silk merchants were sacked on the Quai Saint Clair because they had been used as headquarters by the National Guard.[102] But after this incident the *canuts* organized squads to patrol the area and to protect the warehouses. As Louis Blanc later wrote: "The city of Lyon was never better guarded than during that astounding day of the 23rd of November."[103]

The November rebellion began as an economic dispute, preceded by public meetings, demonstrations, negotiations, and a strike. This should not obscure the fact that some persons had attempted to channel the fighting toward a political goal. A few individuals had exhorted the crowd with Republican proclamations at the barricades and the Provisional General Staff, whatever its aim, had tried to declare itself the government of the city. If the Lyonnais workers were not as uniformly "apolitical" as local politicians believed, they were confused and hesitant after their unexpected victory. And most "patriots" (or "political Republicans" as Fernand Rude calls them[104]) were either neutral or fought on the other side of the barricades. When trouble came again in April 1834, the lines would be differently drawn.

The "moral influence" of the November uprising on the worker community was immense. The Orleanist editor and local historian, Monfalcon, predicted:

> their victory, so singularly the result of a succession of accidents and the incapacity of the authorities, will make them [the *canuts*] more demanding . . . Perhaps for a hundred years the marvelous tale of the defeat of the National Guard and the garrison of Lyon by the unarmed workers will charm the leisure of the workshop. This tradition will pass from generation to generation; a son will say with pride . . . "My father was one of the conquerors of Lyon."[105]

Responding to those who expressed relief that the rebellion had not been political, François Guizot stated perceptively:

> A very different question has arisen. The Revolution of July only raised political questions, only questions of government. Society was by no means menaced by those questions. What has happened since? Social questions have been raised. The troubles of Lyon have raised them . . . Social questions, domestic questions, discussions of society have joined political questions, and today we have the difficulty of constructing a government and defending a society.[106]

Nowhere would these questions be more ardently debated than in Lyon.

IV

Bouvier Dumolard was recalled to Paris in disgrace and Minister
of the Interior Perier ordered Gasparin, the prefect in nearby Grenoble, to move to Lyon. Called to a temporary post, he remained for
over three years as "a prefect with the special mission of preventing
a [second] insurrection."[107]

Count Adrien Étienne Pierre de Gasparin was a *grand notable* of
the July Monarchy.[108] Obscure members of the provincial Protestant
nobility before 1789, his family made its name with the Revolution.
The prefect's father, a former captain in the royal army, was elected
to both the Legislative Assembly and the Convention. Briefly a member of the Committee of Public Safety (where he was replaced by
Robespierre), it was the elder Gasparin's decision which gave Napoleon Bonaparte command at the seige of Toulon. When he died
suddenly in 1793, the Convention voted to have Gasparin's heart
buried in the Pantheon.

The future prefect intended to follow his father's military career.
His name won him favor with the General Staff and by the age of
twenty he was already a cavalry officer attached to Murat's command. A wound suffered at the battle of Eylau necessitated his
premature retirement and he spent the remaining years of the Empire
in a series of administrative jobs near the family home in Orange.
He shunned politics during most of the Restoration and spent his
time reading and writing on agricultural problems.

The Revolution of 1830 opened a new career for Gasparin. Elected
a deputy from the Vaucluse to the chamber which was dissolved by
the July Ordinances, he never took his seat because by the time the
assembly finally convened in August 1830 he had been appointed
prefect of the Loire department. In October of the same year he was
transferred to the Isère (Grenoble). When he arrived in Lyon he was
forty-eight years old and had two grown children; his daughter was a
member of Guizot's religious circle in the capital. His personal annual
income was 25,000 francs. Gasparin had twice profited as the result
of revolution, but now he was pledged to prevent a third one.[109]

The new prefect's immediate goals were to restore order, calm the
merchants and workers by resolving the *tarif* issue, and assess the
means of preventing future trouble. Persons accused of serious crimes
were arrested, but an amnesty was declared for the other insurgents.
Efforts were made to disarm the civilian population and a number of

journeymen *canuts* were enrolled in the army. All *livrets* were annulled and new ones granted only upon presentation of a certificate of good conduct from the police. A number of foreign-born workers were expelled from the city to create jobs for local residents.[110]

The continued presence of the Legion of the Volunteers of the Rhône worried Gasparin, but he believed no local jury would dare convict its leaders and feared violent repercussions if he attempted to disband the units which met in the cafés of the Croix Rousse and drilled outside the city every Sunday. The prefect estimated their membership at 800 men, while Police Commissioner Prat typically exaggerated it to be 2,500.[111] Police spies told the authorities that the Volunteers were self-declared enemies of the government and Gasparin called them "our *sans culottes.*"[112] At the time of minor disturbances in Grenoble in March 1832, he was afraid they might march on that city as they had departed for Savoy the year before.[113] References to the Legion began to fade from the prefectoral correspondence by the middle of 1832 and we may presume that it was considered to be less dangerous.

Compromise on the tarif issue proved impossible since the prefect had little choice but to uphold the decision that the rate agreement was illegal. Instead, three concessions were offered to the worker community. First, a *mercuriale* was established, "a common price for the manufacture of silk goods to serve as a rule for jurisprudence when there is a disagreement between the merchant and the worker." The *canuts* at first saw little difference between the *mercuriale* and a *tarif* and later discovered that it, too, was not legally binding on the merchants.[114]

Second, a government-subsidized loan office called the *caisse des prêts* was created. A worker savings bank (*caisse d'épargne*) had been founded in 1821, in a period when the *fabrique* flourished; it served little purpose during years of protracted depression, however.[115] The inability of the *canuts* to borrow money was a major source of antagonism, but the new loan office aided only the "aristocrats" of the community. Directed by a committee of *prud'hommes,* municipal counselors, and members of the Chamber of Commerce, it loaned funds at 5 per cent interest but only to married master weavers. In addition, the amount available was proportionate to the number of looms an individual already owned and payments were deducted from the weaving contracts by the silk merchants.[116] Not only did these rules fail to save those who wished to purchase a Jacquard loom from having to borrow directly from the merchants but they also left the poorer masters and all journeymen to deal with the municipal pawn shop, the *Mont-de-Piété,* whose interest rate was 17 per cent. Its salesroom was in the Place Confort in the heart of a bourgeois quarter and the auction of its unclaimed items was advertised regularly in the newspapers.[117] The creation of a *caisse des prêts,* in other words, left most *canuts* untouched, while their request for more substantial reforms of the *octroi* and other taxes was rejected in Paris despite the fact that it had the support of Mayor Prunelle and Prefect Gasparin.[118]

The third and most important concession was a reform of the *Conseil des Prud'hommes.* Membership was expanded from seventeen (including four merchants and three master weavers from the silk industry) to twenty-five persons (nine merchants and eight master weavers), and electoral requirements were lowered to include all masters owning four or more looms.[119] Since the masters had petitioned for equal representation and the eligibility of masters owning two or more looms, this change fell short of their expectation. Furthermore, the journeymen continued to be totally excluded. Nevertheless, the *Écho de la Fabrique* pledged its support. The turnout for the last election for the unreformed *conseil* was apathetic in January 1832, but as the special election for the new board approached in April anticipation was high in the workshops. "It is the spirit of November, no more and no less," wrote Prefect Gasparin.[120] His observation was confirmed when the eligible masters streamed to the polls in the expressed hope that the election would launch a new era in the *fabrique.*[121]

In restoring order and arranging a truce between the merchants and *canuts* Prefect Gasparin was aided by luck. By March 1832 the silk industry had recovered from the effects of the uprising and even appeared to have shaken off the recurrent depression which had plagued it for several years. One local official said the workshops were "in a state of great activity."[122] The next month, however, the cholera epidemic struck France and the amount of raw silk registered by *La Condition Public* fell to its lowest level in a decade. With popular hysteria gripping Paris, Gasparin was alarmed when a traveller who had recently arrived from the capital fell ill with the disease. Yet, for no explicable reason, only a few cases of cholera were reported locally.[123] We cannot predict the reaction

of the *canuts* had an epidemic been added to the unexpected slump
in the market in the aftermath of the November rebellion. Happily
for the authorities, they were spared this grim situation.

Gasparin's first priority in seeking to prevent future trouble was
to improve the defense of the city. The National Guard was dissolved
for a year on the grounds that only a fraction of the bourgeois units
had responded to the moblization and those in the worker neighborhoods had joined the insurgents. The garrison was increased and
troops assumed certain police powers, a situation that was bitterly
opposed by Mayor Prunelle.[124] In addition, plans were set in motion
to build a series of "detached forts" around the city and also to
repair the wall which separated Lyon from the Croix Rousse suburb.[125]

The new prefect encountered opposition when he attempted to
reorganize the local police, however. Although Mayor Prunelle
acknowledged that he had arrived "in the most critical circumstances
in which our city has ever been found," he overrode the recom-
mendations of Minister of the Interior Perier and Minister of War
Soult and refused to yield any administrative authority.[126] Criticism
of Police Commissioner Prat came from all directions except the
Hôtel-de-Ville. At one point Minister of the Interior Montalivet, who
replaced Perier in May after the latter contracted cholera, wrote in
exasperation:

> He [Prat] speaks vaguely of money distributed. By whom? To
> whom? Where? When? . . . What does it mean to announce that
> there are Carlist and Republican maneuvers going on with regard
> to the working class without any facts, some names, details?[127]

Such high official frustration notwithstanding, Casimir Perier had
already told Gasparian that control over the local police would have
to remain with Mayor Prunelle, a man "jealous of his rights."[128]

Gasparin also desired to establish guidelines for the administration
of labor policy. The two principles which the government said it
honored in these matters perforce caused it to misunderstand the
character and goals of the Lyonnais worker community. The first
principle was a kind of self-deceiving "neutrality." As Minister
of Commerce Thiers wrote to Gasparin sometime later:

> One must not intervene between worker and merchant for the

regulation of rates. Avoid a collision if possible, but never retreat for that will be seen as weakness.

The workers have their muscles and the entrepreneurs their capital. If the workers choose to absent themselves from labor, they give the entrepreneurs the right to protect their money.

These are your principles; I am not telling you anything [new]. I am confirming our accord with regard to these deplorable questions.[129]

Even where privately angered by the merchants' intransigence, local officials were publicly prepared to reject all worker requests for mediation and to intervene only to prevent the destruction of property.[130] The tragic result of his predecessor's efforts in October 1831 served to confirm the wisdom of this policy in Gasparin's mind.[131]

A corollary to this principle was the belief that the *canuts* would be content so long as there was work available. Because the merchants convinced them that the prosperity of the silk industry depended on low weaving rates, the local authorities condemned agitation for higher pay not simply because it was illegal, but because they judged it would hurt business and, therefore, was contrary to the *canuts'* best interest.[132] Such circular reasoning made it difficult to convince the worker community that Gasparin's administration was not the handmaiden of the silk merchants.

The second principle was that since political issues and economic matters were discrete and separate it was the government's duty to protect workingmen from the seductive appeals of radicals. As Monfalcon wrote:

Politics degrades the worker by taking away the very character which recommends him to the protection of society and involving him in matters whose principles he does not understand.[133]

The *Courrier de Lyon* piously added that "much time and care is necessary to inculcate the masses with a feeling for law and respect for institutions."[134]

This attitude was doubly self-defeating: not only did it implicitly assume that the *canuts'* politization would guarantee their opposition to the philosophy of the *juste-milieu,* but it also openly ignored their traditions and popular culture. The July Monarchy had little intention of offering them "the protection of society" or taking the "time and care" to convert them to its institutions, yet its supporters refused to believe that the workers could discover this for themselves. After the November rebellion Casimir Perier had stated that "the workers must learn they can expect no remedies other than patience and resignation."[135] If the *canuts* proved remarkably patient, many of them were no longer resigned.

3   The Republican Party in Lyon

Although it interrupts the discussion of the Lyonnais worker movement, it is necessary to recount the history of the local Republican party from its origins until the so-called "episode of the Public Hawkers" in January 1834 in order to place the question of its power and influence in a proper perspective. Because the Republicans became organized at about the same time, some contemporary observers blamed them for the *canuts'* growing militancy after the November rebellion. Many historians have accepted this assessment, moreover. Gabriel Perreux described Lyon as "the premier Republican city in France,"[1] while John Plamenatz says that they "converted the silk workers to their cause."[2] Such opinions notwithstanding, we will learn that the local party was not only small, weak, and faction-ridden, but also that the character of its program long restricted its influence on the worker community. The *canuts* believed their problems were economic and social in nature, while the Republicans tried to convince them they were fundamentally political. The party was composed, however, of a collection of bourgeois radicals whose appeal to the workshops was successful only to the degree that they were able to disprove the popular equation of a Republic with the Terror and learn to see how the future looked through the eyes of threatened artisans.

I

In mid-May 1832, Police Commissioner Prat wrote to Prefect Gasparin: "I avow, Monsieur, that I did not believe there was a frankly Republican party in Lyon. In the last eight or ten days my opinion has changed. I cannot refuse to believe it now."[3] Although Prat offered no specific explanation for this pronouncement, we may conveniently use it to organize our discussion.

The "pre-history" of the local Republican party can only be
vaguely sketched since it is difficult to say why and when individual
Lyonnais became Republicans.[4] For many the decision was likely
the result of dissatisfaction with the policies of Casimir Perier. A
placard, Advice to True Patriots, posted on the first anniversary of
the July Days, condemned the government for its failure to aid the
peoples of Savoy, Piedmont, Belgium, and Poland.[5] It may be that,
just as the expedition of the Volunteers of the Rhône had stirred
elements of the worker community, opposition to a pacific foreign
policy drove some members of the old liberal coalition in the direction of Republicanism. In any case, the few Republican brochures
and articles written then showed little interest in domestic problems. One exception was the announcement of a fund for unemployed weavers. Lyonnais patriots had sent money to the Greeks and
Poles, its author declared, and should now think about their fellow
townsmen.[6]

Several local Masonic lodges had Republican members, but these
seem to have been organized according to profession and social status
rather than political opinion.[7] In the interrogations after the uprising
of 1834, only one person claimed to have been persuaded to join the
Republican party by Masonic acquaintances.[8] The *Carbonari*, the
secret society inherited from the Restoration period, was a more
likely seed-bed. Lyon was one of its three "capitals" and the leaders
of the local party were all identified as members at one time or another. Police Commissioner Prat vastly overestimated the number of
Lyonnais *Carbonari* at a thousand.[9]

The limited appeal of Republicanism at this time can be seen in the
fate of two newspapers. The *Glaneuse* began as a literary review in
mid-1831 but drew little attention even when it adopted the motto,
Prison is the Seminary of Patriots. The November rebellion brought
the paper briefly into the spotlight. Its editor, Adolphe Granier, was
a member of the Provisional General Staff at the Hôtel-de-Ville and
some of its staff fought alongside the rebels. On 25 November, the
paper declared: "Our sympathies are with the largest and poorest
class; today and always we shall be its defenders."[10] Neither the
Republicans nor the *canuts* seemed much concerned, however, and
after a series of trials the *Glaneuse* suspended publication in May
1832. Granier's friends were certain that the venture was dead and
sought a position for him elsewhere after his release from prison.[11]
Seemingly one of the ephemeral journals so common in this period,

the *Glaneuse* reappeared four months later and became the spokes-man for the Jacobin faction of the local Republican party.

Early in 1832, a lone-wolf named Joseph Beuf launched *Le Furet de Lyon.* His previous effort, the *Sentinelle Nationale,* had failed the year before.[12] Despite the fact that Beuf called himself *un prolétaire,* and was jailed for castigating the king for keeping his fellow citizens in "vassalage," *Le Furet de Lyon* lasted only twenty-seven issues.[13] The *canuts'* newspaper attributed its fate to reader indifference.[14]

The *Glaneuse* and the *Furet de Lyon* were shoestring publications without an audience. The *Précurseur,* on the other hand, was a lead-ing provincial journal whose conversion to Republicanism was a significant event in local politics. This transformation was tied to the personal history of its editor, Anselme Petetin.[15] Born in Savoy in 1807, Petetin began his career in Paris as the co-editor of the *Revue Encyclopédique.* Disappointed when it fell under the influence of the Saint Simonians, he heard that the editorship of the *Précurseur* was open and applied for the position. After an interview with a committee of stockholders including such pillars of the establishment as Mayor Prunelle and the local Procureur Général, Petetin began work in November 1831. On the day the *canuts'* rebellion began he declared that despite the nation's "profound sympathy for their misery," no civilized people could tolerate the destruction of prop-erty and order.[16]

The *Précurseur* remained a spokesman for the party of Movement in the first months of 1832. By May, however, it began to doubt the achievements of the July Revolution, stating that "it is always a bit embarrassing to admit that one has been duped."[17] The brutal suppression of the June revolt in Paris caused it to break completely with the regime. In Petetin's opinion the Charter had been violated and he declared: "Henceforth, a river of blood separates us from our enemies."[18] The paper now came under judicial attack and several stockholders mounted a campaign to fire Petetin. Although they mustered a majority against him, their effort was frustrated by a clause in the bylaws which required a four-fifths vote to remove the editor.[19] These influential men then transferred their money and allegiance to the recently-founded *Courrier de Lyon,* which received secret funds from the Minister of the Interior.[20]

In order to save the *Précurseur* Petetin and his supporters estab-lished the Lyonnais Association for the Liberty of the Press. Within three days they claimed to have enrolled 200 persons. Since membership was maintained solely by financial contribution and the executive committee called only one general meeting annually, this association was never a dynamic organization.[21] Nevertheless, it did provide the catalyst for a kind of "right Republicanism," a focus of activity for defectors from the party of Movement. Respectable "patriots" such as Jules Seguin (a financier and builder), Charles Depouilly (the owner of the *Grand Atelier* at La Sauvagère), Pierre Lortet (a physician and captain of the National Guard), and Léon Boitel (a successful printer whose reading room was frequented by young liberals) rallied behind this cause. Prefect Gasparin described them as "honest citizens who legally oppose the regime, but dread trouble and riot."[22]

Those who desired a more vigorous expression of Republican doctrine were cheered by the return of Adolphe Granier. The trial of the Provisional General Staff had been transferred to the town of Riom in order to obtain a verdict favorable to the government. In June 1832, the authorities were scandalized when a jury acquitted the defendants, a decision which helped make Granier a hero to Lyonnais radicals.[23] While awaiting trial he had become acquainted with the deputy mayor of Riom, Edouard Albert, whom he later persuaded to pay the caution-money for his newspaper.[24] Solvent once more, the *Glaneuse* resumed publication on 27 September.

By the middle of 1832, a Republican party existed in Lyon. Its membership divided between the supporters of the *Précurseur* and the *Glaneuse,* Prefect Gasparin called those who read the former "Americans," "legal opportunists," and "Girondists" and those who read the latter "Maratists," "men of action," and "Jacobins."[25] As we shall see these labels not only reflected Republican divisions in France as a whole, but also pertained to specifically local issues and personalities.

II

Banquets were a common form of provincial political activity under the July Monarchy. The celebration of a patriotic holiday or the visit of a popular deputy furnished an occasion for local politicians to display their oratorical skills and to raise money for their projects. In the period between the national elections of July 1831 and June 1834, moreover, they were also a chance to test the strength of rival factions.

In August 1832, the *Précurseur* sponsored a banquet for 500 persons in honor of the leader of the Dynastic Opposition in the Chamber of Deputies, Odilon Barrot, who was defending Anselme Petetin before the Assizes Court. The respectable tone of the affair was ruined when the physician Pierre Lortet offered a toast "To the Union of the People" and the guest of honor took exception with his "violent" language. Prefect Gasparin compared the resulting uproar to the Tower of Babel.[26] Undaunted and perhaps encouraged by its rival's embarrassment, the *Glaneuse* held a banquet in honor of the Republican deputy Garnier-Pagès the next month. In order to promote ticket sales the banquet committee spread the rumor that Étienne Cabet would also attend. The authorities were sufficiently concerned to alert the police, but the event was held without incident. Its climax was a toast by Granier "To the approaching fall of the *juste-milieu.*"[27]

Both banquets had been financially successful and for a short time the Republicans believed they might capture the support of the deputy Couderc, a leader of the local party of Movement. A delegation met to discuss a third banquet in his honor. Granier optimistically predicted "a complete fusion of the two nuances of Lyonnais liberalism," but when the newspapers leaked the story of the private negotiations Couderc withdrew his name and stated that both age and experience had taught him that the Republicans' goals were illusionary.[28] This broke their final tie with the Lyonnais political elite.

Because they focused their activity around the two newspapers Prefect Gasparin had relied on legal harassment of the press to control the Republicans.[29] In the spring of 1833, however, he turned to new methods. A mammoth banquet was planned by the Lyonnais Association for the Liberty of the Press in honor of Garnier-Pagès, who was returning to defend the *Glaneuse* before the Assizes Court. The banquet committee set its attendance goal at 6,000 persons and sent invitations as far as Grenoble, Marseille, and Dijon. Free tickets were distributed in the workshops. Whereas the Prefect had scoffed earlier, he took this occasion to force a confrontation. On 23 April, he issued an ordinance banning all banquets and public meetings until further notice. When the Republicans indicated they would ignore this order he summoned the chairman of the banquet to say he would use force to uphold the law.[30]

Gasparin had thrown down the gauntlet. The subsequent debate whether or not to pick it up exposed the division in the Republican ranks. As a temporary measure the banquet was postponed from 5

until 12 May, but the question remained whether it should be held at
all. Speaking for the Girondists, Anselme Petetin argued that the
party might destroy itself if it challenged the ordinance. Adolphe
Granier and his Jacobin supporters, on the other hand, contended
that they could not afford the humiliation of bowing to an order
they had already declared illegal. The Prefect predicted that if the
banquet was prevented the Republican party would collapse and its
moderate members could be won back to the side of the government.[31]

Party division, in fact, had been growing wider for some time.
Although it outwardly took the form of theoretical and tactical dis-
agreements, at its heart lay the subtler issues of style and political
respectability. Both factions were drawn from essentially the same
social stratum, but the Girondists considered the Jacobins an embarrassment.[32] As early as November 1832, one of the former
castigated the latter as "those young, immoral madmen, who have
consideration neither for the masses nor for the middle classes . . .
[and whose] vain efforts discredit the work of more worthy and
sane Republicans."[33] To the Jacobins, however, the Girondists had
failed to shed "the habits of the old opposition."[34] Furthermore,
personal relations between the newspaper editors, Petetin and
Granier, were strained. The former believed the latter to be a fa-
natic.[35] Such squabbling always surfaced at times of crisis and played
an important role in the fortunes of the local party.

As was often the case, the Republicans papered over their differences with a feeble compromise. On the day of the banquet a
token group was sent to be turned away by the troops who surrounded the hall. Having symbolically challenged the ordinance, the
affair was cancelled. Gasparin was amazed there was no resistance.[36]
The *Courrier de Lyon* noted that "the July Monarchy is more often
compromised by the softness of its friends than by the . . . real
strength of its enemies."[37] The Republican newspapers tried to save
face by protesting the Prefect's action. The *Glaneuse* chided him
for thinking that they had a June revolt of their own in mind and the
Précurseur claimed that the party had suffered no defeat because it
had not officially endorsed the Garnier-Pagès banquet.[38] Gasparin
dismissed all this as "the rage of a vanquished party."[39]

The Assizes Court soon dealt the Republicans a second blow.
Anselme Petetin of the *Précurseur* was found guilty on two counts
of *délit de la presse* and received a prison term of three months and
fines totaling 3,200 francs, while Adolphe Granier of the *Glaneuse*
was sentenced to fifteen months in prison and fined 4,000 francs.

Even the local judicial officials admitted their surprise at these verdicts.[40]

Prefect Gasparin had reason to be pleased by these setbacks. Always a cautious administrator, his letters to Paris betrayed constant nervousness over Republican machinations. At one time he actually complained that the city was too quiet and speculated that plots were being brewed for the future.[41] Although he estimated that no more than 200 persons were active members of the Republican party,[42] he mistakenly believed he lacked sufficient means to restrain them. On 2 May 1833, therefore, he proposed the introduction of legislation to ban all unauthorized organizations, whether or not they were divided into sections of less than twenty members.[43] Here originated the idea for the national "law on associations." The impact on the worker community of its subsequent adoption eleven months later was the principal cause of the Lyon uprising of 1834.

Ironically, one result of the authorities' success in curbing its activities was to compel the local Republican party to swallow its pride and to affiliate with the burgeoning national organization. The Lyonnais' attitude prior to the middle of 1833 is recaptured in the comment by one Republican: "All I ever hear is 'They want this meeting in Paris. The provisional committee will be chosen in Paris. Finally, the money will be spent in Paris.'"[44] At one point the national secretary of the Society for the Liberty of the Press complained that he had received no news from Lyon for months.[45] In contributions to a national fund drive the city ranked not only behind Paris but also Metz, Perpignan, Auxerre, and Strasbourg.[46] The Girondist faction, moreover, was committed to a program of decentralization, or "federalism" as they called it. In April 1833, Anselme Petetin proposed Lyon as the center for an Association of the East. In a circular which he sent to newspaper editors in the region he argued:

> Our departments, isolated from the influence of Paris, having different resources and different interests, need such an association . . . Moreover, it is time to give the provinces an independent life of their own. The geographical division of our country . . . will eventually force us there later, if our political interests do not direct us there now.[47]

This interest in provincial independence was sacrificed as the Republicans were forced to look to the capital for help.[48] Crippled by the verdicts of the Assizes Court and its stockholders ("those

men of the party who have something to lose," according to Gasparin[49]) in rebellion, the *Précurseur* was in serious trouble. The
lawyer Jules Favre wrote to Petetin's friend Armand Carrel, the
editor of the *National,* to remind him: "as you yourself have said,
it is important that Lyon—the center of an inevitable future explosion—maintain an organ of calm and moderate Republican opinion."[50] Henceforth the *Précurseur* and the *National* frequently
exchanged articles. The *Glaneuse* faced a similar crisis. "Until today,"
Granier wrote to the national secretary of the Society for the Liberty
of the Press, "the style of the *Glaneuse* has been fresh, free, and
detached from all outside influence. I have not recoiled from any
sacrifice to preserve this independence." Circumstances, however,
now required that the paper seek stockholders and he asked for the
names of wealthy Republicans throughout France. Granier also
allied the *Glaneuse* with the *Tribune* in Paris.[51] As they sought funds
from its societies, solicited articles from influential figures, and
begged the distribution of their trial brochures the Lyonnais consequently became part of the national network.[52]

In July the Parisians intervened directly in Lyonnais politics for
the first time. While on a vacation trip Armand Carrel had visited the
city and seen for himself the factionalism there.[53] He later wrote to
Petetin to tell him that Godfrey Cavaignac, an editor of the *Tribune*
and the head of the Society of the Rights of Man, intended to
come to Lyon for the purpose of mending fences. Carrell advised
Petetin:

> You have a part to play in this rapprochement. Your conver-
> sation will prove to you that our three Republics—yours, his and
> mine—can mingle very easily into a single school which will
> triumph.[54]

The circumstances of Cavaignac's trip were clouded with misunderstanding and recrimination, however. He visited the editor in prison
for an amicable talk, but trouble arose when Petetin learned that
Cavaignac had gone to the office of the *Précurseur* to hold a secret
meeting. Leaping to the conclusion that his friends were conspiring
against him, Petetin wrote Carrel accusing him of treason to the
cause of moderate Republicanism. Carrel replied that he knew nothing of the meeting and said that his situation in Paris was as "delicate" as was Petetin's in Lyon.[55] The real purpose of the meeting was
to discuss the formation of an association similar to the Society of
the Rights of Man. Ten persons representing the two factions of the

local party attended. Cavaignac himself chose an "Invisible Committee" and correspondents for the new group, but underestimated
the depth of local hostility. As Edouard Albert later testified: "The
lack of homogeneity of the selected members caused the project
to remain completely sterile."[56]

Hitherto, with the exception of their newspapers and banquets,
the Lyonnais Republicans had succeeded in harassing the authorities
only over the issue of the city's defense. As soon as the order which
had dissolved the National Guard expired Mayor Prunelle held elections for its officers. To his embarrassment the turnout of guardsmen
was low and with a concerted effort the Republicans elected several
of their candidates, including a batallion commander. Confronted by
these "imperfect results," the government chose to keep the Guard
on inactive status.[57] If only monarchists were permitted to be
officers, why not call it the Royal Guard, asked the *Précurseur?* Did
Louis Philippe consider his fellow citizens too dangerous to trust
with weapons?[58] This decision, in fact, had serious consequences:
because it was now necessary to summon the garrison to deal with
minor disturbances, friction was created between the troops and the
worker community which may have helped induce violence in April
1834.[59] The Republicans also protested the construction of the
so-called "detached forts" around Paris and Lyon. They disputed
the claim that they were necessary to prevent a seige during an invasion and (correctly) charged they were intended to be used in case
of domestic disorder. "One bastille was demolished in 1789," said
the *Glaneuse,* "and fourteen are raised in 1833."[60]

Commenting on a band of "patriots" who had marched through
the streets to celebrate the third anniversary of the July Days, the
local Procureur Général wrote: "One saw the Republic passing under
the windows as a band of drunks."[61] The Minister of the Interior
added: "The population viewed these excesses with disgust . . . Lyon
has not lost her memories of the Republic."[62] Indeed, the authorities
feared only the local party's potential influence on the *canuts.* And,
as Prefect Gasparin stated at the time of the suppressed banquet for
Garnier-Pagès: "The Republicans are not counting on the worker
population."[63]

III

Mutual indifference, fear, and misunderstanding restricted contact
between the Republicans and the *canuts* for more than a year after
the November rebellion. To better understand why this was so we

will examine two early and three later Republican discussions of the
weavers' plight. These obscure works merit attention because they
reveal how much the party's political, economic, and social assumptions had to change for it to tap the potential audience in the workshops.

Eugène Baune was a lycée instructor, leader of the Jacobin faction,
and later president of the local chapter of the Society of the Right
of Man. His *Essay on the Means to End the Distress of the Silk
Industry* was begun before the November rebellion and published
early in 1832.[64] The *Essay* was addressed to the government, the silk
merchants, and the weavers, who Baune believed shared the burden
for reform. While critical of the intervention in the *tarif* dispute, he
thought that a "moral and paternal government" should promote
foreign sales and encourage the domestic use of silk cloth. The local
authorities were advised to suppress the lottery, reduce the *octroi,*
and establish a worker savings bank. The silk merchants were to help
to lower rents and the *canuts* were urged to join mutual aid societies.[65]

Baune also proposed the establishment of a Society of Encouragement to make the silk industry "more efficient," finance a worker
insurance fund, support a nonpolitical "popular" newspaper to edify
the *canuts* on matters such as the introduction of machines, and
found a Special Commercial School, whose graduates would travel
abroad to observe the latest industrial methods.[66] These suggestions
were an appeal for more of the same kind of liberal programs already
in operation. If Doctor Monfalcon, that paragon of local *juste-milieu*
sentiment, read this little book he would have found nothing to
criticize.

Baune's *Essay* was not directed at the worker community and it is
doubtful if many *canuts* ever saw it. During the fall of 1832, however, Anselme Petetin of the *Précurseur* exchanged heated opinions
with the master weaver Bouvery, who was a *Prud'homme*, a Mutualist, and a former member of the Central Commission on the *Tarif.*
This debate between an important Republican and a leader of the
canuts was carried on in the *Écho de la Fabrique.*[67]

The exchange originated with an article in which Bouvery expressed the community's traditional opposition to machines. Petetin,
believing that a man with such influence should not be permitted to
spread "the old arguments of the old political economy" unchal-
lenged, responded with a letter to the editor. Second and third
rounds followed. The Republican presented his case on explicitly

political grounds, openly seeking to confound the idea that politics
and "social economics" could be separated. Describing himself as
"a partisan of industrial perfection," he said that under a democrat-
ically chosen government the state would take care (*prendrait
quelque soin*) of workers made idle by machines. Laissez-faire,
therefore, was in the interest of all.

Bouvery's reply indicated that he had not been overwhelmed by
Petetin's case. The master weaver accused him of misjudging human
nature like the Saint Simonians and warned that any government
which abandoned property qualifications for active citizenship risked
tyranny. Taken aback by this criticism, Petetin admitted that France
might not be ready for democracy and defended himself against what
he called Bouvery's "false notions" of a Republic by stating that
"today Republican institutions can be nothing more than a collection of laws made in the interests of all, which give to each an equal
advantage." He then asked the hypothetical question: would a single
machine capable of accomplishing all work done in France be bene-
ficial to society? The answer, he concluded, depended on the nature
of the government. Bouvery ended the debate by saying that the
reason he opposed machines was not because they reduced work and
concluded that he was still unconvinced by his opponent.

These examples reveal the differences which initially separated the
Republicans from the weavers. Both Baune and Petetin at this point
favored the introduction of machines and the increased "efficiency"
of the silk industry and opposed official intervention to regulate
weaving rates. Bouvery, on the other hand, believed the proposals
of these "partisan[s] of industrial perfection" were misguided at
best. Paraphrasing E. P. Thompson, we may say that Bouvery recognized that the rewards of the "march of progress" were going to be
gathered by someone else.[68] Moreover, his articles reveal him as a
conservative, who was unswayed by democratic appeals and tacitly
accepted the government's declared separation of economic and
political problems. The worker community, in other words, was not
naturally inclined to support radical political formulas.

The first Republicans to win acceptance in the *canuts'* neighborhoods were not journalists or leaders of political associations, but
individuals who were willing to defend them before the courts or
offer medical advice. During the threat of an epidemic in the spring
of 1832, for example, the physician Pierre Lortet wrote articles
on public hygiene for the worker paper and joined with the monarchist master weaver Pierre Charnier to organize the sixty-man

Sanitary Association of the Saint Paul Quarter, which was pledged to come to the aid of cholera victims. The *Écho de la Fabrique* said that these volunteers gave "to the worker population the means to combat the devastating plague of which it is the first victim."[69] In this unromantic (and for the most part unrecorded) fashion the members of the Republican party began to educate and be educated by the *canuts*. For the former this meant abandoning economic liberalism, while for the latter it meant shedding fear of a Republic.

Among the first to cross these barriers was Charles Monier, who proposed to write a "History of the Proletarians in the Nineteenth Century," the story of "the true people who earn their bread by the sweat of their brow [and who] have been forgotten or unknown for too long."[70] Monier intended a four volume work in fifty weekly installments, but only the preface and first chapter were ever printed. In them he described 1789 and 1830 as "brother and sister revolutions" and admonished the workers to love institutions more than individuals [a reference to the popular veneration of Napoleon]. In December 1832, Monier spoke in a café in the Croix Rousse suburb. "Robespierre did not love blood," he told the *canuts*. "He was the only friend of the working class." His speech went unfinished, however, for the police burst in and arrested him for holding an unauthorized meeting of more than twenty persons.[71] Monier was later acquitted by the Assizes Court when the prosecution was unable to produce a single civilian witness to testify against him[72]

The Monier affair had a double significance. Not only had he told the workers that they had a history and need not be "forgotten or unknown" any longer, but also by presenting Robespierre as the "only friend of the working class" he had addressed a sensitive issue: the Revolutionary tradition in France.[73]

Both factions of the Lyonnais Republican party rejected the Convention as the model for a future government.[74] In an article called "The Republic of 1830," the *Glaneuse* told the story of a man born under the Empire and raised to fear a Republic who encounters an old friend shortly after July 1830. The friend admits he is a Republican but adds: "Calm yourself. Times have changed. '93 was a cruel necessity . . . but we don't desire the guillotine any more than you do. In fact, the first decree of the Republic will be the abolition of the death penalty."[75]

This fictitious conversation reflected a real situation. With one exception, the leaders of the local party had no personal memories of the first Republic.[76] While the Jacobins later adopted its symbols in their clubs, all sought to explain, not defend, the Revolutionary heritage.

The most important presentation to the worker community of a modern Republican alternative was the "New Republican Catechism by a proletarian," a pamphlet expanded from a series of articles which had appeared in the *Glaneuse*.[77] Divided into twenty "lessons," it adopted the catechismal question and answer format familiar to most Frenchmen. Allegedly written by one who "issued from the pure and glorious blood of the proletarians," the Catechism's "holy and useful mission" was to carry the "religion of the future" into the workshops and cottages of the region. To examine the "New Republican Catechism" as a contribution to political theory is to recognize the imprecision which Paul Bastid has pointed out in Republican doctrine for the entire July Monarchy.[78] Nevertheless, its arguments were specifically designed for workingmen who feared the Republic and the future.

The central thesis of the "New Republican Catechism" was the interconnection of political, economic, and social problems. Those who labored only to enrich the merchant or landowner were said to be exploited by existing society. This situation would be remedied by means of equal representation, fair distribution of taxes, a revision of the educational system, and the limitation of the right of inheritance: all part of the standard Republican program of the time. In addition, the reigning spirit of competition would be ended. "An Egoist [the term used by the *canuts* to describe an economic liberal] will never be a Republican," the Catechism said.

In order to accomplish this radical transformation of society it would be necessary to re-examine the nature of property and work. The Catechism regarded property as a creation of society and said that where it was "no more than the right of exploitation" the Republic would modify the law to protect its citizens. Work, too, was a product of human history. In an earlier era, the Catechism explained, all men owned property and worked for themselves. After a "social revolution due to various causes," however, two classes had arisen: those who owned the instruments of production and those who did the work. The idle class had imposed a law code which permitted it to set wages without regard to the labor performed, but "by a new social progress" the workers later began to dispute it with the result of a conflict in which they found themselves presently vanquished. The establishment of a Republic, however, would aid "the moral and material amelioration of the worker and farmer."

Idleness and the exploitation of one man by another would be
replaced by a new "pact of association" which would place "the
instruments of work in the hands of those who employ them" and
"organize [and] encourage work."[79]

The "New Republican Catechism" recognized that many "proletarians" feared a future Terror and devoted an entire section to the
question: "What should one think of those who cry that the Republic means the scaffold, agrarian laws, and the pillage of property?"
Cleverly citing Thiers's history of the Revolution as its source, the
pamphlet stated that the government of 1793 was forced to act out
of necessity rather than ideology. It totally avoided mention of
other elements of the Revolutionary tradition such as Babeuf and
his "Conspiracy of the Equals."

In presenting "The advantages of a Republic over a Monarchy,"
further effort was made to dispel anti-Republican attitudes in the
worker community: free elections were described as a better guarantee of stability than the clamoring after royal favor which characterized the present regime, the example of the United States was used
to prove that order was possible without monarchical succession,
and a Republic was said to be a cheaper and more peaceful system
of government. Finally, Louis Philippe was specifically attacked for
substituting "the aristocracy of money for that of nobility," as well
as for pursuing a cowardly foreign and repressive domestic policy.[80]

The "New Republican Catechism" delivered the local party's message in an inexpensive, popular format. It little matters that it was
second-rate literature because we know that the *canuts* read it. In his
testimony before the Court of Peers in 1835, Prefect Gasparin
recalled that a group of weavers came to see him and recited pas-
sages from this pamphlet from memory.[81]

The increased communication between Republicans and workers
was not limited to theoretical tracts. In July 1833, Jules Favre defended a group of *canuts* accused of leading an illegal strike. His
deposition was printed as a pamphlet: "On the Coalition of the
Master Weavers of Lyon."[82] Favre began with an exposition of the
problems of the silk industry from the perspective of a master weaver. These men did not consider themselves simple workers (*ouvriers*),
he said, but property owners (*propriètaires*) who, unlike their journeymen, were "fixed" in the community. Nevertheless, while the
merchants grew rich by pleading they would be ruined by higher
weaving rates, the masters faced the stark alternative of extinction
or resistance.

But the *canuts* realized that rebellion was profitless and that they must win their "social emancipation" by other means. Legal or not, Favre declared, it was time to acknowledge the purpose of worker associations. If the establishment of open competition once had helped to spur the economy, its present abuse gave the workers no choice but to oppose it. The great social question of the day, therefore, was: "Can industry, which has grown for forty years by individual efforts and the rivalry between the workers, now live with their association?"

Finally, Favre addressed himself directly to the members of his own class. If the master weavers were now organized, they were only obeying the law of self-defense. He offered reassurance to those who said the *canuts'* demands would destroy the silk industry and lived in fear because events had proven they could defeat the garrison. "If I believe in the power of the people," Favre concluded, "I also believe in its morality and its intelligence."

If their political, economic, and social assumptions are compared with those of the earlier proposals by Baune and Petetin, the three works just examined may be said to constitute the Republicans' "discovery" of the Lyonnais worker community. Their authors had sought to disprove the equation of a Republic with the Terror, present an alternative to the policies of the July Monarchy, and understand the problems of the silk industry from the workers' point-of-view. The *canuts*, of course, had always been there. But not until its members learned to see how the future looked through their eyes was there any opportunity to transform the narrowly-based Republican party into a popular movement.[83]

IV

The Republican party attempted to proselytize the worker community for the first time in the fall of 1833. The local Jacobins initiated this shift in political tactics and in October the *Glaneuse* announced the existence of a local chapter of the Society of the Rights of Man.[84] Although they had earlier sponsored an organization called the Society of Progress,[85] the Girondists now opposed secret societies on theoretical, tactical, and personal grounds. First, with their conviction that French society was moving irresistably toward greater liberty, they believed that freedom of the press superseded the need for them.[86] Second, their vision of the gradual adoption of Republican institutions was predicated on support from an enlightened middle class. Since the bourgeoisie equated Republican clubs with conspiracy, it was argued, they should be discouraged.[87] Finally, they feared the effect the Society of the Rights of Man would have on the local party. Anseleme Petetin privately criticized it for "concentrating on a single point all the young, ardent, eloquent men . . . , all those who lack positive and serious interests in life, all those who have the time, the words, and the anger to spend them without profit."[88]

The *Précurseur* later condemned as retrograde the Society's decision to include Robespierre's version of the Declaration of Rights of Man in its bylaws.[89] The *Courrier de Lyon* could hardly contain its amusement. "Discord reigns in the camp of the Republicans," it wrote. "Ordinarily parties divide after their victory; the latter are so confident that they have split before the battle and already are arguing over the spoils."[90]

Little is known about the actual foundation of the Society of the Rights of Man in Lyon.[91] The first sections were organized in October 1833 and elections for a Central Committee were held at the end of that month. The original Central Committee was composed of Eugène Baune (a lycée instructor), Caesar Bertholon (the son of a local businessman), Antide Martin (a journalist and the author of the "New Republican Catechism"), and Joseph Hugon (a bookbinder). An increase in membership necessitated a special election in December, when Edouard Albert (the publisher of the *Glaneuse* and Joseph Pujol (a battalion commander of the National Guard) were added. Two hundred and eight votes were cast in this election.[92]

The Society's formal purpose was stated in its *Règlement:*

> The oppressors and intriguers of all nations have always founded their empires and success on the division, ignorance, and weakness of the people. In order to destroy this tyranny the people must regain its sovereignty; citizens must unite and learn their rights. Association and propaganda are the two powerful levers by which . . . to prepare for the day of emancipation.
>
> To abolish the exploitation of man by man, to destroy the revolting privilege of a few idlers, . . . to summon all men to dignity, liberty, political equality, and especially to a just division of the advantages and burdens of society: there is our goal.[93]

Its structure conformed to its professed democratic principles. The Central Committee was elected annually by direct vote of a majority of all members. Its decisions were administered by commissioners in each arrondissement, who also visited the sections regularly to report on their activity. Each section bore a patriotic name and met weekly under the leadership of its elected section chief. When a section grew to more than twenty members the bylaws provided that it automatically subdivide itself.

The requirements for membership reflect the desire to create a popular movement. Unlike the worker associations, which placed strict moral and professional restrictions on candidates, the Society of the Rights of Man was open to anyone who could pass a patriotic scrutiny. At the time of his initiation a prospective member had to explain why he had become a Republican and swear allegiance to Robespierre's version of the Declaration of the Rights of Man. Two negative votes in a section were sufficient to reject a man. Monthly dues of fifty centimes brought membership within the budget of most Lyonnais workers.

These facts help explain the disproportionate fear of the Society on the part of the government and the silk merchants. Leonard Richards has suggested that the "gentlemen of property and standing" who composed the antiabolition mobs in the United States in this same period were moved to violence because abolition societies were open to everyone; they believed their elite status and political power were threatened by a movement that stirred the passions of *all* citizens.[94] So it was that in Lyon the Association for the Liberty of the Press, an organization of restricted function and bourgeois membership, was tolerated, while the Society of the Rights of Man was perceived as a danger to the deference sacred to *juste-milieu* political life.

The relationship of the Lyonnais chapter to the national organization of the Society of the Rights of Man is (and was) easily misunderstood. Its leaders in Paris saw it as a vehicle for building a national Republican party and, theoretically, the provincial chapters were under their command.[95] In practice, however, they had neither financial nor administrative control over them. Affiliation was accomplished merely by sending a letter to the capital.[96] The authorities incorrectly accused the Lyonnais of blindly obeying the national leaders and the members of the local Central Committee adamantly denied it.[97] More by default than intention, in fact, the Lyonnais actually replaced the Parisians in the vanguard of Jacobin Republicanism. This was true not because they were more militant, but because the government was so confident of controlling events in the capital. We will later learn how the Parisians deferred revolutionary initiative to the Lyonnais.

The local chapter also helped organize associations in neighboring cities such as Vienne, Villefranche, and Saint Étienne. In December 1833, Eugène Baune embarked on a trip to Valence and Romans, where his speech was interrupted by the police and he was ordered to leave before morning.[98] The emergence of Lyon as a regional Republican center undoubtedly contributed to the rumor that help for the insurgents would be forthcoming from the surrounding departments at the time of the April uprising.

The Lyonnais Society of the Rights of Man sponsored no public meetings or demonstrations before the end of 1833, and we know little about what transpired in its section meetings until the well-documented crises of February-April 1834. According to its *Règlement,* meetings began with the minutes and proceeded to the reception of new members, new business, reading of local and national newspapers, and, during the first session of each month, a financial report. This does not tell us anything, however, about their atmosphere or the political discussions which obviously took place. A Russian scholar, Volguine, has speculated that the tone of the latter was more radical than were the organization's publications.[99] Nevertheless, Joseph Benoit said that as a youth in Lyon he was driven out of a section meeting for proposing the abolition of private property.[100] We have concluded, therefore, that if the Society of the Rights of Man was the foyer of what Leo Loubère has called "Jacobin Socialism'" it was not a forerunner of French communism.[101]

Something of the atmosphere of Lyonnais secret associations is recaptured in the report of a police spy who infiltrated the Society of Progress.[102] His account also reveals much that was characteristic of such groups in general. First, there was an exaggerated concern for ritual. The agent was taken blindfolded into the meeting where he was asked to state his name, age, profession, and political and religious opinions. He then received the name of his section (the *Varsovienne*), its password, and motto and chose a patriotic name by which he would be known at all meetings. In part, such clandestine tactics were necessary to skirt the law, for an individual might be unaware of the identity of the members of other sections or the size of the organization as a whole. But ceremony and ritual had other functions as well: they gave each member a political identity, were surrogates for and mirrors of other institutions such as the church, and, as was often the case, substitutes for a substantive political program.

Second, these societies were instruments of socialization. Associations of all types flourished in this period, not only in France but in the United States and elsewhere. Adolphe Thiers privately lamented to Prefect Gasparin that they were "the malady of our epoch."[103] In a sense they were a collective response to what Wolfram Fischer has called "the social disintegration" which accompanied the transition from a traditional to a modern society.[104] Bound together by vows of fraternity and common purpose, members of groups such as the Society of Progress met regularly to discuss newspapers and pamphlets and to pass on the latest political gossip. Often they continued talking over a bottle of wine in a café. Their members' simple sense of belonging helps explain their popularity.

Finally, the police spy's report raises a problem which E. P. Thompson calls "the dilemma of revolutionism."[105] The members of the Society of Progress were said to have been reminded to continue arming themselves for the coming revolution. Did they (and should we) take this exhortation seriously? In this case it seems unlikely,[106] but the general problem remains, nonetheless. Without denying, as Eric Hobsbawm reminds us,[107] that under different circumstances the same men can be either radical reformers or revolutionaries, we have concluded that the leaders of the Lyonnais Republican party were nonrevolutionary. Openly opposed to the July Monarchy, their newspapers waffled in response to the delicate question: under what circumstances is revolution justified? The *Précurseur* said it saw "a distinction between riot, in other words, useless and dangerous uproars, and revolutions, which are always legitimate because they emanate from real necessity and always produce results advantageous to civilization."

The paper added that it was not yet time for a Republic because, without the re-education of society, the new regime would be forced to use the guillotine.[108] And the *Glaneuse* stated: "We approve of insurrection (not riot) . . . when the people have found it impossible *for several years* to change legally the order of things."[109]

While such qualifications helped camouflage the "dilemma of revolutionism" which plagued them, it is equally important that both the Jacobin and Girondist factions frequently resorted to revolutionary rhetoric. The danger inherent in this style of leadership is that in a moment of crisis a few militants may seek to bridge the gap between words and action. This is precisely what would happen in April 1834.

By the end of 1833, the local Jacobins had seized the initiative in the campaign to win worker support. The Girondists attempted to counter the Society of the Rights of Man by reorganizing the Society of Progress for "the instruction of the industrial classes" and stressing its respectability. One of its brochures carried a fictitious conversation between Master Jacques and his friend Guillaume, who says: "In our association, which is composed only of honest workingmen, we don't have *esprit* so much as plain common sense. We had established our principles long before the Society of the Rights of Man published its Manifesto"[110]

In spite of the efforts of men such as Charles Lagrange[111] and Leon Favre (the elder brother of the lawyer, Jules Favre) the Society of Progress disappeared sometime in early 1834. [112]

What was popularly called the "episode of the Public Hawkers (*crieurs publics*)" also originated with the competition between factions of the Republican party.[113] Copying a technique used in Paris to exploit a loophole in the press laws, the Girondists began hawking penny-pamphlets in the streets. Their first sheet, "The *Précurseur* of the People," was printed on 22 December 1833. It and two others were seized by the police, but a fourth number, "The Liberty of the Press Is an Illusion" was sold unhindered on 18 January 1834.[114] By this time the Society of the Rights of Man had its own Public Hawkers and the authorities were more concerned over these "Jacobin carnivals" than by the Girondist vendors, who prided themselves on maintaining strict legality.[115] On one occasion the police attempted to arrest a man distributing copies of Robespierre's version of the Declaration of the Rights of Man and were attacked by a crowd and forced to take refuge in the Prefecture.[116] The Society announced that its members would be out the next Sunday with Phrygian bonnets and boxes labeled "Democratic Writings" in order to distinguish them from the Girondists.[117]

Mayor Prunelle was enraged by the new Republican tactics. As he wrote to Prefect Gasparin:

> We are now at the point where the imprudence of those who disturb the public repose is a daily event. There is no need for

secret agents to uncover plots. The journals . . . are confident . . .
of provoking rebellion . . . with impunity.

Isn't it time to apply the penal code with regard to conspiracy?
What are we waiting for?

Legislation, in fact, was already being prepared to stop the Public
Hawkers. On 24 January, the Minister of Justice introduced a bill
requiring vendors of written or printed materials to have a revokable
license. A second provision brought all publications, regardless of
their format, under the existing tax and caution-money regulations.[119] The bill was supported by the Lyonnais deputy Fulchiron,
who said that sedition was being preached in a city where 100,000
workers were likely to be seduced by Republican promises.[120] A
similar opinion was expressed by Prefect Gasparin: "We must fight
this occult state within the State which is making ceaseless war
against us. [Our enemies], noting the attitude of the workers since
their fatal triumph of November, realize that this city is filled with
the elements of disorder."[121]

Such alarm was exaggerated. Even before the passage of the Law
on Public Hawkers much of the tension might have subsided had
local officials been able to work together effectively. Bureaucratic
rigidity, for example, delayed the adoption of a plan by which a
judicial reading for seditious content could be made when a brochure
was registered.[122] Weeks passed before someone discovered an old
regulation which forbade the public wearing of a Phrygian bonnet.[123]
The administrative and judicial authorities each thought the others
inadequate to the task. At one point the Counselor of the Royal
Court wrote Gasparin: *"Monsieur le Préfet,* I am not entirely satisfied with you either."[124] Although they claimed it was their adherence to legality which hampered them, even apologists such as
Monfalcon and the *Courrier de Lyon* criticized their handling of
the Public Hawkers' affair.[125]

The experience did teach Gasparin a lesson, however. Henceforth,
all agencies of local administration and law enforcement were criti-
cally evaluated and the Prefect began to ignore the advice of Mayor
Prunelle and Police Commissioner Prat and turned instead to Lt.
General Aymard, the commander of the Seventh Military District
whose headquarters was in Lyon.[126] The government's strong action
in the days before the April uprising—which included the coordination of administrative, judicial, and military officials—was in part
a result of the fiasco in January.

Nonetheless, the clumsy efforts at policing the vendors allowed
the Republicans to emerge briefly as popular heroes. Marc Reverchon, who went to prison for hawking Girondist brochures, chided
the authorities: "In seeing the censorship, the seizures, the trials,
the arrests raining down on all those who sold our publications, the
people have understood that we are truly their friends. Particularly
since we were welcomed in such a fashion by the friends of the
King, Louis Philippe."[127]

We can only speculate how many *canuts* read these penny-pamphlets simply because the government tried so hard to suppress
them. Monfalcon reported with unconcealed bitterness how the
Republicans went from workshop to workshop with petitions in
support of the liberty of the press.[128] Although it could not have
been apparent to anyone at the time, the "episode of the Public
Hawkers" marked the apogee of Republican popularity in Lyon.

The Girondists' brochures were largely articles on the necessity
for a free press reprinted from the *Précurseur*,[129] while the Jacobins'
combined original Lyonnais writings with pamphlets distributed
through the Propaganda Committee of the national Society of the
Rights of Man.[130] In citing the November rebellion as proof that
a bourgeois government could never be trusted, one of them, in
particular, showed the impact which the *canuts* had had on the
Republican party. It also summarized the character of its appeal
to the workshops:

> Now, Citizens, you understand that . . . [the] industrial re-
> forms which you so justly desire cannot be accomplished . . .
> without a political revolution . . . Political reform will necessarily
> introduce the industrial revolution [that is, worker owner-
> ship].[131]

By 1834, the Lyonnais Republicans were openly attempting to
politicize the worker community. In later chapters we will discuss
how the *canuts* responded and under what circumstances a temporary rapprochement between them actually occurred. Nevertheless, the party had violated the rules established after 1830 by the
local political elite which blamed it for the simultaneous development of a militant worker movement. In his year-end report for
1833, the commander of the departmental Gendarmerie wrote:
"Material order has not ceased to reign in the Department of the

Rhône . . . But the moral order has been compromised by the violence of writings against the government."[132] Such officials faithfully
reported but failed to register the significance of the fact that the
local party was not only small and faction-ridden, but also that its
members had only recently learned how to appeal to the workers
on their own terms. In addition, the Lyonnais had become affiliated
with the national Republican network largely because of their
inability to survive independently as a party under the harassment
of the government. Perhaps it was because the Republicans now
challenged their system of deference that the supporters of the *juste-
milieu* overrated the party's real strength in Lyon.

4   The Worker Movement

Following the rebellion of November 1831 the government introduced a few reforms and then advised the *canuts* to be patient and resigned. Those who controlled local politics saw little profit in a concern for their cause. As the *Courrier de Lyon* stated: "We do not invite the workers to rally to our flag because we see them as workers not party men. We recommend to them faithfulness to their contracts, respect for the law, activity and economy, but not adherence to our beliefs."[1]

Cast adrift in this manner the weavers sought to organize the worker community in 1832 and 1833 in order to mold the future for themselves. Their attempt followed four lines: the reformed *Conseil des Prud'hommes*, secret associations and strikes, newspapers, and plans for producers' cooperatives in the silk industry. These were bound together in a movement whose purpose was to win for the *canuts* (particularly the master weavers) the respect they believed due them and to wrestle from the merchants the power they wielded by their control over weaving rates. "Our goal," proclaimed Lyon's second worker newspaper, the *Écho des Travailleurs*, "is SOCIAL EQUALITY, . . . a uniform condition of well being, . . . an integral development in all men of their moral and physical abilities; this does not yet exist."[2]

I

The reform of the *Conseil des Prud'hommes*, the arbitration board of the silk industry, was the government's principal concession after the November rebellion. For more than a year the master weavers attempted to use what little authorized power they had to transform it into a legal forum for their grievances. Their failure and the reasons

96

that lay behind it did much to turn them in the direction of illegal associations and strikes.

Eight master weavers were elected to the reformed *Conseil des Prud'hommes* by their fellows who owned four or more looms in April 1832. Each man represented a constituency whose boundaries were drawn to give them a roughly equal number of looms; six of the eight master *Prud'hommes* lived in either the Croix Rousse commune or the 1st (Croix Rousse hillside) and 5th (right bank of the Saône) arrondissements.[3] Prefect Gasparin addressed the *Conseil's* opening session and admonished its members to forget class antagonisms and render impartial justice. Although the initial meetings handled only routine matters, the *canuts* filled the council room. Even when a larger hall was found there were complaints that persons with cases to be heard were unable to reach the *Prud'hommes'* bench.[4]

That the new board operated smoothly in its first months can be illustrated by a case concerning the tulles weavers. At one time among the best-paid workers in the industry, they were severely hurt by the introduction of English competition. According to Prefect Gasparin their weaving rates had fallen more than 60 per cent over a period of years.[5] In June 1832, the *tullistes* asked permission to march in the Place Bellecour to publicize that the merchants were paying them rates based on a standard bolt of cloth while demanding they weave bolts that were much longer. In denying their request the prefect advised them to go to the *Conseil des Prud'hommes,* which thereupon arranged a compromise solution.[6] This model example of cooperation between the local administration, merchants, and *canuts* suggests why John Bowring at this time described the *Conseil* as "one of the most popular institutions which exist in France."[7]

In January 1833, the *tullistes* were once again before the *Prud'hommes* to charge that the merchants had cut their rates. This time, however, the permanent merchant majority on the board told them that such complaints would ruin the industry. The tulles weavers' response was to launch a short and unsuccessful strike in the name of their mutual aid association.[8] Why had the attitude of the *Conseil des Prud'hommes* changed?

It had changed because the master *Prud'hommes* were now attempting to transform the role of the board itself. The merchant *Prud'hommes* did not object because most disputes brought before the *Conseil* were between *canuts* and *fabricants;* the example of the tulles weavers was, in this sense, unusual since the vast majority of its cases dealt only with masters, journeymen, and apprentices. What they rejected was the intention to standardize its procedures and make it a real court of appeals.

Conflict first arose when the master *Prud'hommes* argued that because the merchants were better educated than the average weaver, the latter should be able to bring a lawyer when he appeared before the *Conseil.* When a law clerk tried to defend two printing workers, however, the board's president, a merchant, ordered him placed in jail for contempt. The prefect, acting on orders from the Minister of Commerce, told the merchants that the decision was a correct one. The master weavers, on the other hand, were advised by a number of Republican lawyers that they were within their rights. The *Écho de la Fabrique* solicited the names of *canuts* willing to defend fellow workers and over 5,000 masters and journeymen signed a petition for the right of legal representation. One merchant *Prud'homme,* who strenuously opposed this demand, was vilified by the worker newspaper and resigned his position in anger. In the end the decision of the president was upheld by the government.[9]

The master *Prud'hommes* then campaigned to make the *Conseil's* decisions carry legal precedence. Although the merchants rejected the idea, the *Écho de la Fabrique* began to run a regular column of the "jurisprudence" established at its meetings.[10] A third suggestion, that only representatives of the silk industry should vote in cases involving the *fabrique,* was also defeated.[11]

By the time for new *Prud'homme* elections in January 1833, the *Conseil* was no longer a viable institution. Seven merchant representatives were to be chosen, but only 86 of their 457 eligible colleagues bothered to vote. The only merchant *Prud'homme* who occasionally voted on the workers' side did not stand for re-election and six of those who were selected were known for their opposition to the masters' tactics. "Where could we find men more hostile," asked the *Écho de la Fabrique?*[12] Nevertheless, the master weavers took the election seriously. The worker press called voting "the most important act of your proletarian lives."[13] The most important result from the *canuts'* point of view was the failure of Falconnet to be re-elected in the 1st arrondissement. The defeat of the founder and editor of the *Écho de la Fabrique* was attributed to the fact that he had been unable to fulfill his promise to change the role of the *Conseil des Prud'hommes.*[14] With emotions running high among both groups

perhaps Monfalcon was right when he wrote: "The merchant *Prud'
homme* remains a merchant and the master *Prud'homme* considers
himself not a judge, but a representative of the workers."[15]

A crisis arose when six (and later all seven) new merchant *Prud'
hommes* resigned because "what should be a sanctuary of justice has
become a battlefield," The *Courrier de Lyon* reported that one
merchant had been physically attacked after an unpopular decision.[16]
The *Écho de la Fabrique* alleged that they had conspired to refuse
to accept office until they were assured that all meetings of the
Conseil would be held in secret.[17] Prefect Gasparin feared the board
would simply dissolve in rancor and confusion. Concerned to maintain what he called "a legal channel for the workers," he proposed to
Paris that the *Conseil* be reduced to the size it had been before the
November rebellion. In the meantime he suspended its meetings until
the master *Prud'hommes* promised to maintain order.[18] Adolphe
Thiers, at that time Minister of Commerce, contended that the
masters had to live "with the dangerous results of their conduct."
Accordingly, he ordered new elections for the merchant *Prud'
hommes* and told the prefect to obtain a guarantee that they would
serve.[19]

But the crisis was far from over. Gasparin wrote Paris that "at the
present moment the *Conseil des Prud'hommes* is going nowhere."[20]
He finally won Thiers's support for "reform": five merchants and
four masters were to be regular members of the board (*titulaires*),
while four merchants and four masters served as substitutes (*supplé-
ants*) and could participate only to guarantee a quorum. The public
explanation was that frequent absences by *Prud'hommes* had been
the source of its troubles.[21] The real reason was that the reduction in
size would "facilitate the enjoyment of a majority by the merchants."[22]

Thiers realized that the merchants had contributed to the crisis. He
probably knew, for example, that their newspaper had dismissed
the *Conseil* as "a utopia of some *bons citoyens.*"[23] Privately, he
instructed Gasprin that "you must make the silk merchants understand (and it is about time they heard it) that if they abandon the . . .
Conseil des Prud'hommes either by negligence or by calculation . . .
they will be committing a truly imprudent act that will prejudice
their own interests."[24] Nevertheless, the government refused to
consider giving both sides equal representation and, in its peculiar
self-defeating way, allied itself with the merchants by substituting
reaction for real change. The significance of this fact was not lost on

the worker community. The *Écho de la Fabrique* noted: "We can truthfully say that the ordinance of 21 June was for the workers of Lyon what the July Ordinances were for France, that is to say a veritable coup d'État."[25]

The second reform of the *Conseil* was accomplished by having the *Prud'hommes* draw lots to determine which of them would become substitutes. At the same time they decided which terms of office would expire at the end of the year; the worker constituencies were to alternate being represented by a substitute or regular *Prud'homme*. The government was not through tampering with the board, however. As the elections approached the *Écho de la Fabrique* and its rival, the *Écho des Travailleurs,* demanded that all candidates make a public statement of their goals. The masters' Society of Mutual Duty hoped to elect a slate of its members.[26] Gasparin took steps to block these plans. The term of Labory, who represented the peninsula, was scheduled to end in December 1833. Because he was the most conservative of the master *Prud'hommes,* the prefect issued an ordinance protecting Labory for another two years. Not only would his status change from substitute to regular member, but also the representative from the militant 1st arrondissement would have to face re-election instead. Despite the fact that his constitutents told the prefect that Labory had moved his workshop to another part of the city he stuck by the decision.[27]

"You have violated the law," said the *Écho de la Fabrique.*[28] "This conduct cannot be tolerated for long," warned the *Écho des Travailleurs.*[29] Even the monarchist master Pierre Charnier threatened to resign his seat on the board if Labory kept his.[30] But Gasparin would not be moved: "According to my mind . . . by attempting to transform the *Conseil des Prud'hommes*—an attempt that I constantly opposed—the workers were seeking a *tarif* by other means."[31] In order to understand the development of the Lyonnais worker movement one must realize that only after they had lost faith in accomplishing change by means of established institutions did the *canuts* turn to illegal tactics.[32] Little wonder that the *Écho de la Fabrique* told the government: "Hypocrites! The time for confidence is passed. It is gone with no return."[33]

II

Surveying the proliferation of labor associations, Prefect Gasparin believed it was the master weavers' Society of Mutual Duty which epitomized "the spirit of egotism . . . so fatal to our industrial class."[34] Two surviving versions of the mutualists' *Règlement* permit us to examine the structure and goals of this organization whose development mirrored that of the Lyonnais worker movement as a whole.[35]

The law which forbade unauthorized associations of more than twenty members necessitated that the Society of Mutual Duty be formed like a pyramid with separate lodges at its base. Each lodge was subdivided into four cells headed by an Indicator, who alternated as lodge president and was responsible for communicating messages to four other members. Two delegates from each of ten lodges formed a Central Lodge. The presidents of the Central Lodges comprised the Grand Council, or Council of Presidents, of Mutualism. Although the society's structure was democratic in theory, in practice the Council of Presidents was an oligarchy which frequently acted as a brake on the rank-and-file.

The requirements for membership were strict in keeping with the stated desire that Mutualism help provide order in the community. A candidate had to be at least twenty-five years of age, have worked as a master for one year, and have a reputation for "a good life and manners." Not until 1833 did unmarried men become eligible and even then they had to be proposed by two married members. One became a Brother only after he was scrutinized at a number of meetings and a secret vote was taken. The initiation fee was five francs, monthly dues were one franc, and members were fined if they missed a required meeting. If a mutualist's character was found unacceptable at any time he could be expelled by the Council of Presidents and the reason would be announced in every lodge, or "workshop (*atelier*)" as they were called. The society eventually introduced different ranks of membership: an aspiring master weaver served a period of "apprenticeship," became a nonvoting "journeyman," and received full rights as a "master" after a year's probation.

From its foundation by Pierre Charnier in 1827 until the creation of the so-called Second Lodge in October 1831, the Society of Mutual Duty had no more than 250 members.[36] In March 1833, Prefect Gasparin estimated its membership to be 1,200 master weavers.[37] A high point was reached early in 1834, when one member of the new Executive Council reported there were 3,000 mutualists,[38] or approximately 40 per cent of all *chefs d'atelier.* In any case, the society's influence extended far beyond its formal membership. During their general strike in February 1834, for example, the mutualists succeeded in idling every loom in the *fabrique.*

The Society of Mutual Duty's multiple goals distinguished it from most other worker associations. It was at once a mutual aid society, a secret fraternity for the self-regulation of the weaving community, and a society of resistance against the silk merchants. Funds were available from its treasury in case of accident or illness, as loans for the rental or purchase of new equipment, and as pensions for the widows of deceased Brothers. On the occasion of the death of a mutualist or a member of his family his lodge printed funeral invitations which the Indicators distributed in his neighborhood. A fine of one franc was levied on members who failed to attend a required funeral since this was considered "an act of ingratitude" toward the society. At first glance these activities seem like those of other burial societies and a familiar form of early working class organization. For the mutualists, however, they were an occasion to display their strength. Three days before the uprising of April 1834, for example, more than 5,000 *canuts* participated in the funeral procession of a master weaver.[39]

All other mutualist activities were carried on in secret. Although members might recognize one another by the society's badge of different colored ribbons and repeat its motto, "Equity, Order Fraternity/Indication, Aid, Assistance," they were forbidden to divulge anything to a nonmember. Brothers found guilty of leaking secrets, even unintentionally, were automatically expelled. Each lodge had a special name, such as "Perserverence" or "Unyielding," and held at least one subscription to the *Écho de la Fabrique*.[40] Although articles from the worker press were regularly debated, all discussion of politics or religion was "expressly forbidden" by the *Règlement*. Five times each year the lodges devoted themselves to a discussion of workshop problems. The presidents of the lodges reported to the Council of Presidents which then distributed lists of rules "in order to inform each mutualist so that he can conform uniformly to them in his shop." An annual prize in the form of a special ribbon was awarded to the member who made the suggestion for improving the quality of work performed by the *canuts*.

In addition to distributing mutual aid and seeking to introduce uniform standards in the worker community, the mutualists were pledged "to unite their efforts in order to obtain a reasonable wage for their handwork." To this end every member had to work full-time as a weaving master and could be neither the father nor the son of a silk merchant or his clerk. According to Prefect Gasparin's first extensive report on Mutualism, the society's principal goal was "to protect the interests of its members against what is called the opposition and greed of the merchants."[41] Almost all mutualists agreed that some form of a *tarif* offered the best protection of their interests. They disagreed, however, on the means to achieve one and their debate over tactics informs much of our subsequent story.

About the same time as the masters organized the Second Lodge of Mutualism, the journeymen weavers established their own association called the Society of Ferrandiniers, after a special type of silk and woolen cloth. Their *Règlement* reveals the Ferrandiniers were a mixture of the *compagnonnages* and Mutualism.[42] The ordinary weaver had never enjoyed the benefits provided by the *compagnonnages* to other bachelor journeymen in Lyon. In the Ferrandiniers he now received financial aid in times of illness and found companionship in the *Mère,* the mother house or inn which became his fraternal club. Disrupted after April 1834, the Ferrandiniers were later reorganized and in 1844 they formally associated themselves with the Society of Union, which sought to reform the *compagnonnages.*[43] While it seems natural that the Ferrandiniers eventually merged with the progressive journeymens' movement, it is important to note that at first they were more heavily influenced by the example of their masters' society.

The local authorities believed the Society of Ferrandiniers was "composed of men who have nothing to lose and who find themselves without a place to live, without the means of existence when they are not working, . . . the floating part of the population. They are men without education . . . who belong to whomever gives them money."[44]

For this reason the mayor gave Pierre Charnier 6,000 francs to bribe its leaders. The founder of Mutualism was satisfied, however, that the new association was devoted to the improvement of the industry and described its members as "true and good *compagnons.*" His optimism likely stemmed from the fact that the Ferrandiniers called themselves "the sons of Mutualism" and banned religious and political discussion from their meetings.[45] Although their *Règlement* did pledge them to correct a number of workshop grievances, the chorus of their song stressed solidarity with their masters:

> Forward, march on!
> With our patrons
> And together we will strike all abuses
> To save our industry.

At a banquet to celebrate the first anniversary of the *Écho de la Fabrique,* one Ferrandinier toasted the "Union of Masters and

Workers" because "they have the same goal, the same hope."[46]

Membership in the Society of Ferrandiniers was open to unmarried journeymen weavers between the ages of eighteen and thirty-five whose *livret* indicated they were a *bon ouvrier.* For aspirants who passed the scrutiny of a lodge, the initiation fee was three francs, monthly dues were one franc, and a member could be dropped if he fell three months in arrears. Like the mutualists, the Ferrandiniers were concerned with the moral character of their colleagues; the medical benefits of the society specifically excluded venereal disease, for example. And, like the exclusive *compagnonnages,* they pledged themselves to consider only "men of their profession, religion, and country (*pays*) as friends." Somewhat in contradiction, the names of their lodges suggest they were organized according to regional or national origins and that Swiss, Piedmontese, and Savoyard *canuts* were also members. The number of Ferrandiniers is difficult to estimate. A register from Easter 1834 gives the names of eighty-three men. If these were all leaders of lodges the society might have had around 600 members.[47] While Police Commissioner Prat's estimate of 5,000 members is obviously an exaggeration, he was perhaps correct to consider this society a greater threat to public order than the association of the older and more settled masters.[48] As a verse of the Ferrandiniers' song proclaimed:

> To the parvenu who dispises us
> And enriches himself by our labor
> Let him learn that our motto
> Is 'An honest wage or no work'
> From the first harmony will be born
> From the second would come anarchy.[49]

Not all of the *canuts'* associations were as successful as the mutualists and Ferrandiniers. Among a myriad of still-born proposals was one for an Industrial Circle centered around a worker savings bank. The prospectus for this organization helps reveal their mentality at his time:

> In the present state of civilization, where Egotism . . . conducts men little by little to the point of isolation and cruelty . . . approaching the state of savages and menacing the dissolution of society, those who suffer most . . . are . . . the men who earn

their subsistance through daily work with their hands and who
have come to be called "proletarians."

  The only solution, according to this document, lay "in the spirit
of association, which permits men to reunite for the defense of rights
and common interests."[50] The exhortation to *reunite* against unbridled competition marks a longing for what E. P. Thompson calls
"the old paternalistic moral economy."[51] But the Lyonnais also
looked forward to a time when those for whom work was "a mer-
chandise, the most real and sacred of all," would use their collective
power to guarantee "the value of their property."[52] To cite Thompson again, they perceived that "in both directions lay an alternative
political economy and morality."[53]
  The November rebellion, moreover, had given them a sense that
they were the vanguard of their class. On the second anniversary of
the uprising the *Écho des Travailleurs* proclaimed: "Proletarians of all
classes, you were united for three days by a fraternity of arms, by a
community of danger. Never forget it! From your union comes your
strength!"[54] Prefect Gasparin earlier quoted a couplet sung in the
worker cafés: "The Croix Roussiens are not dogs. The merchants are
all idlers."[55] A local worker poet published a stanza whose final line
was the *canuts'* motto from November 1831:

  The people are dying of hunger.
  You had better open your pockets
  If you don't want to see a day of battle
  Rising to its full height before you
  If you still ignore this burning dilemma:
  "Live working or die fighting."[56]

  And Anselme Petetin reported that the weavers knew they had
been called "barbarians" by supporters of the *juste-milieu* and used
the term with pride when referring to themselves.[57] Class feeling was
forged from such irony.[58]
  It is no surprise that the silk merchants viewed the formation of
secret labor associations with alarm. Their newspaper warned that
"when the organization of the workers into lodges is completed . . .
they will be the masters of the *fabrique*." The solution, it said, was
strict enforcement of the law against strikes and the formation of
a merchants' Commercial Circle to prevent the *canuts* from using

"the weight of their masses" to crush "isolated men."[59] The merchants failed to understand that worker societies were the weavers' response to the sense that they were the ones who were isolated.

A major test for the mutualists and Ferrandiniers came with the selective strike of July 1833.[60] This offensive coalition had two initial targets: two *unies* (plain cloth) houses which refused to raise their rates despite the relative prosperity of the industry at this time, and a *façonnes* merchant accused of paying lower rates than others who specialized in this brocaded material. The strike spread to a small number of other firms which publicly opposed worker associations. One merchant in particular, Monsieur Berlie, was selected because he had refused to sign the *tarif* agreement in October 1831. Eight houses in all were hit and around 1,000 looms idled.[61]

While members of the Society of Ferrandiniers visited the workshops to convince their fellow journeymen of the justice of the strike, representatives of the Society of Mutual Duty called on the selected houses to demand a raise in rates. The merchants refused to talk with anyone but masters with whom they had contracts and the *canuts* said they would not finish the orders mounted on their looms until they were promised higher rates.[62] Although Prefect Gasparin told them there was no legal way to attack the worker societies themselves, he advised the merchants to make no concessions because their members could not afford a long walkout.[63] When the stoppage lasted a second day, however, the government raided the office of the *Écho de la Fabrique* (where no evidence was found) and then arrested fourteen journeymen and masters who were identified as strike leaders by the merchants.[64] This action killed the coalition and soon all looms were working again.

For all its cant about "neutrality" in economic disputes, the government's real attitude is clear in the Gasparin correspondence. The Minister of Commerce called the strike "a damnation," the mutualists "an occult government," and said he would not "allow the master weavers to form a . . . menacing corporation which seeks . . . to impose itself between the merchant, who does not recognize it, and the worker, who appears to support it only out of fear."[65] The next week he advised the merchants to form "a wise union against the tyranny of coalitions."[66] This idea won the praise of the *Courrier de Lyon* which stated that if a master weaver participated in a strike against one firm all others should refuse to give him work.[67] By the government's and the merchants' double standard, in other words, a coalition by the *canuts* was dangerous and illegal, but one by the *fabricants* was sound commercial policy.

To the Minister of the Interior, the worker associations were guilty of preaching "the spirit of coalition, or rather of revolt." He ordered the prefect to forget about the letter of the law and "strike at the heart of the association of mutualists."[68] The local authorities, however, were calmer than their superiors in Paris. In contrast to their hysteria during the general strike in February 1834, they acknowledged that the situation had never been dangerous and that politics played no direct role in the dispute.[69]

The trial of its alleged leaders was more disturbing to these officials than the July strike itself. The prosecution attempted to prove that the mutualists and Ferrandiniers had terrorized the worker community; the police commissioner testified that the nuns in one convent had been warned their looms would be smashed if they continued to weave on them. Rather than reply to such charges the defense lawyer, Jules Favre, concentrated on presenting the role of these associations from the *canuts'* perspective; his speech was reprinted as the brochure "On the Coalition of the Master Weavers of Lyon." The judge of the Correctional Court acquitted four weavers who had been jailed arbitrarily by the police and sentenced the others to the minimum fine of twenty-five francs. In delivering his verdict he criticized the cupidity of the merchants and regretted it was his duty to enforce the unjust law against coalitions.[70]

The Minister of Commerce had predicted maximum sentences of two to five years in prison and even Gasparin expected the strike leaders would spend a few days in jail.[71] Now, however, it not only appeared they were unable to control the activities of the weavers' associations, but also their assumption that the *canuts* would be content so long as there were plenty of contracts had proven invalid. The merchants were both puzzled and angered by the verdict. Writing nearly a year later Monfalcon could not forget that some of them had thought to surrender to the *canuts'* demands. "A necessary solidarity lies between the merchant houses," he wrote: "For four years, what has been the direct cause of the decadence of . . . the most valuable industry in France? Is it the avidity of the merchants? No! It is the indiscipline, it is the ignorance of the workers."[72]

The *canuts* were not the only local workers who were active at this time. During the fall of 1833, five journeymen's societies struck against their masters. A virtually simultaneous series of strikes in Paris made the government suspect that a conspiratorial hand lay behind this agitation. If the strikes in the capital remain a subject for conjecture,[73] however, those in Lyon were part of an attempt to break the stultifying power of the *compagnonnages*. A recent street brawl between rival bands of curriers and cobblers had impressed on many Lyonnais that these archaic fraternities only "forge[d] links in the chains of the workers."[74]

The Society of Union of the Workers of the *Tour de France,* an organization pledged to end hierarchical distinctions between fellow journeymen, originated in Toulon in 1830 when members of the locksmiths' *compagnonnage* expelled a group of aspirants from their crowded restaurant. In 1832, the association transferred its head-quarters to Lyon where a national *Règlement* was written, breaking the tradition that workers in each city prepared their own rules.[75] And in November 1833, 400 local members of the Society of Union demanded a shorter working day and announced their solidarity with the locksmiths of Paris who were also on strike.[76]

The same month a group of journeymen cobblers demanded an average increase of three francs in weekly wages from their masters, who they charged had conspired to pay low rates. This partially successful strike was organized by the local Union of Perfect Accord which had begun to mobilize a trade previously dominated by the *compagnonnages.* Another cobblers' society, the Association of Brothers of Concord, was discussing the establishment of a producers' cooperative staffed by journeymen.[77]

The journeymen wheelwrights' association also struck for higher wages. In refusing their demand the masters stated that as veterans of the *tour de France* themselves they were aware of the hard lot of journeymen. Their advice was to stop taking Holy Monday as an extra day of leisure in order to earn enough without a raise.[78] Little is known about the strike by the journeymen carpenters beyond the fact that the masters sought permission from the garrison com-mander to hire troops to work on their uncompleted projects. The Minister of War found this idea appealing and authorized masters in any trade where the journeymen were on strike to replace them with soldiers. "This measure should contribute much toward restoring the civilian workers to their duties," he wrote.[79]

The Philanthropic Society of Tailors was also in competition with the *compagnonnages.* "Rally to us," it told local journeymen: "Today we are workers, tomorrow we can be masters."[80] The final line of the society's Manifesto suggests the influence of the *canuts'* rebellion on other trades:

> Nobody can forget the numerous peaceful meetings in each
> trade after the July Revolution. It appeared to the people
> that . . . they were the heroes and victors and that the thoughts
> of our legislators would turn toward the laboring classes . . . It is
> not our fault if we are now forced to associate in order to com-
> bat the rapacious spirit which seeks to exploit our misery so long
> as we continue to remain isolated . . . *Vivre en travillent!*[81]

The journeymen tailors worked for a piece-rate which was lowered
when business became scarce. For this reason the Philanthropic
Society, which had earlier adopted the statutes of a Parisian tailors'
association, waited until orders were abundant for the winter season
to strike seven of Lyon's largest shops. Its members said they were
imitating their colleagues in the capital. The coalition lasted for two
days and involved around one hundred persons. It was broken by
the arrest of seven journeymen who were bailed out of jail by their
masters. Six shops later agreed to raise their rates.[82]

By the workers' own admission the wave of strikes in Lyon and
Paris was not coincidental, yet there is no evidence that they were
centrally directed in any formal sense. Taking some hints from
Jean-Pierre Aguet,[83] we have concluded that they were loosely coordinated by journeymen on the *tour de France* and (with the possible
exception of the wheelwrights' strike) were part of the widespread
rebellion against the *compagnonnages.* Their timing and central goal
of a permanent increase in wages (some groups wanted a *tarif*) suggest they were also a natural response of workingmen to France's
recovery from the depression which had begun in 1827 and only
ended around 1832. Indeed, what the *Courrier de Lyon* called "the
coalition mania" the *Écho des Travailleurs* saw as "coalitions of
ascension."[84]

The government, however, suspected a pernicious political influence was at work. The Minister of the Interior told Gasparin he had
proof that the Parisian Republicans had sent emissaries to Lyon
and blamed the Society of the Rights of Man for the strikes in both
cities.[85] We have discovered that the head of the Lyonnais Philanthropic Society of Tailors, a journeyman named Louis Marigné, was
later the chief of the Independence section of the local Society of
the Rights of Man. After his acquittal of charges stemming from the
tailors' strike, Marigné worked for a short time in Marseille and was
in touch with journeymen's association there.[86] Rather than confirming the assertion of the Minister of the Interior, Marigné's partici-

pation seems evidence that the mobility of artisans helped coordinate the revolt against the *compagnonnages.*

Beyond this individual, whose political sentiments the authorities never mentioned at the time, the Lyonnais Republican party played almost no role in the fall strikes. The Society of the Rights of Man was scarcely organized and one of its first communications to its members was an appeal for funds to support the families of arrested workers. "We are going to prove to them that we are truly their brothers," the letter stated.[87] The *Courrier de Lyon* thought they would have little success. "The more the Republicans make an effort to disrupt their shops the more the July Monarchy can count on the support of the masters," it stated.[88]

The *Précurseur* cautioned against a political explanation for the strikes and the United Brothers, an association of masters and journeymen in various embroidery trades, wrote the *Glaneuse* to declare that "the mutualists have shown us the route of emancipation."[89] Even the Minister of the Interior acknowledged there was a long tradition of worker agitation in Lyon.[90] Nevertheless, the government now believed that radical measures were necessary to stop the spread of popular societies. The Minister of Justice drafted a bill banning all unauthorized associations no matter what their membership structure.[91] Prefect Gasparin, who had proposed exactly this idea at the time of the Republicans' second banquet for Garnier-Pagès, requested immediate permission to declare a meeting illegal if anyone present had been previously convicted of breaking the existing laws governing societies.[92] When the wave of strikes subsided the Council of Ministers set aside the bill. The legislative session of 1833 was already concluded, but the Council was determined to submit it to the Chamber of Deputies at an appropriate moment in the new year.

At the height of the journeymen's strikes there were rumors that some weavers had threatened to stop work "just as their masters acted toward the merchants in another epoch." Lyonnais authorities were relieved, therefore, that there were no coalitions in the silk industry during the fall of 1833.[93] This did not mean that the mutualists and Ferrandiniers were inactive, however, for the revolt against the *compagnonnages* in other trades had engaged the *canuts* in a serious debate over the purpose of their own associations.

The *Écho des Travailleurs,* which first appeared in November 1833, said that the mutualists and Ferrandiniers had "adopted the secrecy of earlier times." On the second anniversary of the November rebellion it published a letter from the Fourierist cloth printer Rivère cadet, stating: "The great mistake of the founders of Mutualism . . . is wanting to choose rather than accept their colleagues." And in an article called "A defense of silk workers who are not mutualists," the paper attacked "the industrial church," that proclaimed, "There is no salvation outside Mutualism."[94] These charges, of course, were similar to those being made against the *compagnonnages.*

While we do not know the reaction of the Ferrandiniers, it is clear that many mutualists took this criticism seriously. Having already opened their doors to unmarried masters, they now sought to distribute benefits to nonmembers by creating a board of overseers (*Syndics*), whose function was to keep informed of current rates and investigate grievances in each branch of the silk industry.[95] The association also took the unprecedented step of holding a joint banquet with the master ribbon weavers' association of Saint Étienne. Toasts were offered by the editor of the *Écho de la Fabrique* and Pierre Charnier, the founder of Mutualism, and another master weaver entertained the audience by singing the Song of the Mutualists. The *Écho des Travailleurs* was not impressed, however. It called the affair a workshop masters' version of the Congress of Münchengratz.[96]

Disagreement over the proper role of the Society of Mutual Duty reached a peak in December 1833, with a rank-and-file rebellion against the power of the Council of Presidents. Those who desired an open, more militant organization won approval for the creation of an Executive Council, a board elected by two delegates from each lodge to receive complaints and suggest what action the society might take. One of its first decisions was to recommend a strike against seven firms specializing in plush cloth. When the Council of Presidents refused to transmit this message to the lodges, the Executive Council called for a general vote by which the authority of the former body was suspended.[97]

This successful coup brought new men to power. Master weavers such as Bouvery (aged forty-six), Serre (fifty-five), Souchet (fifty-two) and Douchet (fifty-two) surrendered leadership in the organization to a younger generation represented by Frandon (twenty-eight), Racine (thirty), Pollard (thirty-two), and Girard (thirty-two). Moreover, at least two members of the Executive Council, Girard and Carrier, were also members of the Society of the Rights of Man.[98] Although it continued to recognize the formal ban on political discussion, the Society of Mutual Duty had abandoned its elitist,

conservative origins in response to the internal dynamics of the
worker community. Less than two months later the Executive
Council would seek to test its power by calling a general strike in
the silk industry.

III

The weekly publication of the *Écho de la Fabrique*—the only
worker newspaper in France at this time—imparted information to
the *canuts,* identified issues for them, and molded their opinions and
values. To a great extent it was the public voice of the Lyonnais
worker movement. In an early issue its editors declared: "Our paper
is completely industrial. The single goal in creating it was to provoke
the amelioration of the laboring class which is the glory of our
city . . . the paper which we publish is not political." As if to underline this contention they launched a series of articles on "The Abuses
of the *Fabrique.*"[99]
Given the diversity of the silk industry, where there were hundreds
of merchants, thousands of workshops, and countless types of cloth,
each woven according to a different rate, a central source of information was an essential step toward community organization. Which
merchants were paying high rates? Which were cutting back their
contracts? What were the prospects for the season ahead? Had the
Conseil des Prud'hommes decided what should be done with an
apprentice who quit his loom, a master caught stealing thread, or
a merchant who cheated on his rates? The *canuts* found the answer
by reading the *Écho de la Fabrique.* The merchants were aware of
this fact, moreover. Some were known to refuse to give orders to
masters who subscribed to the paper and one firm sued it for printing its name on a list of alleged unscrupulous merchants. Found
guilty by the Assizes Court, the *Écho de la Fabrique* declared its
only error had been to use a wrong name to describe an almost
universal situation.[100]
The paper constantly exhorted the *canuts* to develop pride in
themselves and their work. "The weaver," it said, "seeks to live by
the fruit of his labor and not be subject to the humiliations of a
Helot or a Muscovy serf." Rather than "resign himself to suffering
and dying while singing psalms to the Virgin and praying She will
send him work," he should recognize that his labor was "the CAPITAL
of the proletarians" and that all men had a "right to work."[101] In
an article called "On the Industrial Revolution in France," it asked

whether another revolution was necessary to raise the "property" of work to a status equal to those of land and money?[102]

The themes of pride and humiliation were woven into its discussion of the problems of daily life. The public water supply, for example, was a matter of serious concern to the residents of the Croix Rousse hillside. During the summer months those who lived around the rue Tolozan drew water from a single fountain that delivered only forty liters an hour. In addition to the obvious inconvenience, there was always a danger of fire when oil lamps were used near the looms. The Municipal Council had promised that the money charged for the use of these fountains would go for the construction of more wells and pumps. There was outrage, therefore, when the *Écho de la Fabrique* revealed that these funds were actually helping finance a new theater where the merchants could enjoy the opera.[103]

Other local institutions also came under attack. The charity hospital, the Hôtel Dieu, charged a small admission fee and the paper questioned if this did not discourage the very persons who required its services? Furthermore, the hospital advertised free vaccinations but required a deposit of two francs to insure each child returned for observation. What worker mother could spare two francs for even a week, it asked?[104] Police harassment was another issue. The *Écho de la Fabrique* reported the case of a journeyman arrested for loitering when he was merely sitting in a café after delivering an order. The poor *canut* was held in custody for a day until his master could be found to vouch for his behavior.[105] Not even the church was immune from criticism. The "terrible intolerance" of the local clergy was exposed by the death of a young Savoyard weaver. When his neighbors sought to have him buried a priest refused to administer the Last Rites because he had not confessed before he died.[106] "You have given us an administration of *cultes,*" said the paper, "which charms us with Gregorian chants and sermons . . . When one seeks prayers of absolution he knows where to go. But to find work! Bread! . . . You have done everything for us to gain eternal life, but nothing for our lives on this earth."[107]

The *Écho de la Fabrique* reserved special venom for the local judiciary. The master and journeymen stonecutters, for example, had agreed to a raise in wages. When one master reneged his journeymen quit his yard and went to work elsewhere. The master took them to court, but they were acquitted by a jury before their lawyer had a chance to speak in their defense. Nevertheless, the counselor of the Royal Court insisted on appealing the decision and received

permission from the judge to keep the journeymen in jail in the
meantime. The paper announced that four of these men had families
and that their treatment showed the contempt which local officials
had for innocent workers.[108]

While the social and economic function of the Lyonnais worker
press seems clear, its ideological role is more difficult to describe.
Christopher Johnson has accurately stated that the *canuts* were "man
for man, the most mature and politically conscious working class on
the continent."[109] Nevertheless, we should not suppose that their
ideas ever existed *en bloc* or changed like a regiment marching from
one camp to the next. Of the four successive editors of the *Écho de
la Fabrique,* one was a Bonapartist and three were Republicans,
yet all of them explicitly placed the political neutrality of their
journal above their personal opinions.[110] This was done not only
to escape the wrath of the local authorities, but also because, as the
paper stated: "To tell the truth, many workers are Republicans,
others are . . . legitimists, and others still retain an almost religious
faith in the MAN whose column in the Place Vendôme July [the
revolution of 1830] has promised."[111]

If it endorsed no single cause, the paper scattered political items
throughout its pages, nonetheless. From these we can trace the
gradual disappearance of references to Napoleon and the Bourbons,
who had served the *canuts* by establishing *tarifs* in the past, and
the appearance of an interest in those groups and individual politicians it believed were presently concerned with their problems. On
one occasion it referred to General Lafayette, Odilon Barrot, Garnier-
Pagès, and Étienne Cabet as "our tribunes," but quickly added "as
to the present, our mission is totally industrial . . . and we are keeping strictly within it."[112]

In the fall of 1832, the *Écho de la Fabrique* devoted its front page
to the debate between Anselme Petetin and Bouvery in which the
latter emphatically denied the Republican's contention that politics
and economic matters were interrelated. After the collapse of confidence in the *Conseil des Prud'hommes* in early 1833, however, it
stated: "The political question complicates all industrial questions . . . No government can remain totally foreign to the society
which it claims to govern."[113] And in September, the paper chose its
words carefully in declaring:

> We entirely share the opinion of the *Précurseur* when it says
> that "the interests of the PEOPLE will be well defended only by

the representation of their rights, and that the philanthropists in
claiming them implicitly demand their moral and material amelioration."

We are also for the opinion of the *Glaneuse* when it says: "All
social reform which is not based on a REPUBLICAN political organization will not offer any guarantee of stability for the future."
For that is also our opinion.[114]

While obviously significant, we should not read too much into this
statement. It did not mean that the *Écho de la Fabrique* had become
a Republican journal (given the faction-ridden local party it would
have been difficult for the paper to support both the *Précurseur* and
the *Glaneuse*[115]), nor did it signal the transformation of the *canuts'*
associations into political clubs. It did indicate, however, that influential spokesmen for the worker community were now politicized
in the sense that they acknowledged the interrelation of political,
social, and economic issues and no longer expected the government
of Louis Philippe to come to their aid.

The worker press also helped introduce the *canuts* to the theories
of Saint Simon and Fourier. *Père* Enfantin had declared Lyon to be
"the Manchester of the European continent" and by the end of 1832
the "transformed men," as the Saint Simonians called themselves,
were constantly active in the community. Some "missionaries"
actually became weavers, while others tried to stir interest by going
to the workshops and convincing wives to bring their husbands to
Saturday evening dances which were preceded by Saint Simonian
services.[116] The authorities were uncertain whether to consider the
Saint Simonians a religious sect or a worker society, but believed
they constituted no great danger because of their bizarre costumes
and ideas. As Prefect Gasparin explained: "Our population is too
practical to become the seat of a new religion."[117] He concluded it
was wiser to allow them to operate virtually unhindered than to
throw them out of the city and risk angering the *canuts.*[118]

The *Écho de la Fabrique* said it admired men who had abandoned
brilliant careers to devote their lives to the common people, but
confessed: "We do not understand the Saint Simonian religion."[119]
The Republican newspapers were less sympathetic: the *Précurseur*
ridiculed their "mystical profundities," while the *Glaneuse* criticized them for "moralizing the poor" much like the supporters of the
juste-milieu.[120] With one specific reservation, therefore, we can
accept Fernand Rude's opinion that: "In spite of the ardent Saint

Simonian propaganda . . . , the Lyonnais workers turned more . . .
toward presyndical and Republican associations, toward direct action
which reached its climax in the *journées* of April 1834."[121]

Although the Fourierists made fewer converts, their doctrines were
probably better known to the readers of the Lyonnais press. Although the editor of the *Écho de la Fabrique* personally thought
Fourier's ideas were "exorbitant and ridiculous," he allowed a series
of articles explaining them to be printed. Written by a cloth printer
named Rivière cadet, this was perhaps the first time that the story of
the Phalansterien settlements was presented directly to a worker
audience.[122] The lectures of a traveling Fourierist speaker on "The
System of Agricultural Colonization" were also advertised and re-
viewed by the worker papers, but no permanent organization
resulted from them.[123]

All this suggests that the *canuts* were not the simple pawns of
either the Republicans or the Utopian Socialists at this time. In fact,
the direction of influence was often reversed.[124] Precisely because
they were "mature and politically conscious," the Lyonnais were
more skeptical of romantic answers to their real problems than often
has been assumed. Recalling the workers who had fallen in November
1831, the *Écho des Travailleurs* said: "Republicans have hymns to
the martyrs of Saint Merri. Bonapartists shed tears for Sainte Hélène.
Simple proletarians, we must . . . raise a funeral chant on the tomb
of those who have died for our cause."[125]

The search for pragmatic solutions eventually caused a schism on
the *Écho de la Fabrique.* During its first year of publication the paper
was committed to no particular worker association and only concerned that the *canuts* agree to concentrate on a single type of
society so as not to dissipate their energy.[126] Gradually, however,
it became a kind of house organ for the Society of Mutual Duty and
in July 1833, its stockholders fired the editor and publisher because
the two opposed such close ties to the master weavers' organization.[127]

By October the departed editor, Marius Chastaing, had printed a
prospectus for the *Écho des Travailleurs,* which appeared in early
November and claimed to have 300 subscribers within a month.
Implying that its rival was content to remain "within the narrow
bounds of a *cahier de doléances*," the new paper boasted on its
masthead: "This journal addresses itself to all classes of workers.
It is not the special journal of one industry, but that of all."[128] In
virtually every issue the *Écho des Travailleurs* criticized the narrow

goals of the *Écho de la Fabrique* and the Society of Mutual Duty,
hinting that two directors of the paper had fought alongside the
troops in November 1831, urging readers to vote for non-Mutualist
candidates in the *Prud'homme* elections, and even announcing a rival
association, the Independent Philanthropists of Lyon.[129]

In spite of their bitter disagreement, the Lyonnais worker newspapers were in accord as to the efficacy of labor associations. In their
opinion, the legality of such organizations was not a consideration
because existing laws were outdated. Associations had the triple role
of curbing anarchy in the community, furnishing a counterforce to
unbridled competition, and providing self-protection for the worker
and his family.[130] Pragmatic about other matters, the *Écho de la
Fabrique* called for "the Holy Alliance of the People . . . born from
the no less holy alliance of the workers."[131] And the *Écho des
Travailleurs* offered a catalogue of contemporary associations in
support of the principle:

> Thus Fourier preached the transformation of the world into a
> vast *phalanstère* . . . Association! Saint Simon, and after him his
> disciples, professed the indispensability of a religion . . . which
> binds the interests and hearts of men. Association! The Catholics,
> under the inspiration of Lamennais, demand a restoration of the
> belief to the Middle Ages with reciprocal charity and Christian
> fraternity. Association! The Republicans, still without an avowed
> plan, but aware of the importance of this great word, are form-
> ing political clubs, binding one to the other with promises, con-
> tributions, and even suffering—and in this union see the assurance
> of their success in the future. Association! Finally, the utilitarian
> economists themselves, of whom M. Bowring [who had visited
> Lyon in 1832] has presently been the best and most salient
> expression, what do they demand? The free exchange of prod-
> ucts, the fraternity of men and their industry, the Holy Alliance
> of crafts, and by this, the lowering of prices and the rise of con-
> sumption for all. Again, Association![132]

Leo Loubère has caught the spirit of the age in his remark that
"during the July Monarchy the word 'association' acquired the cur-
rency of a messianic formula."[133]

The local Republican press also endorsed the worker associations.
The *Précurseur* thought they marked a shift from fruitless violence
to positive programs and said that the first axiom of "the new

politics" was the self-emancipation of the working class.[134] The *Glaneuse* declared that a just wage was not a legal, but a moral question and suggested that "if the workers had formed associations twenty years ago, they would not be fighting today against the malaise which torments the industrial class."[135] This shared faith in associations was a key factor in whatever rapprochement occurred between the Republican party and the worker movement in Lyon: to the Republicans, associations were the route to a popular political movement; to the workers, they were the means of achieving social and economic goals; to the government, however, they posed a threat to the status quo.

IV

We have already learned that while some Lyonnais merchants were presently dispersing their *unies* contracts to cottage industry, others hoped eventually to concentrate the looms in factories near the city. In either case, by radically changing the structure of the silk industry they hoped to undercut or abolish the function of the master weavers. The latter, however, had plans for producers' cooperatives in which the merchants would be eliminated. Each group, in other words, believed that the other's destruction would guarantee a better future for itself. Economic and social conflict can run no deeper.

Although he was critical of the ruthless competition between the merchant houses almost from the moment he arrived in the city, Anselme Petetin of the *Précurseur* had misunderstood the *canuts'* fear of the mechanization of weaving. His published debate with the master weaver Bouvery changed his opinion as to what would constitute "efficiency" in production, however, and in a series of articles in 1833 he proposed a plan for Central Houses in the major branches of the silk industry. Initially funded by the government, each House would be headed by an "active *fabricant*" (presumably an experienced master weaver), elected by the employees' organization and charged with supervising both the manufacture and sale of cloth. The size of each House would depend on the market demand for the type of cloth it produced. The masters and journeymen associated with the Central Houses were to work for a fixed daily wage and receive a percentage of the annual profits.[136]

The *Écho de la Fabrique,* which was critical of those "who occupy themselves so much with our *rights* and would better occupy themselves with our *interests* and our dignity as men,"[137] warmly received the plan for Central Houses because it articulated in positive terms the *canuts'* perception of the problems of the industry. First, it would halt the spread of rural weaving, a development the worker paper said was contrary to the direction of civilization "which serves to separate the agricultural population from the industrial one." Second, the centralization of contracts would eliminate the competition between merchant houses and reduce manufacturing costs. Third, it would permit the base of production to remain in separate workshops rather than becoming concentrated in factories. Fourth, the fixed wage would give the weavers the equivalent of a *tarif.* Fifth, the principles of self-administration and profit sharing would not only serve as incentives, but also prove they were not idlers, rather honest artisans trapped by an exploitive system. Finally, the elimination of the merchants would end social and economic conflict and restore tranquility to Lyon.[138] Reform by means of Central Houses would be "the simplification of the industrial mechanism . . . in the collective name of the master weavers."[139]

The concept of Central Houses was more than a fantasy for the *canuts* since cooperative programs were an explicit goal of their associations and newspapers. In November 1832, the *Écho de la Fabrique* informed readers of a plan for a producers' cooperative in which a loom was considered to be the equivalent of a share of stock.[140] In 1833, a group of masters from the Croix Rousse suburb, who may have been influenced by the ideas of Fourier, published the statutes for a weavers' cooperative and began to solicit stockholders at twenty-five francs a share.[141] And according to Anselme Petetin, the Society of Mutual Duty intended to establish a model Central House with the funds from its treasury.[142] A related project called the Commercial Society was actually launched in October 1834 with a reported 4,000 stockholders and 100,000 francs in capital. Operating in the aftermath of the April uprising, the society encountered difficulties from the start and showed a deficit of 700 francs when it was dissolved in 1837.[143]

The merchants and weavers were not the only persons with "solutions" to the problems of the silk industry. Prefect Gasparin also wrote about them on a number of occasions. In September 1833, he addressed himself to "The Social Condition of Lyon" in an article he sought unsuccessfully to publish anonymously in the *Écho de la Fabrique.*[144] Making reference to the Petetin-Bouvery debate, he wrote: "Look at Liverpool, look at Manchester . . . If the worker does not earn a sufficient wage, it is not the fault of the machine."

The problem, he believed, lay in "the decadence of certain industries." Gasparin then ruled out systematically the *canuts'* ideas:
a *tarif* was illegal and would prevent Lyonnais goods from com-
peting with cheap cloth from abroad, a system of government-funded
Commercial Houses would cripple private enterprise, and public
works projects not only lacked support in a Chamber of Deputies
dominated by rural interests, but also were a proven failure. "We
have dug canals, built roads, constructed forts, and still the evil
endures," he wrote. There was, the prefect said, a solution that did
not require state intervention which would be explained in a future
article. It was never written.

What Gasparin had in mind can be found in his private reports on
the local industrial and administrative situation, as well as in his
article published as an anonymous appendix to Guizot's memoirs.[145]
The prefect believed there was no future for the silk industry as
presently organized in Lyon. Rather than continue to disperse contracts to rural cottages, however, the merchants should construct
factories (*grandes manufactures*) where "the master weavers would
disappear and the general cost of manufacturing will be diminished
by the suppression of a superfluous wheel." In fact, the real hope
for the worker community lay in a future when Lyon would no
longer be tied to the fate of a single industry. Built in "the advanced
suburbs of the industrial metropolis," the new weaving factories
would stimulate the city's expansion. As soon as the canals and railroad under construction were completed, the coal fields of Saint
Étienne would be opened and modern industries would settle in
Lyon.[146] Not only would the workers find better jobs in these enter-
prises, but also the city itself would be transformed: "Lyon will
descend from Fourvières and the Croix Rousse; it will extend itself
leisurely in the peninsula of Perrache and the plain of Les Brotteaux." If Prefect Gasparin accurately foresaw the economic and
geographical development of the Lyonnais region, his "solution"
based on long-term modernization gave little comfort to those faced
with the immediate problem of survival. In fact, it ran counter to
the *canuts'* aspirations.

In the two years which followed the rebellion of November 1831,
the conflict over the *Conseil des Prud'hommes,* the merchants' opposition to the *canuts'* associations, and the verbal battles waged in the
press and in the courts had had a schismogenetic effect: they had
polarized the two communities as a result of their interaction. Now
Prefect Gasparin, who had already supported the merchants over the

"reform" of the *Conseil des Prud'hommes* and at the time of the July strike, made it clear that he rejected the idea of producers' cooperatives and looked forward to the disappearance of the master weavers and the employment of their journeymen in factories.

The Lyonnais worker movement was remarkably pragmatic in its development. For this reason it was only after they became frustrated and disillusioned with the policies of the July Monarchy that the *canuts* began to acknowledge that economic and political issues could not be separated. If it is certain that the local Republicans never "converted the silk workers to their cause" in some monolithic fashion, it seems clear that by 1834 many would have agreed with the *Glaneuse* that "the worker at his loom is the EQUAL of Louis Philippe seated on his throne."[147]

5 The General Strike

In order to underline their separate motives and goals, the development of the Lyonnais worker movement and the activities of the local Republican party have been treated to this point almost as though they existed in isolated compartments. From February 1834, however, the interaction of the *canuts* and the Republicans (on occasion real, but more often exaggerated or imagined by nervous officials) becomes a central theme of our story. In that month a number of bizarre events, including an abortive invasion of Savoy and the murder of a policeman in Saint Étienne, occurred almost simultaneously with a general strike staged by the Society of Mutual Duty. This mammoth demonstration of worker solidarity not only revived memories of November 1831, but also led the government to imagine it was part of a larger conspiracy to foment an insurrection in southeastern France. Gripped by hysteria (or pretending to be so), it introduced the bill to abolish all unauthorized associations which it had prepared the previous fall. The pieces began to fall into place for the confrontation of April 1834.

I

The supposed "conspiracy" began on 1 February, when Guiseppe Mazzini attempted to liberate Savoy and Piedmont in the name of his organization, Young Italy. The event was not unexpected, however, for the Gasparin papers are laced with reports on the machinations of political refugees during the fall and winter of 1833–1834. Mazzini's aide-de-camp, General Romorino, for example, was known to travel frequently to Lyon in order to recruit members for the Geneva-based operation. By the end of January the government was convinced that the invasion would be launched within a matter of days.[1]

When it came, the Young Italy expedition was like something out of Grand Opera. Mazzini and Romorino set out with their tiny army of volunteers in the dead of winter to capture the town of Saint Julien just over the border in Savoy. Their only real weapon was a moral one—a proclamation, written in the style of the *levée en masse* decree, calling on all citizens to rise against their enemies and establish the Republic.[2] Marching through snow and bitter cold the vanguard of Young Italy soon disintegrated. Mazzini's friends took him back to Switzerland in a state of delirium. The French authorities, concerned over a rumor that Romorino thought a Republican insurrection would occur if he appeared again in Lyon, sent troops to close the border.[3]

Although both factions of the Lyonnais Republican party supported the liberation of Savoy in principle, neither had been anxious to support the Young Italy expedition.[4] The *Glaneuse* reported the invasion with the headline, "The European Insurrection has begun!" but failed to call for a resurrection of the Legion of the Volunteers of the Rhône.[5] The *Précurseur,* for its part, explained that while all true patriots had wished Mazzini well, "in our opinion the resolution not to cooperate was wise in all cases."[6]

Under other circumstances Mazzini's failure might have been accurately seen as proof of the weakness and disunity of the Republican party. In the context of subsequent events, however, many officials reached the opposite interpretation. Whereas the invasion was actually delayed for several months,[7] they concluded it had been premature. The explanation for this twisted logic lay in their assumption that it was meant to coincide with the mutualists' general strike. To be sure, the latter was the most important Lyonnais event since the rebellion of November 1831, but it was largely misunderstood by a government that saw everything in political terms.

The silk industry at this time was plagued by a scarcity of orders and the threat of rate reductions. In early February the houses which specialized in *shalls* and *peluches* (cheap cloth used to make men's hats) cut their rates from 1 franc 50 centimes to 1 franc 25 centimes per *aune.* Believing it was better to attack at once rather than wait for the merchants to cut back on other kinds of material, the mutualists' Executive Council proposed a strike to demand a *tarif* for the entire industry. On 12 February, the master weavers who were members of the Society of Mutual Duty voted 1,297 to 1,004 to stop all work on the 14th.[8] Their decision had the support of the journeymen *canuts.* On the 13th the mutualists and Ferrandiniers demonstrated their unity by marching, two masters and two journeymen in each row, in the funeral procession of a deceased weaver. The authorities estimated that over 1,000 persons participated in the parade.[9] The next morning the general strike began. It lasted for eight days, until 22 February, and at its peak it idled all 25,000 looms in Lyon and her suburbs.

The *ordres du jour* sent by the Executive Council to each mutualist lodge reveal an extraordinary concern that their goal be achieved peacefully. Calling for the considerable minority which had opposed the strike to respect their association's "democratic principles," the Executive Council declared that the absence of violence would justify the Lyonnais worker movement and prove that the *canuts,* who it said represented the *peuple ouvrier* of France, were responsible citizens.[10] The Executive Council also sought to keep the strike free of politics. When it learned that Republican brochures were being circulated in some lodges (this was shortly after the Public Hawkers' episode) it warned:

> It is the intention of the authorities to make a completely industrial affair degenerate into politics. Reflect wisely, Brothers. We must be prudent. Beware of police tricks, of cries you may hear day or night. Do not leave your homes. We must remain calm and silent . . . We beg this of you in the very name of Mutual Duty.[11]

The Council also said that if its members were arrested the lodges should quietly hold elections in order to continue the strike. The authorities wanted nothing more, it explained, than to antagonize the weavers, shoot them down, and then announce they had foiled a rebellion.

Five measures facilitated the operation of the general strike. First, in order to broaden support in the community the Executive Council increased its membership from twenty-five to thirty-three persons. Although the journeymen continued to exert influence only through their separate association, representatives of the poorest masters were thereby invited to participate in the strike leadership.[12] Second, in order to present a coordinated and accurate *tarif* proposal, the *Syndics* were instructed to learn which firms had lowered their rates within the past three months and to prepare lists of prevailing rates. The Executive Council advised that the eventual demand must be a reasonable one in order to dispel any claim that their motives were not economic ones.[13] Third, what was called a *ban fraternal,* a kind of mutual pledge, was imposed on all members: no individual master nor sector of the industry was to resume work until the demands of all were met or special permission was given by the Executive Council.[14] Fourth, in order to prevent public disturbances all members were to keep their journeymen, apprentices, and lancers under close supervision. Strangers were forbidden to attend lodge meetings and all talk of direct action was banned. *"Point de bravade,"* stated the *ordre du jour.*[15] Finally, steps were taken—the details remain unclear—to insure that masters who were not mutualists honored the strike. Teams of masters and journeymen circulated in the community to enforce the work stoppage. On occasion there were threats that looms would be smashed or cloth slashed if the master did not comply. Such tactics were highly effective, even halting the looms in the *Grand Atelier* at La Sauvagère.[16] On the evening of the first day of the strike Mayor Prunelle reported to Prefect Gasparin: "I walked today in the Saint Just quarter and the northern part of the town where the workshops are found and I failed to discover a single loom in operation."[17]

Despite the promise of the *Écho de la Fabrique* that "the workers of Lyon have not sought to vanquish the merchants, but gain a living wage (*vivre en travaillant*),"[18] the city was paralyzed by fear. Streets were deserted, shops closed early, theaters were shut, and the annual carnival was canceled. Many merchants locked their warehouses and fled to their country homes.[19]

The rationale behind the general strike was that those few merchants who were sympathetic would initiate negotiations for a *tarif.* At first it appeared that this tactic would succeed. Sometime on the 16th, the third day of the strike, Charles Depouilly, the owner of the *Grand Atelier* at La Sauvagère, and two other merchants persuaded some of their colleagues to raise their rates.[20] It is unclear whether they signed a *tarif*, a pledge not to lower rates again for three months, or what Prefect Gasparin called, "a *tarif* under the name of a *règlement du prix.*"[21] In any case, it is certain that some formal agreement was reached. Proof for this can be seen in the rapid shift which occurred in the character of the strike.

Until this point if the mutualists were optimistic, so were the merchants, at least publicly. The *Courrier de Lyon* boasted that the authorities were prepared to give "a vigorous lesson" to troublemakers and said that if the merchants held out for only a week they could destroy the *canuts'* associations. "Lyon has absolutely nothing to fear," the paper concluded.[22] After the 16th, however, the

Courrier changed its opinion, stating that if any merchant agreed to the weavers' demand he risked disaster for the entire industry. Resistance to the strike was now a matter of the highest principle, for "there is no reason why in a week they will not demand five francs as today they demand five sous."[23]

The attitude of the government also changed. When the strike began Prefect Gasparin assured Paris that there had never been a better time for the merchants to resist because work in the industry was so slow.[24] On the 17th, however, he told the mutualists that he would not be a mediator and that he had decided to enforce the law against coalitions in full measure.[25] Eventually, under the urging of the local authorities, the merchants denied that any of them had ever signed a *tarif* or even "an engagement of honor."[26]

The Executive Council of the Society of Mutual Duty understood the implications of this duplicity. The tone of its *ordre du jour* for the 17th was one of potential failure: "It is no longer a question of whether or not we have acted wisely, rather we must convince ourselves that all concessions on our part, that is to say resuming work without having settled anything, would be to destroy Mutualism."[27] That, of course, was precisely what the merchants and the government had in mind.

With the negotiations stalemated, resentment of the mutualists began to be felt in the worker community. Squads of weavers sought to maintain the *ban fraternal* by means of further threats, but now the authorities were prepared to use force of their own; in one case the mayor ordered troops to stand guard in the rue Tolozan to protect a master who had declared his intention to resume work.[28] In addition, the mutualists' treasury was insufficient to support even their own members much less all the *canuts*. Distribution committees were created in each lodge, but foods and funds were lacking.[29] On the 19th, 300 women marched through the streets crying for food. They threatened to bring their children with them the next day.[30]

As their hopes crumbled the Executive Council exhorted the mutualists with the claim that "our cause is that of the entire city, of all France, even of the universe." If the society was humiliated, it warned, it would weaken every other worker association in the nation. In desperation it vowed to solicit money on street corners and seek help from workers in other departments, whose "immense resources" would soon flow into the strike fund.[31] Nevertheless, the government's support of the merchants' intransigence soon caused the general strike to collapse under its own weight. On 19 February

the mutualists voted 1,382 to 445 to resume work on the 21st.[32]
The Executive Council claimed that the coalition was merely suspended and that if the merchants did not honor their agreement to
raise the rates they would be struck again "until the extinction of
their houses."[33]

Some journeymen weavers initially opposed the decision to resume
work. Perhaps 800 of them refused to return to the looms until they
were paid compensation for the work lost during the strike. This
"quarrel of interest," as the authorities called it, triggered a brawl
in the Croix Rousse suburb between a band of *compagnons* who
were remaining out and others going back to their masters' shops.[34]
This skirmish sent shock waves through the community. The *Précurseur* warned the *canuts* that disunity threatened their cause and
the *Écho de la Fabrique* denied that the mutualists and Ferrandiniers
were in disagreement.[35] Indeed, there is no evidence that the disgruntled journeymen were members of the Society of Ferrandiniers.
Nevertheless, the tension created by the failure of the general strike
opened the first serious crack in the protoindustrial solidarity that
had been the key factor in the development of the Lyonnais worker
movement.[36]

A strike, as Maurice Agulhon has noted, is *"l'événement par excellence"* for labor history, the equivalent of a battle or an election
for military or political history.[37] Judged in terms of its immediate
goal, the general strike was a disastrous error. The Executive Council
had extended the *canuts'* organizations beyond their means and
thus seemed to substantiate the position of the conservative Council
of Presidents that militancy would destroy Mutualism. Under renewed attack from these men, many of them founders of the society,
the Executive Council resigned and called for new elections to
restore the authority of the Council of Presidents.[38] One of the
poorer members of the former body noted that the strike had cost
him his life savings and stated: "In spite of all that I was satisfied
with the outcome . . . because I think it was a stern lesson which will
teach Mutualism never to plunge into such a labyrinth again."[39]
Membership in the Society of Mutual Duty dropped so rapidly that
Prefect Gasparin for a time believed that the association was dead.[40]

Seen in a larger context, however, the general strike was a land-
mark in the history of the European working class. Having democrat-
ically agreed to strike, the mutualists pragmatically collected
information on rates and sought to open negotiations for a *tarif.*
Their ability to impose the strike decision on the entire industry was

an innovation whose significance disturbed the merchants, the government, and even many Republicans.[41] Although the attempt to organize distribution centers for food and strike funds was a failure, the methods employed were remarkably sophisticated for the time. Most important, the mutualists and Ferrandiniers were aware of how their opponents would perceive their actions and took explicit steps to avoid playing into their hands. Their success in preventing serious trouble in a highly volatile situation testifies to the discipline and collective conscience of the worker community. That the second Lyon uprising occurred (under distinctly different circumstances) in April, not February, 1834, suggests that the authorities were wrong to dismiss the *canuts* as "barbarians" and assume that a sequel to November 1831 was somehow inevitable.

The official response to the general strike was essentially the same as it had been the previous July: to maintain a public posture of neutrality while privately supporting the merchants. Recalling that the rebellion of November 1831 had been preceded by a work stoppage, the local authorities took precautions to disperse all demonstrations. In fact, there was only one incident during the entire strike: during the evening of 18 February, a small crowd gathered in front of the Hôtel-de-Ville, and when cries of *Vive la République* were heard the police made a few arrests and sent the others home.[42] The authorities were astonished at the mutualists' and Ferrandiniers' "occult power" in maintaining order. As the Minister of Commerce wrote to Gasparin: "The affectation for public tranquility, the more or less sincere protests against mixing in seditous politics . . . are remarkable signs."[43]

II

The members of the local Republican party were divided over a response to the general strike. The leaders of both factions were convinced they should not meddle in the affair because the government seemed intent on avenging the humiliation of November 1831.[44] They were opposed by a cadre of militants who saw the strike as an opportunity to overthrow the regime. Convinced that any revolt would be crushed, the party's leaders struggled to prevent the *enragés* from fishing in troubled waters.

The *Précurseur* played a conciliatory role throughout. While not wanting to alienate the *canuts,* the paper was clearly alarmed by the magnitude of the strike.[45] It is almost certain that Anselme Petetin brought his friend Charles Depouilly together with representatives of the mutualists, thereby taking the role of mediator that Prefect Gasparin had refused.[46] After the "agreement" of the 16th had fallen through and the mutualists were to vote whether or not to resume work, the *Précurseur* printed an open letter warning them to avoid all "collisions" with the authorities. It was signed by a cross section of Girondist, Jacobin, and "socialist" leaders and reveals their deep desire to prevent violence.[47] Finally, at the end of the strike the paper registered its relief, stating: "What did they [the authorities] want if not to irritate the least prudent Republicans and push them by bravado into an unequal duel against thirty thousand bayonets? Happily . . . the good sense of the Republican party . . . has saved us from that danger."[48]

Nowhere was Republican good sense more sorely tested than within the Society of the Rights of Man. Led by Guillaume Vincent, chief of the Intrepidity section, the militant members of the association wanted to lead the *canuts* to the barricades.[49] Only the prestige of the Central Committee dissuaded them. In one confrontation, Antide Martin bluffed Vincent by producing a letter from Buonarroti which advised that "caution and moderation" were the virtues necessary for good Republicans.[50]

Evidently the members of the Central Committee were not convinced that their victory was permanent, for they sent Edouard Albert to confer with the heads of the Society of the Rights of Man in Paris. The Lyonnais leaders already knew that conditions in the capital were such that any decision to revolt would not come from there. Albert's mission, therefore, was a further bluff: while pretending to seek advice, he was sent to solicit support for the stand of the Central Committee.[51] Cavaignac, the head of the Society of the Rights of Man, and Carrel, the editor of the *National,* were prepared to accompany him to Lyon when they received the news that the strike was over. Instead, Albert wrote: "Paris is not like Lyon. It has no need of being curbed, it rather wants the spur."[52] During the general strike, as they would do again in April, the Lyonnais leaders sought to avoid taking this initiative.[53]

Thus, the general strike ended without a single serious Republican incident in Lyon. The moderation of the local party was overshadowed in the government's mind, however, by scattered evidence which seemed to suggest the existence of a plot. The story seems like detective fiction, more *policier* than history. Nevertheless, it had an important effect on inducing the hysteria which resulted in the passage of the law on associations.

It will be recalled that on the evening of 18 February a crowd had

been chased from near the Hôtel-de-Ville. The next day, as the
mutualists were voting to resume work, a young Republican law
clerk name Laurent Tiphaine and a group of his fellow militants met
in a café and discussed what for them had been a discouraging night.
Someone suggested that they write Marc Caussidière, a Republican
leader in Saint Étienne, to tell of the situation in Lyon. In a letter
which he signed "Nivoise," Tiphaine wrote:

> Tired of the same state of things and fearing that our failure to
> act would only inspire the . . . distrust of the people, we took it
> upon ourselves last night to attempt the *grand coup.* Numbering
> eighteen, we decided that the next morning we would present
> ourselves at different points in the city and call the citizens to
> arms . . . Our plan was well concerted by a night of planning and
> all was set for execution. Then . . . the [Central] Committee,
> which we had accused of inertia and which we had walked out
> on, learned of our intentions and came to stop the effort.

The letter concluded with the admission that "the workers don't
want to resume work, but they don't want to begin [a revolt] ."[54]
The "Nivoise" letter arrived the next day in Saint Étienne, where
Caussidière had had little success in converting the local ribbon
weavers.[55] That evening a group of Republicans capped a session
in a café with a serenade of patriotic songs for the residents of the
city. One participant later testified that he was too drunk to remem-
ber where he was.[56] Their nocturnal songfest was interrupted by
the police and in a scuffle a policeman was stabbed to death. The
"Nivoise" letter was found in one reveler's pocket.
Tiphaine's "Nivoise" letter was a single rash act within a general
pattern of Republican caution. Its contents, moreover, told how the
local leaders had kept a rein on the *enragés* during the general strike.
Yet the authorities assumed they had discovered proof of a conspiracy. Reports received earlier told them that Republicans in Épinal,
Marseille, and Chalons were saying that an insurrection was im-
minent in Lyon. Demonstrations staged by the Society of the
Rights of Man in Paris had been punctuated with cries of *Vive les
Lyonnaise!* The invasion of Savoy, at first dismissed as a farce, now
seemed more serious.[57] A warrant, therefore, was issued for the
arrest of the leaders of the Lyonnais Society of the Rights of Man
and the collection of documents that showed "a plot was formed in
Lyon and in several neighboring towns."[58] Prefect Gasparin was

ordered to furnish "proof" of the mutualists' "political manoeu-vres."[59] And early on the morning of 26 February, only hours after the text of the law on association had been presented to the Chamber of Deputies, the police raided the office of the *Glaneuse* and also arrested the members of the Lyonnais Central Committee in their beds. After extensive interrogation of the prisoners no evi-dence of a plot could be confirmed. The government subsequently dropped the case, but it took two weeks for the local *Procureur Général* to inform Paris of the feeble results of his investigation.[60] By that time the Lyonnais "conspiracy" had been cited by the Minister of Justice as proof for the necessity of repressive legisla-tion and Prefect Gasparin had been assured that "the crisis will have been salutory and you will be given powerful means against the associations."[61]

The events of February 1834 underlined an apparent need to attack all secret societies in France. During the general strike the authorities had hesitated even to arrest the members of the mutualist Executive Council. Once it ended, however, many *canuts* were ex-pelled from the city and six alleged leaders of the strike were taken into custody.[62] Their trial was set for 5 April, as it happened the same day as the text of the law on associations was presented to the Chamber of Peers for final approval. Four days later, as the mutu-alists' trial reconvened, the April uprising exploded in the streets of Lyon.

III

In response to the general strike the Orleanist deputy and liberal economist Charles Dupin published an article in the official journal *Le Moniteur* which purported to be an open letter to the mutualists. Reprinted by the *Courrier de Lyon* and distributed as a pamphlet, the "letter" combined platitudes about patience and resignation with numerous *juste-milieu* misapprehensions of the working class.[63] A brief discussion of Dupin's arguments and the *canuts'* reaction to them illustrates the chasm separating the government's and the weavers' mentalities by this time.

Dupin began by condemning the mutualists for making all workers suffer in the name of a few. With absurd logic he argued that 50,000 persons had been idled because of fifty *peluche* weavers and re-minded them that one day of unemployment for 50,000 was the equivalent of a thousand days' unemployment for 50. While he might expect such a stupid action from "a poor simple *canut* . . . who only uses his intelligence to push the shuttle," Dupin said he hoped for more from a master weaver. Calling the latter "the infamous *juste-milieu* of the silk industry [a most unfortunate phrase in Dupin's case]" and men who manipulated their journeymen like they did a Jacquard loom, he charged: "you simple intermediaries, you wanted to exercise dictatorial power over the worker and the merchant!"

Having called the proud masters "simple intermediaries," Dupin further insulted them by advising that the Society of Mutual Duty was dangerous because: "Under the shadowy veil of secret associations and clandestine coalitions are hidden men who are animated by other ambitions, men who are affiliated with other secret societies, with Republicans, with Carlist and Jesuitic cabals, with foreign agents who count on your ruin."

Worker associations, according to Dupin, only served "the monstrous alliance" which sought to starve them, ruin French industry, and topple the government. "Recall the Republic of '93, of '94, of '95," he reminded them: "Your workshops without contracts, your workers gone, your looms smashed or abandoned—*your* looms, *Messieurs les Mutuellistes!* That is what the Republic gave you."

The brochure concluded with the prediction that the mutualists would drive the *fabrique* from Lyon if they did not recognize the danger, madness, and crime of their strikes.

The *canuts'* reaction was rapid and devastating. On 1 March, the *Précurseur* carried a letter, "The response of a mutualist to M. Charles Dupin," which began by thanking him for his "lessons" and added: "we have been trying to forget precisely what you want to teach us. Egotism [laissez-faire] has made us miserable for a long time. Now permit us to hope for a better life from . . . Mutual Devotion.[64]

The letter continued by ironically complimenting Dupin on his "marvelous talent for arithmetic" and asking him to calculate the amount of wages lost by rate reductions since 1830. In reference to his terrifying picture of the Republic, it asked if he knew how much silk cloth was purchased each year by the "Republicans" in the United States? The letter concluded by suggesting that Dupin "tell your friends in the Tuileries" that "social dignity" for the worker could only be gained under a Republic.

If the *Précurseur's* letter was perhaps written or rewritten by the paper's staff in order to oppose Dupin on political grounds, we may be certain that the response of the *Écho de la Fabrique* was an authentic expression of the sentiments of the worker community itself. On 2 March the paper reminded the authorities that the mutualists had publicly disavowed politics, and on the 9th it proclaimed the *canuts'* faith in the principle of association in an article called "To M. Charles Dupin."[65] Attacking his suggestion that conspirators had organized the general strike, the article stated that the lessons of the past and the needs of the present had been the mutualists' only guides. Only a person such as Dupin, who would equate a *canut's* mind with his shuttle, could believe that the strike had been forced on the community, the paper said:

> Our power is totally moral. We have neither police nor gendarmes to enforce our "dictatorial" decrees. But there is a solidarity between us and the weavers. They know very well that by striving to guarantee our interests, they are striving to guarantee their own.
>
> If we are intermediaries, then the master tailors, cobblers, carpenters and wheelwrights have exactly the same title. We have been and we are all workers (*travailleurs*) . . . !
>
> Thus, the lessons of the past have not been fruitless: *rich* and *poor,* all can march with confidence from the present to the future, from isolated conditions and continual battles to *association.* And from association to *harmony.*

This statement, with its reference to the mutualists' solidarity with the progressive forces in the worker movement and the assertion that master and journeymen weavers alike were *travailleurs,* amounts to a declaration of class consciousness. Its importance is heightened, moreover, by the fact that it appeared at a moment when deputies such as Charles Dupin were debating the suppression of labor organizations as well as political clubs. The law on associations, the *Glaneuse* predicted: "will be a death blow to the . . . mutualists, the Ferrandiniers, the . . . Society of the Rights of Man, the Unionists, the Concordists, the *compagnonnages.* All the people will find themselves attacked at once."[66]

6   The Law on Associations

The law on associations was an act of political hysteria. Despite the
failure of the general strike and the disorder of the Republican party,
the government convinced itself that only this piece of legislation
would forestall anarchy. But, like the Combination Acts had done
in England, it virtually induced the situation it was supposed to prevent. A double fermentation, worker and Republican, existed in
Lyon and the government's action brought them together. Prefect
Gasparin belatedly realized this fact when he wrote to the Minister
of the Interior on the eve of the April uprising that "a mutual interest
has united the two camps."[1]

This was not the sole cause of the uprising of 1834, however. In
the aftermath of the general strike an unexpected slump in international sales threw many *canuts* out of work. In the first days of
April a series of events related to the trial of the mutualist leaders
brought the civilian and military authorities, the worker community,
and the Republican party to a point where a collision seemed inevitable. Once this climate of violence existed only a triggering incident
was necessary to transform an unarmed demonstration into a riot.

I

Repression was the keynote of the legislative session of 1834. In
opening the meeting of the Chamber of Deputies Louis Philippe
warned of the illegal plots afoot in the land. The king's address was
intended as a trial balloon for a return to the so-called "System of
13 March," the law and order policy first articulated by Casimir
Perier. But, whereas the late prime minister had depended on the
strict enforcement of existing laws, the present government was
disposed to seek additional legislation.[2] The bill further abridging
the right of association was not presented, however, until the Dep-

uties' formal reply to the Throne Speech had been received. What the government learned was that the cumulative effect of the strikes of late 1833, the trial of the Twenty-Seven,[3] the Public Hawkers episode, and the alleged February conspiracy had convinced a majority to suspend liberties which the party of Order had not presumed to touch two years earlier.

On 25 February 1834, the Minister of Justice presented the text of the law on associations to the Chamber of Deputies. Debate began on 11 March and the bill passed on the 25th by a vote of 246 to 154. Two days later it was introduced in the Chamber of Peers which devoted only two sessions, 8–10 April, to debate and voting. The king signed it into law on the 10th, the second day of the Lyon uprising.

The law on associations had four major provisions. First, all associations, even those with sections of fewer than twenty members, were required to obtain a revokable authorization. Second, each member of an illegal association, not merely its officers as under the previous statute, was liable for a prison sentence up to a year, fines to 1,000 francs, and police surveillance. Third, any person who knowingly permitted his property to be used for an illegal meeting was liable for punishment as an accomplice to a crime. Fourth, those infractions of the law judged a danger to national security were to be tried before the Chamber of Peers, sitting as the High Tribunal.[4] There was little doubt about the effect of the law on associations in Lyon. Whereas Prefect Gasparin had been powerless against the sections of the Society of the Rights of Man or the lodges of the Society of Mutual Duty, under the new law he could crush them. Furthermore, the penalites which threatened ordinary members would dissuade most persons from joining an illegal organization.

The debate over the bill reveals that the government and deputies were motivated by three interacting conceptions: an exaggerated view of the strength of the Republican party, a concern to stem the militancy of the working class, and a false perception that previous policies had failed. The effect of these views was compounded by a conspiratorial mentality which permeated French political life. Having come to power by means of revolution, the supporters of the July Monarchy were haunted by the spector of violence. Fearing counterrevolution from the Right and continued revolution from the Left, the *juste-milieu* had already reduced itself to a defense of an ever-threatened middle course.[5]

These attitudes were reflected when Minister of Justice Barthe,

himself a former member of the *Carbonari,* condemned all associations as being permanent plots.[6] The Comte d'Argout, then Minister
of the Interior, referred to the February events in southeastern
France saying: "there was harmony in those disorders and no one
can deny it! There was a system, a plan, an organized project."[7] Both
Adolphe Thiers, soon to become Minister of the Interior, and Girod
de l'Ain, who would lead the official investigation of the April
revolts, went on record as believing that associations were "counter-
governments" which commanded total obedience from their members.[8] This was a form of political paranoia, an inability on the part
of men who before 1830 had been considered conspirators themselves to accept the fact that anything happens by chance. The
previous chapters have shown that the Republican party did not
possess the monolythic power these officials imagined. Nevertheless,
the campaign for the law on associations was waged as though it
did. At least one deputy saw the irony of the situation when he
noted: "If there is one thing more disgusting than revolutionary
impudence, it is the impudence of apostacy."[9]

The exaggerated fear of the Republicans grew from the conviction
that they were largely responsible for working class militancy. When
the Comte d'Argout depicted the tragedy of laborers forced to sell
their tools and looms in order to pay their Republican dues, he spoke
from the belief that only official intervention could prevent them
from being duped.[10] On the same grounds Mayor (and Deputy)
Prunelle opposed an amendment which would have restricted the
proposed legislation to political groups. The *canuts* were too igno-
rant, he said, to prevent the Republicans from infiltrating and seizing
control of their societies.[11] Citing his experience as Minister of Commerce, Thiers warned that unless worker associations were suppressed they would continue to corrupt the free competition for
wages and eventually impose their will on the economy.[12]

The general strike had been politically motivated and only the law
on associations could prevent a future disaster in Lyon; so the
deputies were assured by Prunelle and Fulchiron, a deputy from
the Rhône.[13] The latter added: "you cannot leave our most important cities, our great manufacturing centers, under the *dread* of
the sword of Damocles . . . The ancients have said that the muses
need tranquility, and I affirm that our industry *wants* it even
more."[14]

Fulchiron's speech was applauded by the *Courrier de Lyon,* which
reminded its readers that "associations have always been and always
will be the refuge of malcontents."[15]

Behind these speeches were large measures of ignorance and self-
deception. Many deputies would not accept the possibility that
the workers had legitimate grievances or minds of their own. Fulchiron, for example, supported the theory that poverty was a necessary goad to the workingman: "In Lyon, whenever wages are low the
canuts work better. And when the daily rate [sic] is raised they make
enough in three days so that they do nothing else during the rest of
the week."[16]
The Minister of the Interior argued that Republican dues were a
greater burden on the worker than the taxes which the government
necessarily collected.[17] And Guizot, sounding like the Calvinist he
was, told the legislators:

> You . . . who have come here to give your time, your fortune,
> and your repose in public service, you are all "idlers." (Laughter)
> You are the idle who devour the goods of the worker. (Renewed
> laughter)
> That is the new theory of political economy which has been
> created in order to attack the middle class. That is the absurd, the
> barbarous argument with which they seek to instill trouble in
> society in order to menace us with a new social revolution.[18]

Finally, the government failed to recognize that virtually continous
prosecution and frequent conviction of their leaders under existing
laws had already weakened or destroyed many worker and political
associations. "The day after the Revolution of July," declared
Thiers, "we saw our duty to moderate it. In effect it was no longer
liberty, but order which was in danger."[19] If French administrators
were preoccupied in the first years after 1830 with finding a new
balance between liberty and order, the law on associations marked
the end of their quest. The *Courrier de Lyon* said it was "the demar-
cation line between the past and the future."[20] The *Revue des Deux
Mondes* called it "the equivalent of a new declaration of principles"
which "completely changed the situation of the government."[21] And
so it did. But in adopting this measure the deputies and peers seriously miscalculated the practical and symbolic importance of association for the workers of Lyon.

II

The debate over the law on associations also raged in the cafés and
workshops of Lyon. The Republican and worker press vigorously

attacked the bill. The *Glaneuse* called association a right as imperish-
able as the people themselves.[22] The *Écho des Travailleurs* said that
the law would violate the General Will.[23] The *Écho de la Fabrique*
ironically noted that the deputies criticized the *canuts* for resorting
to violence in 1831 and when they struck peacefully in 1834. "What
they want," the paper stated, "is to force the workers back into
their primitive state of isolation where they can be exploited with
full security."[24] And the *Précurseur* declared: "If France resigns
herself to it, if we consent to pass under the yoke of a power which
we created with our own hands, . . . then she will have become the
most cowardly and imbecilic nation of Europe."[25]

In spite of these bold protests, three of the four papers were in
serious trouble. Earlier in the year the *Écho des Travailleurs* had cut
back to a single issue per week and it ceased publication altogether
on 22 March. The *Glaneuse* had nearly gone bankrupt in January and
in March its acting editor was sentenced to over a year in prison and
received a heavy fine for an article praising the rebellion of November
1831. The paper's financial backer, Edouard Albert, attempted to
find new subscribers, but his effort was in vain. Amid recriminations
over lost or stolen funds, the house organ of the local Society of
the Rights of Man published its last issue on 26 March with the
exhortation: "Proletarians! Unite yourselves!"[26] The *Precurseur*,
for its part, denied rumors that its stockholders were in rebellion and
that it, too, would soon fail.[27] Only the *Écho de la Fabrique* remained solvent because of its mutualist and Ferrandinier subscribers.
Official harassment and limited funds, in other words, had taken
their toll of the Lyonnais worker and Republican press well before
the passage of the law on associations.

The local Republican party, in fact, was near collapse. Funds were
drying up in this supposed bastion of political radicalism. A financial
report of the Society of the Rights of Man stated that dues were still
partially unpaid for January, half collected for February, and that
no figures could be given for March. The treasury held only 600
francs.[28] More important, informers within the organization kept
the authorities aware of all its plans. "The best symptom of its
decomposition," Prefect Gasparin reported, "is the large number
of section chiefs who have come to us and entered into the service
of the police."[29]

Although the Central Committee had managed to restrain the
society's *enragés* during the general strike, its authority was more
seriously challenged over a response to the law on associations. Because membership had reached a peak in January and was declining

rapidly by late March the militants had increased their relative influence in the association.[30] At a meeting of section chiefs on 21 March, a majority of those present voted to dissolve the society rather than challenge the pending legislation. Nevertheless, the Central Committee evidently felt it necessary to concede something to the minority. For this reason a petition, bearing the names of seventy-five section chiefs (some of them signed without their permission) and declaring that they would resist, was published in both the *Glaneuse* and the *Précurseur* on the 24th.[31] While striking a strong public pose, the Society of the Rights of Man had privately voted for submission.

The militants had been bluffed into inaction during the general strike and were not going to accept a similar evasion now. Ten sections, renamed "divisions," were organized as the Society of Action, or the Intrepid Knights of God and Justice. The chiefs of these schismatic sections continued to attend meetings of the parent organization, but they established their own motto and secret signs.[32] Although the Lyonnais authorities dutifully reported to Paris on the Society of Action, their letters reveal little trace of the concern shown two years earlier over the Legion of the Volunteers. of the Rhône. Perhaps this was true because there were no *canuts* in the Society of Action or it was led by *agents provocateurs.* In any case, the militants seem to have caused more worry to the party's leaders than to the government.

After the April revolts the authorities would declare there had been a nation-wide conspiracy to overthrow the regime with a series of coordinated insurrections timed to coincide with the passage of the law on associations. Not a single document written before these events was produced to verify this contention, however. Prefect Gasparin, in fact, wrote on 19 March that: "Our associations are preparing some movement . . . but have no confidence in their plans and are only seeking to avoid reproach for inaction."[33] There is no evidence that either the Girondist or Jacobin leadership of the local Republican party sought a do-or-die confrontation with the government at this time. Instead, many in both factions reasoned they should avoid a predictably fatal collision in order to be able to fight another day. On 3 March, the national leaders of the Society of the Rights of Man sent a printed circular to Lyon which failed to even mention the impending legislation, but stated:

> What you have said about centralization appears just and well taken to us. Continue to centralize the departments which sur-

round you. We will send you circulars for the principal towns.
Lyon should be considered as a center of French proletarians and
a school for the application of new theories of social reform . . .
She must furnish men of intelligence and brawn to the future
Republic. What we mean by Parisian centralization is not the
absorption of all abilities and intelligence in one place, rather
their development toward a single goal, under a single thought.
We are counting heavily on you.[34]

The tone of this document is striking, particularly in its deference
to the Lyonnais' provincial pride and desire for independence. But
it is not that of a revolutionary party on the eve of a conclusive
battle.

If there were no plans for an insurrection, Prefect Gasparin predicted that the Republicans would stage demonstrations to protest
the law on associations. Their purpose, in his opinion, would be
to force the authorities to make hundreds of arrests and appear repressive in the public eye.[35] On 20 March, the Society of the Rights
of Man in Paris requested that each provincial chapter send a representative to report on local conditions. Casear Bertholon was Lyon's
delegate and his report from the capital was received on 3 April.
It appeared that the situation there was unchanged since Edouard
Albert's trip during the general strike. As Prefect Gasparin reported
it:

The Republican associations have received letters from Paris in
which the desire was expressed that any resistance to the law on
associations begin in the city of Lyon. The assurance was given
that the Parisian societies are so compromised that nothing less
than the news of success, or at least of serious trouble, in the
capital of industrial coalitions could drive Paris into action.[36]

This admission placed the Lyonnais Republican leaders in a peril-
ous position. The Central Committee resolved that only a direct
confrontation could restrain the *enragés* this time.[37] On 4 April, its
members offered their resignations and called for a special election.
The government later claimed they intended to prepare the Society
of the Rights of Man for insurrection,[38] but their actual purpose
is clearly revealed in this circular letter:

Citizens! The more circumstances have become grave, the more
those whom you have chosen . . . need to know the exact spirit

which animates you . . . The Central Committee has . . . witnessed the discontent indicated by the inconceivable conduct of several section chiefs, who, in violation of our rules, have tried, although they are an infinitely weak minority, to induce the majority to follow them. This is nothing less than division and anarchy in our ranks, just at the moment when we need unity more than ever before . . . You will have a chance to choose. Without consideration of personalities, but only examining services rendered to our common cause, . . . you will make your decision.[39]

The Central Committee had played its final card. Prefect Gasparin assured the Minister of the Interior that factionalism had rendered the local party powerless and that the law on association would find it "in a very advanced stage of decomposition."[40] "Everything," he concluded, "augers a tranquil future for Lyon."[41] If the uprising proved him a false prophet, his analysis of the Republicans' weakness was accurate.

The worker community, too, was bitterly divided over a response to the law on associations. The situation was complicated, moreover, by an unexpected economic crisis which struck the *fabrique.* The American market, which accounted for half of Lyon's annual export sales, traditionally brought the industry out of the slow winter season. In March, however, a financial crisis in the United States caused the sudden cancellation of these contracts. Just when the weavers hoped to recover their losses from the general strike they faced continued stagnation. The number of looms standing idle grew daily. Making matters worse, a number of merchants who had weaving orders refused to let them out for fear they would be intentionally ruined. Other *fabricants* began to recall their goods and flee the city.[42]

The daily police reports are a record of the *canuts'* frustration and rage. Bands of men went about demanding work and declaring they would never permit their societies to be dissolved. The mutualists marched in their holiday dress. The Ferrandiniers paraded with the ceremonial batons of their association. A number of weavers descended from the suburb of the Croix Rousse with a flag and a drum to demonstrate in front of the merchants' warehouses along the Rhône. Others crossed the river from La Guillotière to march in formation on the Place Bellecour. And a crowd estimated at 600 journeymen gathered in front of the Hôtel-de-Ville to salute three of their fellows who were leaving the city.[43]

The *canuts* were not alone in protesting. The journeymen curriers of Les Brotteaux shouted, "If they want a fight, then we'll give them one." The journeymen joiners of Vaise promenaded wearing the ribbons of their society. There was a rumor that several of the cobblers and tailors who lived around the charity hospital, the Hôtel Dieu, were going to try their luck in Saint Étienne. Shouts were heard at night in the respectable Place des Celestins that all the workingmen had gained in 1830 was *"la misère Philippe et choléra."*[44] Prefect Gasparin specifically assured the leaders of the conservative *compagnonnages* that the government would not harass them under the new law.[45] Nevertheless, on 2 April a crowd which the police estimated at 2,000 to 3,000 workers marched along the quais shouting, "No. No. The *compagnonnages* will never end."[46] On the eve of the trial of the leaders of the general strike one police official reported, "There is misery among most of the workers."[47]

Beset by the economic crisis, threatened by the law on associations, and facing the trial of six of its members, the Executive Council of the Society of Mutual Duty was also forced to share its authority in an ambiguous and unresolved manner with the Council of Presidents. Nevertheless, having weathered the humiliation of standing for re-election in the aftermath of the general strike, the Executive Council was determined to continue an aggressive policy. As Gasparin later explained: "After February the language of the mutualists was pacific for a long while. But the presentation of the law on associations, which according to them was the sole safeguard of the workers, caused a great reaction."[48]

On 28 March, the Executive Council sent delegates to a Joint Committee (*comité d'ensemble*) which was discussing the protests by several organizations against the impending law. This action was taken without consulting the general membership and with the knowledge that the Council of Presidents considered such negotiations a violation of the exclusive spirit of Mutualism.[49] On 1 April, the entire Executive Council sent a letter to the *Procureur du Roi* asking to be tried with the six accused men on the 5th.[50] The next day it ordered all mutualists to stop work on the day of the trial and gather in front of the Palais du Justice to await the verdict.[51] And on the eve of the trial it published a petition alleged to have been signed by 2,557 members (only thirteen names were actually printed) in the *Précurseur:*

The Mutualist Society of Lyon, placed by its own choice out-

side political circles and believing that it has nothing to fear from
the men in power . . . has deliberated:

Considering as a general thesis that association is a natural right
for all men, that it is the source of all progress . . .

Considering, in particular, that the association of workers
(*travailleurs*) is a necessity of our age, that it is a condition of
existence . . .

In consequence, the Mutualists protest the libercidal law on
associations and declare that they will never bow their heads
under this arbitrary yoke and that their meetings will never be
suspended. Relying on the most inviolable right, that is to say to
live working (*vivre en travaillant*), they will resist with all the
energy which characterizes free men.[52]

With its evocation of the power of association, the "Mutualists'
Protest," as it was called, was the apotheosis of the Lyonnais worker
movement.[53]

The purpose and plans of the Joint Committee are difficult to discover. In its final form it brought together representatives of the
worker and political societies, but we do not know who proposed
such an assembly or when it was actually organized. The police
reports for March 1834 are full of rumors about secret meetings
between Republicans and workers, but if these were more than the
product of hysterical imaginations, there is no specific mention of
the Joint Committee. Its first known meeting took place in a café in
Les Brotteaux on 28 March, three days after the law on associations
had passed the Chamber of Deputies.[54]

The composition of the Joint Committee is a calculated speculation.[55] Among the worker organizations, the mutualists, the Ferrandiniers, the Philanthropic Society of Tailors, the Union of Perfect
Accord (cobblers), and the United Brothers (goldsmiths, and so
forth) were likely participants. Among the Republican associations,
the Society of the Rights of Man and the Free Men[56] were likely,
the Independent Philanthropists and the Society of Progress possible,[57] and the Association for the Liberty of the Press unlikely
participants. We do not know how its delegates were selected, but
the three worker representatives who can be identified—Girard of the
mutualists, Didier of the Ferrandiniers, and Marigné of the Philanthropic Society of Tailors—belonged to the politically conscious
factions of their organizations.

The only surviving account of a meeting of the Joint Committee is in the unpublished memoir of Anselme Petetin, who first learned of it from a mutualist leader and was encouraged to present the moderate Republican viewpoint. Noting the small number of organizations represented and sensing what he called "subterranean influences," Petetin warned the group not to attempt to speak for those not present.[58] We cannot be certain whether there were *agents provocateurs* on the Joint Committee or whether Petetin was referring to his old Jacobin enemies.

We do know, on the other hand, that it was coordinating local participation in the national project for demonstrations against the law on associations. Its single public act was to send a letter to Paris which appeared in the *Tribune* on 5 April: "The industrial societies, the *compagnonnages,* the political societies, have all formed a federation. Unity reigns. All citizens, whatever body they belong to, consider themselves attacked. The defense will be solid."[59]

Had these demonstrations occurred as scheduled we might know more about the Joint Committee.[60] The unexpected events of 5 April, as we shall soon learn, changed all plans and left its role unclear. Nevertheless, this mutual effort by the Lyonnais worker and Republican societies illustrates how the threat of the law on associations induced the situation it was supposed to prevent.

III

On Saturday, 5 April, the trial of the six mutualists began. Four days later the second uprising in twenty-nine months exploded in the streets of Lyon. In this brief interval long-standing antagonisms and a series of tension-heightening incidents combined to create a climate of violence.

A spontaneous incident in front of the Palais du Justice set the stage. At the hour the trial convened on 5 April the Court chambers and the Place Saint Jean outside were filled with *canuts.* When the clamor of the crowd made it impossible to hear testimony, the president of the Court declared that if the noise continued he would have to hold the trial in a closed session. He then adjourned the case until the following Wednesday, the 9th. Those outside mistakenly thought that he had actually announced a closed trial and began to shout their disapproval. At that moment a witness, who had testified that the mutualists had threatened to destroy his looms if he refused to join the strike, attempted to leave the building. He was attacked by the crowd. The counselor of the Royal Court tried to help his witness and was also pummeled. A single gendarme came to their aid and the three men took refuge in a nearby building. A company of soldiers from the Seventh Infantry Legion arrived in the square and were rapidly surrounded. An accidental shot might have triggered a riot, but the troops turned their gun butts in the air and fraternized with the workers to shouts of "Long live the Seventh! Long live our brothers!"[61]

Each side drew its own conclusions from the incident in the Place Saint Jean. The government feared it would embolden those who opposed the law on association. Even though a massive demonstration was now promised for the 9th, in its mind there was no possibility of postponing or transferring the trial because such an action would be interpreted as a sign of weakness.[62] The *Courrier de Lyon* complained about "the horrible and humiliating disorders" and pointedly reminded the authorities of the insufficient military preparations in November 1831.[63] The incident was indeed humiliating for the garrison. Lt. General Aymard drew a reprimand from the Minister of War and promised that order would be maintained when the trial reconvened.[64] Many *canuts* were convinced, however, that a show of force might win the acquittal of the mutualist leaders. On the 6th, some 5,000 to 6,000 of them marched in the funeral procession of a master weaver. On the way back from the cemetery some were alleged to have sung Republican songs and Lt. General Aymard was afraid they would descend on the Prefecture and demand the release of the six men.[65] The militants in the Republican party, for their part, were now convinced that the troops would not open fire on a crowd.

There was official concern about the loyalty of the garrison, in fact. The infiltration of Republican sentiments, particularly in the artillery corp and among junior officers, was frequently mentioned in dispatches.[66] Reports of soliders in their cups joining in the singing of "patriotic" songs were common. Copies of the local Society of the Rights of Man's *Revue Militaire,* which exhorted the troops not to fire on the people, were distributed near the barracks.[67] Seen in this light the incident in the Place Saint Jean was part of a larger problem. The army was acutely sensitive to the question of honor, a fact which served to escalate an already tense situation. Determined there would be no repetition of the retreat of November 1831, on 6 April Lt. General Aymard called up reinforcements from neighboring departments. By the 10th he expected to have around 13,000 troops at his disposal.[68]

The government's determination to erase all suspicion as to its
intention led some to believe it was seeking to provoke a fight.
Alarmed by the military deployment which he saw throughout the
city, Anselme Petetin sought a meeting with Prefect Gasparin. While
waiting in an anteroom he saw the prefect emerge from his office
with a group of military and judicial officials. Sighting the Republican editor, Gasparin greeted him with the statement: "Well we're at
war!" In the course of their conversation the prefect said that he
was convinced there would be trouble the next day, but predicted:
"It will only be a two hour affair since we are better prepared than
we were in November [1831]."[69] In reality, Gasparin had no authorization to seek a confrontation. His final telegraphed instructions
from the Minister of the Interior, received in Lyon after the fighting
began, read: "I engage you never to go beyond the limits of moderation. But I must tell you that [the incident of] the 5th made a
dangerous impression, which imposes on the authorities the duty
of showing great energy . . . I await your dispatches with impa-
tience."[70]

Nevertheless, the government had maneuvered itself into a position
where its preparations looked like provocation to its opponents,
while anything less would have been cowardice in its own eyes.

The Republican party, ironically, was in a similar situation. The
Central Committee of the Society of the Rights of Man was returned
to office on the 6th, but the effect of this vote in favor of moderation was largely dissipated by the previous day's events. Failure
to support the *canuts'* demonstrations on the 9th would mean that
the party was abandoning them and bowing to coercion. Not even
those who had endorsed submission to the law on association were
willing to endure the ridicule that would result. Many members of
worker associations, by the same token, now believed the trial was
too critical an event for them to fail to show their solidarity. The
local authorities believed that a show of force would convince the
workers and Republicans to abandon their plans.[71] Instead, this
tactic had the opposite effect. The two sides were locked into a fatal
contest of will.

The incident in the Place Saint Jean helped create a climate of
violence in Lyon. Such precipitating factors—unexpected events
which aggravate existing strains and create new ones—play a role in
all riot situations.[72] So it was that on 8 April word was received
of two political decisions which raised the level of tension. First, in
spite of the fact that the present crisis in the silk industry was due to

the loss of American contracts, the Chamber of Deputies rejected an emergency bill to extend credit for trade with the United States. "Our deputies have failed to give serious consideration to our relations with that country as well as our position with regard to a riot," stated the *Journal de Commerce de Lyon*.[73] Second, the formation of a new cabinet was announced, including three men in key positions who were closely associated with the law on associations: Thiers became Minister of the Interior, Persil became Minister of Justice, and Martin du Nord became *Procureur Général*.[74] There could be no doubt that the hated legislation would be enforced vigorously. The timing of this news could not have been worse for the chances of calming the Lyonnais situation.

As they sought to finalize and coordinate their plans the leaders of the worker and Republican societies reached three decisions: the demonstrations on the 9th would be staged at three sites—in the Place Saint Jean in front of the Palais du Justice, in the Place des Jacobins in front of the Prefecture, and in the Place des Terreaux in front of the Hôtel-de-Ville; a common password, "Association, Resistance, Courage," would be used by all participating groups; and the sections and lodges of these organizations would meet early on the morning of the 9th to receive final instructions.[75]

Important elements among the mutualists resisted these plans, however. According to the founder of the society, Pierre Charnier, many lodges were in disorder because of the "insolence" of the Executive Council's policies. When the latter body ordered a work stoppage for the 9th, for example, many Indicators sided with the Council of Presidents and refused to communicate the message to their lodges.[76] The last-minute activities of other worker organizations unfortunately are unknown for the most part.

The leaders of the Republican party, meanwhile, were seeking a modus vivendi. Both moderates and militants agreed to fight only if the troops opened fire on the demonstrators. The Central Committee of the Society of the Rights of Man ordered each section to assemble unarmed at one or another of the demonstration sites. If shooting began they were to retreat to prearranged positions where weapons and further instructions were promised.[77] In retrospect, these plans were no more than a dangerous charade since there were no large caches of guns or ammunition and the strategy was highly vulnerable to provocation either by police agents or the militants themselves.[78] The "dilemma of revolutionism" which had plagued the party's words for so long now haunted its actions with a vengeance.[79]

The city of Lyon stood at the brink of violence. Why had it happened again so soon after the rebellion of November 1831? On one level, a series of recent events, whose significance was magnified because they heightened long-accumulating tensions, had brought the civilian and military authorities, the worker community, and the Republican party to the point where a triggering incident—the seizure of a Republican broadside on the morning of the 9th—was sufficient to precipitate an uprising.[80] On a deeper level, we should recognize that April 1834 was not so much a political as a *politicized* confrontation. Describing a pattern encountered in the study of collective behavior, Neil J. Smelser notes that the "interaction between dissatisfaction (strain) and the closing off of avenues of protest (structural conduciveness) produces a situation which easily gives way to violence."[81] In the case of Lyon, the *canuts'* well-articulated dissatisfaction with the conditions which the merchants and the government imposed on their labor was underlined by the failure of the general strike and the unexpected crisis in the silk industry. The law on associations, moreover, was perceived by the worker community as the final step in a concerted effort to deprive it of all effective means of protest. The trial of the leaders of the Society of Mutual Duty symbolically bound these strands together. Or, as a contemporary writer simply observed, when the powder and fire are combined it is not difficult to predict an explosion.[82]

7   The April Uprising

By dawn on 9 April 1834, the government's emergency plan was in operation: the garrison stood at battle alert; squads of infantrymen with loaded weapons and two days' provisions patrolled the streets and guarded the principal squares and bridges; troops were stationed inside churches and government buildings; cannon in the fortresses were trained on Lyon. As Prefect Gasparin and Lt. General Aymard arrived at the command post near the Palais du Justice a police informer told them that the Central Committee of the Society of the Rights of Man was meeting in the neighborhood. Unwilling to risk an incident, the prefect decided not to arrest them.[1] The second session of the mutualists' trial was to begin at ten o'clock. By that time thousands of unarmed demonstrators were milling around the Palais du Justice in the Place Saint Jean, the Prefecture in the Place des Jacobins, and the Hôtel-de-Ville in the Place des Terreaux. Within the hour trouble occurred in two of the three sites.

It flared first in the Place Saint Jean when an unidentified man began to distribute a Republican handbill. Police Commissioner Prat ordered him arrested but the crowd aided his escape. Copies of the same handbill had been posted on a building at one of the narrow entrances to the square. A barricade was raised to prevent the police from reaching them. Sensing serious trouble, Prat called for reinforcements and the soldiers moved across the square to dismantle the barricade. The crowd pelted them with paving stones and the troops opened fire. The first person to fall was later identified as a police spy. He was carried into the Palais du Justice where he died in the judge's chamber.[2]

Almost simultaneous to these events a second, unrelated incident took place in the Place des Jacobins. Through an oversight only twenty-four soliders had been sent to guard the Prefecture. By ten o'clock, the young official whom Gasparin had placed in charge

of the building became alarmed at the size of the crowd and ordered
the troops to retreat into the courtyard and to close the iron gate.
About a half hour later some of the demonstrators began to pass
copies of the Society of the Rights of Man's *Revue Militaire* through
the fence and the young official himself went out to talk to them.
When they refused to withdraw he ordered the troops to open fire,
but was overruled by the military officer in command because they
were waiting for inforcements. At this point the crowd became
hostile. A group of men seized a wooden beam from a nearby construction site and attempted to storm the gates of the Prefecture.
One person was bayoneted and another shot by the troops. At about
10:45 A.M. the reinforcements arrived and a second order to fire was
obeyed. After the salvo a well-dressed man carrying an old cavalry
sword stepped forward and shouted: "We're your friends, your
brothers. I fought for my country. If you want an enemy, shoot at
me. I'm not afraid to die." As he was pulled back by his friends
another round of shots rang out.[3]

The demonstration on the Place des Terreaux was without incident.
The crowd there had already begun to disperse when the news arrived
of the fighting at the other demonstration sites. A single barricade
was raised, but it was taken down by the troops who remained in
complete control of the Hôtel-de-Ville. Stationed at *octroi* barrier
on the Croix Rousse hillside General Fleury heard the sound of gunfire coming from the city below. The *canuts* heard it, too. About a
half hour later a barricade went up in the Grande Place of the Croix
Rousse.[4] The April uprising had begun.

I

The second Lyon uprising, the largest civil disturbance in France
between 1830 and 1848, lasted six days and left over 300 persons
dead. Because collective violence is inherently chaotic and description of so long an event is difficult, we have attempted to impose
order on our discussion by dividing it into three sections. The first
examines the fighting from the government's position, surveying
it within a framework of military tactics. The second shifts to the
other side of the barricades to search for patterns in the rebels'
actions and to recognize what George Rudé has called the "faces in
the crowd."[5] The final section examines the role of the worker
associations and Republican party in the Lyon uprising and discusses
the character of the April Days elsewhere in France.

The form of the conflict was dictated by a combination of military planning and urban geography. Because the demonstrators had been in three separate sites the fighting initially broke out at several points. But, unlike November 1831 where the resistance had snow-balled, the April uprising was never larger than at its start because the army now had detailed plans for handling a riot situation in Lyon.[6] Using their control of the major public squares and bridges to advantage, the troops cut off communication between the various quarters. All traffic was banned from the streets. The rebels could cross the rivers or move through military lines only with extreme difficulty. Only the suburbs of Vaise, La Guillotière, and Les Brotteaux lay outside this tactical grid. These critical maneuvers assured the government's ultimate victory.

The six-day conflict was divided into three stages: during the 9th and 10th the troops remained on the defensive; on the 11th and 12th they moved on the attack; and the 13th and 14th were devoted to mopping-up operations. On the morning of 15 April, Prefect Gasparin telegraphed Paris: "*Voila!* Our operations are over . . . our troops are masters of the city of Lyon and its suburbs."[7]

Once the fighting had started the army's objective was to contain the rebels. On the right bank of the Saône the demonstrators retreated from the Place Saint Jean into the worker neighborhoods of the fifth arrondissement. The government retained control of the space around the Palais du Justice. On the peninsula the army controlled the Place Bellecour and the Place des Terreaux at either end of the commercial district and the demonstrators who were driven away from the Prefecture were trapped in this area. Some of them erected a barricade in the Passage de l'Argue, directly off the Place des Jacobins. An artillery piece was used to blast them out, the only time such weapons were used in the commercial district. Retreating further, the one group of rebels went toward the Saint Nizier church and another toward the Place des Cordeliers, where the tocsin was rung in the Saint Bonaventure church, food stalls were smashed, and carts overturned to construct barricades.[8] The residents of the first arrondissement waited until they saw the troops hasten down the hillside to reinforce the Hôtel-de-Ville and then they sacked the Bon Pasteur caserne and raised barricades around the Place Sathoney. The fortifications rebuilt after November 1831 along the Croix Rousse barrier served their intended purpose. Massed along this line the army prevented the Croix Roussiens from descending into the city. The barricades constructed at the entrance to the Grande Côte and in the Grande Place of the Croix Rousse were seized and dismantled.[9]

By the end of the first day resistance had been isolated in four major pockets: the right bank of the Saône, the Croix Rousse hillside, the Croix Rousse commune, and the south-central area of the peninsula along the right bank of the Rhône. The Perrache quarter was quiet and, except for incidents of sniper fire in Les Brotteaux, the left bank of the Rhône had not yet joined the uprising.[10] Even more important, the fighting was confined to predominantly worker neighborhoods. With the exception of the tiny island of rebels at the Saint Nizier church the wealthy quarters of Lyon were safely behind the army's lines.[11]

At six o'clock on the morning of 10 April, the tocsin sounded from the Saint Bonaventure church in the Place des Cordeliers. The bells of other rebel-held churches chimed their reply. During the second day fighting began in the suburbs. Around nine o'clock a large barricade was erected to block the Grande Rue of La Guillotière. Fearing that it would impede the arrival of troops which were expected from Grenoble, Lt. General Aymard called for the artillery to clear the route. As the heavy guns were being moved into position the officer in command was killed by a sniper's bullet. His men responded by firing their cannon at the building from which the shot had come. The barrage touched off a fire which burned for over a day and leveled an entire block, the largest incident of property damage in the uprising.[12] When the reinforcements arrived from Grenoble during the afternoon they met fierce resistance in La Guillotière.

In the suburb of Vaise on the other side of the city rebels sacked an evacuated caserne and cut the telegraph communications between Paris and Lyon. A company of soldiers being sent on punishment duty to Algeria were liberated and many of them joined the uprising. Among the leaders of the resistance in Vaise was the former hawker of handbills, Marc Reverchon, who stormed into the mayor's office and demanded that all weapons be surrendered in the name of the Republic. This incident was subsequently cited as proof that the entire uprising was directed by the Republicans.[13]

In the Perrache quarter a few barricades were raised, but were easily removed by troops sent from the military headquarters in the Place Bellecour. Patrols prevented subsequent trouble in Perrache and the only injuries and property damage there were the result of sniper fire from across the Saône and the destruction of a bridge set afire by a burning barge of hay.[14]

In the four original pockets of resistance the barricades were strengthened and a search for weapons and supplies extended. Artillery was used to destroy new barricades in the Croix Rousse suburb. Heavy fighting occurred on the Croix Rousse hillside, particularly in the area round the Jardin des Plantes and the Place Sathoney. An infantry officer was shot near the entrance to the rue Marcel and his enraged men entered a nearby building and killed several innocent persons, including the elderly owner.[15] The president of the local Society of the Rights of Man, Eugène Baune, lived in the Place Sathoney. Although he had no active role in the uprising, Baune was dragged from his sickbed and taken into custody. With the exceptions of those suburbs beyond the army's lines the uprising had been contained after two days of fighting.

During the night of the 10th the military and civilian officials met to determine future strategy. Although the government commanded overwhelming numbers, the troops were not prepared for street fighting and their officers were uncertain how to deploy them. With most of the rebels trapped in densely populated quarters the authorities were faced with the decision of employing cannon to blast their barricades or engaging in house-to-house combat.[16] The resistance in La Guillotière, moreover, threatened to spread along the left bank of the Rhône into Les Brotteaux. And, if captured handbills bearing the name of the Society of the Rights of Man were to be believed, aid for the rebels would soon arrive from neighboring departments. Lt. General Aymard was concerned that supplies might run dangerously low in the event of a protracted conflict. After rejecting proposals that the army evacuate the city or abandon the right bank of the Saône,[17] three decisions were made: to consolidate the military forces, in part by evacuating the Saint-Irénée fortress which dominated the heights of Fourvière; to increase the bombardment of La Guillotière, a tactic judged appropriate because of its broad streets and open areas; and to begin to penetrate the rebel-held areas of the city.[18] The government, in other words, was moving on the offensive.

By 11 April, despite numerous attempts to requisition weapons in the city and in the rural areas of the department the rebels' situation was already desperate.[19] During the third day they failed to break the army's lines, while an artillery barrage temporarily silenced La Guillotière. Their only success was the "capture" of the abandoned Saint Irénée fortress where two cannon unsuccessfully sabotaged by the retreating troops were trained on the military bivouac in the

Place Bellecour. Their gunners were inexperienced, however, and their salvos fell far off the target. One witness reported seeing them load a cannon by placing the ball ahead of the charge.[20]

The troops had taken heavy casualties because they were inexperienced in street fighting. By the third day, however, they had learned tactics such as the use of counterbarricades and sniper posts, as from the dome of the Hôtel-de-Ville.[21] Prefect Gasparin was now confident enough to permit women in protected neighborhoods to leave their homes in order to shop for food. A proposal to reactivate the National Guard units in bourgeois quarters to patrol behind army lines was not adopted, however, because of the difficulty of communicating with the individual guardsmen.[22] The authorities believed it was only a matter of time before the uprising would be suppressed.[23]

On 12 April, Lyon lay under a blanket of snow. The fourth and decisive day was fought in the mud and cold of a spring storm. To protect their communication to the south and east (particularly in light of the rumors of revolts in Grenoble and Saint Étienne), the authorities resolved to bombard La Guillotière into final submission. At six o'clock in the morning the prefect warned residents that they had four hours to remove all barricades before the cannon would open fire. If necessary, his proclamation stated, the entire suburb would be destroyed. Calmer minds prevailed, however, and a reconnoitering party was able to capture the Grande Rue of La Guillotière and reopen the route. In the prefect's words, the "success was more prompt, more complete, and above all less dearly bought than was at first expected."[24]

The suburb of Vaise fell on the 12th, too. Two army columns were sent under the covering fire of cannon in a pincer movement to converge on the Place de la Pyramide where it was estimated that forty-nine persons, many of them innocent bystanders, were killed.[25] The army's record during the April uprising was deeply stained by the tales of atrocities committed by rum-inspired soldiers in Vaise; one man tried to hide in a chimney and was alleged to have been burned alive. Louis Blanc later compared these events to the September Massacres and the slaughter in the rue Transnonain in Paris.[26]

The government's most important victory on the 12th was the capture of the insurgent area in the center of the city. A squad of soldiers bravely climbed the steeple of the Saint Nizier church, which overlooked the wealthy Quai de Retz quarter, and captured four snipers. A message was sent to the rebels in the Place des Cordeliers

informing them that Vaise and La Guillotière had fallen and when
they refused to surrender troops began to penetrate the Saint Bonaventure quarter from two directions. Although outnumbered and
virtually unarmed, the insurgents were so tenacious that the soldiers
actually had to battle their way inside the church, where they found
an improvised hospital and ammunition factory, but the altar un-
molested. The fighting in the Place des Cordeliers added a heroic incident to the Republican tradition, but its fall marked the collapse of
the revolt in the center of Lyon.[27]

On 13 April traffic circulated freely through the peninsula. Resistance continued in the first and fifth arrondissements—the neighborhoods of the *canuts*—but they were captured and subdued by evening
on the 14th.[28] The second Lyonnais uprising had been crushed by
269,000 musket shots and 1,729 rounds of artillery. If the cost was
almost 350 military casualties, nevertheless, the government had
proven that it could maintain order. With the exception of the
Algeria-bound troops in Vaise, moreover, only a handful of soldiers
had defected.[29] As the Minister of War's personal investigator
proudly reported: "The garrison of 1834 avenged the humiliation
of 1831."[30]

Two things should be clear from this review of military tactics: not
only had the government been thoroughly prepared for trouble,
but also the April uprising, unlike the one of November 1831, was
fought largely by isolated pockets of insurgents who never had a
change of success. We are now prepared to re-examine the uprising
from the rebels' side of the barricades and to seek to recognize
the "faces in the crowd."

II

How large was the April uprising? Although we may cherish the
image of the *canuts* rising as a single man, it is certain that the overwhelming majority of Lyon's citizens—worker or otherwise—took
no part in the fighting.[31] Those persons who were at home or managed to return there were generally trapped for the duration of
the conflict. Jules Favre, for example, was defending the mutualists'
case when the shooting started. Returning to his room near the
Palais du Justice he remained there until the evening of the 10th,
when he set out in search of food and was arrested by patrolling
soldiers.[32] Once the demonstrations had been dispersed there were
no bands of insurgents loose in the streets. The rebels in the Croix

Rousse suburb were unable to make contact with those on hillsides below them. And, although the mayor of Vaise insisted that those who troubled his commune were all strangers, the addresses of the men and women arrested there indicate otherwise.[33] It is impossible to calculate exactly the number of insurgents; Prefect Gasparin estimated there were 3,000, while Girod de l'Ain's official claim of 6,000 was widely refuted at the time.[34] Perhaps a few thousand persons participated in the demonstrations on the morning of 9 April, but most of them retreated before the army's overwhelming numbers.

Who were those who stayed to fight? Much information in reply to this question is found in the more than 500 dossiers of individuals arrested during and after the uprising. Many dossiers are incomplete and there is no certainty that all persons arrested were actual participants. Nor can we doubt that many escaped detection. Nevertheless, these sources reveal a great deal about the character of the uprising and the composition of the crowd in April 1834.[35]

Appendix II and figures 5–7 show that the insurgents were recognizable members of the Lyonnais worker community. Unmarried

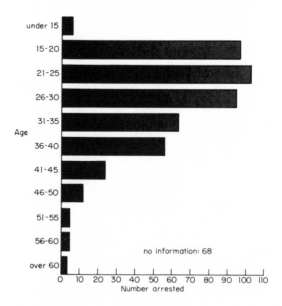

FIGURE 5. Lyon uprising of 1834: arrests
by age
Source: AN CC 559–571.

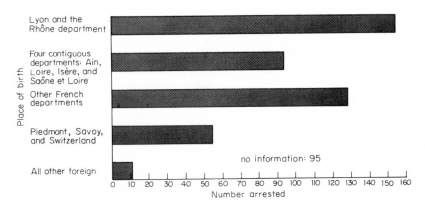

FIGURE 6. Lyon uprising of 1834: arrests by place of birth
Source: AN CC 559–571.

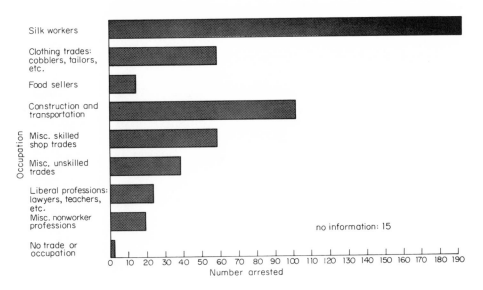

FIGURE 7. Lyon uprising of 1834: arrests by occupation
Source: AN CC 559–571.

males, those who normally characterized the broad stratum of journeymen in all trades, constituted two-thirds of the persons arrested.
Women and married males either stayed out of the fighting or somehow avoided capture. Figure 5 indicates that while the rebels were
young they were adults, nonetheless. Nearly 90 per cent were under

the age of forty, but only 20 per cent were under the age of twenty;
the latter figure may be deceptively low, however, because a number
of juveniles (particularly *lanceurs,* the boys who threw the shuttle
back across the loom) were released without being charged.[36] Figure
6 suggests the magnetic influence which the city exercised over
southeastern France. One-third of those arrested had been born in
Lyon and the Rhône department, 22 per cent came from the four
departments contiguous with the Rhône department, 30 per cent
came from other regions of France, and 10 per cent were foreign
born, principally from near-by Switzerland, Savoy, and Piedmont.
As a group they represented forty-nine French departments and
eleven foreign states, corroborating the fact that immigration was
the principal factor in Lyon's growth during this period.

The faces in the Lyonnais crowd were neither those of the *canaille*
nor the "revolutionaries" and "adventurers" imagined by historians
such as Thureau-Danguin.[37] The insurgents were remarkably well-
educated for the time; two-thirds of those arrested were literate and
only one-fifth were completely illiterate.[38] They were also far from
indigents; only four persons reported having no fixed domicile and
two confessed they had no trade or occupation. And, at a time when
crime rates were climbing rapidly in the city, a mere handful (2.5
per cent) admitted having a criminal record. This is in marked contrast to the 21 per cent of the Parisian Communards of 1871, as
identified by Jacques Rougerie.[39] Finally, approximately 15 per cent
of those arrested for participation in the fighting can be identified
as members of either a worker or a political association. This figure
may seem remarkably low; perhaps it can be explained by the fact
that many persons fled to avoid arrest and that denial under the
circumstances would be understandable. We should also recall that
less than a quarter of the master weavers were ever members of the
Society of Mutual Duty. Young, mobile, and employable, the rebels
were men who had come to Lyon seeking work. Far from being an
uprooted, "dangerous class," they fought only when their future
appeared gravely threatened.

The occupations of persons arrested reflect both the structure of
the Lyonnais worker community and some of the tensions within it.
Jobs which can be described as either rural or representative of
modern industry (for example, a factory machinist) are virtually
absent in the dossiers; this is not surprising since the city itself was
a preindustrial one. Figure 7 contradicts the government's claim that
few *canuts* participated in the uprising;[40] silkworkers constituted

37 per cent of the total number of arrests, a figure larger than for
any other occupational category. All available evidence indicates,
moreover, that the journeymen weavers did far more of the actual
fighting than did their masters. This fact raises four important points.
First, it may confirm the testimony of the members of the Council
of Presidents that many mutualists refused to support the Executive
Council's call for demonstrations on 9 April.[41] It is regrettable that
there is no evidence concerning the last-minute attitude of the journeymen Ferrandiniers. Second, it suggests that the local authorities
were correct in their assessment that the *compagnons* were more
violent than their masters.[42] Third, it raises the possibility that the
journeymen believed they had more to lose by the abolition of their
associations because they were the first to feel the effects of fluctuations in the market. That there was no loom wrecking indicates that
their rage was not directed toward their masters. Finally, it reveals
continuity in the character of the Lyonnais crowd: in the "two sous
riot" of 1786, the November rebellion of 1831, and the April uprising of 1834, the journeymen weavers were the street fighters.

Among the other occupations which took a prominent role in the
fighting, the journeymen tailors, cobblers, carpenters, and masons
have all been previously noted for their associations, strikes, or other
displays of organization. Others, such as the carters and drivers, may
simply have been men who enjoyed a good fight. It is striking that
bakers, butchers, and other foodsellers, one of the largest occupational groups in the city, made up only 3 per cent of the total arrests.
The fact that these tradesmen were frequently attacked in the worker
newspapers for their monopoly and unfair practices suggests that
their absence was less than accidental.

The dossiers further reveal that the insurgents were neither trained
military cadres nor a mob bent on pillage. Only 6 per cent of those
arrested had either army or National Guard training, in contrast to
the large number of Napoleonic veterans whom Fernand Rude has
alleged were in the revolt of November 1831 and David Pinkney has
discovered in the Parisian crowd in July 1830.[43] There is also no
trace of the Legion of the Volunteers of the Rhône which played an
important role in November 1831.[44] In a few cases, individual
Republicans led the resistance. Charles Lagrange in the Place des
Cordeliers, Marc Reverchon and Antoine Drigeard-Desgarniers in the
suburb of Vaise, and Étienne Carrier in the Croix Rousse, to cite the
most important examples, supervised the construction of barricades,
organized the requisition of weapons, and issued orders to men

whom they gave military-sounding titles. Only in the latter case
were those they led gathered except by chance. And Carrier was
known not so much as a Republican, but as a mutualist leader and
a former officer of the commune's National Guard.[45]

In most cases the fighting was chaotic and authority ephemeral. In
the Gourgillon quarter of the fifth arrondissement, for example, a
man named Veyron organized the resistance in the Place de la
Trinité. The barricade there was a masterpiece built from paving
stones and wood taken from a carpenter shop. It permitted the rebels
to shoot through crevices without exposing themselves and a dum-
my's head on a stick was used to draw fire from the troops. A crude
flag of green cloth, symbolic one must suppose of Veyron's Carlist
sentiments, flew over the stronghold. When one of his neighbors,
a mutualist named Muguet, insisted that a red flag be substituted,
Veyron threw down his sword and went home. Without his leadership the Place de la Trinité soon fell.[46]

The fact that most of the rebels were fighting in their own neighborhoods partially compensated for the absence of leadership. The
logistical advantage offered by the narrow streets of the working
class quarters did much to prolong the uprising. But Louis Blanc
accurately measured the situation when he wrote that "the insurrection floated purely on the waves of chance."[47] Incidents of looting
by the crowd were generally confined to pharmacies (in order to
obtain the ingredients for making powder), weapons shops, and food
stores (a necessity in a six-day uprising). Madame Martin, who owned
an *auberge* in the Place des Cordeliers testified that the rebels who
dined in her establishment at first carefully paid for their meals and
that after their funds ran out they wrote her promisory notes.[48]
Necessary items were requisitioned from private homes. This was a
dangerous practice, however, because many individuals were later
denounced by angry neighbors. "Everyone in the quarter knows
that Mazoyer fired on the troops," declared a witness in the Pierre
Scize quarter.[49] But it was unwise to be a stranger in some areas.
One man was later identified because his fine clothing was so con-
spicuous in a worker neighborhood. "I thought that surely his dress
and actions would make him recognizable," said a witness.[50] Nevertheless, Lt. General Aymard believed that most residents offered
at least secret support.[51] While the bookseller Jean Caussidière fought
on the barricade, for example, his wife and children rolled cartridges
at home and took food and drink to the fighters.[52]

Physical damage—even selective destruction[53]—was minimal on the part of the crowd. Barracks abandoned by the troops on duty were a frequent target of looters. The *octroi* stations—the very symbol of Lyon's high prices—were destroyed.[54] Because all important public buildings, as well as the merchants' warehouses along the Rhône, lay behind government lines the crowd had no opportunity to attack them. There is nothing to suggest, however, that the Lyonnais wished to copy the incendiary tactics used by the Bristol rioters in 1831.[55] And there was no evidence of the virulent anticlericalism demonstrated by the Parisian crowd which sacked the archbishop's palace at the time of the trial of the ministers of Charles X in January 1831. Several of Lyon's churches served as makeshift rebel headquarters, but the only reports of pillage—the robbing of poor boxes, theft of precious stones from relics, and the desecration of altars—were attributed to the troops.[56] Two priests from the Saint Bonaventure parish, in fact, were arrested and charged with actively supporting the resistance.[57] Although one witness, the director of the Hôtel Dieu, stated that the rebels had fired at anyone in uniform or bourgeois clothing,[58] the government acknowledged that they made conscious attempts to prevent harm to innocent persons. The example of Charles Lagrange, who spared the life of a police agent unmasked in the Place des Cordeliers, was cited not only by Louis Blanc but also by Girod de l'Ain.[59] Perhaps the crowd was too preoccupied in defending itself, but the fact remains that a wooden bridge across the Saône was the only thing which was put to the torch.[60] A survey of the applications by private citizens for compensation for property loss and personal injury strongly indicates that the main damage suffered by the city was the result of the government's cannon.[61]

The number of Lyon's residents who were wounded or lost their lives during the April events must remain in the realm of speculation because complete information on civilian casualties is unobtainable. Although the public charity hospital remained open and its staff worked without relief for six days treating rebels and soldiers alike, many who were injured in the fighting never sought professional care because they realized that it would likely guarantee their eventual arrest.[62] Girod de l'Ain reported the official figure of 192 civilian dead, but no master list of the victims survives.[63] To complicate matters further, many bodies were never identified. At the Hôtel Dieu, for example, half of the dead persons went unclaimed by friends or relatives.[64] A list we have compiled from documents scattered in three archives furnishes some information, admittedly less certain than that found in the dossiers of persons arrested, concerning 178 men and women. Particularly in the case of an unsuccessful uprising, dead men tell the historian fewer tales.[65]

It was not surprising that a large number of civilian victims were killed accidentally by the artillery bombardments or during the house-to-house fighting. The number of women and children killed far exceeds the number arrested for participation in the fighting and the percentage of males over the age of forty killed is double that of men in the same category arrested. There appears to be little occupational difference between persons killed or arrested, with two interesting exceptions. First, a number of unidentified men were listed as day laborers (*journaliers*), thereby raising the incidence in this category far higher among the dead than among those arrested. We cannot know how many of these persons were actually *canuts.* Second, the number of property owners (*propriétaires*) killed far exceeds those arrested. There is no evidence, however, to suggest that they were the rebels' intentional victims. When he learned of the Lyon uprising, Giuseppe Mazzini wrote: "Ruins cover the second city of France. And each brick covers the tomb of a hero."[66] Unfortunately for us these "heroes" remain largely anonymous.

We have already seen that the most characteristic feature of the April uprising was its fragmentation. Did the composition of the crowd differ in the various parts of the city? If the thesis is to be sustained that Lyon experienced an indigenous worker uprising and not a political insurrection, the patterns of activity in each pocket of resistance should conform to the structure of daily life there. And where exceptions are found, a reasonable explanation must be made.

The map of Lyon used in the official investigation of the April uprising indicates the position of all reported barricades, making it a simple task to identify precisely the areas of resistance: (1) the fifth arrondissement—all or part of the six quarters on the right bank of the Saône; (2) the first arrondissement (with the exception of the Griffon quarter) and the Boucherie quarter of the third arrondissement—most of the Croix Rousse hillside; (3) the south-central portion of the peninsula along the right bank of the Rhône—all or part of the Hospice and Bel Cordière quarters of the second arrondissement and the Saint Bonaventure, Saint Nizier, and Thomassin quarters of the fourth arrondissement; (4) the suburb of the Croix Rousse, including the commune of Saint Clair which was legally separated from it in 1832; (5) the suburb of La Guillotière on the left bank of the Rhône; (6) and the suburb of Vaise, which lay north of the city along the right bank of the Saône.

Why did violence occur in these quarters and suburbs while the others remained generally quiet? At least part of the answer can be found by using the records of the fiscal census of Lyon and the Croix Rousse suburb in 1834.[67] Taking three factors—population density, number of silk looms, and percentage of domestic servants in the total population—as a rough means of approximation, an economic and social profile can be drawn and each quarter placed on a scale ranging from heavily working class on the one end, to haute bourgeois or aristocratic on the other. Three quarters—Saint Clair, Capucins, and La Boucherie—along the base or slope of the Croix Rousse—had distinctly divided profiles. The other twenty-two quarters, plus the Croix Rousse suburb, had more homogeneous populations.

Table 11 shows that the insurgent quarters tended to be those with working class profiles. In the three divided quarters, moreover, the fighting was confined to the worker neighborhoods. The exception to this pattern was the Saint Nizier quarter (and to a certain extent the Thomassin and Saint Bonaventure quarters); an explanation will be offered later. The suburbs of La Guillotière and Vaise, for which we lack adequate census information, lay beyond the army's lines and joined the uprising during its second day. In the case of the former, we know that many *canuts'* shops were clustered near the end of the Pont de la Guillotière, that work stopped in this neighborhood on the ninth, and that the first barricade in the suburb was erected there on the morning of the 10th.[68] With regard to the latter, it was not so much the presence of the *canuts* (although a number of them lived there) as the fact that the village was the obvious place for the residents of the fifth arrondissement to seek reinforcements and weapons. Indeed, it was under such circumstances that Vaise became involved in the uprising.

The April uprising, then, was a conflict of the new worker quarters, the old neighborhoods of the fifth arrondissement, and the suburbs against the wealthy quarters and the commercial center of Lyon. This conforms closely to Jacques Rougerie's vision of the Paris Commune of 1871 as the recapture of the heart of the capital by its post-Haussmann peripheral quarters.[69] In both cases there was a direct relationship between urban development and the patterns of violence.

We must now take an additional step and examine the character of the fighting in the various areas of Lyon. According to Girod de l'Ain, the resistance in the first arrondissement was the most highly organized in the uprising.[70] Nevertheless, the fighting there was essentially a neighborhood affair. A majority of the persons arrested

TABLE 11. Social and economic profiles of the quarters of Lyon, 1834

Greatest working class density	La Croix Rousse[a]
	La Côte[a]
	Saint Vincent[a]
	Gourguillon[a]
	Bel Cordière[a]
	L'Hospice[a]
	Porte-Froc[a]
	Pierre Scize[a]
	La Juiverie[a]
	Place Neuve Saint Jean[a]
	Ancienne Ville[a]
	Perrache
	Thomassin[a]
	Saint Bonaventure[a]
	Villeroy
	Saint François
	Saint Nizier[a]
	Griffon
	Louis le Grand
	Place Confort
	Palais des Artes
Greatest haute bourgeois/aristocratic density	Hôtel-de-Ville
	Orléans
Divided quarters	Saint Clair[a]
	Capucins[a]
	La Boucherie[a]

Source: AM K, "Recensement de la population," 1834.
[a]Insurgent quarter.

on the entire Croix Rousse hillside lived in a four-square block area immediately to the east of the Place Sathoney and the Jardin des Plantes. This was the neighborhood of the rue Tolozan. The principal rebel headquarters was the café Armand in that street and as late as 13 April, the day after the fall of the Place des Cordeliers, its resi-

dents were still gathering paving stones in order to build new barricades.[71] Typical of the crowd in this area was Claude Clocher, a
twenty-seven-year-old native of Savoy who was one of six journeymen weavers working in a shop above the café Armand. When he was
arrested and charged with having manned an observation post at the
end of his block, Clocher's only weapon was a sword given to him
by a neighbor who was a former member of the National Guard.
When asked to explain the uprising, he said that "misery caused it
all."[72]

Much of what the government later believed was organized resistance in the first arrondissement can be attributed to the fact that
men such as Claude Clocher knew the terrain. Four examples serve
to illustrate this point. First, by the time the shooting started on the
morning of the 9th, the hillside was already sealed off from the rest
of the city as a result of troop deployment. The Bon Pasteur caserne,
however, stood less than a block from the rue Tolozan and as soon as
its residents saw the soldiers leave to reinforce the Hôtel-de-Ville
they knew they were free to go there in search of arms.[73] Second,
on the 11th, a handful of rebels were able to use their intimate
knowledge of hidden passageways (the *traboules*) to move unseen
and ambush a squad of soldiers which had entered the rue Bouteille,
two streets down the slope from the rue Tolozan.[74] Third, during
that same day troops were sent to remove an abandoned barricade in
the rue Saint Marcel and were driven off by a rain of tiles and bricks.
Among the residents of the street who took to their roofs were a
master weaver named Satin and his two sons, aged nine and sixteen.[75] Finally, during the night of 13–14 April, when it was certain
that the troops would sweep the hillside next day, most of the rebels
abandoned the barricades and returned home.[76] The success of these
urban guerillas in escaping detection may be seen in the fact that
the authorities were able to make only sixty-two arrests in the entire
arrondissement.

As far as can be determined there was no prior preparation for
resistance in the rue Tolozan. We do not know how many residents
attended one of the demonstrations on the morning of the 9th, but
those who remained first learned of the fighting from the sound of
gunfire coming from the Place des Terreaux and when someone rang
the tocsin in the Saint Louis church a few blocks away on the quai
of the Saône.[77] The band of men and women which set out to look
for weapons in the Bon Pasteur caserne found very few guns, but

took tables and chairs to build a barricade, looted the junior officers' trunks, and stole wine from the kitchen.[78] Had the *canuts* of the first arrondissement given any indication they were getting ready for trouble these quarters would not have been left undefended.

What of the evidence that some insurgents were organized in a paramilitary manner, complete with the use of ranks and titles? The explanation is two-fold. First, the worker associations which already existed in the neighborhood furnished a natural chain of command and communication. For instance, when the journeyman weaver Jacques Didier led an attack on the troops in the Place Sathoney he likely used his position as an officer of the Society of Ferrandiniers to mobilize the *canuts*.[79] Second, three of the other leaders—Joseph Pradel, Louis Marigné, and a man known simply as Correa—were, respectively, an artilleryman home on leave, a former member of the Genevan army, and a former member of the National Guard. Correa lived in the rue Tolozan and Pradel was visiting his mother and brother, a master weaver, who resided there. Only Marigné, an avowed Republican and the head of the Philanthropic Society of Tailors, lived outside the neighborhood. He later claimed that he had been unable to make his way home directly from the demonstration in the Place Saint Jean, had taken a back route, and been trapped on the hillside. In any case, he admitted: "I did not know the area."[80]

One can make too much of military titles, in other words. Among the men who took their meals in the café Armand there were some who were called "lieutenant" or—inevitably—"citizen." But most were referred to by their nicknames—*sans peur, nez à tout, soupe,* and *Bel-Oeil.*[81] These were simply men who saw one another every-day in the streets. And while the red flag (a piece of woolen cloth) flew from the steeple of Saint Polycarpe and the banners of the "Generosité" and "Fecundité" sections of the Society of the Rights of Man were seen elsewhere on the hillside, no flag flew over the rue Tolozan.[82]

We have found the first-hand accounts of two public officials who witnessed the resistance in the first arrondissement. One was a medical officer who was captured by the rebels on the 9th and spent the rest of the uprising on house arrest. He reported that few members of the crowd had guns and that many were children and young men armed only with knives attached to the ends of sticks.[83] The other was a postal courier who arrived from Paris on the 11th and, after first being fired upon by the troops, accidentally fell into the hands of the rebels. Because he wore a strange-looking uniform the rumor spread that the *Procureur du Roi* had been captured and was being held prisoner. There was a demand for his immediate execution, but the crowd was persuaded to spare his life when the elderly owner of one of the buildings told the story of Napoleon's treatment of the Duc d'Enghien.[84] Perhaps his audience included Claude Clocher.

Across the Saône in the fifth arrondissement the pattern of resistance was similar to that on the Croix Rousse hillside. One will recall that by 1834 these quarters, once the heart of the Renaissance city, housed the poorest of the *canuts*. It is not surprising that Monfalcon reported hearing cries there such as a husband shouting to his wife, "Keep calm. In a few days we'll all be rich," or a group of women screaming at the troops, "Down with the rich. It is we who should be sleeping on silken sheets!"[85]

Like their brethren in the first arrondissement, the rebels on the right bank of the Saône were poorly armed and for the most part fought where they lived. Police records describe the barricades as being constructed of *mauvais planches* and *bois de charpentre enléves à pleusieurs marchands du quartier.*[86] Once again the rhythm of daily life was reflected in the fighting. The butcher Rodet, a resident of the rue Tramassac, was reluctant to allow his ancient building to be used as a snipers' nest for fear that it would collapse under cannon fire from the troops.[87] A mutualist named Sabattier, who lived in the rue des Farges, on the other hand, joined the insurgents when his neighbors accused him of being a coward.[88] Another man, a journeyman weaver, was chased away because his brother was known to be a policeman.[89] And the café owners Paulandre of the rue Trouvée and Brunet of the rue Juiverie were later arrested for permitting their establishments to be used as rebel headquarters.[90]

Leadership in the fifth arrondissement came from men such as Joseph Gille, a cobbler who had served in the National Guard; Rockzinski, a Polish officer who had taken refuge in France; Morel, a journeyman weaver who had served in the army; and Butet, a master weaver who was an officer of the neighborhood night patrol (*compagnie des surveillants de nuit*).[91] The crowd there included a higher percentage of outsiders than on the Croix Rousse hillside—likely the result of persons unable to return to their homes from the demonstration in the Place Saint Jean—but only 5 out of the 108 men and women arrested were identified as Republicans. Monfalcon was probably correct when he told Prefect Gasparin in a private letter that he should not be deceived by the relatively small number of insurgents in the fifth arrondissement, for "the neutrality of the working class was certainly a hostile one."[92]

The fighting on the peninsula was somewhat different from the resistance in the first and fifth arrondissements. At the heart of the rebel area there was the triangular Place des Cordeliers, with the Saint Bonaventure church at its base and inns, wineshops, and food stores along its sides. In contrast to streets such as the rue Tolozan and the rue Saint Georges in the *canuts'* quarters, only one master weaver had his shop in the Place des Cordeliers. Many of its 357 residents were hatters and wigmakers. Only one street in the entire quarter, in fact, housed more than fifty silk looms and even there it appears that the common practice was for the wife of a tailor or hatter to operate a single loom to supplement the family income.[93] The Saint Nizier, Thomassin, L'Hospice, and Bel Cordière quarters were also a part of this pocket of insurgency in the center of the city; this area was previously described as being more like the central quarters of Paris than any other Lyonnais neighborhood.

Although the data is skewed to some degree by the fact that many persons were arrested upon the fall of the Place des Cordeliers, it seems clear that the crowd on the peninsula differed in two ways from those in the first and fifth arrondissements. First, it was composed of a mixture of artisans—cobblers, tailors, joiners, tinsmiths, plasterers—whose occupations were familiar in any preindustrial city. Only seventeen men with occupations related to the *fabrique* in any way were among the 118 persons arrested. The dossiers suggest, in fact, that more tailors than *canuts* populated the crowd. Second, almost half of those arrested were not residents of the central peninsula. The typical rebel in the Place des Cordeliers was as likely to live in Vaise as he was to inhabit that nearby *cour des miracles,* the rue Noire.

Two things should be kept in mind when weighing the significance of these facts. First, if many rebels on the peninsula were outsiders, more than half of them *were* fighting on their own ground. And the occupational structure there was not the same as in the first and fifth arrondissements. Men and women such as Pierre-Antoine Girard, a master tailor whose business had suffered because he had opposed the rebellion of November 1831; Adele Krug, the common-law wife of a man named Jomard, who not only forced her husband to fight but also built barricades with her own hands; and the journeyman papermakers Mercier and Gayet, described by their neighbors as *très*

mauvais sujets et des gens dangereux, all fought where they lived.[94]
Second, the Place des Cordeliers and the streets around it were the
natural route of retreat from the Prefecture and the Hôtel-de-Ville on
the morning of the 9th. One will recall that the first barricades in
this area were raised by men fleeing the shooting in the Place des
Jacobins and the artillery fire in the Passage de l'Argue.[95] As for the
insurgents around the Saint Nizier church, some of them were escaping the demonstration sites on the peninsula, while others made
their way across the Pont Sequin while returning from the Place
Saint Jean.[96]

In many ways, such as the shortage of weapons, methods of requisition, and the absence of much selective destruction, the character
of the resistance on the peninsula was like that elsewhere. In one
significant way, however, it was different: some of those fighting in
the Place des Cordeliers claimed they sought to establish a Republic.
Led by Charles Lagrange, an individual who had never had more than
a minor role in the local Republican party, these men distinguished
themselves from the ordinary residents of the square by posting a
copy of the Declaration of the Rights of Man, singing the *Marseillaise,* and shouting *Vive la République.*[97] But they were merely a
handful in the crowd. Only ten persons were later identified as
Republicans among those arrested in the area. The uprising on the
peninsula, in other words, *did* conform in many ways to the rhythm
of daily life there. Where it did not—particularly in the case of the
miniature Republican insurrection in the Place des Cordeliers—we
have suggested a reasonable explanation. The government later dis-
torted the entire rebellion by focusing attention on the Place des
Cordeliers. The events there were colorful and dramatic, but we would
be in error to dwell over them while overlooking other parts of Lyon.

In the suburbs of Vaise, La Croix Rousse, and La Guillotière the
story was much the same as in the first and fifth arrondissements:
local residents fighting with improvised tactics and few weapons.
Since these areas were outside the city it is not surprising to find a
few rural elements in the patterns of resistance: fields set on fire to
delay the troops, a farmer and a gardener arrested, a cow killed
accidentally.[98] When the director of the Veterinary College in Vaise
locked the school gates a few of his pupils scaled the walls to join
the fighting. Because there was no university in Lyon these were the
only students arrested in the uprising.[99]

This examination of the patterns of resistance quarter by quarter
might be extended for pages without adding much to what has

already been said. In order to avoid convincing the reader that even
violence can become tedious, it is sufficient to conclude that much
of what we have found corresponds closely to phenomena other
historians have observed in other preindustrial French crowds.[100] In
fact, the resort to radical action by artisans threatened with loss of
status and changing economic structures has become almost a dogma
of social history.[101] Lyon seems to provide yet another example of
what George Rudé has called "indigenous"[102] and Charles Tilly terms
"reactionary"[103] behavior. What is different about the Lyonnais
crowd (and the dossiers alone would make this a tenuous statement)
is the presence of a protoindustrial occupational concentration and
conscious organization in the worker community. These facts suggest
that the Lyon uprising of 1834 was the first example of "modern"[104]
collective violence in European history.

The argument in support of the "modernity" of the uprising is
strengthened by the circumstances under which the fighting began:
workingmen gathered at the trial of their leaders to protest a law
intended to destroy the institutions they believed would help mold
their future, not resurrect an imagined golden past. Perhaps it was
inevitable that the government—just as a later one sought to blame
the Paris Commune of 1871 on the First International—would single
out the Republicans in the crowd and conclude that the entire affair
had been a political insurrection.[105] We must resist the temptation
to wrestle needlessly with this straw man, however. A minor Republican revolt had occurred during the rebellion of November 1831 and
a larger one took place in Lyon in April 1834. The principal difference between them was not that the worker community had become more receptive to their ideas (one need only recall the role of
the Legion of the Volunteers of the Rhône in 1831), but that in the
second uprising the local Republicans were on the same side of the
barricades as the *canuts*, at least in sympathy if not physically. In
neither case, however, is there evidence that the mass of workers
themselves believed they were fighting to establish a Republic. Many
of the symbols of the Society of the Rights of Man—flags, songs,
handbills, passwords—were in evidence in 1834, but so were those
of the worker societies. Some of the rebels in the Place des Cordeliers
proclaimed Republican motives, but a variety of others—the Bourbon
claimant Henry V, the Bonaparte family, and the expected economic
grievances—are also to be found in the dossiers.

Obviously it is an oversimplification to assign a single motive to
any crowd, but this is precisely what the government did. Because

they wore ideological blinders, the supporters of the *juste-milieu* neglected to ask the critical question: would the Lyonnais workers have rebelled if there had been no economic crisis, no mutualist trial, and only political associations had been threatened?

III

What was the role of the worker associations and the Republican party in the Lyon uprising of 1834? What was the relationship between this event and the other minor revolts which occurred elsewhere in France?

By now it is clear that the uprising did not produce a *levée en masse* of Lyonnais "patriots." Among the hundreds of persons arrested for actual participation in the fighting only thirty-nine could be identified as Republicans and just eight of them were ever brought to trial. A few individual Republicans did have prominent roles in the resistance, but in most cases they were either men with military experience (Lagrange, Rockzinski, Carrier) or also active in a worker association (Carrier, Didier, Marigné, Girard). They did not, in other words, command authority over the crowd simply by announcing their political beliefs.

In discussing earlier the character of the conflict in the Place des Cordeliers it was suggested that this square lay on the route of retreat from the Prefecture and the Hôtel-de-Ville. In addition, the schismatic section of the Society of the Rights of Man which was headed by Guillaume Vincent met regularly in this neighborhood. That *enragé* himself was seen near the Prefecture on the morning of the 9th, but his subsequent escape makes it impossible to report accurately on his movements during the fighting.[106] We can speculate, however, that the order of the Society of the Rights of Man that in the event of trouble its unarmed members should leave the demonstration sites and retreat to secondary positions broke down and left a few militants stranded. In the last analysis, Republican participation in the Lyon uprising of 1834 was a result of the weakness, not the strength, of the local party.

There is evidence, moreover, that the worker associations were at least as active in the resistance. A black flag flew from the steeple of the Saint Nizier church, a red one from Saint Polycarpe on the Croix Rousse hillside, and red and black banners were reported in the suburb of the Croix Rousse.[107] The mutualists and Ferrandiniers were ordered by their leaders to attend the demonstrations on the

9th and the same methods as had been used during the general strike
in February were employed to generate a work stoppage on that
morning.[108] Although the members of *compagnonnages* were forbidden to attend the demonstrations because Prefect Gasparin had
assured their leaders that the law on associations would not be
applied to them, the leaders of the progressive journeymens' organizations had participated on the Joint Committee and summoned
their fellows to join the *canuts'* protest.[109] Once the fighting began
these men did not shy away. Pierre Ayel, a section chief of the
cobblers' Society of Perfect Accord in Vaise, testified that late on
the morning of the 9th two men came to the shop where he worked
and told him to convene his section because the troops had fired
on the crowd in the Place Saint Jean. Ayel and his followers were
unable to proceed beyond the Pierre Scize quarter of the fifth arrondissement before they were stopped by the troops and sent back to
Vaise.[110] Not all workers understood why they were fighting, however. One man later said "there was much confusion among us. A
cloth printer told me one thing, others said other things. No one
knew the motive of the insurrection."[111] But others, such as a young
day laborer, expressed at least a vague notion that it was a social
conflict: "They said that if the workers were the strongest they
would win."[112]

The relationship between the Lyon uprising and the troubles elsewhere in France was a double one: it triggered them and some of
them in turn influenced events in Lyon. Since November 1831 the
city had had a reputation as the nation's most explosive spot, and
given the tension created by the law on associations it is easy to
understand how the arrival of the news of the clash of 9 April would
bring Republicans elsewhere into the streets. In Arbois, Chalons-
sur-Saône, Clermont-Ferrand, Grenoble, Lunéville, Marseille, Saint
Étienne, Paris, and Vienne, this is what happened. Small groups
staged minor revolts, but there was no coordination in their timing
and all were quickly suppressed.

In Arbois, for example, the coach from Lyon arrived on 13 April
and a passenger reported that the Republic had been proclaimed
there. Local Republicans rushed to seize the Hôtel-de-Ville and met
no resistance. Late the next day they received the news of the suppression of the Lyon uprising and simply faded away. On the 15th, a
small squad of soldiers "recaptured" the Hôtel-de-Ville without
incident.[113] At Lunéville, a group of cavalry officers led by Clémont
Thomas had been converted to Republicanism. On the morning of

16 April–after Lyon had returned to normal–the *Tribune* arrived
from Paris with the false information that the garrison of Belfort
had proclaimed the Republic. Thomas and his followers attempted
to capture the Lunéville military headquarters but their *coup* was
stifled.[114] In Saint Étienne, where many of the master ribbon weavers were organized in much the same manner as the mutualists, local
Republicans tried to stir the worker community and succeeded only
in generating a strike against a few notorious shops. As one man
explained the attitude of the masters' association:

> It is forbidden to speak of politics in the meetings . . . , and
> those who do receive severe penalties. Porte [one of the leaders]
> was certainly a Republican, he told me so himself. But in our
> committee meetings he never talked about politics for that was
> forbidden.[115]

The other revolts were best described by Louis Blanc: "Bodies of
men walking around for awhile in a menacing manner, threatening
shouts and cries, tumultuous assemblies soon dispersed, a few senti-
nels disarmed, false information circulated."[116] The exception to
this was in Paris where the news of the Lyon uprising arrived on the
10th. Three days later, after the Republican newspapers had printed
the rumor that the city had fallen to the rebels, the government
closed down the *Tribune* and arrested the leaders of the Society of
the Rights of Man. That night and the next day there was trouble
in the quarters of the Marais and the Temple, which was suppressed
with a considerable number of innocent victims. The situation in the
capital was never out of control, a fact of which the Minister of the
Interior hastened to inform Prefect Gasparin by telegraph.[117] Nevertheless, it is Daumier's lithograph of the slaughter in the rue Transnonain in Paris which we generally associate with the events of April
1834.

If the troubles elsewhere were launched by accurate and inaccurate
news from Lyon, they had only an indirect bearing on the uprising
there. The Lyonnais authorities expected coordinated demonstrations against the passage of the law on associations and it is understandable that they became alarmed by reports of violence in
Grenoble, Saint Étienne, and Vienne. Although this news was later
discovered to have been substantially exaggerated, it did influence
Lt. General Aymard's decision to delay the commitment of his entire
force for fear that his promised reinforcements might never arrive.

On the other side of the barricades, the rumors of these revolts may have bolstered the spirit of the crowd and certainly gave credence to the Republicans' promise that help from patriots in other departments was on the way. In no case, however, did persons in one city actually come to the aid of those in another town.

The Lyon uprising was the only revolt of serious consequence during the entire *journées d'avril.* It can most accurately be explained as the combined result of an unexpected economic crisis and popular resentment of the law on associations. It was the government's hysterical response to a supposed political threat which provided the catalyst for whatever belated rapprochement occurred between the local Republican party and the worker community. This action estranged it far more than radical propaganda. While counseling that resignation alone was the workers' proper response to their lot, the defenders of the *juste-milieu* said they saw no reason to modify the revolutionary settlement since no legal barriers to advancement remained. The *canuts,* the elite of French workers, perceived this was not so. Defeated in their efforts to organize and politicized by repression, they had come to see the government of Louis Philippe as a natural enemy. This was the reason why April 1834 was a greater challenge to the regime than was November 1831. For, as one eyewitness reported: "The workers of Lyon did not revolt as Republicans, but as workers united by a mutual interest."[118]

8   *Autrefois Les Canuts*

The April events were like a self-fulfilling prophecy. Even before the fighting ended numerous public officials charged that France had been the victim of a Republican conspiracy. The subsequent investigation was a political witchhunt and told the government exactly what it wished to hear. After a year of preventive detention many of the Lyonnais prisoners were sent to Paris to be tried for sedition before the Court of Peers. Once in the capital they became embroiled with the Parisian Republicans, who wanted to turn the trial into an indictment of the regime. Perhaps because the outcome of the *procès monstre,* as it was popularly called, was a foregone conclusion the peers and the Republicans sacrificed concern for justice and competed for the national attention focused on the Luxembourg Palace. The *canuts,* meanwhile not only had their associations suppressed by the government, but also found themselves largely abandoned by those who had claimed to share their cause.

I

On 15 April 1834, the Peers of France met in a special session to receive a royal ordinance transforming them into the nation's High Tribunal. So began the longest and most spectacular legal battle of the July Monarchy. Sitting for nearly two years, the court received more than 17,000 depositions, reports, and interrogations and passed judgment on 168 political prisoners. The trial was organized by Baron Pasquier, the president of the Court of Peers,[1] Thiers, the Minister of the Interior, Persil, the Minister of Justice, and Martin du Nord, the *Procureur Général* of France. Special assistants were appointed to collect evidence in each of the insurrectionary cities; in Lyon the task fell to Chégaray, the counselor of the Royal Court.[2] Girod de l'Ain, a former prefect of police in Paris and now a deputy, was asked to write the official report on the April events. Martin du Nord's initial communication to the court stressed the theme of premeditated rebellion and when they adjourned on 30 April to await the results of the investigation only one peer saw fit to remind his colleagues that there was only a presumption of guilt which remained to be proven.[3]

Official sentiment was much the same in Lyon. The assistant mayor, who was in charge in Prunelle's absence, expressed gratitude to the garrison for saving the city from the "civil war" which "the sedition-mongers from every province" had prepared for Lyon. Now, his proclamation stated, "the friends of law and order" had triumphed and France herself was saved.[4] The Municipal Council's report on the extent of property damage argued that the state should reimburse the city because it had been the chosen battlefield in a plot of national proportions.[5]

It is instructive to trace the development of this conspiracy theory. During the evening of 9 April, the local *Procureur Général* informed the Minister of Justice by telegraph that "the inevitable combat" had begun and predicted the government's certain victory would end Lyon's role as "the hearth of conspiracies." Warrants, he reported, were already being prepared for the arrest of the "known leaders."[6] Three days later the same official stated that an insurrection had been planned for three months and that the mutualists' trial was only a pretext for disorder.[7] On the 13th, the counselor of the Royal Court ordered the arrest of the section chiefs of the Society of the Rights of Man who had signed the petition protesting the law on associations as "the principal leaders of the armed insurrection."[8] On the 29th, his preliminary report for the official investigation stated that the violence had been premeditated, completely political in character, and that the leaders of the Society of the Rights of Man were "in the first rank of the guilty." A few days later, Martin du Nord passed this document to the Minister of Justice with the notation that it "correctly" explained the Lyonnais events.[9]

Partisan politics had an explicit role in the subsequent investigation. In urging Prefect Gasparin to gather evidence which suggested the existence of a conspiracy the Minister of the Interior promised to accept full authority for all searches and arrests. As the latter put it, the April events constituted open warfare and the government "like a general after a successful battle [should] take full advantage of the enemy."[10] Gasparin was also ordered to give attention to possible Carlist complicity, but after searching the homes of local legitimist leaders he reported that no evidence of their participation could be found. The government soon abandoned this line of investigation.[11]

Although still convinced of a Republican plot, the authorities were obliged to revise an important part of their original explanation. Immediately after the uprising Gasparin claimed to believe that the Society of the Rights of Man was alone responsible for the Lyonnais events. At that time he noted the neutrality of the worker associations and commented that the fighting would have been "much more terrrible" had they been involved.[12] As late as 1 May, he reiterated his conviction that the *canuts* had generally remained passive.[13] As the interrogation of prisoners proceeded, however, the discovery of the mutualists' Order of the Day for 9 April ("Association, Resistance, Courage") forced both Gasparin and Chégaray to admit the participation of the worker associations. A month after the revolt they informed their superiors of the new development.[14]

The reaction in Paris was striking. Persil, the Minister of Justice, complained about "these curious details" and demanded that evidence be found to prove that the Republicans had infiltrated the worker associations.[15] Thiers, the Minister of the Interior, instructed the Lyonnais officials to distinguish between the mutualist Executive Council and the rank and file membership.[16] A published rumor in the *Revue des Deux Mondes* hinted that the investigation was producing "much uncertainty" with regard to the alleged conspiracy and they clearly did not want to weaken the government's case by any suggestion that the Lyon uprising stemmed from economic and social grievances.[17]

The Republicans themselves harbored no illusions. The *Précurseur* told Prefect Gasparin that "the interest of your party is to discover a Republican plot in the Lyonnais events."[18] And the editor of the *Tribune,* Armand Marrast, accurately predicted that the political opponents of the regime would be accused of obeying a single order to revolt. "Only the victorious have spoken," he wrote, "and among the vanquished the happiest are the dead."[19]

The roundup of insurgents and others accused of complicity in the alleged plot began during the uprising and continued for weeks afterward. We do not know the exact number of arrests. The official figure for the Lyonnais *inculpés* was set at 679, but other lists range from a high of 858 to a low of 639.[20] Whatever the correct figure, local jails were overflowing and it was necessary to release minor criminals and transfer other prisoners in order to make room for the rioters. One of those to be moved was Adolphe Granier, the former editor of *La Glaneuse* and a leader of the Jacobin faction of the local Republican party. Although only a few months remained in his sentence from the previous year, Granier escaped from his guards along the route and fled into exile. After two years in Geneva he would return to France and become a police informer.[21]

Other political fugitives found Switzerland the safest refuge. Among them was the local Carlist leader Adolphe Sala, who busied himself writing a history of the Lyon uprising.[22] Dozens of ordinary workers fled the city, also. Men such as Billie *le Algérien,* a native Lyonnais, and Onkle de Wurth [sic?], an English-born weaver, left only dossiers marked *absent* as their place in history.

With the members of the mutualist Executive Council, most of the section chiefs of the Society of the Rights of Man, and two members of its Central Committee[23] in custody the police busied themselves with mopping-up operations. Neighboring departments were notified of the description of important fugitives and the records of local hospitals were checked when the wounded were released. In one of many acts of administrative justice the license of a tobacconist alleged to have been the treasurer of the Society of the Rights of Man was reassigned to the widow of a policeman killed in the uprising.[24]

Meanwhile the judicial authorities were searching for evidence, questioning witnesses, and interrogating prisoners. Some who were obviously innocent were anxious to respond, but others took the advice of lawyers and refused to cooperate.[25] A search of Republican homes and newspaper offices failed to reveal new information. In fact, neither the financial records nor the membership lists of any local Republican organization were ever produced. Counselor Chégaray's preliminary report was based on a few documents which had been seized in the office of the *Glaneuse* at the time of the "Nivoise" letter incident in February. Prefect Gasparin was unable to send a complete set of local Republican brochures to Paris for the trial.[26]

A number of repressive measures were imposed on the worker community in the aftermath of the uprising. In an effort to control the "floating population" all masters were required to obtain *livrets* for their journeymen and to deliver them to the police for inspection. Those who refused to comply were subject to a heavy fine.[27] Official xenophobia was widespread. One army report tried to reconcile an obvious contradiction with the explanation that since many foreign-born *canuts* were known to be Republicans, they had stayed out of the uprising only because they realized it could not succeed.[28] Counselor Chégaray received permission from Paris to expel any foreigner suspected of participation in the revolt for whom there was insufficient evidence to make an arrest. At least sixty persons were deported in this manner.[29] Prefect Gasparin noted that while their expulsion had opened a few jobs for native-born workers, the local economy was likely to remain stagnant for some time.[30] In fact, the *fabrique* made a sharp recovery in the second half of 1834, but the uprising nonetheless seemed to substantiate the merchants' fears and to justify the law on associations.[31]

The new legislation proved exactly the means of control the government had long desired. Although the Minister of the Interior refrained from applying it against all French worker organizations, in the case of Lyon he ordered the law used to destroy "offensive associations" whatever their character.[32] The trial of the six members of the mutualist Executive Council, which had been suspended on the 5th and the 9th, was again interrupted by gunfire on 16 April. When it reconvened on the 21st all six men received harsh penalties and were bound over to face a second trial for sedition alongside the Republicans.[33] In the same month a strike by the journeymen thread dyers was quickly halted by the arrest of twenty-one alleged leaders. Tried before the Correctional Court they received sentences ranging from one to six months in prison. The local *Procureur Général* applauded the verdict as a return to firmness on the part of the courts. He also reported widespread discouragement among the tattered remnants of the worker associations.[34]

The police kept close watch on the worker neighborhoods. When the mutualist lodges met in May to arrange small loans for members their sessions were interrupted and in September a group of master weavers was arrested and mistakenly charged with trying to resurrect the society. Although they were acquitted, the Society of Mutual Duty itself was moribund.[35] Most workers were afraid to belong to a labor association any longer. The Ferrandiniers resorted to strong-arm tactics to restore their depleted ranks. One *canut* told the police that he and several friends were ordered to either leave the city or marry (thereby losing eligibility for membership), but that they could not remain an inactive member of the association. Refusing, he was summoned before his old lodge, stripped of his membership ribbon, and saw it burned before his eyes.[36]

Only the worker press continued. The *Écho des Travailleurs* had

gone under in March and the *Écho de la Fabrique* failed to appear
after the uprising. As early as July 1834, however, there were rumors
of a new journal.[37] When the project was realized two newspapers
appeared to perpetuate the dispute between their predecessors. The
Indicateur took its name from the administrative office of the Society of Mutual Duty and pursued the "narrow" program of the *Écho
de la Fabrique.* (The "mutualists" arrested in September were
actually the directors of the *Indicateur* and the paper's subscription list was seized in the raid.)[38] The *Tribune Prolétaire* was edited
by Marius Chastaing, the former editor of the *Écho des Travailleurs.*
It is unfortunate that little dialogue beyond vituperation ever passed
between them because the *Indicateur* said it supported the economic
theories of Sismondi, while its rival endorsed those of J. B. Say.[39]
When both papers failed for lack of funds in July 1835, Falconnet,
the former *Prud'homme* and founder of the *Écho de la Fabrique,*
launched *Le Nouvel Écho de la Fabrique,* which he dedicated to heal-
ing the divisions in the worker community.[40] Another paper called
the *Union des Travailleurs* also appeared for a short time. If the
worker press persisted under difficult circumstances, the Lyonnais
worker movement had been stripped of the momentum it had
developed between 1827 and 1834. Much as the Le Chapelier law
had ended the master weavers' rebellion within the Grande Fabrique,
the law on associations deprived the *canuts* of the means of organizing to assert control over their own labor.[41]

The local Republican party was fatally compromised by the uprising. The combination of internal divisions and renewed government pressure drove it underground and ended the propaganda
campaign aimed at the workshops. Prefect Gasparin noted the rapid
disappearance of the now-illegal popular associations and a return
to the small secret societies which had characterized the radical
opposition during the Restoration. He optimistically concluded that
the Republicans were no longer a threat in Lyon.[42]

Republican newspapers underwent a concerted official attack
throughout France. In Paris, the *Tribune* was suppressed and the
National constantly harassed. In Lyon, the *Glaneuse's* supporters
made an attempt to resurrect it for a single issue after the uprising,
but Gasparin ordered a raid of the paper's office on the eve of publication.[43] The *Précurseur* was caught between Jacobin insults on the
one hand and official condemnation on the other. In the mind of the
government the paper's reputation for moderation and respectability
counted for little. Because it had been the only active Republican

journal in Lyon at the time of the uprising the authorities were anxious to implicate it in the alleged conspiracy. Its editor, Anselme Petetin, was in poor health and believed he would not survive for long in prison. After writing an open letter to Gasparin accusing him for condemning Jacobinism while himself practicing the "justice" of the Convention, Petetin eluded police surveillance and escaped to Switzerland. Behind him he left the doors of his office sealed by the authorities, two of his closest colleagues in jail, and only a single assistant to run the newspaper. The *Précurseur* soon succumbed to the legal attack and its successor, called *Le Censeur,* did not remain unscathed for long. A month after it first appeared in November 1834, its editor was sentenced to a prison term and fined 1,200 francs for articles critical of the investigation being carried out for the Court of Peers.[44]

The local authorities had followed Thiers's admonition to take advantage of their enemies and they expectantly awaited the thanks of a grateful government. At the request of the prefect decorations and rewards were liberally distributed. Cash bonuses were paid to the regular troops and immediate payment was made on claims from government employees who had suffered injury or property damage. The Minister of the Interior considered such matters to have the highest priority since, as he put it, "in financial matters as in government, it is necessary to pay one's debts in order to receive credit."[45] The cash nexus was never far from the official mind of the July Monarchy.

Not all Lyonnais officials were praised, however. The Minister of the Interior agreed with Prefect Gasparin that Police Commissioner Prat should be fired and told him to override the mayor's certain objection with a special ordinance if necessary.[46] Dr. Prunelle was also embarrassed as a result of the uprising. Because he was a deputy from the Isère the mayor was in Paris when the trouble began. He was about to leave for Lyon when he received word from the Minister of the Interior that his trip was unnecessary. Prunelle angrily submitted his resignation as mayor and to his chagrin it was accepted. He later was forced to withdraw the offer in a humilating personal letter to Thiers.[47] In the struggle for political power between the Prefecture and the Hôtel-de-Ville Gasparin had emerged the winner.

Confident of winning major gains the government held elections in June 1834 to replace the Chamber of Deputies chosen in 1831.[48] The results further enhanced Gasparin's reputation. Minister of the Interior Thiers saw this as a great opportunity to further discredit

the Republicans and settle the course of the July Monarchy. If the
desired returns were obtained the great question of public order
which divided France would be answered. Otherwise, he predicted,
the nation faced an uncertain future.[49] Such dramatic declarations
notwithstanding, the outcome was never in doubt. The preferred
candidates were selected in Paris from local lists and the prefects
supervised their election. When he delivered the entire Rhône delegation to "the constitutional cause," Thiers attributed the victory
to the excellence of Gasparin's administration.[50] Within a few
months the man who had established "order" in Lyon was summoned to the capital to serve as an assistant in the Ministry.

II

More than a year passed between the uprising of 1834 and the
beginning of the *procès monstre* in Paris. For the men waiting in
Lyonnais prisons this was a period which began with a spirit of unity
and ended in factionalism and disillusionment. A major reason for
this transformation was the publication of the official account of the
April events written by Girod de l'Ain.

The first months of confinement were filled with organized activities. The desire to divide equitably the gifts sent to the prisoners
brought about the election of an executive committee. Many citizens
of this little Republic passed the time carding wool and repairing the
prison walls. Others attended the lectures of Eugène Baune, a peda-
gogue in any situation. Discussions with the *canuts* filled long evenings. As a group the prisoners read aloud the *Paroles d'un Croyant*
and were said to have been moved to tears by the religious message.
Some composed short political tracts, but no one appears to have
written an account of the uprising. Prison routine was also broken
by parties and celebrations. The most unusual event was the marriage
of a printshop worker to his faithful sweetheart who visited him
regularly during his captivity.[51]

As the investigation proceeded many persons were released for
insufficient evidence. On 10 November, thirty-five section chiefs of
the Society of the Rights of Man were freed, a fact little publicized
because it so obviously weakened the case for a conspiracy. By
late fall the most common form of literary expression was no longer
the political tract but the petition. Whether to the Court of Peers or
the king, the prisoners spoke not only of their own innocence but
also of the hardship imposed on their families. The individual dossiers
in the Archives Nationales are laced with letters telling a common

story: deprived of the father's income the wife and children found
jobs, but their earnings were still insufficient. Clothing, furniture,
and finally the most precious possession in the house, the worker's
tools or loom, were sold.[52] To make matters worse, the local authorities now forbade public events to raise funds for the prisoners or
their families.

The *esprit* dissolved. All the normal petty politics and jealousies
seemed magnified by the prison bars. One person said his life took on
the disagreeable aspects of that in an isolated village. The executive
committee, a common effort of workers and Republicans, was dis-
banded.[53] Even more significant, the mutualists began to declare
their innocence in separate petitions from the Republicans.[54] As the
months dragged on the desire of each individual to protect his own
interests destroyed the unity of the Lyonnais prisoners.

On 24 November 1834, the Court of Peers reconvened to receive
the report of Girod de l'Ain.[55] Its four volumes included a survey of
Republican activity in France since 1830, detailed sections on each
of the insurrectionary cities, and annexes containing portions of
documents cited in the text. Despite all of the paraphernalia of objective research the report told the peers what they expected to hear:
the April events were the direct consequence of a plot prepared by
the Society of the Rights of Man, an organization which had covered
France with a network (*réseau*) of associations with its center at
Lyon.[56] By distorting events there and oversimplifying them elsewhere the *canuts* emerged from its pages as dupes and the city as the
innocent victim of ruthless political agitators. Girod de l'Ain did alter
Counselor Chégaray's original draft, however, since no mention was
made in the report of the alleged connection between Massini's invasion of Savoy and the general strike or the rumor that 4,000 members of the local Society of the Rights of Man had stockpiled 1,800
guns and 36,000 rounds of ammunition.[57]

With regard to the Lyonnais worker movement, the members of the
Executive Council of the Society of Mutual Duty were charged with
cooperating with the Republicans in the formation of the Joint Committee, as well as issuing the common Order of the Day for 9 April.
The *Écho de la Fabrique* was alleged to have been in liaison with the
Republican party and to have incited the *canuts* to revolt. The *Écho
des Travailleurs* was almost ignored and no other worker association—not even the Society of Ferrandiniers—was implicated. The
economic crisis which struck the *fabrique* shortly before the uprising
went totally unmentioned. Little interested in describing the structure and tensions of the worker community or giving an accurate

estimate of the importance of local issues, traditions, and personalities, the report mirrored the government's stated desire to charge only a few labor leaders and to leave the impression that the Republicans had exploited, as the Act of Accusation later stated, "the resources of disorder . . . offered them by the enormous worker population of Lyon."[58]

The results of official investigations have been challenged enough in our own day for us not to be shocked by the report of Girod de l'Ain. Nevertheless, it is difficult to believe that officials at the highest level, men who were themselves veterans of the "conspiracies" of the Restoration, seriously thought that so vast a plot could have been prepared with or without their foreknowledge. In the uproar which surrounded the publication of the report no one pointed out that six months of digging had failed to uncover a single document proving there had been a conspiracy in the form which the government now claimed existed.

To digress for a moment, a more reasonable explanation might have been advanced had the report compared the events of April 1834 with those of July 1830, when the arrival of news from the capital caused trouble in a number of provincial cities. Had these revolts failed, the victorious Bourbons no doubt would have suspected that a conspiracy lay behind them. The opposition newspapers, political associations, and individual leaders—men such as Thiers, Persil, and Girod de l'Ain—would have been implicated. They would have insisted that there had been no plot and they would have been telling the truth. The situation was remarkably similar in April 1834, when controversial legislation (the law on associations rather than the July Ordinances), the reaction of the political opposition (this time clearly Republican), and the news of a major rebellion (regardless of the actual character of the Lyon uprising) resulted in uncoordinated incidents throughout France. These events need not have been links in a seditious chain for the Republican party to be accused of creating a climate of violence by its rhetoric. If this seems too much in the realm of conjecture, it is less elaborate and closer to the facts than the "paranoid style" of Girod de l'Ain.[59]

The process of legal indictment began soon after the publication of Girod de l'Ain's report. The Requisition, written by Marin du Nord, declared that

the simultaneous [sic] insurrections of April were prepared in advance, calculated, premeditated, organized . . . The Lyon insurrection was prepared over a period of three years in a plot which embraced not only Lyon, but also a notable part of France, the principal seat of which was in Paris. Lyon . . . was chosen by the factions as their principal battlefield.

It also stated that the Society of the Rights of Man bore specific guilt because "without it . . . there would never have been the April Days in Lyon."[60]

The Court of Peers issued its formal statement of accusation on 6 February 1835. Analysis of the indictments underlines the importance of the Lyon uprising in the April events. While less than 8 per cent (164 of 2,318) of the total number of persons arrested in France were formally charged, more than 27 per cent of the Lyonnais prisoners were brought to trial. Twice as many Parisians (1,224) as Lyonnais (679) were arrested, but only forty-nine residents of the capital were charged, as opposed to eighty-eight from the second city. Over half of the defendants in the *procès monstre,* in other words, were Lyonnais.[61]

The Act of Accusation listed three categories of offense: participation in armed revolt, provocation to revolt, and complicity in revolt. Including Louis Marigné (the head of the tailors' Society of Perfect Accord) and Carrier, Girard, and Polard (all members of the mutualist Executive Council), a total of twenty-eighty Lyonnais Republicans were charged. Of this number, however, only eleven persons (including three members of the schismatic Society of Action) were accused of having actually participated in the fighting. According to the logic of the government's case, this handful of men was responsible for an uprising said to have involved 6,000 persons.[62]

The report to the Court of Peers, the Requisition, and the Act of Accusation constitute the official explanation of the events of April 1834. J. B. Monfalcon's *Histoire des insurrections de Lyon en 1831 et en 1834* also merits examination, not only because it looks at the Lyon uprising from the standpoint of local history, but also because it is a source frequently consulted by scholars. The discovery of some of Monfalcon's notes and letters among the Gasparin papers proves conclusively that this book was intended to justify the action of local officials.

A founder of the *Précurseur* and the *Courrier de Lyon,* Monfalcon was a self-appointed expert on local affairs. As the physician for the city's prisons he had access to police information and as a member of the Orleanist elite he was able to consult the highest civilian

and military authorities. Monfalcon sought and received the prefect's
cooperation when he undertook the task of writing a history of
Gasparin's administration. In some cases he revised his manuscript
to incorporate the latter's suggestions.[63] Despite repeated requests,
however, Lt. General Aymard did not respond to his questions until
after the book had been published.[64]

Monfalcon believed that the two uprisings were related events,
action and reaction. The difference between them was that 1831 had
been "essentially industrial" in character while 1834 was "political"
and a defeat for the Republican party and its "political instrument,"
the *canuts*.[65] Somewhat in contradiction, Monfalcon also saw the
second uprising as a bench-mark in the history of the worker community. In a telling analogy in his book he compared the *canuts*
to Figaro and in a private letter he referred to both revolts as battles
of the poor against the rich.[66] With his knowledge of the city and
the silk industry Monfalcon was able to perceive what Girod de l'Ain
did not: that the uprising of 1834 was caused by economic and social
factors whose importance went beyond that of narrowly conceived
political confrontation.

Written in great haste and published before the report of Girod de
l'Ain, Monfalcon's account was a calculated and distinctly partisan
version of the events. While preparing the book he admitted to
Gasparin that he personally had never seen more than sixty or eighty
persons in the Place des Cordeliers and considered the number of
insurgents supplied him by the army to be greatly exaggerated. Privately he also used derogatory terms such as *drôles, garnements,* and
polissons to refer to the members of the crowd.[67] In his published
account, on the other hand, Monfalcon magnified the size of the
uprising and pictured many of the insurgents as hardened rebels who
had constituted a serious threat to the regime. If Monfalcon cor-
rected some of the deficiencies of the official record, it is nevertheless evident that he wrote not so much what he believed as what
he and Prefect Gasparin felt the public should read.[68]

There is no adequate Republican or worker account of the Lyon
uprising of 1834. Antide Martin, a member of the Central Committee
of the Society of the Rights of Man, took many records with him
when he fled the city. Considering them to be "documents and pieces
of the greatest importance," Martin assured a friend "everything is
safe, history has lost nothing." But his promised work never appeared.[69] The unpublished *Mémoire justificatif* of Anselme Petetin
describes the uprising as a worker revolt against the injustice of the

silk merchants and the government.[70] Louis Blanc's chapter on
the April Days, written ten years after the events, remains the principal Republican source. It suffers, however, from a distinctly Parisian
bias and often uses Monfalcon as an unacknowledged source of
information.[71] The public in 1834 or 1835 could turn only to the
accounts of Monfalcon or Girod de l'Ain to learn what had happened
in Lyon. As the *Censeur* predicted, the sale of these works enjoyed
great success.[72]

III

Although legal preparations were completed in early March 1835,
the trial was delayed for two months in order to complete construction of a special courtroom inside the Luxembourg Palace. The
prisoners used this opportunity to formulate a defense strategy.

The fifty-two Lyonnais prisoners (the others had fled and were
charged *in absentia*) were brought to Paris in late March. They had
hardly settled in the Conciergerie prison before they were swept into
a controversy over the Parisian Republicans' desire to use the trial
as a forum. To this end they had already asked deputies, lawyers,
journalists, and men of letters throughout France to serve as defenders. Radicals such as Buonarroti and Blanqui were to join moderates such as Armand Carrel and Ledru-Rollin to form a sort of
popular front of the political opposition.[73] The president of the
Court of Peers sensed the potential trouble and issued an interpretation of the Code of Criminal Instruction as giving the peers the right
to exclude those persons not licensed to practice law before the
Royal Court of Paris. Despite the condemnation of the legal societies
of several cities, including Paris, the "legal coup d'etat," as the
Censeur called it, was upheld.[74]

Frustrated in their original plan the Parisians adopted the opposite
strategy and resolved to maintain complete silence during the trial.
The Lyonnais Republicans were furious at the suggestion they conform to a Parisian plan, while the workers felt that silence would
compromise them by preventing them from telling the court the true
facts about the uprising.[75] At a meeting of the defense committees
from the two cities the Lyonnais Republicans shocked the Parisians
by putting the interests of their city above those of their party.[76] As
the report of a police informer noted: "The one and indivisible
Republic has many heretics."[77]

On the eve of the trial the question was taken before the Lyonnais prisoners as a whole. After a bitter debate the Republicans finally bowed to the appeals for political solidarity and agreed to remain silent, thereby abandoning the *canuts* whose cause they had earlier claimed to share.[78] The next morning the legal committee gathered at the office of the *National*. When Jules Favre announced he would defend any prisoner who asked for his help he was driven from the building. Then the Republicans set out for the Luxembourg Palace with the intention of presenting themselves as defenders and forcing the peers to turn them away. Their march was broken up by the police before they reached the courtroom.[79]

The doors of the courtroom opened on the morning of 5 May 1835 for the first session of the conspiracy trial. The public galleries had been full for hours before Baron Pasquier and the government prosecutors entered in their scarlet robes. The initial sessions were supposed to be devoted to a public reading of the Act of Accusation, but for three consecutive days the court was forced to recess in confusion as the peers sought the legal means to counter the prisoners' disruptive tactics.

The contest between judges and defendants is reminiscent of other trials in more recent times. On the opening day the petition of those Republicans seeking to defend their colleagues was denied.[80] During the second day the prisoners halted the trial by shouting for Cavaignac to speak after he had been refused the floor. And on the third day they interrupted one of their own lawyers who was challenging the court on a technicality.[81] After assigning a police officer to sit beside each prisoner failed to restrain them, the peers sought more radical measures. According to French law the presence of the accused in the courtroom (if he or she was in custody) was obligatory. After three days of closed meetings, however, the peers ruled that if any defendant continued to interrupt the trial the Act of Accusation would be read to him in his cell and thereafter his presence would be required only when his case was heard. In the event of a disturbance at that time an individual might be excluded from his own trial. There was pandemonium when this controversial decision was announced. A few peers withdrew from the trial in disgust, the influential liberal deputy Odilon Barrot thundered that such tactics resembled those used by the Jacobins during the trial of the Girondists, and Daumier draw a cartoon of a smiling judge leaning over the bench to tell a bound and gagged defendant, *Accusé, parlez, la défense est libre!* Nevertheless, the ruling stood and the public reading of the Act of Accusation was completed without further interruption.[82]

One legal hurdle remained to be crossed. If every prisoner exercised his right to challenge the competence of the court the trial might be stalled indefinitely. Anticipating this tactic the peers announced that this question would be decided a single time on 20 May. On that day, not surprisingly, the Court of Peers ruled in favor of its own competence.[83]

Having rendered unsuccessful all Republican attempts to sabotage the proceedings, the peers began the trials of the individual Lyonnais defendants. In seven sessions the cases of twenty-two cooperative prisoners (the others having been returned to their cells) were heard in rapid succession. Most of them were defended by Jules Favre. The sessions were uneventful with the exception of the revelation that a prominent prosecution witness ran an establishment of *filles publique.*[84]

The *procès monstre* gathered momentum with the cases of the uncooperative defendants accused of actual participation in the Lyon uprising. The peers were resolved to use force to assure that each man was present when his case was heard. Many of the twenty-seven in this group were literally dragged from their cells for the six sessions from 12–23 June.[85] Once in the courtroom there was a common spirit of defiance. Having chosen a prominent Republican as a defender and been told that he was unacceptable to the court, the prisoners lapsed into silence and even refused to cross-examine witnesses or respond to questions from the bench. Only three times was the silence broken: one defendant recanted and accepted the jurisdiction of the court and two others spoke out to expose a prosecution witness as a police spy.[86]

The trial reached its climax with the defense of the Lyonnais Republicans. The public galleries were filled with those who had come to see the men accused of inducing the *canuts* to revolt. They were not disappointed. Brushing aside the agreement to remain mute, the former Public Hawker Marc Reverchon set the tone for these eight stormy sessions with a speech which concluded:

> You are not my judges. We are your enemies, the enemies of . . . your so-called Citizen King. So if our heads fall, let it be with pride and honor. They will fall with our conscience's cry which expresses our political faith, our vow: *Vive la République!*[87]

The peers immediately sentenced Reverchon to five years loss of civic rights and a 50,000 franc fine for contempt of court.

Almost all the Lyonnais Republicans delivered speeches. Beneath
their hyperbole and dramatic gestures their defense focused on four
points. First, they accused the government of deliberately provoking
a confrontation.[88] Second, they contended that police agents had
organized the construction of barricades in the Place Saint Jean on
the morning of 9 April 1834. A prosecution witness named Mercé, a
former member of the Society of the Rights of Man, was brutally
cross-examined. When Martin du Nord solemnly assured the Court
that Mercé was not a police spy and that only insufficient evidence
had prevented his arrest he was greeted with caustic laughter and
jeers from the defendants' bench.[89] Third, military brutality, particularly during the suppression of resistance in the suburb of Vaise,
was contrasted with the conduct of the crowd. Counselor Chégaray
admitted that the government had come to regret "the unfortunate
incidents which occur in a civil war," but Lt. General Aymard refused to concede that his men had committed atrocities even after
Caussidière *père* confronted him with the fact that his dead son's
body had been used as a bayonet target.[90] Fourth, they stressed
time and again that although they were accused of a seditious conspiracy, the trial was being conducted as though their alleged crimes
were individual and unrelated ones.[91] Ironically, the peers themselves underlined this point when they subsequently decided to
sentence the Lyonnais prisoners before proceeding to the trial of
those from other cities.[92]

Only occasionally did the subject of the *canuts* enter the Republicans' speeches, as when Charles Lagrange explained the party's
encouragement of worker societies:

> I can understand it particularly having seen in our unfortunate
> city 15,000 women working from five in the morning until mid-
> night without earning enough for the necessities of life. Many
> of them are without fathers, brothers, or husbands, and have
> been forced to deliver themselves into corruption in order to sur-
> vive . . . Yes, we have seen all that, *MM. les pairs,* and that is why
> we have said to the proletarians: *Associez-vous!*[93]

At the conclusion of the final speech on 10 July the Republicans
rose in unison, shouting, "We're leaving . . . We shall not return" and
marched from the courtroom.[94] Only the summations remained
before the Lyonnais portion of the *procès monstre* could be brought
to a close.

Because his fellow Republicans had refused to be defended, Jules Favre's final address to the court technically applied only to the cooperative defendants. In reality, however, he ranged over the entire case and accused the government of deliberately misrepresenting what had occurred in Lyon. In defending the mutualists (and by inference the worker movement as a whole) Favre stated his belief that:

> If the Society had not been harrassed by legislation, if it had not been slandered by the merchants, if it had not been misunderstood by the authorities, and if it had been able to find counsel and protection, then I dare say that it would not have made its fatal mistake.[95]

Affirming his continued faith in the future Republic, Favre defended the right of revolt:

> After the Revolution of July the people were under the influence of two fatal illusions. First, they believed that the new regime would occupy itself with their interests. Second, they thought that if they had been deceived, they retained the right to use force to reconquer rights which were taken from them illegally. That is the lesson of the July Revolution.[96]

This speech launched Favre's national political career which culminated in his appointment as Minister of Foreign Affairs in 1871 in a government headed (ironically enough) by his present enemy Adolphe Thiers. The oration also concluded the Lyonnais defense.

The Lyonnais prisoners were the rage of Paris as the peers withdrew to debate their fate. Small lithographed portraits, some the work of Daumier, were sold in the stalls and bookshops along with thumbnail biographies and copies of their speeches. It must have been the reappearance of portraits of Marshall Ney—condemned to death as a traitor by the peers in 1815 and later proclaimed a hero—which made the greatest impression on the defendants themselves. And when several of the Parisian prisoners escaped by tunneling out of the Saint Pélagie prison they likely felt abandoned. The bravado of the Parisians had crippled the Lyonnais at the start of the trial; their cowardice now condemned them at its end.

The court reconvened on 13 August to announce its decision concerning the Lyonnais defendants. Because their sessions had been

secret the details of the peers' discussion of the individual cases, as
well as their reasons for substituting supervised residence abroad
(*transportation*) for the death penalty, are unknown.[97] Thirteen persons, none of them charged with a political offense, were acquitted.
Eight others, including Edouard Albert, Eugène Baune, Sylvain
Court, Joseph Hugon, Charles Lagrange, and Marc Reverchon, were
sentenced to perpetual *transportation;* these men were all admitted
Republicans of bourgeois origin. The other defendants received
prison terms ranging from one to twenty years. Of the five persons
who had been leaders of worker associations, Girard and Poulard
were acquitted, Didier received fifteen, Marigné ten, and Carrier
five years in prison.[98] Popular emotions were running high in Paris
on account of the prison escape, the Lyonnais' sentences, and the
attempt on the life of the king by means of a so-called "infernal
machine."[99] The peers, therefore, resolved to let matters cool and
adjourned until November before judging the defendants from the
other cities.[100]

After the *Report to the Court of Peers* by Girod de l'Ain, the
procès monstre itself was anticlimactic. Both the defense and the
prosecution had committed glaring errors of inconsistency while
clamoring for public attention. The Republicans justly claimed there
had been no seditious conspiracy, yet they conspired to produce a
uniform policy of silence and defiance. The government claimed that
the revolts had been the result of a single plot, yet chose to prosecute
the prisoners as though they were accused of separate crimes. Since
the outcome of the trial was generally assumed from the start there is
perhaps little reason for us to criticize the illogic of their actions.

Nevertheless, the events surrounding the Lyon uprising of 1834
marked a turning point, a critical hinge, in the development of the
July Monarchy. A period of widespread disorder was inaugurated in
July 1830 and until April 1834 the possibility existed that the
Revolution might have a revolutionary impact on French society.[101]
In serving notice that the Revolution was truly over the supporters
of the *juste-milieu* paid a great price: they made certain that the new
regime they served would never again be a popular one.

IV

Thirteen years later, on the morning of 9 April 1848, artillery
salvos rent the air of Lyon. This time they did not signal an insurrection, rather the celebration of a new patriotic holiday. A procession

made its way from the Hôtel-de-Ville to the Place des Cordeliers
where Joseph Hugon, a former member of the Central Committee
of the local Society of the Rights of Man, delivered an oration. At its
conclusion a Liberty Tree was planted in the square and the crowd
sang the *Marseillaise*. That evening the Municipal Council sponsored
a gala banquet.[102] The Lyon uprising of 1834 was now enshrined
in the Republican Pantheon.

There it has remained. It often happens that when governments
appropriate events as their own the real significance of what occurred
is conveniently forgotten. Such has been the fate of the *canuts*. The
Third and Fourth Republics renamed the streets of Lyon—the rue
Gasparin, the rue Prunelle, the quai Fulchiron—to honor the men
who had suppressed the worker movement, while the Fifth Republic
would not permit the film *Autrefois les canuts* to be seen on tele-
vision because it did not reflect properly on the grandeur of France's
past. By way of a conclusion, therefore, let us rescue the *canuts*
from the condescension of this official posterity.

Lyon during the early years of the July Monarchy was a preindustrial city with particular demographic, residential, and occupational patterns—some of them inherited from the Old Regime, others
the result of post-Revolutionary change—that made possible a remarkable level of working class organization. This conjuncture was
a historical moment in the transition from a traditional to a modern
society. Until mid-century life in the city was enough as it had been
around 1830 for the *canuts* to remain in the vanguard of French
laborers. But with a difference. According to Michelet: "Because
this world would not do they made themselves another in the humid
obscurity of their alleys, a moral paradise of sweet dreams and
visions."[103] This may be more than Romantic hyperbole, for, although the state of current scholarship leaves broad gaps in our
evidence, the *canuts* of the 1840s seem less pragmatic and more
utopian than those a decade earlier.[104] Some, such as Joseph Benoit
and his followers, fell under the influence of Blanqui and formed
cells of a secret Society of Families. Others were attracted to the
local Fourierist organization, the Phalansterian Workers. Still others
hailed Étienne Cabet as *Le Père Cabet* when he visited the city in
1844. Indeed, the ideal-type Icarian recently proposed by Christopher Johnson perfectly fits the description of a master silk
weaver from Lyon.[105]

The Revolution of 1848 anchored the *canuts* to the political Left,
much as Maurice Agulhon has described the response of the workers

of Toulon.[106] With the introduction of universal male suffrage the
Rhône department sent four socialist workers and three local Republicans of long-established reputation to Paris as representatives. In
June 1849, the rumor that President Louis Napoleon and the members of his cabinet had been arrested sent bands of weavers down the
Croix Rousse hillside shouting "Long live the democratic and socialist Republic." Ninety-two persons were killed or injured in this
incident. And on 3 December 1851, the *canuts* were prepared to
take up arms to protest the *coup d'État.* Because the garrison had
been alerted during the night there was no violence, but nearly a
thousand persons were arrested.[107]

Two decades passed. On 4 September 1870, the news of the defeat
at Sedan triggered the overthrow of the Imperial prefect and Lyon
established a municipal Republic almost a full day before Paris. The
red flag flew over the city and Hénon, one of the five Republicans
elected to the Legislative Assembly in 1857, was chosen as mayor.
Later that month the anarchist Michael Bakunin and the local members of the First International Workingmens' Association attempted
to seize the Hôtel-de-Ville. The Municipal Council called for help and
the arrival of the National Guard from the Croix Rousse, the *canuts'*
quarter par excellence, ended the socialist coup without a shot having
been fired.[108]

Speaking from his forty years' experience as a *militant* the master
weaver Joseph Benoit wrote: "I say it with regret—but I must speak
the truth—the high opinion I always had of the Lyonnais workers
was severely shaken. I no longer recognized the people among whom
I had lived after 1830 and in 1848; I found them considerably
changed."[109] In explaining why this was so we have reached the
denouement of the story of the *canuts,* the silk industry, and the
city of Lyon.

The Lyonnais worker movement was predicated on the protoindustrial solidarity between the master weavers and their journeymen.
This phenomenon, unusual among nineteenth century artisans, had
emerged directly from the *canuts'* life in the city and their labor in
the silk industry. By the time of the Second Empire, however, the
era of the journeymen weavers was all but over. What little urbanized
unies production remained was performed by women, while the
masters devoted themselves to *façonnes* cloth. The young *compagnons* who had been the street fighters in 1831 and 1834 were no
longer present in such large numbers and without this cutting edge
the masters' mentality was increasingly that of *petit-bourgeois* crafts-

men who believed themselves superior to the factory workers employed in the new chemical and metallurgical industries. While they remained politically radical, the *canuts* had become socially conservative.[110]

At the same time the composition of the city's work force was changing the silk industry received a series of harsh blows. The American Civil War crippled the *fabrique* by the loss of its most important foreign market. Total sales in the United States fell from 138,000,000 francs in 1859 to only 1,000,000 francs in 1865. More than three-quarters of the city's looms were idle and public works projects were established for the weavers.[111] *Façonnes* cloth never regained its former popularity, moreover, and fell victim to what was called "the democratization of taste" in the last third of the century.[112] With urbanized weaving in a state of decline before 1870, rural production suffered during the first decade of the Third Republic as a result of the national financial crisis and a series of poor silk harvests which combined to raise the market price of *unies* cloth. By the end of the century, however, the Lyonnais merchants had staged a recovery by introducing power-driven looms and making silk cloth a mass commodity. In 1898, the *fabrique* had 30,000 power looms, while only 10,000 hand looms remained, for the most part reserved for special *façonnes* orders.[113] The defeat had been long in coming, but the workshop was finally overtaken by the factory.

Lyon herself had greatly changed by 1870. The suburbs of La Croix Rousse, La Guillotière, and Les Brotteaux were annexed by 1851 and by the fall of the Second Empire the city's population was 323,000, nearly double the number of residents in 1830. The vast urban projects directed by Prefect Vaïsse between 1853 and 1864 had cut broad avenues through the peninsula, constructed quais to prevent the flooding of the Rhône, and built the railroad station at Perrache to serve the Paris-Marseille line.[114] More important still, Lyon had become a regional center of heavy industry. Modern factories and housing for the workers were constructed on the left bank of the Rhône. No longer was the local economy solely dependent on the silk industry, as Prefect Gasparin had lamented thirty years earlier. The silken skein which bound the *canuts* and the city of Lyon had come unraveled and the character of local life was thereby transformed.

The heart of the Roman capital of Ludgudum had been the forums on the two hills. In Renaissance Lyon it spanned the Saône. During the preindustrial era when the city and the *fabrique* were synonymous it moved to the Croix Rousse hillside. And with the development of the modern urban center it crossed the Rhône and came to rest on the plain of Dauphiné. This final transmutation was accompanied by the disappearance of the *canuts* into the industrial labor force. This symbolized, to use Pierre Léon's metaphor, "the triumph of the 'plain' over the 'hills' of Lyon."[115]

Notes   Appendixes   Bibliography   Index

Abbreviations

AN Archives Nationales
AG Archives du Ministère de la Guerre
AD Archives Départementales du Rhône
AM Archives Municipales de la Ville de Lyon
AMDG Documents Gasparin

Notes

Preface

1. "Critical Notes on 'The King of Prussia and Social Reform' (1844)," *Writings of the Young Marx on Philosophy and History,* ed. Loyd D. Easton and Kurt H. Guddat (New York: Anchor Books, 1967), p. 355.

2. Girod de l'Ain, *Rapport fait à la Cour des Pairs,* 4 vols. (Paris, 1834) and J. B. Monfalcon, *Histoire des insurrections de Lyon en 1831 et en 1834 d'après des documents authentiques précédée d'un essai sur les ouvriers et sur l'organisation de la fabrique* (Lyon and Paris, 1834). Both works are discussed in Chap. 8.

3. "Social Tensions at Early Stages of Industrialization," *Comparative Studies in Society and History,* 9 (1966), 76, 69.

4. The terms are taken from the essay by Charles Tilly, "Collective Violence in European Perspective," *The History of Violence in America,* ed. Hugh Graham and Ted Robert Gurr (New York: Bantam Books, 1969), p. 18. They are discussed in Chap. 7.

1. The *Canuts,* the Silk Industry, and the City of Lyon

1. Joanny Augier, "Le Canut," *Les Français peint par eux-mêmes: Provence, tome premier,* ed. Jules Janin and others (Paris, 1841), p. 281.

2. G. Brouchoud, "Histoire du couvent des Grand Carmes de Lyon," *Revue du Lyonnais,* 5th ser., 6 (1888), 163.

3. Louis Trénard, *Histoire sociale des idées: Lyon de l'Encyclopédie au préromantisme,* 2 vols. (Paris: Presses Universitaires de France, 1958), I, 12.

4. The standard histories of the early Lyon silk industry are E. Pariset, *Histoire de la fabrique lyonnaise: étude sur le régime social et économique de l'industrie de la soie à Lyon depuis le XVIe siècle* (Lyon, 1902) and Justin Godart, *L'Ouvrier en soie, première partie: la réglementation du travail, 1466-1791* (Lyon, 1899).

5. Maurice Garden, "Ouvriers et artisans au XVIIIe siècle: l'exemple lyonnais et les problèmes de classification," *Revue d'histoire économique et social,* 48 (1970), 29n.

6. Pariset, *Histoire de la fabrique lyonnaise,* pp. 89, 107.

7. Ibid., p. 139.

8. Ibid., p. 177; Maurice Garden, *Lyon et les lyonnais au XVIIIe siècle* (Paris: Société d'Édition "Les Belles-Lettres," 1970), pp. 577-578.

9. Godart, *L'Ouvrier en soie,* p. 279.

10. Louis Trénard, "La Crise sociale lyonnaise à la veille de la Révolution," *Revue d'histoire moderne et contemporaine,* 2 (1955), 8.

11. Garden, "Ouvriers et artisans," pp. 29-32, 53-54.

12. Cited ibid., p. 31.

13. Pariset, *Histoire de la fabrique lyonnaise,* p. 216.

14. Garden, *Lyon et les lyonnais*, p. 572.

15. Cited in Trénard, "La Crise sociale lyonnaise," p. 15.

16. Ibid.

17. Ibid., p. 24.

18. Cited ibid., p. 30.

19. According to Maurice Garden (*Lyon et les lyonnais*, p. 588) the journeymen played the same role in the riot of 1744.

20. Trénard, "La Crise sociale lyonnaise," p. 24.

21. Pariset, *Histoire de la fabrique lyonnaise*, pp. 244–245.

22. Trénard, "La Crise sociale lyonnaise," p. 40.

23. Ibid., p. 43; Garden, *Lyon et les lyonnais*, p. 591.

24. Pariset, *Histoire de la fabrique lyonnaise*, p. 246.

25. Garden, *Lyon et les lyonnais*, p. 580.

26. Ibid., p. 581.

27. Andre Steyart, *Nouvelle Histoire de Lyon et des provinces*, 3 vols. (Lyon, 1899), III: *La Époque moderne*, p. 475.

28. Trénard, *Histoire sociale des idées*, I, 244.

29. Robert R. Palmer, *Twelve Who Ruled: The Year of the Terror in the French Revolution* (New York: Atheneum, 1965; orig. ed., 1941), pp. 156–157.

30. Richard Cobb, *Les Armées révolutionnaires, instrument de la terreur dans les départements*, 2 vols. (Paris: Mouton, 1963), II, 788–794.

31. Palmer, *Twelve Who Ruled*, p. 170.

32. Renée Fuoc, *La Réaction thermidorienne à Lyon, 1795* (Lyon: I.A.C., 1957).

33. Natalis Rondot, "L'Industrie de la soie en France," *Revue du Lyonnais*, 5th ser., 8 (1894), 348.

34. Maurice Lévy-Leboyer, *Les Banques européennes et l'industrialisation internationale dans la première moitié du XIXe siècle* (Paris: Presses Universitaires de France, 1964), p. 139n.

35. Pariset, *Histoire de la fabrique lyonnaise*, p. 303.

36. E. Leroudier, "Les Agrandissements de Lyon à la fin du XVIIIe siècle," *Revue d'histoire de Lyon*, 9 (1910), 81–102.

37. Théodore Aynard, "Histoire des deux Antoines et du vieux pont Morand sur le Rhône à Lyon," *Revue du Lyonnais*, 5th ser., 2 (1886), 114–141, 161–184.

38. Auguste Bernard, "Histoire territoriale du département de Rhône-et-Loire," *Revue du Lyonnais*, new ser., 31 (1865), 171.

39. Pariset, *Histoire de la fabrique lyonnaise*, pp. 38–39; Garden, *Lyon et les lyonnais*, p. 718 (Plan n. 4: "Les Chefs d'atelier de la fabrique en 1788: leur repartition par quartiers").

40. Trénard, *Histoire sociale des idées*, I, 15–16; Garden, *Lyon et les lyonnais*, p. 700 (Section Nord-Est, Croquis, no. 11, "La Localisation des ouvriers en soie").

41. AMDG, t.1,"Rapport sur le projet de réunion des communes suburbaines à la ville de Lyon," 27 November 1833.

42. L. Galle, "La Place Morel à Lyon," *Revue du Lyonnais*, 5th ser., 22 (1896), 185.

43. AM K, "Recensement de la population," 1820 and 1834.

44. *Traboule* (verb: *trabouler*) is a word unique to Lyon.

45. Galle, "La Place Morel à Lyon," p. 186.

46. *L'Écho de la Fabrique*, 8 July 1832.

47. AM K, "Recensement de la population," 1827 and 1834.

48. Garden, "Ouvriers et artisans," p. 31.

49. *L'Écho des Travailleurs*, 1 March 1834.

50. P. Truchon, "La Vie intérieure de la fabrique lyonnaise sous la Restauration," *Revue d'histoire de Lyon*, 9 (1910), 400–434; Pariset, *Histoire de la fabrique lyonnaise*, p. 259; *Le Courrier de Lyon*, 25 January 1832.

51. Pariset, *Histoire de la fabrique lyonnaise,* pp. 269–274; Truchon, "La Vie intérieure," pp. 418–423; E. Levasseur, *Historie des classes ouvrières et de l'industrie en France de 1789 à 1870,* 2 vols., 2d ed. (Paris, 1903), I, 388–390. Created to conciliate the special problems of the Lyon silk industry, the *Conseil des Prud'hommes* was soon adopted in other cities. Because of political considerations, however, one was not established in Paris until 1844.

52. Great Britain, House of Commons, *Report from Select Committee on the Silk Trade* (London, 1832). This body heard testimony on the question of the abolition of the tariff on foreign silk cloth. Among those speaking in favor of free trade was the Benthamite economist John Bowring (1792–1872), who had spent six weeks in Lyon during the spring of 1832. When the Select Committee failed to recommend abolition of the tariff Bowring expressed his indignation in an article in *The Westminister Review,* 18 (January-April 1833), 1–31.

53. Levasseur, *Histoire des classes ouvrières,* I, 48–56 and 374–385; J. P. Aguet, *Les Grèves sous la Monarchie de Juillet, 1830-1847* (Geneva: E. Droz, 1954), pp. xvii–xx.

54. Pariset, *Histoire de la fabrique lyonnaise,* p. 265.

55. *L'Écho de la Fabrique,* 5 February 1834.

56. Louis Reybaud, *Études sur le régime des manufactures: condition des ouvriers en soie* (Paris, 1859), p. 133.

57. *L'Écho de la Fabrique,* 6 May 1832.

58. AMDG, t.l, "Rapport sur la situation industrielle de la ville de Lyon et les moyens d'améliorer," 29 November 1833.

59. *L'Écho de la Fabrique,* 18 March and 20 May 1832, 26 October 1833.

60. C. Ballot, "L'Évolution du métier lyonnais au XVIIIe siècle et la genèse de la méchanique Jacquard," *Revue d'histoire de Lyon,* 12 (1913), 1–52. By 1832, however, the *Conseil des Prud'hommes* was attempting to convince the government to prohibit the exportation of Jacquard looms (*L'Écho de la Fabrique,* 16 September 1832).

61. House of Commons, *Report from Select Committee,* pp. 512, 635.

62. AM K, "Recensement de la population," 1829.

63. See the comparative figures presented in Claude Aboucaya, *Les Structures sociales et économiques de l'agglomeration lyonnaise à la veille de la Révolution de 1848* (Paris: Sirey, 1963), p. 15n.

64. P. Truchon, "La Vie ouvrière à Lyon sous la Restauration," *Revue d'histoire de Lyon,* 11 (1912), 196–202; J. B. Monfalcon, *Histoire des insurrections de Lyon en 1831 et en 1834 d'après des documents authentiques, précédée d'un essai sur les ouvriers et sur l'organisation de la fabrique* (Lyon and Paris, 1834), p. 35; L. R. Villermé, *Tableau de l'état physique et moral des ouvriers employées dans les manufactures de coton, de laine, et de soie,* 2 vols. (Paris, 1840), II, 364.

65. The tax on each head of beef was 21 francs and for pork it was 9 francs. A bundle of firewood was taxed 3 francs and a sack of coal was charged 40 centimes. The complete Lyonnais *octroi* rates are in the *Almanach historique et politique de la ville de Lyon et du département du Rhône* (Lyon, 1834), pp. 186–187.

66. *Le Précurseur,* 3 January 1833.

67. AMDG, t.1, "Rapport sur le projet de reunion des communes suburbaines."

68. Charles Beaulieu, *Histoire du commerce de l'industrie et fabrique de Lyon depuis leur origine jusqu'à nos jours* (Lyon, 1838), pp. 144–146.

69. Published sources such as the *Nouvel Indicateur des habitants de la ville de Lyon* proved far less accurate than the unpublished logbooks of the city's fiscal census.

70. Louis Chevalier, *La Formation de la population parisienne au XIXe siècle* (Paris: Presses Universitaires de France, 1950), pp. 34–40; Maurice Agulhon, *Une Ville ouvrière au temps de socialisme utopique: Toulon de 1815 à 1851* (Paris: Mouton, 1970), p. 39; William H. Sewell, Jr., "La Classe ouvrière de Marseille sous la Seconde République: structures sociales et comportement politique," *Le Mouvement social,* 76 (1971), 33.

71. Charles Pouthas, *La Population française pendant la première moitié du XIXe siècle* (Paris: Presses Universitaires de France, 1956), pp. 26, 101–102; Aboucaya, *Les Structures sociales et économiques,* p. 15n.

72. F. Dutacq, *L'Extension du cadre administratif et territorial de la cité de Lyon de 1780 à 1852* (Lyon: Impr. des Deux-Collines, 1923), p. 2.

73. See Appendix I for complete tables from AM K, "Recensement de la population," 1820, 1825, 1829, 1831, and 1834.

74. Paul Savey-Casard, "La Criminalité à Lyon de 1830 à 1834," *Revue historique de droit française et étranger,* 40 (1962), 248–265.

75. Louis Chevalier, *Classes laborieuses et classes dangereuses à Paris pendant la première moitié du XIXe siècle* (Paris: Plon, 1958).

76. Villermé, *Tableau,* II, 361

77. The addresses of the major silk merchants are listed in Beaulieu, *Histoire du commerce,* pp. 123–125.

78. A. Audiganne, *Les Populations ouvrières et les industries de la France dans le mouvement social du XIXe siècle,* 2 vols. (Paris, 1854), I, 224. Unlike the suburb of La Guillotière and the Perrache quarter, the Croix Rousse suburb had no prospect of attracting new industries. In 1833, Mayor Prunelle wrote: "Its topographical position condemns it to never be anything but what it is today." Cited in Dutacq, *L'Extension du cadre administratif,* p. 32.

79. AN CC 620, Report from the Chef de gendamerie départementale to Minister of War, 1 April 1834.

80. AMDG, t.4, Gasparin to Minister of the Interior, 4 June 1832.

81. For information on "sweated labor" in London see E. Yeo and E. P. Thompson, eds., *The Unknown Mayhew* (New York: Shocken Books, 1971).

82. AN CC 566, dossier Degly, interrogation.

83. Sewell, "La Classe ouvrière de Marseille," p. 34.

84. AG E5 38, Gasparin to Minister of the Interior, 11 July 1833 (copy).

85. House of Commons, *Report from Select Committee,* p. 560. John Bowring reported a 7 per cent average annual profit, with higher returns for new patterns.

86. AMDG, t.1, Chamber of Commerce to Gasparin, 20 September 1832.

87. France, *Archives statistiques du ministère des Travaux Publics, de l'Agriculture, et du Commerce* (Paris, 1837), p. 267.

88. House of Commons, *Report from Select Committee,* pp. 520–525; Lévy-Leboyer, *Les Banques européennes,* pp. 145–148; Arthur Dunham, *The Industrial Revolution in France, 1815–1848* (New York: Exposition Press, 1955), pp. 167–177. The latter offers a bibliography on the technology of silk production.

89. *L'Écho de la Fabrique,* 5 August 1832.

90. Villermé, *Tableau,* I, 361.

91. House of Commons, *Report from Select Committee,* p. 521.

92. Pariset, *Histoire de la fabrique lyonnaise,* pp. 303–304; Beaulieu, *Histoire du commerce,* p. 172.

93. House of Commons, *Report from Select Committee,* p. 525.

94. Monfalcon, *Histoire des insurrections de Lyon,* p. 47.

95. House of Commons, *Report from Select Committee,* p. 533.

96. *Le Courrier de Lyon,* 17 July 1833.

97. Ibid., 12 April 1832.

98. In table 9 one can see that lace ribbon work (*passementerie*), which once had been almost as important as *unies* and *façonnes* production, had almost disappeared in Lyon. By 1830, ribbon weaving was a specialty of Saint Étienne. See P. Gonnard, "Les passementiers de Saint-Étienne en 1833," *Revue d'histoire de Lyon,* 6 (1907), 81–102.

99. *L'Écho de la Fabrique,* 23 March 1834.

100. According to David Landes, the development of textile production has three stages: small urban workshops; the putting-out system; reconcentration in factories. The size of the Lyonnais *fabrique* and the luxury nature of silk cloth suggest, however, that the disper-

sion of *unies* looms was more than a simple case of economic retardation. See *The Unbound Prometheuse: Technological Change and Industrial Development in Western Europe from 1750 to the Present* (Cambridge: Cambridge University Press, 1969), pp. 43–44.

101. *L'Écho de la Fabrique,* 14 and 28 April, 12 May 1833.

102. Cited in Lévy-Leboyer, *Les Banques européennes,* p. 141.

103. House of Commons, *Report from Select Committee,* p. 694; *L'Écho de la Fabrique,* 25 November 1832 and 27 January 1833.

104. *L'Écho de la Fabrique,* 3 June and 11 November 1832, 28 April 1833; AMDG, t.1, "Rapport sur la situation industrielle"; Dunhan, *The Industrial Revolution in France,* pp. 312–313; Reybaud, *Études sur le régime des manufactures,* pp. 196–200.

105. AMDG, t.1, "Rapport sur la situation industrielle."

106. Fernand Rude, *Le Mouvement ouvrier à Lyon de 1827 à 1832* (Paris: Domat-Montchrestien, 1944), p. 49.

107. Monfalcon, *Histoire des insurrections de Lyon,* pp. 40–41.

108. *L'Écho de la Fabrique,* 26 August 1832.

109. Fernand Rude, "Pierre Charnier, fondateur du mutuellisme à Lyon," *Revue de 1848,* 35 (1938), 26.

110. *L'Écho de la Fabrique,* 19 and 25 February, 13 May 1832.

111. Ibid., 25 March 1832.

112. Ibid., 5 February and 1 April 1832; Villermé, *Tableau,* I, 380.

113. Norbert Truquin, *Mémoires et aventures d'un prolétaire* (Lyon, 1888), p. 213.

114. *L'Écho de la Fabrique,* 11 August 1833; AMDG, t.1, Mayor of La Croix Rousse to Gasparin, 19 March 1832.

115. *L'Écho de la Fabrique,* 9 and 23 March, 30 June 1833; Joseph Benoit, *Confessions d'un prolétaire,* [*1871*] (Paris: Éditions Sociales, 1969), pp. 46, 68.

116. Stephan Thernstrom, "Urbanization, Migration, and Social Mobility in late Nineteenth Century America," *Towards a New Past: Dissenting Essays in American History,* ed. Barton J. Bernstein (New York: Pantheon Books, 1968), p. 168.

117. Savey-Casard, "La Criminalité à Lyon," p. 255.

118. Benoit, *Confessions,* p. 67.

119. *L'Écho de la Fabrique,* 11 August 1833.

120. Ibid., 18 August 1833.

121. Benoit, *Confessions,* p. 70.

122. *L'Écho de la Fabrique,* 23 August 1833.

2. The Rebellion of November 1831

1. Fernand Rude, *Le Mouvement ouvrier à Lyon de 1827 à 1832* (Paris: Domat-Montchrestien, 1944), pp. 172–178; M. Buffenoir, "*Le Précurseur* et la Revolution de Juillet," *Revue d'histoire de Lyon,* 6 (1907), 358–362.

2. *Le Journal des Débats,* 8 December 1831.

3. Édouard Dolleans, *Histoire du mouvement ouvrier,* 2 vols. (Paris: A. Colin, 1937).

4. Louis Chevalier, *Classes laborieuses et classes dangereuses à Paris pendant la première moitié du XIXe siècle* (Paris: Plon, 1958).

5. For a definition of "protoindustrialization" see Charles and Richard Tilly, "Agenda for European Economic History in the 1970s," *Journal of Economic History,* 31 (March 1971), 186–188; for a discussion of the ideological effects of "proletarianization without mechanization" see Christopher H. Johnson, "Communism and the Working Class before Marx: The Icarian Experience," *American Historical Review,* 76 (June 1971), 642–689.

6. Peter N. Stearns, "Patterns of Industrial Strike Activity in France during the July Monarchy," *American Historical Review,* 70 (January 1965), 371–394; P. H. Noyes, *Organization and Revolution: German Worker Associations and the Revolutions of 1848 and 1849* (Princeton: Princeton University Press, 1966); I. Prothero, "Chartism in London," *Past & Present,* no. 44 (August 1969), 76–105.

7. A. Audiganne, *Les Populations ouvrières et les industries de la France dans le mouvement social du XIXe siècle,* 2 vols. (Paris, 1854), I, 234.

8. Great Britain, House of Commons, *Report from Select Committee on the Silk Trade* (London, 1832), pp. 554–555.

9. J. B. Monfalcon, *Histoire des insurrections de Lyon en 1831 et en 1834 d'après des documents authentiques précédée d'un essai sur les ouvriers et sur l'organisation de la fabrique* (Lyon and Paris, 1834), pp. 25–26.

10. L. R. Villermé, *Tableau de l'état physique et moral des ouvriers employés dans les manufactures de coton, de laine, et de soie,* 2 vols. (Paris, 1840), I, 377–378.

11. E. P. Thompson, "Time, Work-Discipline, and Industrial Capitalism," *Past & Present,* no. 38 (December 1967), pp. 79–80.

12. AMDG, t.4, Gasparin to Minister of the Interior, 10 June 1832.

13. *L'Écho de la Fabrique,* 28 October 1832; Villermé, *Tableau,* I, 367.

14. "Le Père Thomas," *Lyon vu du Fourvière* (Lyon, 1833), pp. 48–56; *L'Écho de la Fabrique,* 4 November 1832.

15. AMDG, t.1, "Rapport sur le projet de réunion des communes suburbaines à la ville de Lyon," 27 November 1833.

16. For a discussion of the role of cafés in another community see John Money, "Taverns, Coffeehouses, and Clubs: Local Politics and Popular Articulacy in the Birmingham Area in the Age of the American Revolution," *Historical Journal,* 14 (1971), 15–47.

17. Villermé, *Tableau,* I, 367–369.

18. Maurice Garden, *Lyon et les lyonnais au XVIIIe siècle* (Paris: Société d'Édition "Les Belles-Lettres," 1970), p. 311.

19. AN CC 558, dossier Serre, interrogation.

20. See Appendix II.

21. Georges Weill, "Les journaux ouvriers à Paris, 1830–1870," *Revue d'histoire moderne,* 12 (1907), 92.

22. *L'Écho de la Fabrique,* 15 April, 13 May, and 3 June 1832.

23. Carter Jefferson, "Worker Education in England and France, 1800–1914," *Comparative Studies in Society and History,* 6 (April 1964), 353.

24. *L'Écho de la Fabrique,* 24 June 1832; *Journal des Intérêts Moraux et Matériels* (Lyon), March 1833.

25. *L'Écho de la Fabrique,* 5 February 1832; *L'Écho des Travailleurs,* 9 November 1832.

26. Garden, *Lyon et les lyonnais,* p. 313.

27. Villermé (*Tableau,* I, 392–393) reports the *canuts'* average age at marriage as twenty-four to twenty-seven for men and twenty to twenty-three for women. Garden (*Lyon et les lyonnais,* p. 92) has established that it was twenty-nine years for men and twenty-seven and one-half for women during the eighteenth century.

28. Joseph Benoit, *Confessions d'un prolétaire,* [*1871*] (Paris: Éditions Sociales, 1969), p. 69.

29. *L'Écho de la Fabrique,* 6 May and 19 August 1832, 26 October 1833.

30. Ibid., 30 June 1833. See also the issues of 23 February, 9 and 23 March 1834.

31. M. Terme, "Enfants trouvées," *Revue du Lyonais,* I (1836), 14; M. Terme and J. B. Monfalcon, *Enfants trouvées* (Lyon, 1838), p. 28.

32. Villermé, *Tableau,* I, 393; Garden, *Lyon et les lyonnais,* pp. 127–140.

33. AM, série D1, *Conseil Municipale, 1832: séance du 16 janvier 1832; L'Écho de la Fabrique,* 12 August and 21 October 1832; *Le Courrier de Lyon,* 15 January 1833.

34. Justin Godart, "Guignol et l'esprit lyonnais," *Revue d'histoire de Lyon,* 8 (1909), 250.

35. Georges Droux, "La Chanson lyonnaise," *Revue d'histoire de Lyon,* 5 (1906), 129.

36. *L'Écho de la Fabrique,* 9 September, 28 October, 2 and 11 November 1832.

37. Monfalcon, *Histoire des insurrections de Lyon,* p. 27.

38. Villermé, *Tableau,* I, 363.

39. AMDG, t.1, "Rapport sur la situation industrielle de la ville de Lyon et les moyens de l'améliorer," 29 November 1833.

40. P. Truchon, "La Vie ouvrière à Lyon sous la Restauration, 1814–1830," *Revue d'histoire de Lyon,* 11 (1912), 202–204.

41. Villermé, *Tableau,* I, 374.

42. Jules Favre, *De la Coalition des chefs d'atelier de Lyon* (Lyon, 1833), pp. 29–32; AMDG, t.1, "Rapport sur la situation industrielle."

43. *L'Écho des Travailleurs,* 20 November 1833.

44. Bernard and Charnier, *Rapport fait et présenté à M. le Président du Conseil des Ministres sur les causes généraux qui ont amené les événements de Lyon* (Lyon, 1831), pp. 4–5. Charnier admitted that even he was uncertain about the rates for many types of cloth.

45. House of Commons, *Report from Select Committee,* p. 557.

46. AMDG, t.1, "Rapport sur la situation industrielle."

47. *Le Précurseur,* 18 January 1834; *L'Écho de la Fabrique,* 15 January 1832; E. Labrousse (*Le Mouvement ouvrier et les idées sociales, 1815–1848* [Paris: Cour de Sorbonne, 1848], p. 39) notes a general decline in wages in this period. Indeed, John Bowring (House of Commons, *Report from Select Committee,* p. 60) said he was told that wages had fallen "considerably" in Lyon in recent years.

48. Walter G. Runciman, *Relative Deprivation and Social Justice: a Study of Attitudes in 20th Century England* (Berkeley: University of California Press, 1966).

49. Truchon, "La Vie ouvrière à Lyon," pp. 212–215; Rude, *Le Mouvement ouvrier à Lyon,* p. 75.

50. J. L. and Barbara Hammond, *The Skilled Labourer, 1760–1832* (New York: Harper Torchbooks, 1970; orig. ed., 1919), pp. 216–217, Chapter 7 of this classic work, "The Spitalfield Silkweavers," may be read as a control for the present study of the Lyonnais *canuts.*

51. Justin Godart, "Le Compagnonnage à Lyon," *Revue d'histoire de Lyon,* 2 (1903), 443–445. The most recent survey is by Emile Coornaert, *Les Compagnonnages en France du Moyen Age à nos jours* (Paris: Les Editions Ouvrières, 1966).

52. Truchon, "La Vie ouvrière a Lyon," pp. 139–140. The *Almanach de Lyon* for 1834 lists sixty-four local mutual aid societies and comments that many of them are inoperative.

53. Rude, *Le Mouvement ouvrier à Lyon,* pp. 139–140. Fernand Rude has unraveled the early history of Mutualism in great detail. The fact that he owns the personal papers of Pierre Charnier may be said to give him an advantage over other historians.

54. Rude, *Le Mouvement ouvrier a Lyon,* pp. 136–137. Charnier himself lived on the Montée Saint Barthélemy on the Fourvière hillside and employed five journeymen at the time of the foundation of Mutualism. He was, therefore, the rarest sort of *canut:* a master who no longer worked a loom (Fernand Rude, "Pierre Charnier, fondateur du mutuellisme à Lyon," *Revue de 1848,* 35 [1938], 22).

55. Rude, "Pierre Charnier," p. 67. For a discussion of the general economic crisis in France see Paul Gonnet, "Esquisse de la crise économique en France de 1827 à 1832," *Revue d'histoire économique et sociale,* 33 (1955), 249–291.

56. Pierre Ansart, *Naissance de l'anarchisme: esquisse d'un explication sociologique du prudhonisme* (Paris: Presses Universitaires de France, 1970), p. 142.

57. F. Baud, "Caractères généraux du parti libéral à Lyon sous la Restauration," *Revue d'histoire de Lyon,* 12 (1913), 217–219; F. Dutacq and A. Latreille, *Histoire de Lyon de 1814 à 1940,* vol. III of *Histoire de Lyon,* ed A. Kleinclausz, 3 vols. (Lyon, 1952), pp. 38–39.

58. I have placed "party" in the lower case to indicate that I am using it in the sense of the French word *parti,* which connotes a more loosely structured organization than those groups which dominate modern political life.

59. *Le Courrier de Lyon,* 12 April 1833.

60. AMDG, t.4, Gasparin to Minister of the Interior, 11 May 1832.

61. *Le Courrier de Lyon,* 11 February 1832; Rude, *Le Mouvement ouvrier à Lyon,* pp. 258–261, 274.

62. The banker Laffitte headed the first cabinet of the July Monarchy. In March 1831, however, the king abandoned support for his policy of "movement" and turned to Casimir Perier to restore "order" in France. The "System of 13 March" refers to the date of Perier's speech to the Chamber of Deputies in which he vowed to attack the king's enemies, whether to the Left or the Right.

63. Dutacq and Latreille, *Histoire de Lyon*, p. 83; *Almanach Royale: 1834*, p. 537. Approximately 8 per cent of the population of the Rhône department were eligible voters.

64. For a discussion of the role of prefects in the day-to-day administration of a department see Alan B. Spitzer, "The Prefect as Proconsul: The Restoration Prefect and the *Police Générale*," *Comparative Studies in Society and History*, 7 (1965), 371–392.

65. Prunelle (1777–1853) was a veteran of the battle of Austerlitz and a successful physician whose summer practice in Vichy, as well as his duties in Paris, kept him away from Lyon for long periods. Married to the daughter of a silk merchant, he was in the capital at the time of both uprisings.

66. *Almanach historique et politique de la ville de Lyon: 1834.*

67. Prefect Gasparin said: "If Monsieur Vachon-Imbert leaves, the municipality of Lyon will cease to exist" (AMDG, t.11, Gasparin to Minister of the Interior, 3 May (1834).

68. Mayor Prunelle defended Prat on the grounds that as a former *Carbonaro* he would be able to think like a conspirator (AMDG, t.13, Prunelle to Gasparin, 2 March 1834). For a discussion of the problems of the French police system see Howard C. Payne, *The Police State of Louis-Napoleon Bonaparte, 1851–1860* (Seattle: University of Washington Press, 1966), chap. 1. Comparison with the British police in the same period may be made by consulting F. C. Mather, *Public Order in the Age of the Chartists* (Manchester: University of Manchester Press, 1959).

69. Rude, *Le Mouvement ouvrier à Lyon*, pp. 172–178.

70. Cited by F. Dutacq, *L'Extension du cadre administratif et territorial de la cité de Lyon de 1789 à 1852* (Lyon: Impr. des Deux-Collines, 1923), p. 34.

71. Rude, *Le Mouvement ouvrier à Lyon*, p. 185.

72. Ibid., pp. 113, 157, 188–189.

73. AN BB18 1218, Avocat Général of Lyon to Minister of Justice, 6 November 1830; Monfalcon, *Histoire des insurrections de Lyon*, p. 55. For a discussion of the use of public works in the early July Monarchy see David H. Pinkney, "Les Ateliers de sécours à Paris (1830–1831)," *Revue d'histoire moderne et contemporaine*, 12 (1965), 65–70.

74. Rude, *Le Mouvement ouvrier à Lyon*, pp. 193, 203.

75. Fernand Rude, "La Première expedition de Savoie," *Revue historique*, 189 (1940), 413–443.

76. AN F7 4144, Commander Gendarmerie du Rhône (report), February 1831. This document describes the Legion's membership as "for the most part unemployed workers." Fernand Rude (*Le Mouvement ouvrier à Lyon*, pp. 313, 325–335) notes that its leadership was a mixture of petit bourgeois elements (shop clerks, and so forth) and master weavers. One of the latter, Lacombe, owned six looms and employed eight weavers.

77. Rude, *Le Mouvement ouvrier à Lyon*, pp. 241, 622.

78. Fernand Rude, "Les Saint-Simoniens et Lyon," *Actes du 89e congrès des sociétés savantes: Lyon, 1964* (Paris, 1965), III, 334–336.

79. Rude (*Le Mouvement ouvrier à Lyon*, p. 305) estimates there were around 250 members of the Society at this time.

80. Rude (ibid., pp. 319–322) rejects the opinion of some contemporaries that this demonstration was led by the Legion of the Volunteers of the Rhône.

81. Ibid., p. 319; Dutacq and Latreille, *Histoire de Lyon*, p. 87. It was not unknown for a prefect to intervene in a labor dispute during the first year of the July Monarchy. After the November rebellion in Lyon, however, the government abandoned this policy. See David H. Pinkney, "Laissez-faire or Intervention? Labor Policy in the First Months of the July Monarchy," *French Historical Studies*, 2 (1963), 123–128.

82. *L'Écho de la Fabrique*, 30 October 1831.

83. Rude, *Le Mouvement ouvrier à Lyon*, pp. 324–325; "Pierre Charnier," pp. 45–46, 76.

84. After the November rebellion Charnier went to the police to denounce Falconnet and Bouvery as "dangerous men." He also circulated the rumor that they had taken money which local officials had intended should be distributed in the worker community (Rude, "Pierre Charnier," pp. 168–169). In his article "Social Structure and Politics in Birmingham and Lyon, 1825–1848," *British Journal of Sociology,* 1 (1950), p. 75, Asa Briggs has missed the point that Charnier was already fighting a rearguard action by October 1831.

85. Dutacq and Latreille, *Histoire de Lyon,* p. 90.

86. Ibid.; Rude, *Le Mouvement ouvrier à Lyon,* p. 348.

87. Rude, *Le Mouvement ouvrier à Lyon,* p. 348.

88. Ibid., p. 351.

89. Contrary to popular legend and drawings of the period, the *canuts* did not carry a banner reading *Vivre en travaillant ou mourir en combattant.* This motto was coined during the fighting by a worker named Jean-Claude Romand. For his account, see *Confessions d'un malhereux* (Paris, 1846).

90. The 4,000-man garrison still included some units which had proven their incompetence by the retreat of July 1830.

91. Rude, *Le Mouvement ouvrier à Lyon,* pp. 357–358; Dutacq and Latreille, *Histoire de Lyon,* pp. 91–93.

92. Rude, *Le Mouvement ouvrier à Lyon,* pp. 372–418; Maurice Moissonier, *La Révolte des canuts, Lyon. Novembre 1831* (Paris: Éditions Sociales, 1958), chap. 4.

93. Rude, *Le Mouvement ouvrier à Lyon,* pp. 421–423.

94. Ibid., pp. 463–475.

95. Ibid., pp. 469–470.

96. Charpentier had once been a journeyman weaver for Pierre Charnier (Rude, "Pierre Charnier," p. 22).

97. Rude, *Le Mouvement ouvrier à Lyon,* p. 528.

98. Ibid., p. 538.

99. Ibid., pp. 355–356.

100. Ibid., p. 434.

101. Ibid., pp. 426–428.

102. Dutacq and Latreille, *Histoire de Lyon,* pp. 95–96.

103. Louis Blanc, *History of Ten Years,* no trans. given, 2 vols. (London, 1845), I, 541.

104. Rude, *Le Mouvement ouvrier à Lyon,* p. 409.

105. Monfalcon, *Histoire des insurrections de Lyon,* pp. 98–99.

106. *Moniteur Universel,* 22 December 1831.

107. Monfalcon, *Histoire des insurrections de Lyon,* p. 164.

108. The prefect signed his name Gasparin, rather than de Gasparin. I have adopted his usage.

109. AN FI bI 161 (5), personnel administratif, dossier Gasparin; Eugène and Émile Haag, *La France Protestante,* 6 vols., 2d ed. (Paris, 1888), VI, 860–876. There is a brief and inadequate biography by Jean Vermorel, *Un Préfet du Rhône sous la Monarchie de Juillet: M. de Gasparin* (Lyon: Impr. des Deux-Collines, 1933).

110. Rude, *Le Mouvement ouvrier à Lyon,* pp. 611, 619–620, 626. The government purchased 500 guns from the Legion of the Volunteers of the Rhône.

111. AMDG, t.4, Gasparin to Minister of the Interior, 10 June 1832; ibid., t.5, "Rapport sur les differentes sociétés sécretes établies à Lyon," n.d. [April 1833].

112. Ibid., t.4, Gasparin to Minister of the Interior, 30 January 1832.

113. Ibid., 20 March 1832. See Charles Breunig, "Casimir Perier and the 'Troubles of Grenoble': 11–13 March 1832," *French Historical Studies,* 2 (1962), 3–23.

114. Police Commissioner Prat, quoted in Rude, *Le Mouvement ouvrier à Lyon,* p. 605; *L'Écho de la Fabrique,* 22 and 29 July 1832. After the November rebellion, Pierre Charnier was summoned to Paris to present the *canuts'* plight to the Minister of the Interior, Perier. Because Charnier was opposed to a *tarif* it is possible that the minister became convinced that the worker community would accept the substitution of a *mercuriale.*

115. Truchon, "La Vie ouvrière à Lyon," pp. 210–211.

116. The *caisse des prêts* opened in November 1832 with initial funds of 90,000 francs (10,000 of which were a donation from Prefect Gasparin). The government later gave the city an interest-free loan of 150,000 francs for this institution. France, Office du travail, *Les Associations professionelles ouvrières,* 4 vols. (Paris, 1894–1904), I, 252–253.

117. *L'Écho de la Fabrique,* 16 December and 5 February 1832; Truchon, "La Vie ouvrière à Lyon," p. 211.

118. AMDG, t.2, Minister of the Interior to Gasparin, 11 December 1831; ibid., t. 13, Prunelle to Gasparin, 22 December 1831; Rude, *Le Mouvement ouvrier à Lyon,* p. 623.

119. Rude (*Le Mouvement ouvrier à Lyon,* p. 634) states that 1,760 masters became eligible electors to the reformed *Conseil des Prud'hommes.* John Bowring (*Report from Select Committee,* p. 541) said the number was 778.

120. AMDG, t.4, Gasparin to Minister of the Interior, 16 April 1832.

121. *L'Écho de la Fabrique,* 8 January, 5 February, and 22 April 1832.

122. AN BB18 1326, Procureur Général Lyon to Minister of Justice, 7 March 1832; AMDG, t.1, report of Chamber of Commerce, 17 March 1832.

123. AMDG, t.4, Gasparin to Minister of the Interior, 14 April 1832. As Asa Briggs points out ("Cholera and Society in the Nineteenth Century," *Past & Present,* no. 19 [1961], 76–96), there is no evident reason why a commercial center should have escaped the epidemic.

124. AMDG, t.13, Prunelle to Gasparin, 25 April 1832.

125. Monfalcon, *Histoire des insurrections de Lyon,* pp. 133–135.

126. AMDG, t.2, Minister of the Interior to Gasparin, 11 December 1831; ibid., t.13, Prunelle to Gasparin, 14 and 18 December 1831, and 25 April 1832.

127. Ibid., t.2, Minister of the Interior to Gasparin, 21 May 1832.

128. Ibid., 9 May 1832.

129. Ibid., t.1, Minister of Commerce to Gasparin, 27 February 1834. For a general discussion of this topic see Claude Fohlen, "Bourgeoisie française, liberté économique et l'intervention de l'État," *Revue économique,* 7 (1956), 414–428.

130. AG E5 46, Commander Gendarmerie du Rhône to Minister of War, 16 February 1834: "the merchants and businessmen of Lyon have lost the memory of what happened in 1831. Always the same egotism . . . everything for themselves and nothing for the maintenance of order."

131. AMDG, t.2, Minister of the Interior to Gasparin, 5 January 1832.

132. Ibid., t.1, "Rapport sur la situation industrielle"; AN BB18 1326, Procureur Général Lyon to Minister of Justice, 7 March 1832.

133. Monfalcon, *Histoire des insurrections de Lyon,* p. 87.

134. *Le Courrier de Lyon,* 11 June 1833.

135. Quoted by Dolléans, *Histoire du mouvement ouvrier,* I, 69.

3. The Republican Party in Lyon

1. Gabriel Perreux, *Aux Temps des sociétés secrètes: la propagande républicaine au début de la Monarchie de Juillet* (Paris: Hachette, 1931), p. 99.

2. John Plamenatz, *The Revolutionary Movement in France, 1815–1870* (London: Longmanns & Green, 1952), p. 54.

3. AMDG, t.4, Prat to Gasparin, 14 May 1832.

4. Some, of course, were already Republicans before 1830. For a discussion of this question see Elizabeth L. Eisenstein. "The Evolution of the Jacobin Tradition in France: The Survival and Revival of the Ethos of 1793 under the Bourbon and Orleanist Regimes," Ph.D. diss., Radcliffe College, 1952.

5. Fernand Rude, *Le Mouvement ouvrier à Lyon de 1827 à 1832* (Paris: Domat-Montchrestien, 1944), p. 274.

6. *La Glaneuse,* 6 November 1831.

7. [Bibliothèque Nationale] ; Fonds Franc-Maçonnerie, FM2 272, 275, 276, see also, E. Vacheron, *Ephémérides des loges maçonniques* (Lyon, 1875).

8. AN CC 570, Dossier Diano, interrogation.

9. AMDG, t.5, Minister of the Interior to Gasparin, 26 March 1834; ibid., t.10, "Rapport sur les différentes sociétés secrètes établies à Lyon," n.d. [April 1833] ; Louis Blanc, *The History of Ten Years,* no trans. given, 2 vols. (London, 1845), II, 242–243, 245, 247. Gabriel Perreux (*Au Temps des sociétés secrètes,* pp. 77–78) attributes the strength of the Republican party in eastern France not only to its proximity to the border (which he believes made patriots more aware of foreign events) but also to the fact that the Carbonari were never destroyed in the region. The best history of this movement is by Alan B. Spitzer, *Old Hatreds and Young Hopes: The French Carbonari against the Bourbon Restoration* (Cambridge, Mass.: Harvard University Press, 1971).

10. *La Glaneuse,* 25 November 1831.

11. AN CC 557, dossier Granier, Trélat (Clermont-Ferrand) to Marchais (Paris), 19 May 1832.

12. *La Sentinelle Nationale,* 29 June–14 October 1831.

13. *Le Furet de Lyon,* 15 January–15 April 1832; "Procès et defense de Joseph Beuf, prolétaire" (Lyon, 1832).

14. *L'Écho de la Fabrique,* 5 August 1832.

15. I uncovered Petetin's *Mémoire justificatif* in the Archives Nationales (CC 572, dossier Petetin) and have deposited a copy in the Archives Municipales in Lyon.

16. *Le Précurseur,* 22 November 1831.

17. Ibid., 12 May 1832.

18. Ibid., 9 June 1832. The revolt of 5–6 June 1832 began during the funeral procession of General Lamarque, a popular figure among Republicans. It failed to win the support of the party's leaders in the capital and the rebels finally barricaded themselves in the cloister of the Saint Merri church in the Marais quarter. In its final hours only workers from the neighborhood participated. One of them, named Jeanne, was quickly canonized by the Republicans as "the martyr of Saint Merri" Georges Weill, *Histoire du parti républicaine, 1814–1870* (Paris: Librairie Félix Alcan, 1928), pp. 69–70.

19. AMDG, t.4, Gasparin to Minister of the Interior, 19 June 1832.

20. The *Courrier de Lyon,* the bête noire of the local Republican party, was founded on 1 January 1832. Its first editor was the same Doctor Monfalcon who later wrote a history of the two Lyonnais uprisings. The Ministers of the Interior and Justice sent funds to Prefect Gasparin to aid this paper "which has rendered and can yet render such great services" (AMDG, t.9, Minister of the Interior to Gasparin, 22 August 1833).

21. *Le Précurseur,* 11 and 13 June 1832; AM I2 59, piece 51: *Règlement;* Petetin, *Mémoire justificatif,* p. 57.

22. AMDG, t.11, Gasparin to Minister of the Interior, 24 April 1833.

23. According to J. B. Monfalcon, this verdict was due to the influence of "emissaries of the secret societies" on the jurors. *Histoire des insurrections de Lyon en 1831 et en 1834 d'après des documents authentiques précédée d'un essai sur les ouvriers et sur l'organisation de la fabrique* (Lyon and Paris, 1834), pp. 121–122. When the coach bearing Granier and the other "Riom prisoners" reached Lyon it was met by a crowd shouting *Vive la République.* AMDG, t.4, Gasparin to Minister of the Interior, 20 June 1832; *L'Echo de la Fabrique,* 24 June 1832.

24. Some historians have confused Pierre Edouard Albert with the worker Albert (whose real name was Alexandre Martin) who served in the provisional government in 1848. For the former's financial role see AMDG, t.4, Gasparin to Minister of the Interior, 18 September 1832; Louis Blanc, *The History of Ten Years,* II, 244.

25. AMDG, t.4, Gasparin to Minister of the Interior, 26 July, 5 August, and 12 October 1832.

26. Ibid., 28 and 31 August 1832; ibid., t.3, Minister of the Interior to Gasparin, 6 September 1832; *Le Précurseur,* 10–11 and 13 September 1832.

27. AMDG, t.4, Gasparin to Minister of the Interior, 25 September 1832; AM I2 19, La Guillotière, Gasparin to Mayor of La Guillotière, 28 September 1832; *La Glaneuse,* 2, 10, and 16 October 1832.
28. *La Glaneuse,* 30 October 1832; *Le Précurseur,* 29–30 October, 1 November 1832.
29. Without counting the seizures which did not result in a trial, the *Glaneusue* made eight and the *Précurseur* ten appearances before the Assizes Court in 1832 and the first half of 1833. AN BB20 61 and 66, comptes rendus d'assises [Rhône], 1832–1833.
30. AMDG, t.10, Gasparin to Minister of the Interior, 28 April 1833; ibid., Banquet Committee to Gasparin, 27 April 1833; AM I2 19, La Guillotière, police report, 1 May 1833; AN CC 554, inventoire 2, "Arrête: réunions, banquets, et bals publiques," 27 April 1833.
31. AMDG, t.10, Gasparin to Minister of the Interior, 30 April, 7, 9, and 10 May 1833.
32. For every Girondist merchant or lawyer such as Charles Depouilly and Jules Favre one can match a Jacobin such as Edouard Albert or M. A. Perier. The ages of the members of both factions were also relatively the same. Since so many were under thirty-five years of age the question of the role of youth is raised. For a discussion see Anthony Esler, "Youth in Revolt: The French Generation of 1830," *Modern European Social History,* ed. Robert J. Bezucha (Lexington, Mass.: D. C. Heath, 1972), pp. 301–334.
33. AN CC 631, liasse 1, T. de Seynes to Marchais, 27 November 1832.
34. *La Glaneuse,* 1 January 1833.
35. AN CC 572, dossier Petetin, Petetin to Granier, 2 February 1833; AMDG, t.10, Gasparin to Minister of the Interior, 27 May 1833.
36. AMDG, t.10, Gasparin to Minister of the Interior, 12 May 1833.
37. *Le Courrier de Lyon,* 13 May 1833.
38. *La Glaneuse,* 1 and 12 May 1833; *Le Précurseur,* 13 and 14 May 1833.
39. AMDG, t.10, Gasparin to Minister of the Interior, 13 May 1833.
40. AN BB20 61 and 66, comptes rendus d'assises [Rhône], 1832 and 1833; AN BB18 1355, Procureur Général Lyon to Minister of Justice, 18 May 1833.
41. AMDG, t.10, Gasparin to Minister of the Interior, 13 April 1833.
42. Ibid., 15 April 1833.
43. AN BB21 407, Gasparin to Minister of the Interior, 2 May 1833. It is significant that this letter is found in the archives of the Ministry of Justice.
44. Girod de l'Ain, *Rapport fait à la Cour des Pairs,* 4 vols. (Paris, 1834), IV, Annex 55, p. 117.
45. AN CC 613, laisse 2, no. 266, Marchais to Lortet, n.d.
46. Ibid., no. 143, 391, and 395.
47. Petetin, *Mémoire justificatif,* pp. 56–57; "Lettre circulaire: Association de l'Est, Avril 1833: Confidentielle" (Lyon, 1833).
48. Provincial pride was also reflected in Lyonnais literature of the period. See M. Roustan and C. Latreille, "Lyon contre Paris après 1830: le mouvement de décentralisation littéraire et artistique," *Revue d'histoire de Lyon,* 3 (1904), 24–42, 109–126, 306–320, 384–401.
49. AMDG, t.10, Gasparin to Minister of the Interior, 11 May 1833.
50. AN CC 572, dossier Petetin, Jules Favre to Armand Carrel, 5 July 1833.
51. AN CC 557, dossier Granier, Granier to Marchais, 26 July 1833; AN CC 613, liasse 2, no. 43, Ferton to Marchais, 20 July 1833.
52. The Marchais papers (AN CC 614) as well as the dossiers of Granier, Albert, and Petetin are full of such requests.
53. AMDG, t.10, Gasparin to Minister of the Interior, 10, 17, and 19 April 1833.
54. AN CC 572, dossier Petetin, Carrel to Petetin, n.d.
55. Ibid., 9 September 1833; Petetin, *Mémoire justificatif,* pp. 58–59.
56. AN CC 556, dossier Albert, interrogation. Louis Blanc (*The History of Ten Years,* II, 245–246) tactfully explains that "disunion had crept in among the Lyonnais democrats" and that "after a close investigation into the resources of the party it was admitted that

there was no opportunity for an open display of force." Consistent with his tendency to read strength where there was weakness, Girod de l'Ain (*Rapport*, I, 155) states that the sole purpose of Cavaignac's visit was to launch a Lyonnais chapter of the Society of the Rights of Man.

57. Monfalcon, *Histoire des insurrections de Lyon*, pp. 176–179; Louis Girard, *La Garde Nationale* (Paris: Plon, 1964), p. 225; AMDG, t.11, Gasparin to Minister of the Interior, 3 May 1833. The exact number of Republican officers is not given in the Gasparin papers or elsewhere to my knowledge.

58. *Le Précurseur*, 3–4 April and 20 July 1833. The authorities used every opportunity to remove Republicans from office. A battalion commander, Joseph Pujol, for example, was relieved of his duties for having signed his rank along with his name to an article praising the June revolt of 1832. AN BB18 1355, Procureur Général Lyon to Minister of Justice, 25 April 1833.

59. There are many examples in the Gasparin papers of fights between troops and *canuts*. To cite one from another source, in July 1833, a sergeant from the 23d Regiment got drunk and fought with some weavers near the Croix Rousse barrier. A crowd of 150 persons formed and it was necessary to call out part of the garrison. AG E5 39, Lt. General Aymard to Minister of War, 29 July 1833.

60. *La Glaneuse*, 23 July 1833.

61. AN BB18 1217, Procureur Général Lyon to Minister of Justice, 3 August 1833.

62. AMDG, t.9, Minister of the Interior to Gasparin, 4 August 1833.

63. Ibid., t.10, Gasparin to Minister of the Interior, 16 April 1833.

64. Eugène Baune, *Essai sur les moyens de faire cesser le détresse de la fabrique* (Lyon, 1832). For more information on Baune see my doctoral dissertation, "Association and Insurrection: The Republican Party and the Worker Movement in Lyon, 1831–1835," University of Michigan, 1968, p. 76, nn. 86 and 87.

65. *Essai*, pp. 14–16, 20–37, 46, 54, 59.

66. The proposal for a Special Commercial School went beyond the pages of Baune's brochure. After setbacks earlier in 1833 he opened such an establishment in Lyon. *La Glaneuse*, 31 March 1833; *Journal des Intérêts Moraux et Matériels*, March 1833.

67. Petetin, *Mémoire justificatif*, pp. 57–58; *L'Écho de la Fabrique*, 9, 16, and 23 September, 7 and 21 October, 4 and 18 November 1832.

68. E. P. Thompson, *The Making of the English Working Class* (New York: Vintage Books, 1966), p. 248.

69. *L'Écho de la Fabrique*, 8 April and 19 August 1832.

70. "Prospectus: Histoire du prolétaire du XIXe siècle, par des prolétaires," n.p., n.d.; "Histoire du prolétaire au XIXe siècle: première livraison" (Lyon, 1832). Monier was a painter and a former Saint Simonian. Members of the movement attended his trial. AN BB20 66, comptes rendus d'assises [Rhône], 1833.

71. AN CC 554, inventoire 8. This dossier contains interrogations of workers taken into custody during the raid.

72. *L'Écho de la Fabrique*, 24 March 1833; *Le Précurseur*, 18 March 1833.

73. Plamenatz (*The Revolutionary Movement in France*, pp. 35–50) offers a discussion of how the Republican party in general related to this issue.

74. *Le Précurseur*, 28 August, 12 September, and 2 October 1833; *La Glaneuse*, 24 March and 16 April 1833.

75. *La Glaneuse*, 21 January 1833.

76. Joseph Pujol, a member of the Central Committee of the Society of the Rights of Man, was born in 1784 or 1785.

77. "Nouveau Catéchisme Républicaine, par un prolétaire, prix 60 centimes" (Lyon, 1833). The author of the brochure was Antide Martin, a law clerk who later served on the Central Committee of the Society of the Rights of Man.

78. Paul Bastid, *Doctrines et institutions politiques de la Seconde République* (Paris: Hachette, 1945), p. 48.

79. It should be obvious from this that the *Manifesto* did not spring from the foreheads of Marx and Engels in 1847, but came from a long-established explanation of social change.

80. To attack the July Monarchy for its cowardly foreign policy on the one hand and to state that a Republic was a more peaceful form of government on the other is a contradiction typical of Republican thought at this time.

81. Cour de Pairs, *Affaire du mois d'avril 1834,* 15 vols. (Paris, 1834–1835, X, 15.

82. "De la Coalition des chefs d'atelier de Lyon" (Lyon, 1833). Not even Favre was immune from criticism, however. On 18 November 1832, the *Écho de la Fabrique* attacked him for entering a case where back rents were being collected from poor *canuts.* There is an excellent official biography by Marice Reclus, *Jules Favre, essai de biographie historique et morale d'après des documents inédits* (Paris, 1912).

83. If the Republicans sometimes found it possible to overcome class attitudes, the Stalinist historian F. Potemkin has not. In his essay *Lionskie vosstaniia 1831 i 1834 g* [The Lyonnais Insurrections of 1831 and 1834] (Moscow: Archiv Marxa i Engelsa, 1937), p. 338, he is openly troubled by this bourgeois attempt at rapprochement with the "proletarians," He makes his way out of the dilemma with a quotation from Lenin: "There are Jacobins and Jacobins."

84. *La Glaneuse,* 24 October 1833. The Society of the Rights of Man originated as a special committee of the Friends of the People society which was authorized to promote Republican attitudes among the workers of Paris. By December 1832, the parent organization had been absorbed by the newer group. Declared illegal by a Paris court in April 1833, the society continued to operate and sought to extend its influence into the provinces by means of its Committee of Republican Affiliations. By November 1833, the society may have had 3,000 members in the capital. Perreux, *Au Temps des sociétés secrètes,* pp. 65–67.

85. AMDG, t.10, "Rapport sur les differentes sociétés secrètes."

86. Petetin, *Mémoire justificatif,* p. 33. The *Glaneuse* (24 October 1833) denied that true freedom of the press existed in France.

87. *Le Précurseur,* 4 August 1833.

88. Petetin, *Mémoire justificatif,* p. 32.

89. *Le Précurseur,* 28–29 and 30 October 1833.

90. *Le Courrier de Lyon,* 5 September 1833.

91. The disappearance of the financial and administrative records of the local Society of the Rights of Man will be discussed later. Information about the organization in this early period is doubly meager because the police had not yet infiltrated its sections.

92. AN CC 556, dossier Hugon, interrogation; ibid., dossier Ferton, "Aux Sections lyonnaises: 20 décembre 1833"; Girod de l'Ain, *Rapport,* I, 159. The number of votes cast conforms closely to Prefect Gasparin's estimate that, while the association claimed to have 1,200 members, it could only mobilize 300 persons for any occasion. AMDG, t.11, Gasparin to Minister of the Interior, 21 January 1834.

93. "Règlement des sections du département du Rhône de la société des droits de l'homme et du citoyen: janvier 1834." Although the Lyonnais rules were modeled on the Parisian ones, a comparison of the two reveals twenty-six specific differences. Some were due to the fact that the Parisian society was much larger, but others indicate an explicit Lyonnais social program absent in the parent organization.

94. Leonard Richards, *"Gentlemen of Property and Standing": Anti-Abolition Mobs in Jacksonian America* (Princeton: Princeton University Press, 1970), pp. 60–61.

95. AN CC 554, inventoire 5, circular letter dated 1 December 1833. In this notice the secretary of the Parisian Society of the Rights of Man stated: "There is one thing which has been missing until today in the organization of the Republican party in France: that is a means of unified correspondence between the patriots of the departments and the

popular societies of the capital, an association between the provinces and Paris."

96. Perreaux, *Au Temps des sociétés secrètes*, pp. 235–236.

97. Girod de l'Ain, *Rapport*, I, 163; AN CC 554, dossier "Société des droites de l'homme et du citoyen," interrogations.

98. AN BB18 1354, Procureur Général Grenoble to Minister of Justice, 6 January 1834; AN CC 554, dossier Baune, third interrogation; *Le Précurseur*, 4 January 1834; *La Glaneuse*, 5 January 1834.

99. Pierre Angand, " 'Les Tendances égalitaires et socialistes dans les sociétés secrètes françaises, 1830–1834,' par V. Volguine: publication de l'academie des sciences de l'U.R. S.S., Questions d'histoire, 1947," *1848 et les révolutions du XIXe siècle*, 39 (1948), 37.

100. Joseph Benoit, *Confessions d'un prolétaire, [1871]* (Paris: Éditions Sociales, 1969), pp. 52–53.

101. Leo A. Loubère, "The Intellectual Origins of French Jacobin Socialism," *International Review of Social History*, 4 (1959), 415–431; George Morange, *Les Idées communistes dans les sociétés secrètes et dans la presse sous la Monarchie de Juillet* (Paris, 1905). The latter (p. 29) incorrectly states that "the essential ideas" of Communism were "favorably welcomed" in the Republican societies between 1832 and 1834.

102. AMDG, t.10, Prat to Gasparin (report), 21 January 1833.

103. Ibid., t.1, Minister of Commerce (Thiers) to Gasparin, 12 December 1832.

104. Wolfram Fischer, "Social Tensions at Early Stages of Industrialization," *Comparative Studies in Society and History*, 9 (1966), 76–77.

105. Thompson, *The Making of the English Working Class*, p. 160: "Again and again, between 1792 and 1848, this dilemma was to recur. The Jacobin or Chartist, who implied the threat of overwhelming numbers but who held back from actual revolutionary preparation, was always to be exposed, at some crucial moment, both to the loss of his own supporters and the ridicule of his opponents."

106. The police agent reported that the members of his section were given a message from "our good cousin Anselme Petetin" concerning a group of Polish officers in Lyon. Petetin, of course, was opposed to Republican violence. Our information, on the other hand, comes from a police spy whose purpose we may assume was to alarm his employers enough to justify the continued use of his services.

107. Eric J. Hobsbawm, *Primitive Rebels: Studies in Archaic Forms of Social Protest*, 2d ed. (New York: W. W. Norton, 1959), p. 11.

108. *Le Précurseur*, 22 August and 1 November 1833. On 23 November, the first anniversary of the November rebellion, the paper had stated: "We would break our pens if we thought that our words could be interpreted as a provocation to disorder."

109. *La Glaneuse*, 19 December 1833; emphasis added.

110. "Les Principes de la République: lettre d'un prolétaire sur l'association du progrès" (Lyon, February 1834).

111. Lagrange cut the most Romantic figure among the Lyonnais Republicans. For this reason, and also because of his prominent participation in the 1834 uprising, historians have tended to equate him with the entire local party. In fact, he was only at its periphery. For more biographical information see A. Robert, E. Bourlotan, and G. Cougy, eds. *Dictionnaire des parlementaires françaises*, 5 vols. (Paris, 1889–1891), IV, 592–593.

112. "Association du progrès: souscription pour l'instruction du peuple, règlement générale" (Lyon, 1834); AN CC 559, dossier Lagrange, notes of meeting of 25 December 1833. This meeting was held on the same day as the special election for the Central Committee of the Society of the Rights of Man and indicates the rivalry between the two organizations.

113. The Lyonnais authorities at first failed to recognize the influence of local politics and assumed the Republicans were acting on orders from Paris. AN BB18 1353, Counselor Royal Court Lyon to Minister of Justice, 24 December 1833.

114. Petetin, *Mémoire justificatif*, pp. 58–59; *Le Précurseur*, 22 December 1833. For a discussion of the press law of the period see Irene Collins, *The Government and the Newspaper Press in France, 1814–1881* (London: Oxford University Press, 1959).

115. *Le Courrier de Lyon*, 19 January 1834; *Le Précurseur*, 4 and 18 January 1834; *La Glaneuse*, 16 January 1834.

116. *L'Écho de la Fabrique*, 26 January 1834.

117. AN BB18 1343, Gasparin to Minister of the Interior, 20 January 1834 (copy); AN F7 6782, liasse 16, Commander Gendarmerie Rhône to Minister of the Interior, 20 January 1834.

118. AMDG, t.13, Prunelle to Gasparin, 18 January 1834.

119. E. Laurent, J. Mavidal, and others, *Les Archives parlementaires de 1789 à 1860: recuil complet des débats legislatifs et politiques des chambres française, deuxieme série: 1800 à 1860* (Paris, 1862–1919), vol. 85, p. 78.

120. Ibid., vol. 86, p. 201.

121. AN BB18 1353, Gasparin to Minister of the Interior, 18 January 1834 (copy).

122. AMDG, t.13, Prunelle to Gasparin, 29 January 1834.

123. Ibid., 1 February 1834.

124. Ibid., t.7, Chégaray to Gasparin, 3 February 1834.

125. *Le Courrier de Lyon*, 28 January 1834; Monfalcon, *Histoire des insurrections de Lyon*, pp. 198–199; Perreux, *Au Temps des sociétés secrètes*, p. 323.

126. AG E5 45, Lt. General Aymard to Minister of War, 13 January 1834; AMDG, t.13, Gasparin to Prunelle, 16 January 1834; ibid., Prunelle to Gasparin, 10 March 1834. In the latter letter the mayor admitted that Prat had little ability, but commended his zeal and refused to dismiss him as Gasparin and General Aymard had requested.

127. Marc Reverchon, "Lettre des républicains à M. le Procureur du Roi: nouvelle de la France et de l'exterior–publication républicaine" (Lyon, 1834); AN BB20 74, comptes rendus d'assises [Rhône], 1834.

128. Monfalcon, *Histoire des insurrections de Lyon*, p. 199.

129. "La Presse populaire–17 janvier 1834" stated: "Thus, people of Lyon, you do not have the right to read what the rich read." The *Écho de la Fabrique* (2 February 1834) agreed, commenting that the authorities thought the common man was a beast who, if he learned too much, would be a danger to society.

130. For a discussion of the work of this committee see Perreux, *Au Temps des sociétés secrètes*, chap. 8.

131. Marc Dufraisse, "Societe des droits de l'homme: associations des travailleurs" (Paris, 1833).

132. AN F7 4144, Report (December 1833).

4. The Worker Movement

1. *Le Courrier de Lyon*, 13 July 1833.

2. *L'Écho des Travailleurs*, 9 November 1833.

3. *L'Écho de la Fabrique*, 22 April 1832.

4. Ibid., 2, 20, and 27 May 1832; AMDG, t.4, Gasparin to Minister of the Interior, 4 May 1832.

5. AMDG, t.4, Gasparin to Minister of the Interior, 15 January 1832.

6. Ibid., 22 June 1832; *L'Écho de la Fabrique*, 10 and 24 June 1832.

7. Great Britain, House of Commons, *Report from Select Committee on the Silk Trade* (London, 1832), p. 41.

8. AMDG, t.10, Gasparin to Minister of the Interior, 22, 24, and 29 January 1833; *L'Écho de la Fabrique*, 10 February 1833.

9. *L'Écho de la Fabrique*, 1, 22, and 29 July, 12 and 19 August 1832; AMDG, t.1,

Minister of Commerce to Gasparin, 15 August 1832; ibid., Pierre Charneir to Gasparin, 7 September 1832.

10. *L'Écho de la Fabrique,* 14 October 1833.

11. Ibid., 7 October and 9 December 1833.

12. Ibid., 20 January 1833.

13. Ibid., 13 January 1833.

14. Ibid., 20 January 1833. On 30 September and 7 October 1832, the paper had admonished the master *Prud'hommes* to work harder to transform the role of the *Conseil.*

15. J. B. Monfalcon, *Histoire des insurrections de Lyon en 1831 et en 1834 d'après des documents authentiques précédée d'un essai sur les ouvriers et sur l'organisation de la fabrique* (Lyon and Paris, 1834), p. 106.

16. *Le Courrier de Lyon,* 27 January 1833.

17. *L'Écho de la Fabrique,* 3 March 1833.

18. AMDG, t.1, Gasparin to Minister of Commerce, 25 January 1833; ibid., t.10, Gasparin to Minister of the Interior, 14 January 1833.

19. Ibid., t.1, Minister of Commerce to Gasparin, 4 and 18 February 1833.

20. Ibid., Gasparin to Minister of Commerce, 21 May 1833.

21. Ibid., Minister of Commerce to Gasparin, 6 May 1833; *L'Écho de la Fabrique,* 7 July 1833.

22. AMDG, t.1, Minister of Commerce to Gasparin, 24 May 1833.

23. *Le Courrier de Lyon,* 27 January 1833.

24. AMDG, t.1, Minister of Commerce to Gasparin, 27 June 1833.

25. *L'Écho de la Fabrique,* 14 July 1833.

26. *L'Écho des Travailleurs,* 7, 21, and 28 December 1833.

27. Ibid., 25 December 1833 and 11 January 1834.

28. *L'Écho de la Fabrique,* 29 December 1833.

29. *L'Écho des Travailleurs,* 11 January 1834.

30. Ibid., 15 January 1834.

31. AMDG, t.8, Gasparin to Monfalcon, n.d.

32. Ibid., t.10, Gasparin to Minister of the Interior, 27 January 1833.

33. *L'Écho de la Fabrique,* 15 December 1833.

34. AMDG, t.1, Gasparin to Minister of Commerce, 18 March 1833.

35. A document called the "Règlement of the Second Lodge of Mutualism," dated 30 October 1831, is printed as an appendix to Louis Blanc's *Histoire de dix ans,* 5 vols. (Paris, 1848), IV, 493–503. Another *règlement* is published in the Office du Travail, *Les Associations professionelles ouvrières,* 4 vols. (Paris, 1894–1904), II, 245–251. According to Octave Festy (*Le Mouvement ouvrier au début de la Monarchie de Juillet* [Paris, 1908], p. 97), the former document was merely the constitution of the society and not a full list of its regulations. In my judgment both documents are authentic *règlements,* but the latter dates from a period when the society was not only larger but also had a more defined sense of its goals. In fact, it may postdate April 1834 and refer to the revival of Mutualism in the 1840s.

36. Fernand Rude, *Le Mouvement ouvrier à Lyon de 1827 à 1832* (Paris: Domat-Montchrestien, 1944), p. 305.

37. AMDG, t.1, Gasparin to Minister of Commerce, 18 March 1833.

38. AN CC 558, dossier Berthelier, interrogation.

39. Monfalcon, *Histoire des insurrections de Lyon,* p. 218.

40. Ibid., p. 150.

41. AMDG, t.1, Gasparin to Minister of Commerce, 18 March 1833.

42. Portions of the Ferrandinier's *règlement* are found in Justin Godart, "Le Compagnonnage à Lyon," *Revue d'histoire de Lyon,* 2 (1903), 453–456. Jean Alazard ("Le Mouvement politique et sociale à Lyon entre les deux insurrections de novembre 1831 et d'avril 1834," *Revue d'histoire moderne,* 16 [1911], 46) suggests that the Ferrandiniers were founded after November 1831. But Fernand Rude ("Pierre Charnier, fondateur du

mutuellisme à Lyon," *Revue de 1848,* 35 [1938], 146) has proven that they were organized before the rebellion. In any case, it is likely that the mutualists and Ferrandiniers were in flux for several months.

43. Office du Travail, *Les Associations professionelles ouvrières,* II, 254–255.

44. AMDG, t.10, "Rapport sur les différentes sociétés secrètes établies à Lyon," n.d. [April 1833].

45. Rude, "Pierre Charnier," p. 146; Festy, *Le Mouvement ouvrier,* p. 161.

46. *L'Écho de la Fabrique,* 9 December 1832 and 7 April 1833.

47. AM I2 47A, "Livre matriculer [sic]."

48. AMDG, t.10, "Rapport sur les différentes sociétés secrètes."

49. *L'Écho de la Fabrique,* 7 April 1833.

50. "Projet des chefs d'atelier de Lyon et des villes-faubourges" (Lyon, [1832]); Justin Godart, "Les Origines de la coopération lyonnaise," *Revue d'histoire de Lyon,* 3 (1904), 417.

51. E. P. Thompson, *The Making of the English Working Class* (New York: Vintage Books, 1966), p. 66.

52. *L'Écho de la Fabrique,* 3 March 1833. The reference to "proletarians" is also significant. Whereas Blanqui (and the local journalist, Joseph Beuf) used the term to refer to the nine-tenths of Frenchmen lacking political rights, here it is used in a narrower economic and social context. For more information on this topic see Alan B. Spitzer, *The Revolutionary Theories of Louis Auguste Blanqui* (New York: Columbia University Press, 1957), p. 83; Michel Collinet, "La Notion de prolétariat," *Contract Social,* 3 (1959), 192.

53. Thompson, *The Making of the English Working Class,* p. 552.

54. *L'Écho des Travailleurs,* 23 November 1833.

55. AMDG, t.4, Gasparin to Minister of the Interior, 23 January 1832. "Les Croix Roussiens/ ne sont pas les chiens/ Les fabricants/ sont des fainians."

56. *L'Écho de la Fabrique,* 16 June 1833: "Le peuple meurt de faim/ Ouvrez mieux votre bourse à ses travaux sans fin/ Si vous ne voulez pas qu'en un jour de bataille/ Se levent devant vous, grand de toute sa taille/ Si vous rejette encore ci dilémme brulant:/ Mourir en combattant ou vivre en travaillant." For more on this poet and his works see Fernand Rude, "Un Poete oublié: L. A. Berthaud (1810–1843)," *1848 et les révolutions du XIXe siècle,* 38 (1947), 5–19.

57. AN CC 572, dossier Petetin, *Mémoire justificatif,* p. 23.

58. The best definition of "class" in this period comes from E. P. Thompson, *The Making of the English Working Class,* pp. 9–10: "Class happens when some men, as the result of common experience . . . feel and articulate the identity of interests as between themselves and as against other men whose interests are different from (and usually opposed to) theirs. The class experience is largely determined by the productive relations into which men are born—or enter involuntarily. Class consciousness is the way these experiences are handled in cultural terms: embodied in traditions, value systems, ideas and institutional forms."

59. *Le Courrier de Lyon,* 24 February and 17 July 1833.

60. In addition to the *tullistes'* strike, there was a small strike by weavers who had contracts with a firm that sold vests in February 1833. Although they won an increase of 25 centimes in their piece rates, five weavers were later arrested. *L'Écho de la Fabrique,* 17 February 1833.

61. AMDG, t.1, Report of Chamber of Commerce to Gasparin, 30 July 1833 and Gasparin to Minister of Commerce, 25 July 1833; ibid., t.9, Minister of the Interior to Gasparin, 13 July 1833; *L'Écho de la Fabrique,* 23 June 1833. For a discussion of offensive and defensive strikes see J. P. Aguet, *Les Grèves sous la Monarchie de Juillet, 1830–1847* (Geneva: Droz, 1954), p. 370.

62. AN BB18 1217, Procureur Général Lyon to Minister of Justice, 29 July 1833; *L'Écho de la Fabrique,* 1 September 1833; *Le Courrier de Lyon,* 14 July 1833.

63. AMDG, t.1, Gasparin to Minister of Commerce, 25 July 1833; ibid., t.9, Minister of Commerce to Gasparin, 14 July 1833.

64. AN BB18 1217, Procureur Général Lyon to Minister of Justice, 29 July 1833.
65. AMDG, t.1, Minister of Commerce to Gasparin, 12 and 22 July 1833.
66. Ibid., 6 August 1833.
67. *Le Courrier de Lyon,* 14 July 1833.
68. AMDG, t.9, Minister of the Interior to Gasparin 16 and 22 July 1833.
69. AG E5 38, Gasparin to Minister of the Interior, 11 July 1833 (copy) and Lt. General Aymard to Minister of War, 14 July 1833.
70. *La Glaneuse,* 27 and 29 August 1833; *L'Écho de la Fabrique,* 1 September 1833; Festy, *Le Mouvement ouvrier,* pp. 174–175. The local *Procureur Général* did express satisfaction, however, that the decision might teach the merchants a lesson. AN BB18 1339, Procureur Général Lyon to Minister of Justice, 5 December 1833.
71. AMDG, t.1, Minister of Commerce to Gasparin, 22 July 1833.
72. Monfalcon, *Histoire des insurrections de Lyon,* pp. 190–192.
73. J. P. Aguet (*Les Grèves sous la Monarchie de Juillet,* pp. 75–87) has done the most recent research on the Parisian strikes. While noting their size (perhaps 21,000 strikers at their height) he minimizes Republican influence on the workers. Octave Festy (*Le Mouvement ouvrier,* chap. 8) also failed to find specific examples of Republican intervention. Gabriel Perreux (*Au Temps des sociétés secrètes: la propogande républicaine au début de la Monarchie de Juillet* [Paris: Hachette, 1931], pp. 300–304) speculates that there was some activity by the newly-created Propaganda Committee of the national Society of the Rights of Man.
74. *L'Écho de la Fabrique,* 6 October 1833; Office du Travail, *Les Associations professionelles ouvrières,* I, 133.
75. Maurice Agulhon, *Une Ville ouvrière au temps du socialisme utopique, Toulon de 1815 à 1851* (Paris: Mouton, 1970), 131–136; Office du Travail, *Les Associations professionelles ouvrières,* vol. 1, pp. 148–150.
76. *L'Écho de la Fabrique,* 24 November 1833; *La Glaneuse,* 19 December 1833.
77. *La Glaneuse,* 3 and 28 November 1833; *L'Écho de la Fabrique,* 8 December 1833; Aguet, *Les Grèves sous la Monarchie de Juillet,* pp. 94–95; Festy, *Le Mouvement ouvrier,* pp. 250–257; Godart, "Le Compagnonnage à Lyon," pp. 449–450. According to the *Écho de la Fabrique* (6 January 1834), the Union of Perfect Accord was not formally organized until after the strike. The journeymen themselves told the *Écho des Travailleurs* (4 December 1833), however, that they had struck "in the name of the associations."
78. AMDG, t.1, "Rapport sur la situation industrielle de la ville de Lyon et les moyens de l'améliorer," 29 November 1833; *La Glaneuse,* 10 November 1833; *L'Écho de la Fabrique,* 1 December 1833.
79. AG E5 43, Lt. General Aymard to Minister of War, 23 November 1833 and Minister of War to Lt. General Aymard, 28 November 1833; AN BB18 1339, Procureur Général Lyon to Minister of Justice, 5 December 1833.
80. *L'Écho de la Fabrique,* 28 December 1833.
81. *La Glaneuse,* 3 November 1833.
82. Ibid., 27 October and 3 November 1833; *L'Écho de la Fabrique,* 27 October and 3 November 1833; *L'Écho des Travailleurs,* 2 November 1833; AMDG, t.1, "Rapport sur la situation industrielle"; AN BB20 66, comptes rendus d'assises [Rhône], 1833.
83. Aguet, *Les Grèves sous la Monarchie de Juillet,* pp. 95–96, 367–368, 386.
84. *L'Écho des Travailleurs,* 16 November 1833.
85. AMDG, t.9, Minister of the Interior to Gasparin, 7 and 29 November 1833; AN BB18 1339, report of Prefect of Police (Paris), 7 November 1833.
86. AN CC 557, dossier Marigné, *livret.* Marigné's papers indicate that he remained in Marseille until 20 February 1834. He was back in Lyon by March.
87. AN CC 557, dossier Ferton, "Aux Sections lyonnaises, 9 novembre 1833."
88. *Le Courrier de Lyon,* 28 November 1833.
89. *Le Précurseur,* 28 November 1833; *La Glaneuse,* 21 November 1833.
90. AMDG, t.9, Minister of the Interior to Gasparin, 16 November 1833.
91. Aguet, *Les Grèves sous la Monarchie de Juillet,* p. 115. The latter points out the

significance of the fact that the Minister of Justice, not the Minister of Commerce, proposed the bill.

92. AMDG, t.9, Minister of the Interior to Gasparin, 2 November 1833.

93. AG E5 43, Lt. General Aymard to Minister of War, 4 November 1833; AN BB18 1339, Procureur Général Lyon to Minister of Justice, 5 December 1833.

94. *L'Écho des Travailleurs,* 6, 20, and 23 November 1833.

95. Festy, *Le Mouvement ouvrier,* p. 165.

96. *L'Écho des Travailleurs,* 16 November 1833.

97. AN CC 558, dossier Rivière cadet, testimony of numerous members of the Council of Presidents. Octave Festy (*Le Mouvement ouvrier,* pp. 300–301) mentions the Executive Council but was unaware of the details of its establishment or exactly how it operated. One member of the new body spelled it out in his interrogation: "There is also an Executive Council . . . whose function consists of receiving various reports from the lodges, corresponding with the Central [lodge], and the superior committee [the Council of Presidents], which merely verifies these complaints and demands." AN CC 558, dossier Berthelier.

98. AN CC 558, dossiers of Carrier and Girard. Neither man was an active propagandist, however. One of Carrier's journeymen testified that he had worked for him for twelve years and never discussed politics with his master. AN CC 563, dossier Regnier, interrogation.

99. *L'Écho de la Fabrique,* 22 and 29 January, 5, 19 and 26 February, 3 and 25 March, and 1 and 15 April 1832.

100. Ibid., 15 January, 24 February, 3 March, and 2 June 1832.

101. Ibid., 24 March, 13 May 1832, and 14 December 1833.

102. Ibid., 6 October 1833.

103. Ibid., 8 and 22 July 1832 and 24 February 1833.

104. Ibid., 8 July 1832.

105. Ibid., 24 February 1833.

106. Ibid., 16 March 1834.

107. Ibid., 1 December 1833.

108. Ibid., 7 April 1833.

109. Christopher H. Johnson, "Communism and the Working Class Before Marx: The Icarian Experience," *American Historical Review,* 76 (1971), 658.

110. AMDG, t.2, Minister of the Interior to Gasparin, 17 December 1832; *L'Écho de la Fabrique,* 12 August 1832 and 18 August 1833; *La Tribune Prolétaire,* 10 May 1835.

111. *L'Écho de la Fabrique,* 13 January 1832.

112. Ibid., 23 September 1832.

113. Ibid., 17 March 1833.

114. Ibid., 1 September 1833.

115. The government was unable to understand the motivation of the editors of the *Écho de la Fabrique* and later claimed that the paper had been converted to the Republican cause by the Petetin-Bouvery debate. Girod de l'Ain, *Rapport fait à la Cour des Pairs,* 4 vols. (Paris, 1834), I, 173.

116. AMDG, t.4, Gasparin to Minister of the Interior, 24 November and 26 December 1832.

117. Ibid., t.10, Gasparin to Minister of the Interior, 26 March 1833.

118. Ibid., 21 January and 10 March 1833; AM I2 46A, Gasparin to Prunelle, 4 January 1833. A few Saint Simonian meetings were raided by the police and one banquet was canceled by official order.

119. *L'Écho de la Fabrique,* 8 July and 31 October 1833.

120. *Le Précurseur,* 2–3 January 1833; *La Glaneuse,* 3 September 1833.

121. Fernand Rude, "Les Saint-Simoniens et Lyon," *Actes du 89e congrès des sociétés savantes, Lyon, 1964* (Paris, 1965), III, 342.

122. *L'Écho de la Fabrique,* 17 February, 17, 24, and 31 March, 21 April, 5 May, and 30 June 1833. For an account of Rivière cadet's conversion from Republicanism to

Fourierism see "Mémoire justificatif présente à la Cour des Pairs par l'accusé Rivière cadet de Lons-le Saunier, imprimeur sur étoffes" (Paris, 1834).

123. M. Buffenoir, "Le Fouriérisme à Lyon, 1832–1848," *Revue d'histoire de Lyon,* 12 (1913), 444–450.

124. Pierre Ansart, *Naissance de l'anarchisme: esquisse d'une explication sociologique du prudhonisme* (Paris: Presses Universitaires de France, 1970), for example, discusses the impact on the thought of the master weavers' Society of Mutual Duty.

125. *L'Écho des Travailleurs,* 23 November 1833. The Saint Merri cloister was the rebels' last refuge during the June 1832 uprising in Paris.

126. *L'Écho de la Fabrique,* 26 February 1832.

127. AMDG, t.9, Minister of the Interior to Gasparin, 13 July and 10 August 1833. In a letter in the *Glaneuse* on 25 August 1833 the two men stated that the *Courrier de Lyon* was wrong to attribute their firing to political differences: "We loudly proclaim ourselves to be Republicans and we think the new editor has only to make a profession of faith to reassure the paper's numerous friends and put an end to the congratulations of the *juste-milieu* paper." Chastaing later repudiated this statement (*L'Écho de la Fabrique,* 20 October 1833), an act which caused the *Glaneuse* (27 October and 3 November 1833) to sever ties with him and his new newspaper. The resulting confusion has led a number of historians to assume that the rivalry between the two worker papers was political when it was not. In any case, a check of the stockholders of the *Écho de la Fabrique* reveals only eleven persons who can be identified as Republicans; three of them were later members of the Society of the Rights of Man.

128. *L'Écho des Travailleurs,* 5 October (prospectus), 2 November, and 21 December 1833. The paper was registered at the Prefecture on 16 October and its first issue was published on 2 November 1833. It appeared twice a week, on Wednesdays and Saturdays, to avoid direct competition with the *Écho de la Fabrique,* which appeared on Sundays. Prefect Gasparin initially thought he could keep all political material out of the *Écho des Travailleurs.* Given Chastaing's reputation the reason for this optimism is obscure to say the least. AN CC 572, dossier Petetin, Gasparin to Procureur Général of Paris, 13 November 1833.

129. *L'Écho des Travailleurs,* 21 and 25 December 1833 and 8 and 11 January 1834; AN CC 617, dossier *La Tribune,* petition and letter, 15 November 1833. The petition was intended to indicate the solidarity of the Independent Philanthropists with the Parisian Society of the Rights of Man. Because of Chastaing's quarrel with the *Glaneuse* he never joined the local chapter. Although he claimed that his "political and industrial society" had 300 members, there is little surviving information on this organization.

130. *L'Écho des Travailleurs,* 7 December 1833 and 1 February 1834; *L'Écho de la Fabrique,* 1 December 1833.

131. *L'Écho de la Fabrique,* 12 May 1833.

132. *L'Écho des Travailleurs,* 30 December 1833.

133. Leo A. Loubère, "The Intellectual Origins of French Jacobin Socialism," *International Review of Social History,* 4 (1959), 422.

134. *Le Précurseur,* 11 January, 25 February, and 25 May 1833.

135. *La Glaneuse,* 17 November and 22 December 1833.

136. *Le Précurseur,* 27–28 February, 3 and 5 March, 13 and 27 July 1833.

137. *L'Écho de la Fabrique,* 12 May and 23 August 1833.

138. Ibid., 12 May and 4 August 1833.

139. *Le Précurseur,* 21 July 1833.

140. *L'Écho de la Fabrique,* 25 November 1832.

141. *L'Écho des Travailleurs,* 13 November 1833; Justin Godart, "Les Origines de la coopération lyonnaise," *Revue d'histoire de Lyon,* 3 (1904), 411.

142. AN CC 572, dossier Petetin, *Mémoire justificatif,* p. 16.

143. Office du travail, *Les Associations professionelles ouvrières,* IV, 256–257; Godart, "Les Origines de la coopération lyonnaise," pp. 411–412.

144. AMDG, t.7, Gasparin to editor of *L'Écho de la Fabrique,* 30 September 1833. The

paper refused to publish the article on the grounds that it did not print anonymous works. The manuscript and accompanying letter are found in the Gasparin papers.

145. AMDG, t.1, "Rapport sur la situation industrielle" and "Rapport sur le projet de réunion des communes suburbaines à la ville de Lyon," 27 November 1833; F. Guizot, *Mémoires pour servir à l'histoire de mon temps,* 8 vols. (Paris, 1860–1868), III, 496–499.

146. For more information on this topic see Félix Rivet, *La Navigation à vapeur sur la Saône et le Rhône, 1783–1863* (Paris: Presses Universitaires de France, 1962).

147. *La Glaneuse,* 8 December 1833.

5. The General Strike

1. AMDG, t.5, Prefect of the Ain to Minister of the Interior, 22 January 1834 (copy) and Minister of the Interior to Gasparin, 24 January 1834. A detailed account of the invasion is found in Jean-Charles Biaudet, *La Suisse et la Monarchie de Juillet* (Laussane: F. Roth, 1941), pp. 119–202.

2. In the general correspondence of the Ministry of War for February 1834 there is a tattered copy of the decree proclaiming Mazzini's "Insurrectionary Provisional Government." It is dated, "Saint Julien, 1 février 1834." Mazzini never reached the town.

3. AG E5 146, Lt. General Aymard to Minister of War, 1 and 6 February 1834; ibid., Minister of War to Lt. General Aymard, 6 February 1834.

4. *La Glaneuse,* 5 September and 27 December 1833; *Le Précurseur,* 17 June 1833 and 17 January 1834. According to Louis Blanc (*The History of Ten Years,* no trans. given, 2 vols. [London, 1845], II, 221), the Parisian Republicans were asked to create a diversionary incident in the capital. The Lyonnais were likely asked to do the same, but they clearly refused. As the Minister of the Interior put it: "The Lyonnais demagogues have other views and other interests." AMDG, t.5, Minister of the Interior to Gasparin, 27 January 1834).

5. *La Glaneuse,* 4 February 1834.

6. *Le Précurseur,* 8 February 1834.

7. Blanc, *The History of Ten Years,* II, 221–223. According to Blanc, General Romorino spent 40,000 francs in an unsuccessful attempt to raise a volunteer batallion in Lyon. His repeated failures were the principal reason for the delay. J. B. Monfalcon, however, was certain that the invasion was supposed to coincide with the general strike but was launched prematurely. *Histoire des insurrections de Lyon en 1831 et en 1834 d'après des documents authentiques précédée d'un essai sur les ouvriers et sur l'organisation de la fabrique* (Lyon and Paris, 1834), p. 201.

8. Octave Festy, *Le Mouvement ouvrier au début de la Monarchie de Juillet* (Paris, 1908), p. 302; *L'Écho des Travailleurs,* 15 February 1834; AMDG, t.11, Gasparin to Minister of the Interior, 8 February 1834; AMDG, t.13, "Ordre du jour, 12 union, AN 6." The mayor, dissatisfied with the police reports of the strike, had the mutualists' *ordres du jour* collected and sent to the prefect. AMDG, t.13, Prunelle to Gasparin, 6 March 1834.

9. AMDG, t.13, Prunelle to Gasparin, 13 February 1834; AG E5 46, Lt. General Aymard to Minister of War, 16 February 1834.

10. AMDG, t.13, "Ordre du jour, 14 union, AN 6."

11. Ibid., "16 union, AN 6."

12. AN CC 558, dossier Berthelier, interrogation.

13. AMDG, t.13, "Ordre du jour, 14 union, AN 6 *bis.*"

14. Ibid., "14 union, AN 6."

15. Ibid., "15 union, AN 6."

16. Ibid., Prunelle to Gasparin, 14 February 1834; ibid., t.1, Minister of Commerce to Gasparin, 24 February 1834; Monfalcon, *Histoire des insurrections de Lyon,* p. 202.

17. AMDG, t.13, Prunelle to Gasparin, 14 February 1834.

18. *L'Écho de la Fabrique,* 16 February 1834.

19. Monfalcon, *Histoire des insurrections de Lyon,* pp. 202–203; *Le Courrier de Lyon,*

16 February 1834; *Le Précurseur,* 17 February 1834. The latter commented that "the exodus" was "almost univèrsal."

20. *L'Écho de la Fabrique,* 24 February 1834; AMDG, t.13, Prunelle to Gasparin, 14 and 17 February 1834.

21. AMDG, t.13, Prunelle to Gasparin, 23 February 1834; ibid., "Ordre du jour, 19 union, AN 6 *bis*"; ibid., t.11, Gasparin to Minister of the Interior, 19 February 1834; *L'Écho de la Fabrique,* 23 February 1834.

22. *Le Courrier de Lyon,* 13 and 15 February 1834.

23. Ibid., 17 and 19 February 1834.

24. AMDG, t.11, Gasparin to Minister of the Interior, 14 February 1834.

25. Ibid., 17 February 1834.

26. AMDG, t.13, Prunelle to Gasparin, 19 February 1834; *Le Courrier de Lyon,* 23 February 1834.

27. AMDG, t.13, "Ordre du jour, 17 union, AN 6."

28. Ibid., Prunelle to Gasparin, 17 and 19 February 1834; AM I2 47A, *Affiche,* signed by Prunelle.

29. AMDG, t.13, "Ordre du jour, 17 union, AN 6."

30. Ibid., Prunelle to Gasparin, 20 February 1834.

31. Ibid., "Ordre du jour, 17 union, AN 6."

32. Ibid., "19 union, AN 6 *bis.*"

33. Ibid., "20 union, AN 6."

34. AM I2 39B, Rapport journalier de police, 21–22 February 1834; AMDG, t.5, Minister of the Interior to Gasparin, 26 February 1834; Monfalcon, *Histoire des insurrections de Lyon,* p. 308.

35. *Le Précurseur,* 22 February 1834; *L'Écho de la Fabrique,* 2 March 1834.

36. The Gasparin papers contain several references to friction between master and journeymen weavers. In one case the masters were rumored to be discussing cutting the weavers' portion from one-half to one-third of the rate. AMDG, t.4, Gasparin to Minister of the Interior, 12 July 1832. On another occasion a group of weavers walked off the job to protest conditions in some shops. Ibid., t.10, 6 February 1833. Nonetheless, the solidarity among the *canuts* was remarkable in light of the fact that the wave of strikes in Lyon in the fall of 1833 had been by journeymen tailors, and so forth against their masters.

37. Maurice Agulhon, *Une Ville ouvrière au temps du socialisme utopique: Toulon de 1815 à 1851* (Paris: Mouton, 1970), p. 328.

38. AMDG, t.13, "Ordre du jour, 20 union, AN 6."

39. AN CC 558, dossier Durriere, interrogation.

40. Girod de l'Ain, *Rapport fait à la Cour des Pairs,* 4 vols. (Paris, 1834), I, 186.

41. Monfalcon (*Histoire des insurrections de Lyon,* p. 207) remarked on the "tyranny" of the mutualists. In a letter to the Minister of the Interior, Prefect Gasparin said they were "robbing" other *canuts* of their jobs. AMDG, t.5, 21 February 1834. The *Précurseur* (21 February 1834) called the strike "imprudent for the industrial cause" and the *Écho des Travailleurs* (15 February 1834) warned that "the mutualists should calculate the responsibility which they have assumed, for the measure is one that success alone can justify."

42. AN F7 6782, liasse 6, Commander Gendarmerie Rhône to Minister of War, 13 February 1834; AN BB18 1353, Procureur Général Lyon to Minister of Justice, 18 February 1834. The *Écho des Travailleurs* (1 March 1834) listed the names and occupations of thirty-four persons arrested near the Hôtel-de-Ville. Fourteen of them were *canuts.* Out of forty-six other arrests in the city between 18–20 February, only six were *canuts,* a further indication of the discipline of the worker community. AG E5 46, Lt. General Aymard to Minister of War, 21 February 1834; AMDG, t.13, Prunelle to Gasparin, 18 February 1834.

43. AMDG, t.1, Minister of Commerce to Gasparin, 24 February 1834.

44. AN CC 572, dossier Petetin, *Mémoire justificatif,* pp. 60–61.

45. Both local Republican newspapers were ambivalent with regard to strikes. While

the *Précurseur* endorsed them in principle (23 November 1833), it also warned that workers often lost more than they gained by them (10 February 1834). The *Glaneuse* earlier warned the workers that most troubled situations only served the authorities (13 January 1834) and remained silent rather than comment at all on the general strike.

46. AN CC 572, dossier Petetin, *Mémoire justificatif,* p. 62.

47. The letter was signed by Anselme Petetin, Jules Favre (the lawyer who had defended the mutualists in July 1833), Léon Favre (a former head of the Society of Progress), Charles Depouilly (the owner of the Sauvagère factory), M. A. Perier (a Jacobin lawyer who had fought alongside the *canuts* in November 1831), Arlès-Dufour (a businessman and leading Saint Simonian), and Rivière cadet (who had written the Fourierist articles for the *Écho de la Fabrique*).

48. *Le Précurseur,* 19–20 February 1834.

49. AN CC 556, dossier Frézet, interrogation. Frézet, the subchief of Vincent's sections testified to the debate between "those who wanted action . . . to profit from the favorable circumstances presented by the cessation of work, and the others who wanted to operate by persuasion and propaganda."

50. Blanc, *The History of Ten Years,* II, 254–255. It is likely that Blanc received his information about this confrontation from Eugène Baune, with whom he worked on La Réforme in Paris in the 1840s. All of the standard works on Buonarroti give Blanc as the source for the incident. See Armando Saitta, *Fillippo Buonarroti,* 2 vols. (Rome: Storia ed economia, 1951), I, 169; Alessandro Galente Garrone, *Fillippo Buonarroti e i rivoluzionari dell'Ottocento, 1828–1837* (Turin: Biblioteca di cultura storica, 1951), p. 388; Elizabeth Eisenstein, *The First Professional Revolutionary: Fillippo Michele Buonarroti* (Cambridge, Mass.: Harvard University Press, 1959), pp. 100 and 124. It seems unlikely that Buonarroti in Paris could have learned of the general strike and written an unsolicited letter to Lyon in time for it to arrive within the first days of the strike. One may speculate that the letter actually referred to Mazzini's invasion of Savoy, which he was known to oppose and about which the Lyonnais Republicans may well have asked his advise. We know that the local *enragés* had wanted to cooperate with the Young Italy expedition. AN CC 557, dossier Courtois et al., testimony of Racine.

51. AMDG, t.11, Gasparin to Minister of the Interior, 31 January 1834. The prefect reported that the local Society of the Rights of Man had received a letter from Paris stating that any revolt in the capital was likely to fail. This letter was probably written in the context of the decision whether or not to support Mazzini's plans.

52. Blanc, *The History of Ten Years,* II, 252–254.

53. During the general strike Republican leaders from at least two other cities wrote to Lyon to warn patriots there against any rash action. An unknown writer from Nîmes said that Louis Philippe sought to "assassinate the Republic in the streets of Lyon." AN CC 557, dossier Ferton, unknown (Nîmes) to Ferton, 19 February 1834 and Berleir (Montbrison) to Ferton, 20 February 1834.

54. Girod de l'Ain, *Rapport,* I, 182–184. In fact, Tiphaine wrote two letters to Saint Étienne. The first, also reprinted by Girod de l'Ain, was dated 13 February (the eve of the general strike) and stated that the local Republicans were watching the situation closely.

55. Ibid., pp. 320–321. When Caussidière attempted to make a speech during the funeral of a *passementier* he was shouted down by the crowd of workers.

56. Cour des Pairs, *Affaire du mois d'avril 1834,* 15 vols. (Paris, 1834–1835, VIII, 51 (testimony of Journet).

57. AMDG, t.5, Minister of the Interior to Gasparin, 21, 23, and 24 February 1834; AD M "Journées d'avril 1834," pacquet 1, Prefect of Saône et Loire to Gasparin, 22 February 1834; AG E5 47: Minister of the Interior to Minister of War, 2 March 1834.

58. AN CC 557, dossier Ferton, Counselor Royal Court Lyon to Minister of Justice, 25 February 1834.

59. AMDG, t.5, Minister of the Interior to Gasparin, 18 February 1834.

60. AN BB18 1354, Procureur Général Lyon to Minister of Justice, 11 March 1834.

61. AMDG, t.5, Minister of the Interior to Gasparin, 1 March 1834.

62. Ibid., 25 February 1834.

63. Charles Dupin, "Aux Chefs d'atelier composant l'association des mutuellistes lyonnaise" (Paris and Lyon, 1834).

64. *Le Précurseur,* 1 March 1834.

65. *L'Écho de la Fabrique,* 2 and 9 March 1834.

66. *La Glaneuse,* 23 February 1834.

6. The Law on Associations

1. AMDG, t.11, Gasparin to Minister of the Interior, 8 April 1834.

2. S. Charléty, *La Monarchie de Juillet,* vol. V of *Histoire de la France contemporaine,* ed. E. Lavisse, 10 vols. (Paris: Hachette, 1920-1922), pp. 99–100; Paul Thureau-Dangin, *Histoire de la Monarchie de Juillet,* 7 vols. (Paris, 1884-1892), II, 288.

3. Twenty-seven Parisian Republicans were arrested after an incident related to the third anniversary of the July Days. Charged with sedition and brought to trial in December 1833, several of them openly admitted they desired a revolution. Nonetheless, a jury acquitted them. For more information see Georges Weill, *Histoire du parti républicaine en France, 1814-1870* (Paris: Librairie Félix Alcan, 1928), pp. 94–95.

4. A. de Faget de Casteljau, *Histoire du droit d'association de 1789 à 1901* (Paris, 1905), pt. 4.

5. Vincent E. Starzinger, *Middlingness: "Juste-Milieu" Political Thought in France and England, 1815-1848* (Charlottesville: University Press of Virginia, 1965).

6. E. Laurent and J. Mavidal, eds., *Les Archives parlementaires de 1787 à 1860: receuil complet des débats legislatifs et politiques des chambres française. Deuxième série: 1800 à 1860* (Paris, 1862-1913), vol. 85, p. 718.

7. Ibid., vol. 87, p. 396.

8. Ibid., vol. 88, p. 303; Adolphe Thiers, *Discours parlementaires, 1830-1836,* 3 vols. (Paris, 1879), III, 267-268.

9. Cited in Louis Blanc, *The History of Ten Years,* no trans. given, 2 vols. (London, 1845), II, 233. Alexis de Tocqueville, who was writing the first volume of *Democracy in America* at this time, was swept up in the hysteria over the law on associations. Discussing "Political Associations in the United States" (chap. 12), de Tocqueville refers to them as "a government within the Government," an "army," and a "weapon" against the state. Members are called "soldiers on duty" awaiting orders from leaders who exercise "tyrannical control" over them. He suggests that associations are a lesser danger in a democracy where their members realize they are not a majority, but finds a considerable threat in Europe because "they consider themselves . . . the legislative and executive council of the people who are unable to speak for themselves." Having supported the abridgement of the right of association in 1834, de Tocqueville had altered his opinion by the time he published his second volume in 1840. In the latter (chap. 5) he condemns the desire of European governments to limit freedom of association and declares this a risk which all free societies must take. For an interesting comparison of the two volumes see Seymour Drescher, "Tocqueville's Two 'Democracies,' " *Journal of the History of Ideas,* 25 (1964), 201–216.

10. *Archives parlementaires,* vol. 87, p. 401. As early as November 1833, d'Argout had warned of "a Republican conspiracy on the workers." AMDG, t.9, Minister of the Interior to Gasparin, 19 November 1833.

11. *Archives parlementaires,* vol. 87, p. 623.

12. Thiers, *Discours parlementaires,* II, 256.

13. *Archives parlementaires,* vol. 87, pp. 392–395 and 622–624.

14. Ibid., p. 394.

15. *Le Courrier de Lyon,* 12 March 1834.

16. Cited by Justin Godart, "Les journées d'avril 1834 à Lyon," *La Révolution de 1848*, 30 (1934), 134.

17. *Archives parlementaire,* vol. 87, p. 401.

18. Ibid., pp. 410–412.

19. Thiers, *Discours parlementaire,* II, 359.

20. *Le Courrier de Lyon,* 29 March 1834.

21. "Chronique de la quinzaine," *Revue des Deux Mondes,* 31 (March 1834).

22. *La Glaneuse,* 4 March 1834.

23. *L'Écho des Travailleurs,* 8 March 1834.

24. *L'Écho de la Fabrique,* 9 March 1834.

25. *Le Précurseur,* 11 March 1834.

26. AMDG, t.11, Gasparin to Minister of the Interior, 24 March 1834; AN BB20 74: Comptes rendus d'assises [Rhône], 1834; AN CC 556, dossier Albert, interrogation and miscellaneous papers; AD M4 258, dossier Granier, report dated 10 March 1834; *La Glaneuse,* 26 March 1834.

27. AMDG, t.11, Gasparin to Minister of the Interior, 24 March 1834; *Le Précurseur,* 28 March 1834.

28. "Le Comité central du département du Rhône: Aux citoyens composant les sections (Lyon, 15 Germinal, AN 42 de l'ère républicaine [4 April 1834])"; AMDG, t.11, Gasparin to Minister of the Interior, 24 March 1834. The prefect noted: "The members recall that they have contributed ceaselessly for a year."

29. AMDG, t.11, Gasparin to Minister of the Interior, 30 March 1834.

30. The loss of the records of the Lyonnais Society of the Rights of Man makes it difficult to estimate the size of its membership. Two documents suggest a figure around 1,600 persons. First, in reporting on the meeting of 21 March, Prefect Gasparin stated that only sixty-four of the eighty-three section chiefs were present (AMDG, t.11, Gasparin to Minister of the Interior, 22 March 1834). Taking the maximum of twenty persons per section this would indicate no more than 1,600 members. Second, the Section Chief Frêzet stated that normal monthly dues came to 800 francs (AN CC 557, dossier Frêzet, interrogation). At the known monthly rate of fifty centimes per member this works out to 1,600 members.

It appears that membership in the Society reached a peak in January when the Public Hawkers episode made it seem that the Republicans could operate with impunity. The open structure of the association at this time is suggested by the fact that Frêzet became a section chief almost as soon as he joined. Although the government would later argue that the ranks of the Society of the Rights of Man swelled with disgruntled mutualists after the failure of the general strike, it appears that the opposite was true. In the testimony of persons arrested after the April uprising there is a recurrent theme: an individual joined the association in December 1833 or January 1834, became alarmed at the action of the militants during the general strike, and quit attending his section in March because of the impending law on associations. To be sure, such a defense is understandable in the light of the uprising, but it is too frequently found to be pure fiction. The cotton weaver Jean Sic, for example, said that he joined the Society in January, but resigned in March because it had not found him work as he had been lead to expect. AN CC 557, dossier Sic, interrogation.

31. AN CC 557, dossier Frêzet, interrogation; AMDG, t.11, Gasparin to Minister of the Interior, 22 March 1834.

32. AMDG, t.11, Gasparin to Minister of the Interior, 17, 22, and 25 March, and 1 April 1834. In his letter of 22 March, the prefect states that the Intrepid Knights were founded on 10 February by a member of Vincent's section named Chabert. This individual was alleged to have participated in the incident in front of the Hôtel-de-Ville on 18 February. According to Gabriel Perreux (*Aux Temps des sociétés secrètes: la propagande républicaine au début de la Monarchie de Juillet* [Paris: Hachette, 1931], p. 242) a Society of Action was formed in Paris in July 1833 after a split between militant and moderate Republicans

in the capital. He implies that the Lyonnais and Parisian Societies of Action were somehow related, but offers no evidence on this point. Since the Society of the Rights of Man itself originated with a schism in the Help-Yourself (Aide-Toi) Society, there is no reason why separate, unrelated Societies of Action could not have been formed in Paris and Lyon. In time they might have united, but there is no evidence to prove that this had occurred before April 1834.

33. AMDG, t.11, Gasparin to Minister of the Interior, 19 March 1834.

34. "Société des droits de l'homme, comité de correspondence générale et d'affiliations républicaines: Aux sections lyonnais (Pluvoise, AN 42 de l'ère républicaine [3 March 1834])."

35. AMDG, t.11, Gasparin to Minister of the Interior, 17 March 1834.

36. Ibid., 1, 2, and 4 April 1834.

37. One member of the Central Committee, Antide Martin, later explained the decision: "at that time certain men who will be unmasked later were causing trouble in the association. The committee of which I was a member wanted to give its resignation solely to destroy the influence of the *agents provocateurs* who existed in the society." AN CC 556, dossier Martin, interrogation.

38. Girod de l'Ain, *Rapport fait à la Cour des Pairs*, 4 vols. (Paris, 1834), I, 204.

39. "Le Comité central du département du Rhône: Aux citoyens composant les sections."

40. AMDG, t.11, Gasparin to Minister of the Interior, 30 March 1834.

41. Ibid., 24 March 1834.

42. Ibid., 30 March 1834; AM I2 39B, Rapport journalier de police, 3–4 and 6–7 April 1834. All previous accounts of the Lyon uprising of April 1834 have failed to mention the economic crisis which played such an important role in creating a climate of violence.

43. AM I2 39B, Rapport journalier de police, 23–24 March and 3–4 April 1834.

44. Ibid., 20–21, 28–29 March and 2–3, 3–4 April 1834.

45. AMDG, t.11, Gasparin to Minister of the Interior, 4 April 1834.

46. AM I2 39B, Rapport journalier de police, 2–3 April 1834.

47. Ibid., 3–4 April 1834. The local police strained their imaginations trying to discover Republican machinations behind these worker protests. In his report dated 9–10 March, one officer stated that four men dressed in black hats and wearing long black beards had been seen in the shadows of the Hôtel-de-Ville. It was rumored, so he said, "these men were the heads of the Society of the Rights of Man."

48. Cour des Pairs, *Affaire du mois d'avril 1834*, 15 vols. (Paris, 1834–1835), X, 104–105.

49. AN CC 558, information générale, testimony of Douchet; Octave Festy, *Le Mouvement ouvrier au début de la Monarchie de Juillet, 1830–1834* (Paris, 1908), p. 321.

50. AN CC 558, information générale, letter to Procureur du Roi, 1 April 1834.

51. AG E5 49, Lt. General Aymard to Minister of War, 3 April 1834. The authorities were aware of the fact that the mutualists hoped to "intimidate the judges." Perhaps because such gatherings in front of the Palais du Justice were a local custom they neglected to take special precautions on the 5th. This was a serious mistake because the regular contingent of four guards was unable to control the crowd.

52. *Le Précurseur*, 4 April 1834.

53. Activity in the worker community, too, argues against the existence of a seditious conspiracy. In late March journeymen cobblers staged a short strike for higher wages and the thread dyers were on strike for better pay when the uprising began. AM I2 39B, Rapport journalier de police, 20–21, 21–22 March and 4–5 April 1834.

54. AN CC 558, information générale, Police Commissioner Prat to Gasparin, 20 May 1834.

55. Another list of possible participants is found in Festy, *Le Mouvement ouvrier*, p. 321.

56. The Free Men were a small Republican society founded by a café owner named François Gauthier in the Croix Rousse suburb.

57. It is impossible to know whether these two societies still existed. After the failure

of the *Écho des Travailleurs*, Marius Chastaing, the founder of the Independent Philanthropists, dropped out of sight until after the April uprising. If the Society of Progress was defunct, the Ferrandiniers' delegate, Didier, had been a member and could have kept his friends informed of its activities.

58. AN CC 572, dossier Petetin, *Mémoire justificatif*, pp. 63–64. Prefect Gasparin reported that Petetin attended a meeting of "the Republican committee" and that he was physically attacked for advocating moderation. AMDG, t.11, Gasparin to Minister of the Interior, 3 April 1834.

59. *La Tribune*, 5 April 1834.

60. Two sources suggest that the national demonstrations were planned for Sunday, 13 April. See J. B. Monfalcon, *Histoire des insurrections de Lyon en 1831 et en 1834 d'après des documents authentiques précédée d'un essai sur les ouvriers et sur l'organisation de la fabrique* (Lyon and Paris, 1834), pp. 221–222 and Lucien de la Hodde, *Histoire des sociétés secrètes du parti republicaine de 1830 à 1848* (Paris, 1850), p. 180. Information received from Chalons-sur-Saône mentions a "day of movement" was to take place before the 18th. AN F7 6782, liasse 16, Commander Gendarmerie Rhône to Minister of the Interior, 4 April 1834. Prefect Gasparin predicted that the Republicans would try to persuade the worker associations to join their demonstrations, but at no time did he mention a specific date. AMDG, t.11, Gasparin to Minister of the Interior, 2 April 1834.

61. *Le Précurseur*, 6 April 1834; Monfalcon, *Histoire des insurrections de Lyon*, pp. 214–218.

62. AMDG, t.11, Gasparin to Minister of the Interior, 5 and 8 April 1834.

63. Ibid., 6 April 1834; *Le Courrier de Lyon*, 6 April 1834. The prefect actually wrote a public letter of apology to the newspaper and said that he had counted on the mutualists to maintain order themselves. He also vowed that he would not make the same mistake twice.

64. AG E5 49, Lt. General Aymard to Minister of War, 5 April 1834; AG E5 51, Minister of War to Lt. General Aymard, 8 April 1834.

65. AM I2 39B, Rapport journalier de police, 7–8 April 1834; AN CC 620, Commander Gendarmerie Rhône to Minister of the Interior, 7 April 1834; AG E5 49, Lt. General Aymard to Minister of War, 7 April 1834; Monfalcon, *Histoire des insurrections de Lyon*, p. 218.

66. AN F7 4144, Gendarmerie report dated December 1833; AMDG, t.5, Minister of the Interior to Gasparin, 16 January, 3 and 15 April 1834; AMDG, t.11, Gasparin to Minister of the Interior, 29 March 1834; AG E5 146, Minister of War to Lt. General Aymard, 1 March 1834; AG E5 147, Lt. General Aymard to Minister of War, 26 March 1834. The work by P. Montagne, *Le Comportement politique de l'armée à Lyon sous le Monarchie de Juillet et la Seconde République* (Paris: Librairie Générale de Droit et de Jurisprudence, 1966) disappointingly offers only three pages (pp. 186–189) on this important question.

67. "Revue militaire: le régiment ordonné d'obéir" (Lyon, 1834). The government considered this brochure so seditious that is sentenced its author, Sylvain Court, to a year in prison and a fine of 3,000 francs. AN BB20 74, Comptes rendus d'assises [Rhône], 1834; AG E5 49, Lt. General Aymard to Minister of War, 6 April 1834.

68. AG E5 49, "État de la garnison de Lyon à l'époque des événements d'avril."

69. Petetin, *Mémoire justificatif*, pp. 67–68. The Counselor of the Royal Court, Chégaray, was without doubt a member of this group. One may speculate to what extent the rough treatment he had received from the crowd on the 5th influenced his desire for firmness on the 9th. Louis Blanc (*The History of Ten Years*, II, 257) voices the Republican opinion that Chégaray hoped for a military confrontation.

70. AMDG, t.5, Minister of the Interior to Gasparin, 9 April 1834 (telegraph message). The Minister of the Interior had made similar statements in two letters to Gasparin which were written in Paris on 8 April 1834.

71. AG E5 49, Lt. General Aymard to Minister of War, 8 April 1834.

72. Neil S. Smelser, *Theory of Collective Behavior* (New York: The Free Press, 1962), p. 250.

73. *Le Journal de Commerce de Lyon,* 9 April 1834.

74. *Le Précurseur,* 8 April 1834.

75. AN CC 559, dossier Ayel, interrogation. The journeyman cobbler Pierre Ayel testified that the leaders of the Society of Perfect Accord ordered him to attend the demonstration in the Place Saint Jean on the morning of 9 April.

76. AN CC 558, information générale, testimony of Pierre Charnier and Douchet.

77. AN CC 556, dossiers Richeme and Miciol, interrogations; AN CC 557, dossiers Morel and Courtois, interrogations; Petetin, *Mémoire justificatif,* p. 69. According to Petetin, he received a visit from Eugène Baune and Antide Martin of the Central Committee of the Society of the Rights of Man shortly after his meeting with Prefect Gasparin. The two men informed him of the group's plans and when he suggested that they would be wiser to cancel the demonstrations they said they agreed but that this was impossible under the circumstances.

78. Despite the Republican bravado about citizens arming themselves, the authorities failed to discover a single cache of weapons before, during, or after the uprising. Frêzet, the subchief of Vincent's militant section, admitted hearing talk of hidden guns but said that he had never seen any and did not know if they actually existed. AN CC 556, dossier Frêzet, interrogation. Another section chief named Mercé, who may have been a police informer, said that whenever he asked the Central Committee about weapons he always received the same answer: "It isn't wise to talk about that. Keep calm." Mercé was convinced that none existed. AN CC dossier Mercé, interrogation.

79. A moderate section chief named Offrey witnessed a confrontation which occurred sometime during the morning of 9 April: "as the situation became more and more serious, some of the exalted members of the society entered the meeting of the Central Committee fully armed . . . Citizen Antide Martin spoke to them and observed that those who wanted to meet force with force would compromise themselves and those around them. The militants responded energetically that the time had come to put an end to such talk. 'For a long time,' they said, 'you have promised that as soon as the authorities violated our rights we would take to the streets. They're killing our brothers. Listen to the shooting!' The members of the committee, seeing how far things had come and fearing that they could no longer impose their will, gave in." AN CC 557, dossier Offrey, interrogation. Louis Blanc (*The History of Ten Years,* II, 258-259) presents an account of this meeting which is remarkably similar to Offrey's.

80. For the importance of triggering incidents in riot situations see George Lefebvre, "Foules révolutionnaires," *Études sur la Révolution française* (Paris: Presses Universitaires de France, 1954), p. 278.

81. Smelser, *Theory of Collective Behavior,* pp. 237-238.

82. Adolphe Sala, *Les Ouvriers lyonnaise en 1834* (Paris, 1834), p. 43.

7. The April Uprising

1. AN CC 556, dossier Ravachol, interrogation; J. B. Monfalcon, *Histoire des insurrections de Lyon en 1831 et en 1834 d'après des documents authentiques précédée d'un essai sur les ouvriers et sur l'organisation de la fabrique* (Paris and Lyon, 1834), p. 225; Louis Blanc, *The History of Ten Years,* no trans. given, 2 vols. (London, 1845), II, 258. Monfalcon, who was privy to the prefect's thoughts, argues that Gasparin was afraid of provoking an incident. Louis Blanc, on the other hand, states that if the prefect actually suspected a seditious conspiracy he should have arrested its leaders immediately.

2. AD M, "Journées d'avril 1834," pacquet 1, handbill dated 8 April 1834; AN CC 554, inventoire 8, "Minute du rapport de l'insurrection Place Saint Jean, 9 avril 1834"; "Les

événements d'avril 1834 et M. Ranvier de Bellegarde, juge au tribunal de Lyon" (Lyon, 1870); Monfalcon, *Histoire des insurrections de Lyon,* pp. 223–232.

3. Girod de l'Ain, *Rapport fait à la Cour des Pairs,* 4 vols. (Paris, 1834), II, 229–230; Cour des Pairs, *Affaire du mois d'avril 1834,* 15 vols. (Paris, 1834–1835), X, 93–95. The official account of the Lyon uprising skims over the incident in the Place des Jacobins, and Monfalcon and Louis Blanc fail to mention it at all. The most damaging piece of evidence is a letter from the young official to Gasparin in which he admits that he gave the order to fire before the crowd stormed the gates of the Prefecture. AMDG, t.8, Alexander to Gasparin, 9 April 1834. In his anonymous account published as an appendix to Guizot's memoirs Gasparin states that the incident occurred before the trouble in the Place Saint Jean. F. Guizot, *Mémoires pour servir à l'histoire de mon temps,* 8 vols. (Paris, 1858), III, 431.

4. Cour des Pairs, *Affaire,* X, 18–20, 22–23, and 383.

5. George Rudé, *The Crowd in History: Popular Disturbances in England and France, 1730–1848* (New York: John Wiley and Sons, 1964), p. 195.

6. AG E5 44, "Instruction confidentielle sur les bases arrêtées par M. le Lt. Général Aymard à Lyon en cas d'alerte," 1 December 1833. This document describes in detail the tactics which the army employed in April 1834.

7. AMDG, t.11, Gasparin to Minister of the Interior, 15 April 1834.

8. Cour des Pairs, *Affaire,* X, 164 and 178.

9. Ibid., pp. 18–19.

10. Girod de l'Ain (*Rapport,* I, 252) repeats the allegation of a police official from La Guillotière that "the leaders of the Society of the Rights of Man" met in that suburb during the night of 9–10 April to plan tactics for the next day. It seems impossible, however, that anyone but the residents of the suburb itself could have attended such a meeting (if it occurred) because the troops held all the bridges across the Rhône.

11. On the peninsula the troops' lines were drawn along major streets so that the insurgents were prevented from entering the wealthy Villeroy and Place Confort quarters.

12. Girod de l'Ain, *Rapport,* I, 255–256.

13. Ibid., p. 258.

14. Ibid., p. 260.

15. Ibid., pp. 264–266.

16. AMDG, t.11, Gasparin to Minister of the Interior, 11 April 1834.

17. When Minister of the Interior Thiers learned of the discussion he ordered that evacuation should be avoided at all costs. The seige which would have been necessary to recapture the city, he warned, would be much worse than the uprising itself. AMDG, t.5, Minister of the Interior to Gasparin, 12 April 1834. According to Monfalcon (*Histoire des insurrections de Lyon,* p. 253) the idea of abandoning the right bank of the Saône was rejected because the legal archives of the Palais du Justice would have fallen into the hands of the crowd.

18. According to one eyewitness, Lt. General Aymard had overestimated the number of insurgents in areas such as the Place des Cordeliers. When he learned of the real situation the General decided to move to the offensive. Dr. J. Pointe, "Fragments pour servir à l'histoire de Lyon pendant les événements du mois d'avril 1834" (Lyon, 1835), p. 10.

19. Because many of these requisitions were made in the name of the Society of the Rights of Man, Girod de l'Ain (*Rapport,* I, 286) regarded them as certain proof that the entire uprising was the result of a Republican plot.

20. M. Lambert, "Le Courage civil en action" (Lyon, 1835).

21. According to the official military figures there were eighty-six soldiers and officers killed or wounded on each of the first two days of the uprising. This number fell to fifty-five and fifty-four on the 11th and 12th respectively, despite the fact that the government was then on the offensive. AN CC 554, inventoire 6, "Tableau des tués et blessés."

22. Guizot, *Mémoires,* III, 441.

23. In his excellent article, F. Dutacq ("L'Insurrection lyonnaise d'avril 1834," *Revue des cours et conférences,* 41 [1940], 270) makes the point that the government's subse-

quent *Acte de Accusation* made it appear as though the evening of the 11th was the turning point of the uprising when it clearly was not.

24. Guizot, *Mémoires,* III, 443–444.

25. Girod de l'Ain, *Rapport,* II, 293.

26. Blanc, *The History of Ten Years,* II, 268.

27. Cour des Pairs, *Affaire,* X, 179–180.

28. This is not to say, however, that the resistance of the last two days was unimportant. In order to identify the "faces in the crowd" and the character of the uprising quite the opposite is true, as we shall shortly see.

29. Guizot, *Mémoires,* III, 451; AN CC 554, inventoire 1, "État numerique des tués et blessés militaire" (129 killed and 211 wounded).

30. AG E5 51, *Aide de camp du ministre en mission* to Minister of War, 18 April 1834.

31. AG E5 50, Lt. General Aymard to Minister of War, 12 and 14 April 1834.

32. Maurice Reclus, *Jules Favre: essai de biographie historique et morale d'après des documents inédits* (Paris, 1912), p. 55.

33. AN CC 570, Vaise.

34. Guizot, *Mémoires,* III, 451; Girod de l'Ain, *Rapport,* I, 237; AN CC 572, dossier Petetin, *Mémoire justificatif,* p. 71; Adolphe Sala, *Les Ouvriers de Lyon en 1834* (Paris, 1834), p. 54.

35. AN CC 559–571. Tables using the full data from these dossiers are presented as Appendix III. A typical dossier might contain administrative materials (covering letters, and so forth), personal letters of the arrested person, witness reports, and stenographic accounts of interrogations. The latter, when complete, include information on name, age, place of birth, literacy, marital status and number of children, address, occupation, and previous criminal record. Other information, such as length of time an individual had lived in Lyon and previous military record, is more difficult to obtain because these questions were not asked every person as a matter of course.

36. Girod de l'Ain, *Rapport,* I, 159–160. Even before the uprising Gasparin predicted that if there were trouble the lancers and young weavers would be in the middle of it. He did not see a conspiracy or ideology as their spur, rather he described them as "the same ones who daily fight one another with bricks." AMDG, t.7, Gasparin to Lt. General Aymard, 8 April 1834.

37. Paul Thureau-Dangin, *Histoire de la Monarchie de Juillet,* 7 vols. (Paris, 1884–1892), II, 246.

38. Literacy is here determined by the standard test of the ability to read and sign one's own name. We know which of the persons arrested were literate because each was asked to read each page of the record of his interrogation and sign his name at the bottom. The "semiliterate" category includes those who could sign their names but not read the records for themselves.

39. For local crime rates see Paul Savey-Casard, "La Criminalité à Lyon de 1830 à 1834," *Revue historique de droit français et étranger,* 40 (1962), 248–265 and Jacques Rougerie, *Procès des Communards* (Paris: Julliard, 1964), pp. 132–133.

40. AMDG, t.11, Gasparin to Minister of the Interior, 18 April 1834.

41. AN CC 558, dossier Rivière cadet, testimony of members of Council of Presidents of the Society of Mutual Duty.

42. AM "Croix Rousse, troubles 1831, 1834, 1848, 1849," "Rapport fait au conseil municipale de la Croix Rousse dans le séance du 18 avril 1834." The authors of this hastily written report were anxious to deny that the master weavers of the suburb had participated in the fighting. A marginal note on a judicial ledger dated 26 December 1834 states that "the Ferrandiniers and *compagnons*" composed the majority of persons arrested in April. AN BB20 74, Comptes rendus d'assises [Rhône].

43. David Pinkney, "The Crowd in the French Revolution of 1830," *American Historical Review,* 70 (1964), 15.

44. AN CC 559, dossier Charles Arnaud, interrogation. This individual was the only

veteran of the Legion of the Volunteers of the Rhône arrested on the barricades in April 1834. We can be certain that if the government had uncovered any trace of the Legion itself its participation would have been strongly emphasized. Accurate information on persons who fought in both 1831 and 1834 is almost impossible to discover since the dossiers of those arrested in April have yielded only a handful of admitted two-time insurgents and the printed list, "Notice par ordre alphabétique des morts et des blessés civils et militaires à la suite des evenements de Lyon de 21, 22, et 23 novembre 1831" (Lyon, n.d.), is not useful for purposes of comparing the two crowds.

45. AN CC 564, information générale, deposition of police informer Picot; ibid., dossier Carrier, interrogation; ibid., 565, dossier Garnet, interrogation.

46. Girod de l'Ain, *Rapport,* II, 222-223.

47. Blanc, *The History of Ten Years,* II, 264.

48. Girod de l'Ain, *Rapport,* II, 103.

49. Ibid., p. 209.

50. Ibid., p. 114.

51. AG E5 50, Lt. General Aymard to Minister of War, 14 April 1834.

52. AN CC 559, dossier Caussidière, interrogation. Jean Caussidière, a veteran of Bonaparte's Egyptian campaign, had two sons. One was killed in the fighting of Lyon and his body was mutilated by bayonets. The other, Marc, was a resident of Saint Étienne and a leader of the Republicans there. He became Prefect of Police of Paris after the Revolution of 1848.

53. Selective destruction reflects a conscious correlation between the motives of a crowd and the objects or persons destroyed or injured. Thus, an anticlerical riot would likely involve the harassment of priests and the destruction of church property.

54. Girod de l'Ain, *Rapport,* II, 280; AN CC 554, inventoire 3: "Note sur les vols ... commis dans les casernes et autre établissements militaires par les insurgés ..."

55. In October 1831, a crowd sacked and burned buildings in Queen's Square in Bristol in what has been called "the last great urban riot in English history." George Rudé, "English Rural and Urban Disturbances on the Eve of the First Reform Bill, 1830-1831," *Past & Present,* no. 37 (1967), 98.

56. Guizot, *Mémoires,* III, 453.

57. Another cleric, a defrocked priest named Noir, was arrested, but his case seems more an example of mental instability than clerical support for the rebels. AN CC 568, dossier Noir.

58. Pointe, "Fragments," p. 15.

59. Girod de l'Ain, *Rapport,* II, 312; Blanc, *The History of Ten Years,* II, 266.

60. Girod de l'Ain, *Rapport,* II, 310.

61. AD M "Journées d'avril 1834," pacquets 5-16.

62. *Le Précurseur,* 17 April 1834; AN CC 668, Pres. Conseil des hôpitaux civils de Lyon to Procureur du Roi, 1 June 1834. The head of the hospital board was furious because the police were demanding to see the records of each released person. He reminded the judicial officials that "the Hôtel-Dieu is a house of charity and not a prison."

63. Girod de l'Ain, *Rapport,* I, 313.

64. Pointe, "Fragments," p. 14.

65. AN CC 554, information générale (list); AM I2 39B (3 lists); AD M, "Journees d'avril 1834," pacquet 3 (list).

66. Giuseppe Mazzini, *Scritti editi ed inediti,* 10 vols. (Imola, 1907), IV, 32.

67. AM K, "Recensement de la population," 1834.

68. AN CC 570, information générale, undated report by the mayor of La Guillotière.

69. Jacques Rougerie, *Paris libre 1871: la Commune de Paris par elle-même*)Paris: Éditions du Seuil, 1971), pp. 18-19.

70. Girod de l'Ain, *Rapport,* I, 303.

71. The number of café owners, *aubergistes,* and *marchands du vin* arrested indicates the role which these establishments played in the uprising.

72. AN CC 563, dossier Clocher, interrogation. Claude Clocher was not a typical *canut* only in the sense that he worked in an usually large shop.

73. Girod de l'Ain, *Rapport,* I, 243.

74. Ibid., p. 283.

75. Ibid., AN CC 563, dossier Satin, interrogation.

76. Girod de l'Ain, *Rapport,* I, 302.

77. Ibid., pp. 242-243; AN CC 563, information générale, testimony of Bernard.

78. Cour des Pairs, Affaire, XI, 334, 345-346.

79. Ibid., pp. 144-153.

80. AN CC 563, dossiers Correa, Pradel, and Marigné, interrogations.

81. Ibid., information générale, testimony of Ruty.

82. Cour des Pairs, Affaire, VI, 68-72. Louis Marigné did issue a proclamation in the name of the Republic, however.

83. AN CC 563, information générale, testimony of Meunier; dossier Rous, interrogation.

84. Ibid., testimony of Cadier and Souliard.

85. Monfalcon, *Histoire des insurrections de Lyon,* p. 270.

86. AM I2 39A (police reports on barricade materials).

87. Cour des Pairs, *Affaire,* XI, 495.

88. AN CC 558, information générale, testimony of Sabbatier.

89. Girod de l'Ain, *Rapport,* II, 497.

90. Ibid., p. 210.

91. AN CC 565, dossiers Gille, Rockzinski, Morel, and Butet.

92. AMDG, t.8, Monfalcon to Gasparin, n.d.

93. AM K, "Recensement de la population," 1834.

94. AN CC 559, dossiers Girard, Krug, Mercier, and Gayet.

95. It is clear, nonetheless, that Charles Lagrange knew this neighborhood. During the night of 9-10 April he called at the home of a man named Guyotti, a Piedmontese refugee, and demanded to know whether he still had the weapons he had collected for the planned invasion of Savoy. Girod de l'Ain, *Rapport,* II, 201.

96. Sala, *Les Ouvriers lyonnaise en 1834,* p. 54.

97. Girod de l'Ain, *Rapport,* II, 201-206.

98. Guizot, *Mémoires,* III, 459; AN CC 570, information générale, miscellaneous testimony.

99. Girod de l'Ain, *Rapport,* II, 298.

100. In addition to the previously cited works by Pinkney, Rougerie, and Rudé, see Rémi Gossez, "Diversité des antagonismes sociaux vers le milieu du XIXe siècle," *Revue économique,* 1 (1956), 439-457; and the unpublished paper by Charles Tilly, "Urbanization and Political Disturbances in Nineteenth Century France" (Society for French Historical Studies, Ann Arbor, Michigan, 1966).

101. As examples, see E. P. Thompson, *The Making of the English Working Class* (New York: Vintage Books, 1963) and P. H. Noyes, *Organization and Revolution: Working Class Associations and the German Revolutions of 1848-1849* (Princeton: Princeton University Press, 1966).

102. George Rudé, "The 'Preindustrial' Crowd," *Paris and London in the 18th Century* (London: Fontana Books, 1970), p. 20.

103. Charles Tilly, "Collective Violence in European Perspective," in Hugh Graham and Ted Robert Gurr, eds., *The History of Collective Violence in America* (New York: Bantam Books, 1969), p. 18. According to Tilly's use of the term, "reactionary" violence is when "the participants were commonly reacting to a change depriving them of rights they had once enjoyed."

104. Ibid. Tilly describes "modern" collective violence as when "the participants commonly regard themselves as striking for rights due them but not yet enjoyed. They are . . . forward looking." George Rudé's equivalent for this term is "derived" violence, but he confines it to the context of "preindustrial" crowds ("The 'Preindustrial' Crowd," p. 32).

105. An extended discussion of the official investigation is found in Chap. 8.

106. AN CC 556, dossier Vincent (*absent*), testimony of witnesses.

107. Cour des Pairs, *Affaire,* XI, 19, 23–24, 323.

108. AN CC 556, dossier Collier, interrogation. Collier was a master weaver of tulles cloth.

109. Ibid., information générale, testimony of Barillet.

110. Girod de l'Ain, *Rapport,* II, 306.

111. AN CC 556, dossier Nocher, interrogation.

112. AN CC 571, dossier Meyniel, interrogation.

113. Félix Broutel, "L'Insurrection républicaine d'Arbois," *Nouvelle revue Franc-Comptoise,* 1 (1954), 1–15.

114. Blanc, *The History of Ten Years,* II, 272–273; Thureau-Dangin, *Histoire,* II, 248–249. The latter notes with ironic pride that Thomas was later a general and was executed by the Paris Communards in 1871.

115. Cour des Pairs, *Affaire,* XI, 115.

116. Blanc, *The History of Ten Years,* II, 273.

117. AMDG, t.5, Minister of the Interior to Gasparin, 14 April 1834.

118. Bibliothèque Municipale de Lyon, "Lettre de M. le Comte de Skarzinsky à Cracovie écrite par son cousin qui se trouvait à Lyon." This manuscript was intercepted by the Austrian secret police.

8. *Autrefois Les Canuts*

1. Pasquier's career rivals that of Talleyrand in its successful navigation of the currents of French politics. A member of the Parliament of Paris before 1789, a prefect under the Empire, and Minister of Justice during the Restoration, he became a peer after the Revolution of 1830. Paul Thureau-Dangin, *Histoire de la Monarchie de Juillet,* 7 vols. (Paris, 1884–1894), II, 299.

2. AN BB18 1355, Minister of Justice to Procureur Général Lyon, 15 April 1834.

3. Cour des Pairs, *Affaire du mois d'avril 1834,* 15 vols. (Paris, 1834–1835), XIII, meetings of 21 and 30 April 1834.

4. AM D1 Conseil Municipale de Lyon (1834), *affiche* dated 15 April 1834.

5. AMDG, t.11, "Note à l'appui des réclamations de la ville de Lyon."

6. AN BB18 1355, Procureur Général Lyon to Minister of Justice, 9 April 1834.

7. AN CC 619, Procureur Général Lyon to Minister of Justice, 12 April 1834.

8. AN CC 557, dossier Ferton, Chégaray to Minister of Justice, 19 April 1834.

9. AN BB18 1354, report signed by Chégaray (29 April 1834); Martin du Nord to Persil, 10 May 1834.

10. AMDG, t.5, Minister of the Interior to Gasparin, 11, 17 and 19 April 1834.

11. Ibid., 17, 19, and 23 April 1834.

12. AMDG, t. 11, Gasparin to Minister of the Interior, 18 April 1834.

13. Ibid., 1 May 1834.

14. Ibid., 16 May 1834; AN CC 558, information générale, report on mutualists, 14 May 1834.

15. AN BB18 1354A, Persil to Martin du Nord, 16 May 1834.

16. AMDG, t.5, Minister of the Interior to Gasparin, 20 May 1834.

17. "Chronique de la quinzaine," *Revue des Deux Mondes,* 14 (May 1834).

18. *Le Précurseur,* 1–2 May 1834.

19. Armand Marrast, "Vingt jours de secret ou le complot d'avril" (Paris, 1834).

20. Cour des Pairs, *Affaire,* VIII, Tableau 1; AN CC 554, undated list and "État général de situation de la procédure instruite à Lyon par suite des événements d'avril," 27 July 1834.

21. AD M, "Journees d'avril 1834," pacquet 1, order signed on 24 May 1834; AN CC 620, Commander Gendarmerie Rhône to Minister of War, 27 April 1834; AN BB20 407, undated petition to Louis Philippe signed by Granier.

22. AMDG, t.5, Minister of the Interior to Gasparin, 12 June 1834.

23. Eugène Baune and Joseph Pujol were arrested in their homes. Antide Martin, Joseph Hugon, and Edouard Albert escaped to Switzerland. Sylvain Court disappeared without a trace. See Antide Martin, "Un Tir fédéral en Suisse: souvenirs d'exil," *Revue du Lyonnais,* 3 (1836), 194–196.

24. AN CC 554, "Signalmens de révoltes récherches par la justice," n.p., n.d.; AN CC 668, President Hôpitaux Civils Lyon to Chégaray, 1 June 1834; AMDG, t.11, Gasparin to Minister of the Interior, 17 May 1834.

25. AMDG, t.11, Gasparin to Minister of the Interior, 3 May 1834.

26. Ibid., t.12, 8 September 1834; AN CC 572, dossier Petetin, Chégaray to Martin du Nord, 15 May 1834. It was only by chance that the records of the Parisian sections of the Society of the Rights of Man were discovered. Reasoning that the safest place for them was inside a prison, the Republican leaders in the capital had smuggled them into the Saint Pélagie prison in March 1834. They remained in the cell of a man named Facconi until a police spy informed the authorities. Thus, the papers of the Society of the Rights of Man which were introduced as evidence during the trial were those seized in Lyon in February and others hidden in Paris in March. All predated the April events. M. Gisquet, *Mémoires de M. Gisquet, ancien préfet de police,* 4 vols. (Paris, 1840), III, 414–415.

27. AM Croix Rousse, "Troubles 1831, 1834, 1848, 1849," police ordinance, 15 May 1834.

28. AMDG, t.5, General Ferrand to Minister of the Interior, 24 April 1834.

29. AN BB18 1354, Martin du Nord to Minister of Justice, 7 July 1834; AD M, "Journées d'avril 1834," pacquet 1, "Expulsion du territoire française" (list), n.d.

30. AMDG, t.11, Gasparin to Minister of the Interior, 26 April 1834.

31. *Le Courrier de Lyon,* monthly tables of raw silk registered by *La Condition Public* (May–December 1834).

32. AMDG, t.5, Minister of the Interior to all Prefects (*lettre circulaire*), 29 April 1834; Minister of the Interior to Gasparin, 19 and 21 April 1834.

33. Jules Favre, *Plaidoyers politiques et judicaires publiés par Mme Vve Favre,* 3 vols. (Paris, 1882), I, 26; AN BB18 1354, Procureur Général Lyon to Minister of Justice, 21 April 1834.

34. AN BB18 1354, Procureur Général Lyon to Minister of Justice, 23 May 1834.

35. AN CC 558, information générale, Police Commissioner Prat to President Court of Peers, 20 May 1834; AMDG, t.11, Gasparin to Minister of the Interior, 26 April 1834.

36. AMDG, t.12, Administrative Assist. Prefect Rhône to Minister of the Interior, 23 September 1834.

37. Ibid., Gasparin to Minister of the Interior, 20 July 1834.

38. *L'Indicateur,* 21 September 1834.

39. *La Tribune Prolétaire,* 15 February 1835.

40. *Le Nouvel Écho de la Fabrique,* August 1835.

41. Octave Festy, *Le Mouvement Ouvrier au début de la Monarchie de Juillet, 1830–1834* (Paris, 1908), p. 348.

42. AMDG, t.11, Gasparin to Minister of the Interior, 1, 5, 21, 28 May and 20 July 1834.

43. Ibid., 17 April and 6 May 1834; AN CC 557, dossier Ferton, Ferton to [unknown], 18 April 1834.

44. AMDG, t.11, Gasparin to Minister of the Interior, 26 April and 5, 6, and 7 May 1834; AN CC 572, dossier Petetin, *Mémoire justificatif,* p. 73 and Petetin to Armard Carrel, 6 May 1834; AN BB18 1354, Procureur Général Lyon to Minister of Justice, 19 April

1834; *Le Précurseur*, 1–2 and 6 May 1834; *Le Censeur*, 20 November 1834; AN BB20 74, Comptes rendus d'assises [Rhône], 1834.

45. AMDG, t.11, Gasparin to Minister of the Interior, 14 May 1834; t.5, Minister of the Interior to Gasparin, 28 April 1834.

46. AMDG, t.5, Minister of the Interior to Gasparin, 19 April, 20 and 28 May 1834.

47. Ibid., Prunelle to Thiers (copy), 15 May 1834.

48. Sherman Kent, *Electoral Procedure Under Louis Philippe* (New Haven: Yale University Press, 1937), p. 193.

49. AMDG, t.5, Minister of the Interior to Gasparin, 19 May 1834.

50. Ibid., 3 July 1834.

51. Amédée Roussillac, "Description de la prison de Perrache" (Lyon, 1834) and "Prison de Perrache: variétes politiques et littéraires" (Lyon, n.d.); AN CC 554, inventoire 8, Police Commissioner Prat to Procureur Général Lyon, 2 August 1834 and 27 February 1835.

52. As an example see AN CC 565, dossier Ratigné, Mme Ratigné to her husband, 4 August 1834.

53. Roussillac, "Prison de Perrache"; F. A. Gauthier, "Chronique de Perrache" (Lyon, n.d.).

54. AN BB18 1354B, petetin dated November 1834 and signed by Poulard, Berthelier, Girard, and others.

55. Girod de l'Ain, *Rapport fait à la Cour des Pairs,* 4 vols. (Paris, 1834). This report also constitutes the first four volumes of the Cour des Pairs, *Affaire du mois d'avril 1834,* 15 vols. (Paris 1834–1835).

56. Girod de l'Ain, *Rapport,* I, 25.

57. The text of Chégaray's draft is found in AN CC 570, information générale, "Insurrection de Lyon: journées d'avril 1834–rapport général," unsigned and undated with marginalia in several hands.

58. Cour des Pairs, *Affaire,* VIII ("Acte de accusation: arrêt du vendredi, 6 février 1835"), p. 61.

59. Richard Hofstadter's discussion of "the paranoid style in American politics" merits consideration with regard to the French government's reaction to the events of April 1834: "The central image [of the paranoid style] is . . . of a vast and sinister conspiracy . . . The typical procedure of higher paranoid scholarship is to start with . . . defensible assumptions and facts, or what appear to be facts, toward an overwhelming 'proof' of the particular conspiracy that is to be established. It is nothing if not coherent—in fact, the paranoid mentality is far more coherent than the real world, since it leaves no room for mistakes, failures, or ambiguities." *The Paranoid Style in American Politics and Other Essays* (New York: Alfred Knopf, 1965), pp. 29, 36.

60. Cour des Pairs, *Affaire,* V ("Réquisitoire de M. le Procureur Général presenté a la Cour des Pairs, le 8 décembre 1834"), pp. 28–29, 128, 240.

61. Cour des Pairs, *Affaire,* XIV, Tableaux 1–2.

62. My own research in the dossiers reveals nine other persons who were likely Republicans but who were not so indicted by the Court of Peers for some reason.

63. AMDG, t.8, Monfalcon to Gasparin, 16 May 1834.

64. Ibid., 20 June 1834 and "Note pour servir à réctifier l'histoire des insurrections de Lyon . . . pour ce qui concerne les opérations militaires," a brochure sent to the prefect by Lt. General Aymard on 27 June 1834. The army was particularly angry that Monfalcon had revealed the discussion of a possible evacuation of the city. The pamphlet was prepared "to rectify the perfidious accusations and material errors" made in Monfalcon's volume.

65. J. B. Monfalcon, *Histoire des insurrections de Lyon en 1831 et en 1834 d'après des documents authentiques précédée d'un essai sur les ouvriers et sur l'organisation de la fabrique* (Lyon and Paris, 1834), pp. 1–2, 99–100, 221–222.

66. Ibid., p. 264; AMDG, t.8, Monfalcon to Gasparin, n.d.

67. AMDG, t.8, Monfalcon to Gasparin, n.d.

68. In contrast to Monfalcon's Orleanist account, Adolphe Sala's *Les Ouvriers de Lyon en 1834* (Paris, 1834) presents the viewpoint of a local Carlist leader. Sala, too, was concerned with explaining the politization of the *canuts* and believed it was the result of their rejection by the men of the *juste-milieu* (p. 27). He minimizes the size of the uprising (p. 57) and rejects any notion of a conspiracy (p. 66), noting the division within the leadership of both the worker movement and the Republican party (p. 67). Sala concludes that the uprising was one of "the popular masses" of Lyon (p. 135).

69. AM I2 46A, Antide Martin to Sébastien Rosat, 6 July 1834.

70. Petetin, *Mémoire justificatif,* pp. 73–75.

71. A number of cheap brochures claimed to give eyewitness accounts of the Lyon uprising. Most of them were inferior in quality and distinctly anti-Republican in tone. A complete list of them is found in the bibliography.

72. *Le Censeur,* 29 November 1834.

73. AN F7 7682, liasse 16, Commander Gendarmerie Rhône to Minister of the Interior, 8 March and 6 May 1835. Five Lyonnais lawyers—Jules Favre, Kauffman, Chanay, Charassin, and M-A Perier—were invited to join the defense team.

74. Louis Blanc, *The History of Ten Years,* no trans. given, 2 vols. (London, 1845), II, 321, 326; Le Comte d'Alton Shee, *Mes Mémoires, 1826–1848,* 2 vols. (Paris, 1869), I, 126; Paul Bastid, "Les Accusés d'avril devant la Cour des Pairs," *Politique,* 3 (1958), 263. This article is the only scholarly analysis of the *procès monstre.* Rather than exploring the deeper implications of political justice. Bastid is concerned with the legal precedents established by the trial.

75. Blanc, *The History of Ten Years,* II, 321; *Le Censeur,* 3 May 1835; AN CC 665, report of Prefect of Police of Paris, 30 April 1835.

76. AN CC 665, report of Prefect of Police of Paris, 27 April 1835.

77. Ibid., 1 May 1835.

78. Blanc, *The History of Ten Years,* II, 326–328.

79. AN F7 3888, "Bulletin de Police," 5 May 1835.

80. Cour des Pairs, *Affaire,* XIV, 529. The official record of the trial exists only in summary form with occasional direct quotations from speeches. It omits testimony and evidence which reflected poorly on the government or the case against the Republicans. For this reason I have also used the most detailed of the Republican accounts of the trial: *Procès des accusés d'avril devant la Cour des Pairs, publie de concert avec les accusés,* 4 vols. (Paris, 1834–1835).

81. Blanc, *The History of Ten Years,* II, 330–331.

82. Ibid., pp. 332–333; Odilon Barrot, *Mémoires posthumes,* 3 vols. (Paris, 1875), I, 279; Bibliothèque Nationale, Cabinet des estampes, Q1 (1833–1847).

83. Cour des Pairs, *Affaire,* IX, session of 20 May 1835.

84. Ibid., session of 23 May 1835.

85. Ibid., session of 12 June 1835; Blanc, *The History of Ten Years,* II, 353.

86. *Procès des accusés d'avril,* II, 149.

87. "Discours de Reverchon, accusé de Lyon, pronouncé devant la Cour des Pairs, le 30 juin 1835" (Paris, 1835).

88. Cour des Pairs, *Affaire,* XIV, session of 1 July 1835.

89. *Procès des accusés d'avril,* II, 260–265. The official trial record passes over this confrontation in half a page of veiled prose.

90. Cour des Pairs, *Affaire,* XIV, session of 1 July 1835.

91. Ibid., sessions of 4 and 10 July 1835.

92. A puzzling sidelight to this portion of the trial was the appearance of Anselme Petetin, who had returned from exile to testify as a defense witness. Only one paragraph of the official record is devoted to his testimony and the Republican accounts are strangely reticent also. At one point Petetin made reference to his *Mémoire justificatif* and received a sign from Baron Pasquier to pass on to other matters (*Procès des accusés d'avril,* III, 20). When he referred to a plot on the part of the government he was reminded that he was

making a deposition, not entering a defense plea himself. Neither the prosecution nor the defense sought to cross-examine Petetin. It seems that neither side wished to extract more information from the man who had headed the moderate faction of the Lyonnais Republican party.

93. "Discours de Lagrange, accusé de Lyon, pronouncé devant la Cour des Pairs, séance de 2 juillet 1835" (Paris, 1835).

94. *Procès des accusés d'avril*, III, 56.

95. Ibid., 142.

96. Ibid., 136.

97. In 1849, when he was a candidate for the Chamber of Deputies, Chégaray was forced to defend his reputation as an enemy of the Republicans. At that time he declared that he had played the central role in convincing Baron Pasquier and Martin du Nord not to envoke the death penalty. Following the *procès monstre* in 1836, Chégaray was appointed the *Procureur Général* in Orléans. "Pieces justificatives produites par M. Chégaray dans son procès contre 'L'Éclaireur des Pyrénées'" (Pau, 1849).

98. Cour des Pairs, *Affaire*, XV, sessions of 13–17 August 1835; "Tableau synoptique des accusés d'avril jugés par la Cour des Pairs," n.p., n.d.

99. While the peers were debating the fate of the Lyonnais defendants an attempt was made on the life of the king by means of a machine gun-like weapon which was popularly called "the infernal machine." The attack, the famous *attentat de Fieschi*, came during a review and parade and killed several spectators, but left Louis Philippe unharmed. Three former members of the Society of the Rights of Man were indicted for this very real conspiracy. See S. Charléty, *La Monarchie de Juillet*, vol. V of *Histoire de France contemporaine*, ed. E. Lavisse, 10 vols. (Paris: Hachette, 1920–1922), pp. 112–113.

100. The Court of Peers met again in November 1835 until January 1836 to hear the cases against the other defendants. With the Lyonnais prisoners already sentenced and most of the other flamboyant Parisian Republicans being tried in absentia, these sessions passed almost unnoticed by the public. Thureau-Dangin, *Histoire de la Monarchie de Juillet*, II, 305. The men sentenced during the entire *procès monstre* were granted an amnesty at the time of the marriage of the King's eldest son in 1837. Bastid, "Les accusés d'avril," p. 267.

101. Charles Tilly and James Rule, "1830 and the Un-natural History of Revolution," forthcoming in *The Revolution of 1830 and the Origins of the Social Question in France*, ed. John Merriman (New York: Franklin Watts, 1974).

102. F. Dutacq, *Histoire politique de Lyon pendant la Révolution de 1848* (Paris, 1910), pp. 268–271.

103. Quoted by E. J. Hobsbawm, *The Age of Revolution, 1789–1848*, 2d ed. (New York: Mentor Books, 1962), p. 254.

104. Fernand Rude has never written the companion volume to his study of the Lyonnais worker movement from 1827 to 1832, which he promised in 1944. Hopefully the doctoral research of Mary Lynn McDougall of Columbia University will help fill this lacuna.

105. Christopher H. Johnson, "Communism and the Working Class Before Marx: The Icarian Experience," *American Historical Review*, 76 (1971), 677.

106. Maurice Agulhon, *Une Ville ouvrière au temps du socialisme utopique: Toulon de 1815 à 1851* (Paris: Mouton, 1970), p. 330.

107. F. Dutacq and A. Latreille, *Histoire de Lyon de 1814–1940*, vol. III of *Histoire de Lyon*, ed. A. Kleinclauz, 3 vols. (Lyon: Librairie Pierre Masson, 1939–1952), pp. 146–147, 152, 162–163, 167.

108. Louis Greenberg, *Sisters of Liberty: Marseille, Lyon, Paris, and the Reaction to a Centralized State, 1868–1871* (Cambridge, Mass.: Harvard University Press, 1971), pp. 236–237.

109. Joseph Benoit, *Confessions d'un prolétaire, [1871]* (Paris: Les Éditions Sociales, 1968), p. 273.

110. Stretan Maritch, *Histoire du mouvement social sous le Second Empire à Lyon* (Paris: Rousseau et cie., 1930), pp. 61, 113, 227.

111. E. Pariset, *Histoire de la fabrique lyonnaise: étude sur le régime social et économique de l'industrie de la soie de Lyon depuis le XVIe siècle* (Lyon, 1901), pp. 376–377, 415.

112. Maritch, *Histoire du mouvement social*, p. 59.

113. Pariset, *Histoire de la fabrique lyonnaise*, pp. 384–385, 398–399.

114. Charlene Leonard, *Lyon Transformed: Public Works of the Second Empire, 1853–1864* (Berkeley and Los Angeles: University of California Press, 1961).

115. Pierre Léon, "La Région lyonnaise dans l'histoire économique et sociale de la France (XVIe–XXe siècles)," *Revue historique,* 237 (1967), 49.

Appendixes

APPENDIX A. Population of Lyon and number of silk looms by quarter, 1820–1834

	1820	1825	1829	1831	1834
First arrondissement: *Jardin des Plantes*					
Saint Clair					
residents	4,811	4,731	5,238	5,749	6,454
looms	253	463	622	801	957
La Côte					
residents	8,593	7,727	8,245	7,121	7,892
looms	2,362	2,904	2,387	2,370	2,962
Griffon					
residents	3,940	3,019	4,557	4,348	4,800
looms	242	118	78	– [a]	35
Capucins					
residents	2,474	5,604	5,723	5,904	6,281
looms	131	374	474	431	573
Saint Vincent					
residents	5,636	7,604	7,176	7,287	7,632
looms	1,150	1,822	1,676	– [a]	1,825
Total					
residents	25,454	28,685	30,939	30,409	33,059
looms	4,138	5,681	5,237	– [b]	6,352
Second arrondissement: *Louis-le-Grand*					
L'Hospice					
residents	8,058	6,093	6,080	6,027	6,229
looms	1,348	1,086	1,063	1,095	983

continued

APPENDIX A, continued

	1820	1825	1829	1831	1834
Bel Cordière					
residents	6,406	7,555	7,213	7,020	6,906
looms	1,428	1,353	1,266	1,024	1,086
Place Confort					
residents	4,327	3,781	3,638	3,470	3,468
looms	174	71	37	47	22
Louis le Grand					
residents	6,068	6,277	5,477	5,290	5,494
looms	340	330	252	— [a]	221
Palais Royal					
residents	10,970	11,733			
looms	809	1,411			
Saint François					
residents	— [a]	— [a]	7,794	6,957	6,728
looms	[a]	[a]	554	606	352
Perrache					
residents	— [a]	— [a]	6,135	— [a]	6,476
looms	— [a]	— [a]	854	— [a]	790
Total					
residents	35,829	35,439	36,337	— [b]	35,301
looms	4,099	4,251	4,026	— [b]	3,454
Third arrondissement: *Hôtel-de Ville*					
La Boucherie					
residents		3,182	4,689	— [a]	4,208
looms		322	233	— [a]	181
Orléans					
residents		4,116	3,356	3,966	3,261
looms		128	38	39	2
Palais des Artes					
residents		3,244	3,159	3,170	3,486
looms		11	35	54	23
Hôtel de Ville					
residents		6,968	4,175	3,711	3,186
looms		110	69	47	18
Total					
residents	22,094	17,510	15,379	— [b]	14,141
looms	857[c]	571	375	— [b]	224

	1820	1825	1829	1831	1834
Fourth arrondissement: *Halle aux Blès*					
Saint Bonaventure					
residents	5,292	5,616	5,498	5,200	5,088
looms	901	479	454	471	340
Saint Nizier					
residents	4,426	5,019	4,819	4,212	4,436
looms	140	95	74	55	62
Thomassin					
residents	3,243	5,069	4,373	4,163	3,607
looms	313	578	441	265	302
Villeroy					
residents	4,503	4,746	4,429	3,850	4,091
looms	123	117	73	53	63
Total					
residents	17,464	20,450	19,119	17,425	17,222
looms	1,477	1,269	1,042	844	767
Fifth arrondissement: *Métropole*					
Pierre Scize					
residents	4,322	4,696	4,218	4,536	4,155
looms	1,382	1,400	1,094	1,739	1,262
La Juiverie					
residents	6,325	6,597	5,849	3,271	3,206
looms	1,884	1,839	1,387	523	643
Place Neuve Saint Jean					
residents	6,318	6,714	5,370	4,997	5,090
looms	832	857	626	531	579
Porte Froc					
residents	4,723	4,862	4,339	7,108	6,278
looms	959	938	743	1,427	1,483
Gourgillon					
residents	7,246	7,854	6,495	5,015	6,217
looms	2,373	2,687	1,830	1,956	2,624
Ancienne Ville					
residents	4,083	4,270	3,934	3,880	4,673
looms	492	608	484	646	955

continued

APPENDIX A, continued

	1820	1825	1829	1831	1834
Total					
residents	33,017	34,993	30,205	28,807	29,619
looms	7,922	8,329	6,164	6,822	7,546
La Croix Rousse					
residents	— [a]	— [a]	— [a]	16,120	17,475
looms	— [a]	— [a]	— [a]	6,223	6,763

Source: AM K, "Recensement de la population," 1820–1834.
[a]No record.
[b]Incomplete.
[c]The internal boundaries of the third arrondissement were changed after the 1820 census. Because the boundaries of the surrounding arrondissements remained uniform the total figures for 1820 may be presumed to be accurate.

APPENDIX B. Crowd information: persons arrested for actual participation in the Lyon uprising of 1834

		Number arrested	Percent
Place of birth			
Lyon and Rhône department		155	36.0
Lyon	114		
Rhône	41		
Four contiguous departments		94	22.0
Ain	29		
Loire	14		
Isère	33		
Saône et Loire	18		
Other French departments		129	30.0
Allier, Ardèche, Aude, Bas Pyrenees, Bas Rhin, Basses Alpes, Bouche-du-Rhône, Cantal, Charente, Correze, Côte d'Or, Creuze, Daubs, Drôme, Gard, Gaud, Gers, Hte. Alpes, Hte. Loire, Hte. Marne, Hte. Rhine, Hte. Vienne, Herault, Indre, Jura, Larente, Loir et Chere, Loraine, Maine et Loire, Manche, Meurthe, Meuse, Moselle, Nord, Puy de Dôme, Rhin infer., Seine, Seine et Marne, Seine et Oise, Seine infer., Valais, Varre, Yonne			
Foreign born		54	12.0
Savoy	29		
Piedmont	11		
Switzerland	15		
Belgium	2		
Prussia	2		
Hungary	2		
Bohemia, England, Poland, Portugal, Spain (1 each)			
No information:		95[a]	
Literacy			
literate		269	68.0

continued

APPENDIX B, continued

		Number arrested	Percent
semiliterate (can sign name)		41	10.5
illiterate		86	21.5
no information		132	
Marital status			
married		142	32.5
women	7		
men with children	80		
unmarried		287	66.5
widowers		5	1.0
no information		91	
Age			
under 15		6	1.2
15–20		96	20.0
21–25		103	22.0
26–30		95	20.0
31–35		63	13.5
36–40		56	13.0
41–45		24	5.0
46–50		12	2.5
51–55		5	1.0
56–60		5	1.0
over 60		4	.8
No information		68	
Occupation			
Silk cloth manufacture		193	37.0
master weavers	34		
journeymen weavers	112		
undifferentiated weavers	27		
dyers	4		
silk cloth printers	12		
designers	4		

	Number arrested	Percent
Clothing trades	59	12.0
tailors	23	
cobblers	20	
hatters	5	
wigmakers	7	
buttonmakers	4	
Building and transportation trades	102	20.0
carpenters and joiners	29	
painters	7	
woodworkers and decorators	4	
plasterers	3	
masons	12	
smiths and iron mongers	9	
tin smiths	11	
coopers	1	
tanners	6	
saddlers	2	
carters and drivers	16	
wheelwrights	1	
railroadmen	1	
Independent and artisan trades	59	12.0
cafe owners and employees	23	
locksmiths	2	
cutlers	2	
printers	4	
book sellers	7	
book binders	2	
paper and cardboard sellers	4	
money changers	2	
tobacco sellers	2	
jewelers	7	
pharmacists	2	
florists	1	
instrumentmakers	1	

continued

APPENDIX B, continued

		Number arrested	Percent
Unskilled and misc. trades		39	8.0
street vendors	2		
fuel sellers	9		
day laborers	14		
domestics	5		
agricultural workers	9		
Food sellers		15	3.0
bakers	4		
grocers	5		
butchers	1		
wholesale merchants	5		
Professional men		23	5.0
lawyers	2		
teachers	4		
propriétaires	8		
misc. administrative and judicial employees	9		
Miscellaneous professions		19	3.0
priests	2		
students	6		
actors	2		
military on active duty	1		
military on leave or retired	8		
No trade or occupation		2	
No information		15	

Other Information

Admitted membership in association		74	14.5
Society of the Rights and Man	37		
Society of Progress	2		
Society of Mutual Duty	12		
Society of Ferrandiniers	4		
Union of Perfect Accord (tailors)	3		

	Number arrested	Percent
Cobblers association	4	
compagnonnages and mutual aid societies	12	
Military or national guard training	29	6.0
Previous criminal record	13	2.5

Source: AN CC 559–571.
[a]I have adopted the statistically valid procedure of presenting the number of "no information" cases and then computing percentage on only those cases for which information is available.

APPENDIX C. Breakdown of population of Lyon by quarter, 1834

	Married men	Married women	Widowers	Widows
First arrondissement				
St. Clair	1,099	1,146	60	252
La Côte	1,333	1,962	57	267
Griffon	803	837	59	173
Capucins	1,125	1,179	56	276
St. Vincent	1,428	1,463	62	298
Second arrondissement				
L'Hospice	1,097	1,120	82	230
Bel Cordière	1,299	1,316	74	276
Place Confort	674	707	26	189
Louis le Grand	967	985	96	255
St. François	1,160	1,185	75	355
Perrache	1,359	1,385	68	225
Third arrondissement				
La Boucherie	810	841	37	187
Orléans	633	657	26	147
Palais des Artes	645	629	34	156
Hôtel de Ville	594	607	18	161
Fourth arrondissement				
St. Bonaventure	1,048	1,060	37	229
St. Nizier	924	945	49	234
Thomassin	824	846	54	175
Villeroy	796	804	52	211
Fifth arrondissement				
Pierre Scize	793	818	53	203
La Juiverie	672	682	53	224
Place Neuve St.Jean	985	1,020	79	309
Porte-Froc	1,155	1,181	72	297
Gourguillon	1,182	1,205	86	333
Ancienne Ville	888	900	70	182
La Croix Rousse	3,569	4,059	—	—

Bachelors	Children	Servants	Journey-men and apprentices	Others in house-hold	Total popu-lation	Looms
539	1,594	530	978	256	6,454	957
681	1,846	198	1,498	710	8,552	2,962
1,562[a]	1,562[a]	369	588	413	4,804	35
632	1,536	315	888	274	6,281	573
406	2,400	300	1,096	219	7,672	1,825
238	1,844	134	610	874	6,229	983
309	1,904	107	640	981	6,906	1,086
248	981	365	99	179	3,468	22
348	1,356	1,009	193	287	5,496	221
457	1,417	516	257	1,306	6,728	352
368	1,907	347	364	452	6,475	790
425	1,003	226	285	354	4,168	181
406	886	240	95	171	3,261	2
302	802	305	301	312	3,486	23
367	910	272	115	142	3,186	18
362	1,433	259	341	319	5,088	340
407	1,068	316	166	327	4,436	62
245	881	83	164	335	3,607	302
366	1,041	341	192	288	4,091	63
429	969	132	466	292	4,155	1,262
263	1,014	79	147	72	3,206	643
530	1,289	272	304	302	5,090	579
577	1,880	243	436	437	6,278	1,483
509	1,717	142	619	424	6,217	2,624
332	1,096	250	382	579	4,679	955
5,253[a]	5,253[a]	409	3,501	694	17,475	6,763

Source: AM K, "Recensement de la population," 1834.
[a]Bachelors and children.

Bibliography

ARCHIVES

Archives Nationales

BB18 Ministère de la Justice, division criminelle: correspondence générale, 1201, 1203, 1205, 1209, 1217, 1220, 1222, 1318, 1325, 1335, 1339, 1353–1355, 1357, 1360.

BB20 Ministère de la Justice: comptes rendus d'assisses dans l'ordre alphabetique

    56   Cour d'assises de Lyon: départements du Rhône, Ain, et Loire (1832)

    66   Cour d'assises de Lyon: départements du Rhône, Ain, et Loire (1833)

    74   Cour d'assises de Lyon: départements du Rhône, Ain, et Loire (1834)

BB21 Ministère de la Justice: grâces collectives, 1821–1859

The inventory of this section reveals no information on the amnesty given the Lyonnais defendants.

BB30 Ministère de la Justice: affaires politiques

With the exception of a small amount of information in carton 294 this series has no material on the Rhône department in the period 1830–1848.

CC   554–669 Cour des Pairs: Evénéments d'avril 1834

    554–572 Lyon:

        554–558   General information including dossiers on the Society of Mutual Duty and the Society of the Rights of Man

        559–562   Centre

        563   Nord

        564   La Croix Rousse

        565   Saint Just

        566   Saint Paul, Saint Claire, Saint Jean

        567   Saint Georges

        568–569   La Guillotière and Les Brotteaux

        570   Vaise

        571   Miscellaneous other communes

        572   Miscellaneous journals and journalists

        576   Saint Étienne

        585   General information on Paris

        612–614   Papers seized *chez* Marchais (Paris)

615   Papers seized *chez* Dolley (Paris)
616   Papers seized in the Saint Pélagie prison (Paris)
617–618   Papers seized in the office of *La Tribune* (Paris)
619   Information from Ministries of the Interior and Justice
620   Information from Ministry of War
644   Pieces relative to persons indicted in absentia
664   Miscellaneous information from Ministries of the
             Interior, Justice, and War
666   *Démentis* (persons claiming to have been misquoted
             by Girod de l'Ain)
669   Inventory

F7   Police Général
3888   Bulletins de Paris (police reports), 1835–1836
4144–4145   Bulletins et rapports de gendarmerie (Rhône), 1826–
             1835 (monthly reports)
6782   Rapports de gendarmerie, situation politique (Meurthe-
             Sarthe, 1829–1835).

F9   Affaires Militaires
1162–1169   Victimes d'avril 1834 (damage claims)
FI   bI 161 (5)   Personnel administratif: dossier Gasparin

Archives du Ministère de la Guerre

E5   Correspondence militaire générale et divers (1830–1861) January 1833–
       April 1834

Archives Départementales du Rhône
Because of the enormous amount of material sent to Paris for the *procès d'avril,*
the holdings of the departmental archives are thin for the period 1832–1834.

M   (uncatalogued) Journées d'avril 1834 (16 paquets)
M4   Police politique: affaires politiques, 1830–1837

Archives Municipales de la Ville de Lyon

K   Recensement de la population, 1820, 1825, 1829, 1831, 1834.
I2   Police politique
       36   Émeutes et troubles politiques, 1831–1845
       39   A & B Émeute d'avril 1834
       46   A Sociétés politiques, clubs, conferences, 1789–1870
       47   A & B Compagnonnages et corporations
       59   Presse et imprimerie, 1791–1870
       60   Imprimeries, libraires, vente de périodiques, 1802–1870
I1   Police locale
       71 and 71 *bis* Police de sûreté, 1833–1834
D1   Conseil Municipale: séances, 1832–1834
Unclassified documents
       La Croix Rousse, troubles 1831, 1834, 1848, 1849
       La Guillotière, troubles politiques, 1830–1834
Les Documents Gasparin (13 volumes)
   According to the municipal archivist, Henri Hours, the Gasparin papers were

purchased by the city from the former prefect's family around 1920. Because they remained unbound until around 1940, citations before that date are no longer applicable. Given the lacuna with regard to prefectoral correspondence for the July Monarchy in the Archives Nationales, this is virtually a unique source for the study of national and local administration in this period. There are two gaps in the papers: letters from Paris to Lyon (December 1832–June 1833) and from Lyon to Paris (May–December 1833).

Bibliothèque Nationale
Salle des manuscrits, fonds Franc-Maçonnerie, 272, 275, 276

National Archives and Records Service (Washington, D.C.)

T 169-1 U.S. Counselor Office Lyon
    Unfortunately only three letters exist for the period 1830–1835.

ARCHIVAL GUIDES

Chaumié, Jacqueline. *Archives Nationales: Police Générale: objets généraux des affaires politiques: F7 6678-6784 (1815-1838): inventaire et table.* Paris, 1954.
État sommaire des versements fait aux Archives Nationales par le ministères et les administrations qui en dépendent (Série BB: Justice). Paris, 1947.
Schmidt, Charles. *Les Fonds de la Police Générale aux Archives Nationales.* Paris, n.d.
—— *Les Sources de l'histoire d'un département aux Archives Nationales.* Paris, 1902.
—— *Les Sources de l'histoire de France depuis 1789 aux Archives Nationales.* Paris, 1907.
Tulard, Jean. *La Préfecture de police sous la Monarchie de Juillet.* Paris, 1964.

UNPUBLISHED WORKS

Bezucha, Robert J. "Association and Insurrection: The Republican Party and the Worker Movement in Lyon, 1831–1835." Ph.D. dissertation, University of Michigan, 1968.
Eisenstein, Elizabeth A. "The Evolution of the Jacobin Tradition in France: The Survival and Revival of the Ethos of 1793 under the Bourbon and Orleanist Regimes." Ph.D. dissertation, Radcliffe College, 1951.
Servettas, Irène. "L'Opinion politique et sociale de la haute bourgeoisie lyonnais sous la Monarchie de Juillet." Thesis: Diplôme d'Etudes Supérieures, Faculte des Lettres et Sciences Humaines de Lyon, 1967.
Tilly, Charles. "Urbanization and Political Disturbance in Nineteenth Century France." Paper presented to the Society for French Historical Studies, Ann Arbor, Michigan, 1966.

PUBLIC DOCUMENTS

Almanach historique et politique de la ville de Lyon et du département du Rhône. Lyon, 1830–1834.

Almanach Royal et National. Paris, 1834.

Archives parlementaires de 1787 à 1860: receuil complet des débats legislatifs et politiques des chambres française. Deuxieme série: 1800 à 1860. (Edited by E. Laurent and J. Mavidal. Paris, 1862–1913.

Archives statistiques du ministère des Travaux Publics, de l'Agriculture, et du Commerce. Paris, 1837.

Cour des Pairs: Affaire du mois d'avril 1834. 15 vols. Paris, 1834–1835.

Documents statistiques sur la France. Paris, 1835.

Girod de l'Ain. *Rapport fait à la Cour des Pairs.* 4 vols. Paris, 1834.

Great Britain. House of Commons. *Report from Select Committee on the Silk Trade.* London, 1832.

Nouvel indicateur des habitants de la ville de Lyon et des faubourgs d'après le dernier recensement administratif. Lyon, 1834.

Office du Travail. *Les Associations professionelles ouvrières.* 4 vols. Paris, 1894–1904.

U.S. President (Johnson). *Report of the National Advisory Commission on Civil Disorders.* Washington, D.C., 1968.

NEWSPAPERS AND JOURNALS

Le Censeur
Le Courrier de Lyon
L'Écho de la Fabrique and *Le Nouvel Écho de la Fabrique*
L'Écho des Travailleurs
Le Furet de Lyon
La Glaneuse
L'Indicateur
Le Journal des Intérêts Moraux et Materiéls
Le Journal du Commerce de Lyon
Lyon vu de Fourvière
Le Précurseur
Le National (Paris)
Revue des Deux Mondes (Paris)
Revue du Lyonnais
La Sentinelle Nationale
La Tribune (Paris)
La Tribune Prolétaire

MEMOIRS, LETTERS, AND SPEECHES

Barrot, Odilon. *Mémoires posthumes.* 4 vols. Paris, 1875–1876.

Benoit, Joseph. *Confessions d'un prolétaire, [1871].* Paris, 1969.

Bertholon, Caesar. *Recueil posthume de poésies, chansons, et fables.* Saint Étienne, 1885.

Caussidière, Marc. *Mémoires de Caussidière, ex-Préfet de Police et représentant du peuple.* 2 vols. Paris, 1849.

Favre, Jules. *Mélanges politiques, judiciaires et littéraires.* Paris, 1882.

—— *Plaidoyers politique et judicaires, publiés par Mme le Vve Jules Favre.* 2 vols. Paris, 1882.

Gisquet, M. *Mémoires de M. Gisquet, ancien Préfet de Police.* 4 vols. Paris, 1840.
Guizot, François. *Mémoires pour servir à l'histoire de mon temps.* 8 vols. Paris, 1858–1864.
de la Hodde, Lucien. *Histoire des sociétés secrètes et du parti républicain de 1830 à 1848.* 2 vols. Paris, 1850.
Mazzini, Giuseppe. *Scritti editi ed inediti.* 10 vols. Imola, 1907.
de Remusat, Charles. *Mémoires de ma vie.* Edited by Charles Pouthas. 6 vols. Paris, 1960–1966.
Romand, J. C. *Confessions d'un malheureux.* Paris, 1846.
Shee, Le Comte d'Alton. *Mes mémoires.* 2 vols. Paris, 1869.
Thiers, Adolphe. *Discours parlementaires, 1830–1836.* 3 vols. Paris, 1879.
Truquin, Norbert. *Mémoires et aventures d'un prolétaire.* Paris, 1888.
Vidalenc, Jean. *Lettres de J. A. M. Thomas, Préfet des Bouches-du-Rhône à Adolphe Thiers, 1831–1836.* Gap, 1953.

WORKS PUBLISHED BEFORE APRIL 1834

A l'armée: association lyonnaise des droits de l'homme. Lyon, n.d.
Adresse des lyonnais aux parisiens à propos des forts détachés: le comité de l'association pour la liberté de la presse. Lyon, 25 July 1833.
Association de propagande démocratique: prospectus et règlement: société des droits de l'homme. Paris, n.d.
Association du progrès: souscription pour l'instruction du peuple: règlement général. Lyon, January 1834.
Association lyonnaise des droits de l'homme et du citoyen: de la civilité et de la fraternité, par un membre de l'association. Lyon, 1833.
Association lyonnaise des droits de l'homme et du citoyen' réponse à ceux qui accusent le parti républicain de vouloir l'anarchie et le bouleversement de la propriété. Plaidoyer de M. Dupont pour le Capitaine Kerkausie dans le complot des 27. Clermont-Ferrand, 1833.
Association pour la liberté de la presse. N.p., n.d.
Aux citoyens composant les sections: le comité central du départment du Rhône de la société des droits de l'homme. Lyon, 4 April 1834.
Baune, Eugène. *Histoire de Lyon pendant les journées de 21, 22, et 23 novembre 1831, contenant les causes, les conséquences et les suites de ces déplorables événements.* Lyon and Paris, 1832.
—— *Essai sur les moyens de faire cesser la détresse de la fabrique.* Lyon, 1832.
Bernard and Charnier. *Rapport fait et presenté à M. le Président du Conseil des ministères sur les causes généraux qui ont amené les événements de Lyon.* Lyon, 1831.
Beuf, Joseph. *A l'ex-sans culotte Egalité, provisoirement Louis Philippe Ier, Roi des français, par le grace de . . . 219 fripons.* Lyon, n.d.
—— *Aux prolétaires.* Lyon, 1832.
—— *Procès et défense de J. Beuf, prolétaire.* Lyon, 1832.
Bureau lyonnais de propagande démocratique: chansons. Lyon, n.d.
Cours public d'histoire de France depuis 1789 jusqu'en 1830, par le citoyen Laponneraye. Paris, n.d.
Discours du citoyen Desjardins sur la misère du peuple et sur les moyens de l'en préserver. Paris, n.d.

Dupin, Charles. *Aux chefs d'atelier composant l'association des mutuellistes lyonnaise.* Paris and Lyon, n.d.

Favre, Jules. *De la coalition des chefs d'atelier de Lyon.* Lyon, 1833.

—— *Sixième procès du 'Précurseur': plaidoyer de M. Jules Favre, défense de M. Anselme Petetin.* Lyon, 1833.

Ferton, Joseph. *Moyens de défense qui devaient être présenter à la cour d'assises du Rhône le 12 mars 1834.* Lyon, 1834.

Granier, Adolphe. *Appel du peuple polonais, belge, et italien aux bons français, amis de la patrie et de la liberté.* Lyon, n.d.

—— *Cri du peuple, ou esprit du patriotisme français et l'idée que la nation doit avoir d'un roi vraiment patriote.* Lyon, 1831.

—— *M. Lacombe.* Lyon, 1831.

—— *Un pamphlet par J–A Granier, gérant de 'La Glaneuse.'* Lyon, n.d.

Grigon. *Réflexions d'un ouvrier-tailleur sur la misère du people en général.* Lyon, n.d.

Kauffman, M. *"L'anniversaire," lu au banquet patriotique de 'La Glaneuse.'* Lyon, 1831.

Lacombe. *Aux amis de la verité. Lyon, 10 décembre 1831.*

La liberté de la presse—Nouvelles de la France et de l'extérieur—Publication républicaine—Cet écrit vend pour un sou. Lyon, n.d.

Marc-Dufraisse. *Société des droits de l'homme: Association des travailleurs.* Paris, n.d.

Martin, Antide. *Nouveau catéchisme republicain, par un prolétaire.* Lyon, 1833.

Monier, Charles. *Histoire du prolétaire du XIXe siècle par des prolétaires: prospectus et souscription.* Lyon, n.d.

—— *Histoire du prolétaire du XIXe siècle: première livraison.* Lyon, n.d.

Notice sur les individus mort et blessés—novembre 1831. Lyon, n.d.

Petetin, Anselme. *Circulaire relative à la fondation d'une association politique entre les patriotes des départements de l'Est.* Lyon, n.d.

—— *Procès du 'Précurseur': plaidoyer de M. Odilon Barrot . . . avec les articles incriminés.* Lyon, 1832.

Les Principles d'un vrai républicain: société des droits de l'homme. Réception de plusieurs membres. Discours par le citoyen Adrien. Paris, 1833.

Les Principles de la République: lettre d'un prolétaire sur l'association du progrès. Lyon, n.d.

Procès de 'La Glaneuse': association républicaine pour la liberté individuelle et la liberté de la presse, 11 mai 1833. Paris, 1833.

Procès de 'La Glaneuse,' 12 mars 1834. Lyon, n.d.

Procès de 'La Glaneuse' contenant les douze articles incriminés. Lyon, 1833.

Projet d'association des chefs d'atelier de Lyon. n.p., n.d.

Publication républicain pour un sou: des droits et des devoirs d'un républicain. Lyon, n.d.

Réglement des sections du département du Rhône de la société des droits de l'homme: janvier 1834. n.p., n.d.

Réponse aux détracteurs du peuple et réflexions sur la crise industrielle. Lyon, n.d.

La République, le Consulat, l'Empire, la Restauration, 1789–1834. n.p., n.d.

Reverchon, Marc. *La liberté de la presse est un mensonge: publication républicaine.* Lyon, n.d.

——*La presse populaire: publication républicaine: confiscation de 'La voix du peuple.'* Lyon, n.d.

de Seynes, Théodore. *Le patriotisme a expiré avec la République. La Révolution de 1830 ne l'a pas vu renaître.* Lyon, n.d.

Société des droits de l'homme: comité de correspondance général et d'affiliations républicaine: Aux sections lyonnaises des droits de l'homme. Pluvoise, an 42 de l'ère républicain. n.p., n.d.

Société des droits de l'homme: la question du salaire ne peut être résolvé équitablement pour l'ouvrier sans l'intervention de la politique. Lyon, n.d.

Souscription en faveur des condamnés des 5 et 6 juin. Lyon, n.d.

Statute: Association lyonnaise pour la liberté de la presse. Lyon, n.d.

Sur les fortifications de Paris. Lyon, n.d.

Sylvaincourt. *Revue militaire, ou le régiment ordonné d'obéir.* Lyon, 1834.

CONTEMPORARY WORKS ON THE APRIL 1834 UPRISING

Aperçu complet des événements de Lyon pendant les six fatales journées des 9, 10, 11, 12, 13 et 14 avril, rendu jour par jour. Paris, 1834.

Bonnardet, Louis. *Des événements de Lyon à propos de l' indemnité réclamée par cette ville.* Paris, 1835.

Événements de Lyon dans les journées des 9, 10, 11, 12, 13, 14 avril 1834 d'après les renseignements officiels fournis par l'autorité militaire et par l'autorité administrative. Valence, 1834.

Histoire des événements de Lyon dans les journées des 9, 10, 11, 12, 13, et 14 avril, par un témoin oculaire. Paris, n.d.

Lambert, Antoine. *Le courage civil en action, ou mémoire sur la belle conduite d'un habitant du faubourg de Vaise pendant les journées des 9, 10, 11, 12, avril 1834.* Lyon, 1835.

Marrast, Armand. *Vingt jours de secret, ou le complot d'avril.* Paris, 1834.

Monfalcon, J. B. *Histoire des insurrections de Lyon de 1831 et de 1834 d'après des documents authentiques précédée d'un essai sur les ouvriers et sur l'organisation de la fabrique.* Lyon and Paris, 1834.

Petetin, Anselme. *Extrait du 'Courrier Français': lettre de M. Anselme Petetin, ancien rédacteur de 'La Précurseur,' le 5 décembre 1834.* Paris, n.d.

Pointe, J. P. *Fragment pour servir à l'histoire de Lyon pendant les événements du mois d'avril 1834.* Lyon, 1836.

Précis historique des mouvements insurrectionnels républicains de Lyon, Paris, Saint Étienne, Grenoble, et Arbois en avril 1834, suivi d'un dialogue entre les membres d'un société secrète qui s'est dissoute dans les 24 heures de la promulgation de la loi de 10 avril sur les associations. Belfort, n.d.

Relation historique des événements de Lyon de 5 à 17 avril, avec un précis des troubles qui ont éclate à la même époque dans plusieurs villes et notamment à Saint Étienne et à Paris, par A *** D ***. Paris, 1834.

Ranvier. *Les événements d'avril 1834 et M. Ranvier de Bellegarde, juge au tribunal de Lyon.* Lyon, 1870.

Sala, Adolphe. *Les ouvriers de Lyon en 1834.* Paris, 1834.

La Verité sur les événements de Lyon au mois d'avril 1834. Paris, 1834.

CONTEMPORARY WORKS ON PRISON LIFE AND THE APRIL TRIAL

Baune, Eugène. *Discours de Beaune [sic], accusé de Lyon, prononcé devant la Cour des Pairs, le 10 juillet 1835.* Paris, n.d.

Biographie des accusés d'avril, de leurs défenseurs, des pairs, des juges, du procès, etc. 2 vols. Paris, 1835.

Donndorf, M. *"Amnistie et les contumaces.* Paris, 1837.

Fastes de la Cour des Pairs: Procès d'avril, première partie. Paris, 1835.

Ferton, Joseph. *Fragments politiques, écrits à la prison de Perrache.* Lyon, n.d.

—— *Ordre public et amnistie.* Lyon, 1834.

Gauthier, F. A. *Chronique de Perrache.* Lyon, n.d.

Histoire impartiale du procès des accusés avril, ou relation exacte et détaillée contenant les débats, les plaidoyers, les interrogaires des accusés, les dépositions des témoins, etc., etc. 2 vols. Paris, n.d.

Lagrange, Charles. *Discours de Lagrange, accusé de Lyon, prononcé devant la Cour des Pairs, le 2 juillet 1835.* Paris, 1835.

Lasfon, A. J. *La Hécatombe d'avril, ou les ouvriers lyonnais, les républicains, les légitimistes, les membres de l'opposition, devant la Cour des Pairs.* Brussels, 1834.

Mollard-Lefevre. *Ce que seraient les républicains s'il une république dominait en France.* Lyon, n.d.

Pièces justificatives produites par M. Chégaray dans son procès centre 'L'Éclaireur des Pyrénées' au sujet des événements d'avril 1834. Paris, 1849.

Procès des accusés d'avril devant la Cour des Pairs, publié de concert avec les accusés. 4 vols. Paris, 1834–1835.

Procès des prévenus d'avril, suivi de celui des défenseurs: catégorie de Lyon (avec portraits). Lyon, 1835.

Protestation lyonnaise contre la procédure des pairs. n.p., n.d.

Reverchon, Marc. *Discours de Reverchon, accusé de Lyon, prononcé devant la Cour des Pairs, le 30 juin 1835.* Paris, 1835.

—— *Lettre des républicains à M. le Procureur du Roi.* Lyon, 1834.

Rivière cadet. *Mémoire justificatif presenté à la Cour des Pairs.* Paris, 1835.

Roussillac, Amédée. *Variétés politiques et littéraires.* Lyon, n.d.

Sesmaisons, Le Comte de. *Réflexions contre la compétance de la Chambre des Pairs dans l'affaire d'avril 1834.* Paris, 1834.

Tableau synoptique des accusés d'avril jugés par la Cour des Pairs. Paris, 1837.

SECONDARY WORKS

Books

Aboucaya, Claude. *Les Structures sociales et économiques de l'agglomération lyonnaise à la veille de la Révolution de 1848: esquisse d'une application de la méthode quantitative à l'analyse historique.* Paris, 1963.

Aguet, J. P. *Les Grèves sous la Monarchie de Juillet, 1830–1847.* Geneva, 1954.

Agulhon, Maurice. *Une Ville ouvrière au temps du socialisme utopique: Toulon de 1815 à 1851.* Paris, 1970.

Ansart, Pierre. *Naissance de l'anarchisme: esquisse d'un explication sociologique du prudhonisme.* Paris, 1970.

Audiganne, Armand. *Les Populations ouvrières et les industries de la France dans le mouvement social du XIXe siècle.* 2 vols. Paris, 1854.

Bastid, Paul. *Doctrines et l'institutions politiques de la Seconde République.* Paris, 1945.

—— *Les Institutions de la monarchie parlementaire française, 1816–1848.* Paris, 1954.

Bertier de Sauvigny, G. de. *La Restauration.* Revised ed. Paris, 1955.

Beaulieu, Charles. *Histoire du commerce de l'industrie et fabrique de Lyon depuis leur origine jusqu'à nos jours.* Lyon, 1838.

Biaudet, Jean-Charles. *La Suisse et la Monarchie de Juillet: 1830–1848.* Lausanne, 1941.

Blanc, Louis. *History of Ten Years.* No trans. given. 2 vols. London, 1845.

—— *Histoire de dix ans.* 5 vols. Paris, 1848.

Charléty, Sébastien. *Bibliographie critique de l'histoire de Lyon.* 2 vols. Paris and Lyon, 1903.

—— *Histoire du Saint-Simonisme (1825–1864).* Paris, 1896.

—— *La Monarchie de Juillet.* Vol. V. of *Histoire de France contemporaine.* E. Lavisse. 10 vols. Paris, 1920–1922.

Chapman, Brian. *The Prefects and Provincial France.* London, 1955.

Chevalier, Louis. *Classes laborieuses et classes dangereuses à Paris pendant la première moitié du XIXe siècle.* Paris, 1958.

Cobb, R. C. *Les Armées révolutionnaires: Instrument de la Terreur dans les départements.* 2 vols. Paris, 1963.

Collins, Irene. *The Government and the Newspaper Press in France, 1814–1881.* Oxford, 1959.

Coornaert, Émile. *Les Compagnonnages en France du Moyen Âge à nos jours.* Paris, 1966.

Cuvillier, Armand. *Un Journal d'ouvriers 'L'Atelier', 1840–1850.* Paris, 1954.

Deschamps, M. *Les Sociétés secrètes et la société.* 6th ed. Paris and Avignon, 1882.

Dolléans, Édouard. *Histoire du mouvement ouvrier.* 3 vols. Paris, 1936–1953.

Dunham, Arthur. *The Industrial Revolution in France, 1815–1848.* New York, 1955.

Dutacq, F. *L'Extension du cadre administratif et territoriale de la cité lyonnaise.* Lyon, 1922.

—— *Histoire politique de Lyon pendant la Révolution de 1848.* Paris, 1910.

Dutacq, F., and Latreille, A. *Histoire de Lyon de 1814 à 1940.* Vol. III. of *Histoire de Lyon.* Edited by A. Kleinclauz. 3 vols. Lyon, 1939–1952.

—— *The First Professional Revolutionary: Filippo Michele Buonarroti.* Cambridge, Mass., 1959.

Faget de Casteljau, A. de. *Histoire du droit d'association de 1781 à 1901.* Paris, 1905.

Festy, Octave. *Le Mouvement ouvrier au début de la Monarchie de Juillet, 1830–1834.* Paris, 1908.

Fournière, Eugène. *La Règne de Louis Philippe.* Vol. VIII of *Histoire Socialiste.* Edited by Jean Jaurès. 13 vols. Paris, 1901–1908.

Fuoc, Renée. *La Réaction thermidorienne à Lyon.* Lyon, 1957.

Garden, Maurice. *Lyon et les lyonnais au XVIIIe siècle.* Paris, 1970.

Garrone, Alessandro G. *Filippo Buonarroti e i rivoluzionari dell'Ottocento, 1828-1837*. Rome, 1951.

Gaucheron, Jacques. *Les Canuts*. Lyon, 1956.

Gille, Bertrand. *Les Sources statistiques de l'histoire de France: des enquêtes du XVIIe siècle à 1870*. Paris and Geneva, 1964.

Girard, Louis. *La Garde nationale, 1814-1871*. Paris, 1964.

Godart, Justin. *L'Ouvrier en soie, première partie: la règlementation du travail, 1466-1791*. Lyon and Paris, 1899.

Gossez, Rémi. *Les Ouvriers de Paris: livre premier, l'organisation, 1848-1851*. La Roche-sur-Yon, 1967.

Greenberg, Louis M. *Sisters of Liberty: Marseille, Lyon, Paris and the Reaction to a Centralized State, 1868-1871*. Cambridge, Mass., 1971.

Gurr, Ted Robert. *Why Men Rebel*. Princeton, 1970.

Haag, Eugène and Émile. *La France Protestante*. 6 vols. 2d ed. Paris, 1888.

Hales, E. E. Y. *Mazzini and the Secret Societies: The Making of a Myth*. London, 1956.

Halévy, Daniel. *Le Courrier de M. Thiers*. Paris, 1921.

Hammond, J. L., and Hammond, Barbara. *The Skilled Laborer, 1760-1832*. Orig. ed., 1919. New York, 1970.

Hobsbawm, Eric J. *The Age of Revolution, 1789-1848*. 2d. ed. New York, 1962.
—— *Primitive Rebels: Studies in Archaic Forms of Social Movements in the 19th and 20th Centuries*. 2d. ed. New York, 1959.
—— *Laboring Men: Studies in the History of Labor*. 2d ed. New York, 1964.

Hofstadter, Richard. *The Paranoid Style in American Politics and Other Essays*. New York, 1967.

Johnson, Douglas. *Guizot: Aspects of French History*. London, 1963.

Kessel, P. *Le Prolétariat avant Marx*. Paris, 1968.

Kent, Sherman. *Electoral Procedure under Louis Philippe*. New Haven, Conn., 1937.

Kuczynski, Jurgen. *The Rise of the Working Class*. Translated by C. T. A. Ray. New York, 1967.

Labes, M. *Les Pairs de France sous la Monarchie de Juillet*. Paris, 1938.

Labrousse, E. *Le Mouvement ouvrier et les idées sociales pendant la première moitié du XIXe siècle*. Paris, 1948.

Landes, David. *The Unbound Prometheus: Technological Change and Industrial Development in Western Europe from 1750 to the Present*. Cambridge, Eng., 1969.

Lefebvre, Georges. *La Monarchie de Juillet* [Cour de Sorbonne]. Paris, 1951.

Leonard, Charlene. *Lyon Transformed: Public Works of the Second Empire, 1853-1864*. Berkeley and Los Angeles, 1961.

Levasseur, Émile. *Histoire des classes ouvrières et de l'industrie en France de la Révolution à nos jours*. 2 vols. 2d ed. Paris, 1903.

Lévy-Leboyer, Maurice. *Les Banques européennes et l' industrialisation internationale dans la première moitié du XIXe siècle*. Paris, 1964.

Loubère, Leo A. *Louis Blanc: His Life and His Contribution to the Rise of Jacobin-Socialism*. Evanston, Ill., 1961.

Magnin, E. *Les Lortets*. Lyon, 1913.

Maitron, Jean, ed. *Dictionnaire bibliographique du mouvement ouvrier français*.

Première partie: 1789-1864, de la Révolution française à la fondation de la Première Internationale. 3 vols. Paris, 1964.

Malo, H. *Thiers, 1797-1877.* Paris, 1932.

Mather, F. C. *Public Order in the Age of the Chartists.* Manchester, 1959.

Marius, Joseph. *Galerie des lyonnaises célèbres de 1850 à 1903.* Lyon, 1903.

Maritch, S. *Histoire du mouvement social sous le Second Empire à Lyon.* Paris, 1930.

Moissonnier, Maurice. *La Révolte des canuts. Lyon, Novembre 1831.* Paris, 1958.

Monfalcon, J. B. *Code moral des ouvriers, ou traité des devoirs et des classes laborieuses.* Lyon 1836.

Montagne, Pierre. *Le Comportement politique de l'armée à Lyon sous la Monarchie de Juillet et la Seconde République.* Paris, 1966.

Morange, G. *Les Idées communistes dans les sociétés secrètes et dans la presse sous la Monarchie de Juillet.* Paris, 1906.

Morel-Journel, Henri. *La Famille Morel à Lyon et ses alliances: 1274-1550-1911.* Montbrison, 1911.

Noyes, P. H. *Organization and Revolution: Working Class Associations and the German Revolutions of 1848-1849.* Princeton, 1966.

Palmer, R. R. *Twelve Who Ruled: The Year of the Terror in the French Revolution.* Orig. ed., 1941. New York, 1965.

Pariset, E. *Histoire de la fabrique lyonnaise: étude sur le régime social et économique de l'industrie de la soie à Lyon depuis le XVIe siècle.* Lyon, 1901.

Payne, Howard C. *The Police State of Louis-Napoleon Bonaparte, 1851-1860.* Seattle, 1966.

Perreux, Gabriel. *Au Temps des sociétés secrètes: la propagande républicaine au début de la Monarchie de Juillet, 1830-1835.* Paris, 1931.

Plamenatz, John. *The Revolutionary Movement in France, 1815-1870.* London, 1952.

Ponteil, Felix. *Les Institutions de la France de 1814 à 1870.* Paris, 1966.

Potempkin, F. *Lionskie vosstaniia 1831 i 1834 g.* [The Lyonnais Insurrections of 1831 and 1834.] Moscow, 1937.

Pouthas, Charles. *La Population française pendant la première moitié du XIXe siècle.* Paris, 1956.

Ragon, M. *Histoire de la littérature ouvrière du Moyen Âge à nos jours.* Paris, 1953.

Reclus, Maurice. *Jules Favre: essai de biographie historique et morale d'après des documents inédits.* Paris, 1912.

Reybaud, Louis. *Études sur le régime des manufactures: condition des ouvriers en soie.* Paris, 1859.

Ribe, Georges. *L'Opinion publique et la vie politique à Lyon lors des premières années de la seconde Restauration.* Paris, 1957.

Richards, Leonard. *"Gentlemen of Property and Standing": Anti-Abolition Mobs in Jacksonian America.* Princeton, 1970.

Robert, A., Bourlutan, E., and Caguy, G. *Dictionnaire des parlementaires français.* 5 vols. Paris, 1889-1891.

Rigaud-Weiss, H. *Les Enquêtes ouvrières en France entre 1830 et 1848.* Paris, 1936.

Rivet, Felix. *La Navigation à vapeur sur la Saône et le Rhône, 1763-1863.* Paris, 1962.

Rohr, Donald. *The Origins of Social Liberalism in Germany.* Chicago, 1963.
Rougerie, Jacques. *Paris libre 1871: la Commune de Paris par elle-même.* Paris, 1971.
—— *Procès des Communards.* Paris, 1964.
Rude, Fernand. *Le Mouvement ouvrier à Lyon de 1827 à 1832.* Paris, 1944: new ed. 1969.
Rudé, George. *The Crowd in History: Popular Disturbances in England and France, 1730–1848.* New York, 1964.
—— *The Crowd in the French Revolution.* Oxford, 1959.
Runciman, Walter G. *Relative Deprivation and Social Justice: A Study of Attitudes in 20th Century England.* Berkeley, 1966.
Saitta, Armando. *Filippo Buonarroti.* 2 vols. Rome, 1950.
Sée, Henri. *La Vie économique de la France sous la monarchie censitaire, 1815–1848.* Paris, 1927.
Sencier, G. *Le Babouvisme après Babeuf: sociétés secrètes et conspirations communistes, 1830–1848.* Paris, 1912.
Smelser, Neil J. *Theory of Collective Behavior.* New York, 1962.
Spitzer, Alan B. *Old Hatreds and Young Hopes: The French Carbonari against the Bourbon Restoration.* Cambridge, Mass, 1971.
—— *The Revolutionary Theories of Louis-Auguste Blanqui.* New York, 1957.
Starzinger, Vincent. *Middlingness: "Juste-Milieu" Political Theory in France and England, 1815–1848.* Charlottesville, Virginia, 1965.
Stearns, Peter N. *European Society in Upheaval: Social History Since 1800.* New York, 1967.
Steyert, A. *Nouvelle histoire de Lyon et des provinces.* 4 vols. Lyon, 1899.
Talmon, J. L. *Political Messianism: The Romantic Phase.* 2d ed. New York, 1960.
Tchernoff, J. (Iouda). *La Parti républicaine sous la Monarchie de Juillet: formation et évolution de la doctrine républicaine.* Paris, 1901.
Thernstrom, S., and Sennett, R. *Nineteenth Century Cities: Essays in the New Urban History.* New Haven, Conn., 1969.
Thompson, E. P. *The Making of the English Working Class.* 2d ed. New York, 1963.
—— and Yeo, Ellen, eds. *The Unknown Mayhew.* New York, 1971.
Thureau-Dangin, Paul. *Histoire de la Monarchie de Juillet.* 7 vols. Paris, 1884–1892.
Tocqueville, Alexis de. *Democracy in America.* Translated by Henry Reeve. 2 vols. New York, 1945.
Trénard, Louis. *Histoire sociale des idées: Lyon de l' Encyclopédie au pré-romantisme.* 2 vols. Paris, 1958.
Vacheron, E. *Ephémérides des loges maçonniques.* Lyon, 1875.
Varille, M. *Les Journées d'avril 1834 à Lyon.* Lyon, 1923.
Vermorel, J. *Un Préfet du Rhône sous la Monarchie de Juillet: M. de Gasparin.* Lyon, 1833.
Villermé, L. R. *Tableau de l'état physique et moral des ouvriers employées dans les manufactures de coton, de laine, et de soie.* 2 vols. Paris, 1840.
Vingtrinier, A. *Le Docteur Amédée Bonnet et les journées d'avril à Lyon.* Bourg-en-Bresse, 1901.
—— *Histoire de l'imprimerie à Lyon de l'origine jusqu'à nos jours.* Lyon, 1894.

Articles

Alazard, Jean. "Le Mouvement politique et social à Lyon entre les deux insurrections de novembre 1831 et d'avril 1834." *Revue d'histoire moderne*, 16
  (1911), 27–49, 281–299.
Angand, Pierre. " 'Les Tendances égalitaires et socialistes dans les sociétés
  secrètes français, 1830–1834,' par. V. Volguine. Publication de l'Académie
  des Sciences de l' U.R.S.S., Questions d'histoire, 1947." *1848 et les
  révolutions du XIXe siècle*, 39 (1948), 11–38.
Augier, Joanny. "Le Canut." *Les Français peint par eux-mêmes: Province, tome
  premier*, ed. Jules Janin and others (Paris, 1841), 281–288.
Aynard, Théodore. "Histoire des deux Antoines et du vieux pont Morand sur le
  Rhône à Lyon." *Revue du Lyonnais*, 5th ser., 2 (1886), 114–141, 161–184.
Ballot, C. "L'Évolution du métier lyonnais au XVIIIe siècle et la genèse de la
  méchanique Jacquard." *Revue d'histoire de Lyon*, 12 (1913), 1–52.
Bastid, Paul. "Les Accusés d'avril 1834 devant la Cour des Pairs." *Politique*, 30
  (1958), 260–270.
Baud, F. "Les Caractères généraux du parti liberal sous la Restauration." *Revue
  d'histoire de Lyon*, 10 (1911), 217–226.
—— "La Presse liberale à Lyon." *Revue de la Révolution de 1848*, 9 (1913), 119–
  125.
Bernard, Auguste. "Histoire territoriale du département de Rhône-et-Loire."
  Revue du Lyonnais, new ser., 31 (1865), 52–68, 126–146, 218–237, 295–
  307, 396–411, 517–528.
Bezucha, Robert J. "Aspects du conflict des classes à Lyon, 1831–1834. *Le
  Mouvement social*, 76 (1971), 5–26.
—— "The Preindustrial Worker Movement: The Canuts of Lyon." *Modern
  European Social History*, ed. Robert J. Bezucha (Lexington, Mass., 1972),
  93–123.
Boyer, F. "La France et l'émigration politique italien de 1815 à 1861."
  L'Information historique, 26 (1964), 146–151.
Breunig, Charles. "Casimir Perier and the 'Troubles of Grenoble.' " *French
  Historical Studies*, 1 (1962), 3–23.
Briggs, Asa. "Cholera and Society in the Nineteenth Century." *Past & Present*,
  19 (1961), 76–96.
—— "Social Structure and Politics in Birmingham and Lyons (1825–1848)."
  British Journal of Sociology, 1 (1950), 67–80.
Brisac, Marc. "Lyon et l'insurrection polonaise de 1830–1831." *Revue d'histoire
  de Lyon*, 8 (1909), 160–204.
Broutet, Felix. "L'Insurrection républicain d'Arbois en avril 1834." *Nouvelle
  revue Franc-comtoise*," 1 (1954), 1–15.
Brouchard, G. "Histoire du couvent des Grandes Carmes de Lyon." *Revue du
  Lyonnais*, 5th ser., 6 (1888), 161–174, 229–247, 326–340, 406–434.
Buffenoir, M. "Le Communisme à Lyon de 1834 à 1848." *Revue d'histoire de
  Lyon*, 8 (1909), 347–361.
—— "Le Feminisme à Lyon avant 1848," *Revue d'histoire de Lyon*, 7 (1908),
  348–358.
—— "Le Fourierisme à Lyon (1832–1848)." *Revue d'histoire de Lyon*, 12 (1913),
  444–460.

—— " 'Le Précurseur' et la Révolution de Juillet." *Revue d'histoire de Lyon*, 6
    (1907), 358–362.
Coornaert, Émile. "La Pensée ouvrière et la conscience de classe en France de
    1830 à 1848. *Studi in ononore di Gino Luzzato*, 3 (Milan, 1950),
    12–33.
Courtheoux, J. P. "Naissance d'un conscience de classe dans le prolétariat textile
    du Nord (1830–1870)?" *Revue économique*, 8 (1957), 114–139.
Dautry, Jean. "De la première révolte des canuts à la mort de Blanqui." *Pensée*,
    82 (1958), 95–102.
Drescher, Seymour. "Tocqueville's Two 'Democracies.' " *Journal of the History
    of Ideas*, 25 (1964), 201–216.
"Deux lettres inédites de l'imprimeur Louis Perrin sur les événements d'avril
    1834." *Revue d'histoire de Lyon*, 4 (1905), 150–152.
Droux, Georges. "La Chanson lyonnaise." *Revue d'histoire de Lyon*, 5 (1906),
    426–439; 6 (1907), 20–52, 103–133.
Dunham, Arthur L. "The Economic History of France: 1815–1870." *Journal of
    Modern History*, 21 (1949), 121–139.
Dutacq, F. "L'Insurrection lyonnaise d'avril 1834." *Revue des cours et confér-
    ances*, 41 (1940), 16–32, 262–278.
Ehrmann, Henry. "Recent Writings on the French Labor Movement." *Journal of
    Modern History*, 22 (1950), 151–158.
Esler, Anthony. "Youth in Revolt: The French Generation of 1830." *Modern
    European Social History*, ed. Robert J. Bezucha (Lexington, Mass, 1972),
    301–334.
Fischer, Wolfram. "Social Tensions at Early Stages of Industrialization." *Com-
    parative Studies in Society and History*, 9 (1966), 64–83.
Fohlen, Claude. "Bourgeoisie française, liberté économique et intervention de
    l'État." *Revue économique*, 7 (1956), 414–428.
—— "Recent Research in the Economic History of Modern France." *Journal of
    Economic History*, 18 (1958), 1–15.
Galle, L. "La Place Morel à Lyon." *Revue du Lyonnais*, 5th ser., 22 (1896), 185–
    196.
Garden, Maurice, "Ouvriers et artisans du XVIIIe siècle: l'exemple lyonnais et
    les problèmes de classification." *Revue d'histoire économique et sociale*,
    48 (1970), 28–54.
Godart, Justin. "Le Compagnonnage à Lyon." *Revue d'histoire de Lyon*, 2
    (1903), 425–447.
—— "Guignol et l'esprit lyonnais." *Revue d'histoire de Lyon*, 8 (1909), 241–
    254.
—— "Les Journées d'avril 1834 à Lyon." *La Révolution de 1848*, 31 (1934),
    135–154.
—— "Les Origines de la coopération lyonnaise." *Revue d'histoire de Lyon*, 3
    (1904), 330–348, 401–425.
Gonnard, P. "Les Passementiers de Saint Étienne en 1833." *Revue d'histoire de
    Lyon*, 6 (1907), 81–102.
Gonnet, Paul. "Esquisse de la crise économique en France de 1827 à 1832."
    Revue d'histoire économique et sociale, 33 (1955), 249–291.
Gossez, Rémi. "Diversité des antagonismes sociaux vers le milieu du XIXe siècle.
    Revue économique, 1 (1956), 439–454.

Jefferson, Carter. "Worker Education in England and France, 1800–1914." *Comparative Studies in Society and History,* 6 (1964), 345–366.

Johnson, Christopher. "Communism and the Working Class before Marx: The Icarian Experience." *American Historical Review,* 76 (1971), 642–689.

Landes, David. "Recent Work in the Economic History of Modern France." *French Historical Studies,* 1 (1958), 73–94.

Léon, Pierre. "La Région lyonnaise dans l'histoire économique et sociale de la France (XVIe–XXe siècles)." *Revue historique,* 237 (1967), 31–62.

Leroudier, E. "Les Agrandissements de Lyon à la fin du XVIIIe siècle." *Revue d'histoire de Lyon,* 9 (1910), 81–102.

Levy, C. "La Fabrique de soie lyonnaise et la Révolution de 1830." *1848 et les révolutions du XIXe siècle,* 38 (1947), 20–47.

Levy-Schneider, L. "Le Gouvernement insurrectionnel de l' Hôtel-de-Ville en novembre 1831." *Revue d'histoire de Lyon,* 9 (1910), 161–198.

—— "Le Projet d'associaton entre les fabricants lyonnais par le publiciste Kauffman en 1845." *Revue d'histoire de Lyon,* 7 (1908), 430–445.

Loubère, Leo. "The Intellectual Origins of French Jacobin Socialism." *International Review of Social History,* 4 (1959), 415–431.

Money, John. "Taverns, Coffeehouses, and Clubs: Local Politics and Popular Articulacy in the Birmingham Area in the Age of the American Revolution." *Historical Journal,* 14 (1971), 15–47.

Pinkney, David H. "Les Ateliers de sécours à Paris (1830–1831): précurseurs des ateliers nationaux de 1848." *Revue d'histoire moderne,* 12 (1965), 65–70.

—— "The Crowd in the French Revolution of 1830." *American Historical Review,* 70 (1964), 1–17.

—— "Laissez-faire or Intervention? Labor Policy in the First Months of the July Monarchy." *French Historical Studies,* 3 (1963), 123–128.

Prothero, I. "Chartism in London." *Past & Present,* no. 44 (1969), 76–105.

Putz, H. "Documents sur la fabrique de Lyon, 1831–1834, et sur l'insurrection de 1834." *Actes du 89e congrès des sociétés savantes, Lyon, 1964,* 3 (Paris, 1965), 367–379.

Rath, John. "The *Carbonari*: Their Origins, Initiation Rites, and Aims." *American Historical Review,* 69 (1964), 353–370.

"Report from Select Committee on the Silk Trade." *Westminster Review,* 18 (1833), 1–31.

Rondot, Natalis. "L'Industrie de la soie en France." *Revue du lyonnais,* 5th ser., 8 (1894), 217–251, 324–361, 416–444.

Rose, D. J. "The London Workingmens' Association and 'The Peoples' Charter.' " *Past & Present,* no. 37 (1967), 73–86.

Roustan, P., and Latreille, A. "Lyon contre Paris après 1830: le mouvement de décentralisation littéraire et artistique." *Revue d'histoire de Lyon,* 3 (1904), 24–42, 109–126, 306–320, 384–401.

Rude, Fernand. "Entre le liberalisme et le socialisme: quelques médicins lyonnais aux temps romantiques." *Lyon et la médecine,* special issue of *Revue lyonnais de la médecine* (1958), 170–190.

—— "Le Mouvement ouvrier à Lyon," *Revue psychologie des peuples,* 2 (1958), 223–246.

—— "Pierre Charnier, fondateur du mutuellisme à Lyon," *Revue de 1848,* 35 (1938), 18–49, 65–117, 140–179.

—— "La Première expédition de Savoie," *Revue histoirique,* 88 (1940), 413–443.

—— "Un Poete oublié: L. A. Berthaud (1810–1843)." *1848 et les révolutions du XIXe siècle,* 38 (1947), 5–19.

—— "Les Saint simoniens et Lyon." *Actes du 89e congrès des sociétés savantes, Lyon, 1964,* 3 (Paris, 1965), 331–349.

Rudé, George. "English Rural and Urban Disturbances on the Eve of the First Reform Bill, 1830–1831." *Past & Present,* no. 37 (1967), 87–102.

—— "The 'Preindustrial' Crowd." *Paris and London in the 18th Century* (London, 1970), 17–34.

Rougerie, Jacques. "Composition d'une population insurgée: l'example de la Commune." *Le Mouvement social,* 48 (1964), 31–47.

Savey-Casard, P. "La Criminalité à Lyon de 1830 à 1834." *Revue historique de droit français et étranger,* 40 (1962), 248–265.

Sewell, William, Jr. "La Classe ouvrière de Marseille sous la Seconde République: structure sociale et comportement politique." *Le Mouvement social,* 76 (1971), 27–66.

Spitzer, Alan B. "The Bureaucrat as Proconsul: The Restoration Prefect and the *Police Générale, "Comparative Studies in History and Society,* 7 (1965), 371–392.

Stearns, Peter. "Patterns of Industrial Strike Activity in France during the July Monarchy." *American Historical Review,* 70 (1965), 371–394.

Terme, M. "Enfants trouvées." *Revue du lyonnais,* 1 (1836), 25–35.

Thernstrom, Stephan. "Urbanization, Migration, and Social Mobility in Late Nineteenth Century America." *Towards a New Past: Dissenting Essays in American History,* ed. Barton J. Bernstein (New York, 1968), 158–175.

Thompson, E. P. "The Moral Economy of the English Crowd in the Eighteenth Century." *Past & Present,* no. 50 (1971), 76–136.

—— "Time, Work-Discipline, and Industrial Capitalism." *Past & Present,* no. 38 (1967), 56–97.

Tilly, Charles. "Collective Violence in European Perspective." *The History of Collective Violence in America,* ed. Hugh Graham and Ted Robert Gurr (New York, 1969), 1–45.

—— "Reflections on the Revolutions of Paris: An Essay on Recent Historical Writing." *Social Problems,* 12 (1964), 99–121.

—— and Tilly, Richard. "Agenda for European Economic History in the 1970s." *Journal of Economic History,* 31 (1971), 184–198.

—— and Rule, James. "1830 and the Un-natural History of Revolution," forthcoming in *The Revolution of 1830 and the Origins of the Social Question in France,* ed. John Merriman (New York, 1974).

Trénard, Louis. "La Crise sociale lyonnaise à la veille de la Révolution." *Revue d'histoire moderne et contemporaine,* 2 (1955), 5–45.

Truchon, P. "La Vie intérieure de la fabrique lyonnaise sous la Restauration." *Revue d'histoire de Lyon,* 9 (1910), 409–434.

—— "La Vie ouvrière à Lyon sous la Restauration." *Revue d'histoire de Lyon,* 11 (1912), 195–225.

Voog, Roger. "Les Problèmes réligieux à Lyon pendant la Monarchie de Juillet et la Seconde République d'après des journaux ouvriers." *Cahiers d'histoire,* 8 (1963), 404–420.

Weill, Georges. "Les Journaux ouvriers à Paris, 1830–1870." *Revue d'histoire moderne,* 12 (1907), 90–105.
—— "Philippe Bunonarroti." *Revue historique,* 76 (1901), 241–275.

Film

Chardère, Bernard (director). *Autrefois les canuts* (1960).

Index

Harvard Studies in Urban History

DATE DUE
